LITERARY/LIBERAL ENTANGLEMENTS

Literary / Liberal Entanglements: Toward a Literary History for the Twenty-First Century

EDITED BY CORRINNE HAROL
AND MARK SIMPSON

UNIVERSITY OF TORONTO PRESS
Toronto Buffalo London

Toronto Buffalo London
www.utppublishing.com

ISBN 978-1-4426-3090-1 (cloth)

Library and Archives Canada Cataloguing in Publication

Literary/liberal entanglements : toward a literary history for the twenty-first century / edited by Corrinne Harol and Mark Simpson.

Includes bibliographical references and index.
ISBN 978-1-4426-3090-1 (cloth)

1. Literature and history. 2. Liberalism – History. I. Simpson, Mark, 1967–, editor II. Harol, Corrinne, editor

PN50.L58 2017 809′.93358 C2017-902481-7

University of Toronto Press acknowledges the financial assistance to its publishing program of the Canada Council for the Arts and the Ontario Arts Council, an agency of the Government of Ontario.

Canada Council for the Arts
Conseil des Arts du Canada

Funded by the Government of Canada
Financé par le gouvernement du Canada
Canada

Contents

Acknowledgments

This collection would not have been possible without the commitment, effort, and support of a number of people and institutions. English and Film Studies at the University of Alberta provided a dynamic environment in which to hold the symposium that brought many of the contributors represented in this volume together in April 2014. The department also provided crucial financial support, as did the University of Alberta's Faculty of Arts, Provost and VP Academic, and Kule Institute for Advanced Study. The Killam Trusts and the Canadian Society for Eighteenth-Century Studies provided further support. The Connections Grant we received from the Social Sciences and Humanities Research Council of Canada, meanwhile, supported both the symposium and some of the publication costs of this book. We thank our colleagues who generously agreed to participate in the symposium: Brent Bellamy, Adam Carlson, Megan Farnel, Susan Hamilton, Lois Harder, Dan Harvey, Nat Hurley, Eddy Kent, Brandon Kerfoot, Sarah Krotz, Katherine Meloche, Sean O'Brien, Michael O'Driscoll, Carolyn Sale, Anna Sajeki, Peter Sinnema, Katherine Starks, Melissa Stephens, Zeina Tarraf, and Teresa Zackodnik. We are especially grateful to those people who read and offered comments on the manuscript: Amanda Anderson, John Frow, Susan Hamilton, Teresa Zackodnik, and the two anonymous readers and the Manuscript Review Committee at UTP, who provided uncommonly generous and rigorous feedback. Katarina O'Briain provided expert assistance with manuscript preparation in the final stages, for which we are most grateful. Jessica MacQueen worked on the project from beginning to end, as research assistant, event organizer, graphic designer, copy editor, indexer, and intellectual interlocutor. Her tireless commitment and high standards continually surprised and inspired us, and the project would not have been possible without her. Richard Ratzlaff's supportive, concise, and expeditious truth-telling made him the ideal editor for this project. We thank him for his abiding commitment to its realization.

LITERARY/LIBERAL ENTANGLEMENTS

Introduction: Toward a Literary History for the Twenty-First Century

CORRINNE HAROL AND MARK SIMPSON

Book Trades and Twenty-First Century Entanglements

Amazon – the online giant that used the book trade to become a global purveyor of everything – continually imagines ever more fantastic methods for eclipsing space and time in the very process of delivering goods to customers. Take for instance anticipatory shipping, a patented strategy awaiting implementation that would draw on extensive data generated from established purchasing patterns in order to predict choices to come – and so, in a sense, to preempt choice altogether – by packaging in advance what consumers have yet to discover they actually want. In a warehouse loading bay somewhere near you, a box may one day wait to be filled with the artefacts of someone's emergent longings: the complete collection of that sitcom in a near-dead format, Slavoj Žižek's latest treatise, radish seeds, roofing nails in bulk … and on and on and on. Mobile 3-D shipping, similarly merely virtual for now, would up the ante on just-in-time production so as to gratify the abiding plasticity of contemporary desires. The very possibility of truck-borne 3-D printing labs – cruising through ex-urban streets, the first responders to our consumerist emergencies, poised to generate on-the-spot replacements for the broken car part, the burnt-out hand-mixer, the threadbare chew toy – reverberates uncannily, some three centuries on, with a foundational moment of the literary/liberal entanglement: the printing press mobilized by William of Orange en route in 1688–9 to the liberation – or was it conquest? – of Britain.[1]

Considered as formal processes, anticipatory shipping and mobile 3-D printing together constitute a telling symptom of neoliberalization in what Mark McGurl calls "the Age of Amazon,"[2] by which market reason supplies the precept and template for absolutely everything. Underscoring Amazon's competitive ingenuity and aggression, these practices indicate (or even allegorize) the power of the economic realm to supply the operative mode and common sense that govern judgment, action, and desire in contemporary social life. As both marketing strategies and forms of everyday governance, anticipatory shipping and mobile 3-D printing suit perfectly (because they help to educe) the requisite mode of subjectivity today – a mode less about consumption, surprisingly enough, than about entrepreneurial (self) investment and (self) valuation. Put another way, the predictive, proleptic bent in Amazon's competitive strategy reflects as it produces the *what's next?-ness* of neoliberal subjects: flexible, fungible, and, as Eva Cherniavsky argues, no longer fixed by discipline but instead receptive to control, "minutely sensitive to the smallest fluctuations of the market."[3] The condition at issue, epitomized by Amazon's ingenious methods yet manifest pervasively across social, cultural, and political settings today, serves what Michel Feher calls "the promotion of human capital – that is, the presentation of the individual as 'investor in himself or herself'" – a turning of the screw on possessive individualism to arrive instead at that liberal model's more properly speculative counterpart.[4]

As scholars and educators trained in the professional study of literature and other cultural forms (an undertaking historically emergent within the hegemonic disciplinary ambit of the liberal university), we cannot help but recognize – because we endure – the profound impact of these dynamics on the institutions and endeavours of higher education today. The contemporary university is a learning market, a place to trade in the futures and derivatives, hedges and risks that qualify by quantifying the speculative individuals subject to neoliberalism: students now entrepreneurial self-investors, teachers now skill managers and content providers, and all of them – all of us – bound together by a fungible capacity for "lifelong learning."[5] And precisely because of these tendencies in higher education, it does not seem especially far-fetched to look for resonances – yet also dissonances – between Amazon's book trade and the current state of that other book trade, literary studies. One similarity is immediately evident: both encompass a great deal more than books. Just as Amazon has used the book market to turn itself into the master retailer for every conceivable commodity, so over a longer time span literary studies, moving beyond its traditional diet in literature, has developed an omnivorous appetite for all objects, concepts, and paradigms across culture broadly understood. What's more, the methods and emphases enabling anticipatory shipping as a retail innovation – the aggregation of big data, the attention to everyday desires, the bid for predictive assessment – have their counterparts within contemporary manifestations of literary study (distant and algorithmic reading, affect theory, speculative realism) that do not rely on recognizably liberal modes of argumentation and critique. The point here is not to suggest that such literary-critical practices are – in a sort of methodological determinism – merely symptomatic of neoliberal governance. They do, however, entail nodes of engagement with the texture and temperature of neoliberal culture: heterogeneous efforts on the part of literary and cultural critics to reckon, to analyse, to historicize, and sometimes to contest the aesthetics and politics of subjection and governance today.

The project for which this collection marks the culmination developed under the long shadow of neoliberalism. It took shape, more specifically, in the aftermath of the financial crisis of 2007–8, an event significant less as a break than as a reframing or recalibration produced from within the neoliberal passage: not so much a rupture, as the term crisis might imply, as an aleatory rescaling of neoliberalism's chronic condition – a rescaling dramatically manifest in the democratic yet vicious embrace of Brexit and Donald Trump in 2016.[6] Although the financial industry's speculative malfeasance was catastrophic for millions around the world, it nevertheless supplied not just the alibi or happy accident but, indeed, the conditions of possibility through which austerity's well-worn narrative might thrive, percolate, and circulate. Thus in the university sphere, the global financial crisis enabled academic administrations to accelerate the implementation of austerity measures and neoliberal management strategies. This process of austerity, capitalizing on the recession but part of a longer trajectory, has revealed how unvalued literature and other humanities disciplines – or indeed any intellectual pursuit not adjunctive to economic norms and practices – have become.[7] Ironically enough, this same process, so ubiquitous over the past decade, may also signal a turning point, heralding the future impossibility, as Angela Mitropoulous has argued, of treating the economic realm as natural (oikonomic) and separate from cultural concerns, both literary and political.[8]

Literary critics, trained in the workings of narrative, know how to offer insight into both the historical unfolding and the contemporary import of such dynamics. A major practice of literary studies, after all, has been to reckon how the politics of narrative discourse animate culture and to understand the codes and collateral effects of such discourse. Literary critics have long noticed the tendency of liberalism – and now neoliberalism – to operate on a model of continued crisis. Yet as theorists of liberal sovereignty in its relation to literary and other cultural production, we have enjoyed a kind of liberal agency, not to mention material and cultural capital, that has allowed us to feel dissociated, even emancipated, from the liberal mechanisms we have often studied. The financial crisis helped fuel the clamour about a "crisis" in the humanities, shifting the centre of gravity in the discipline of literature as we had known it.[9] Long-standing debates about the value of literary history, the complicity of literature in liberal ideology, or the potential of literary studies to influence economic, racial, or sexual equality/justice came evermore increasingly to seem, in the period from 2007 to 2017, at once less consequential and more urgent, perchance a turning point for English departments, which had long survived by analysing the entanglement of economics and culture yet had long been buffered from the consequences of neoliberalism. If the financial crisis incited university administrations and public funders to double down on austerity, the effects of events during the past decade on the literary engagement with liberalism have been rather more confounded – in ways that we hoped, in imagining this project, could be productive.

The perspectives informing this collection build on a diverse array of recent scholarly approaches in English studies and the humanities more generally, approaches that venture to rethink the history of the relationship between liberalism and literary history in light of critiques of these concepts in poststructuralism, ethnic studies, cultural studies, feminism, and Indigenous studies. Literary scholars have made key interventions in the relationship between the financial crisis and the crisis in the humanities. In addition, recent scholarship has sought to recover political alternatives to liberalism and to re-narrate its history, whether by focusing on political theology, republicanism, or secularization. Some scholars have defended the nineteenth-century valuation of literature's service to liberalism, others have disarticulated literary history from liberalism in order to recover some of its conservative critique of liberal ideals, while still others have tried to rehabilitate the relationship of literature and liberalism. An important contribution, particularly in the fields of Deleuze studies and ecocriticism, has offered a critique of the abstraction of a rights-bearing subject of liberalism grounded in a philosophical monism. The individual essays in this collection engage such developments heterogeneously, while the collection as a whole highlights the question of *entanglement itself* as a constitutive condition of literature and liberalism and therefore as a pressing matter for scholarly interrogation.[10]

Entanglement as Method

Rather than defining either liberalism or literature categorically for the entire collection, we and the writers of the essays take up key controversies entangling literature and liberalism in specific historical contexts. In general we take liberalism to mean a commitment to freedom, rights, and self-determination as facts and norms of human culture. Influential controversies about liberalism that inform the collection include positive and negative freedom, economic and individual freedom, the poesis of politics and culture, and the anti-foundationalist quality of political systems.[11] We treat literary history, also generally, as the institutionalization of a national narrative of cultural development giving the original justification for English studies as a discipline. For us the literary realm is a subset of aesthetics and liberalism is a subset of politics, making the literary/liberal entanglement a special case of the aesthetics/politics entanglement. Mindful of the internal variability of liberalism and literary history, we treat them as paradigms in order to signal their shared historical ability to mediate facts and norms, abstractions and practices. These paradigms share a history of entanglement: emerging in the late seventeenth century, they have since engaged in an intimate if tempestuous relationship, one foundational to politics and culture across English-speaking liberal modernity and to the institutional and disciplinary formation of English studies in particular. Over this conjoined history, literary history and liberalism have often served as the alibi, symptom, or shadow for one another. Literature has alternately been seen as the foremost fortification for liberal ideas of progress or as the principal conscientious objector to liberalism's excesses and blind spots. Whether correlated negatively or positively – whether estranged or collaborating – literature and liberalism have always been entangled, and this entanglement has always been central to the discipline of English studies.

We deploy "entanglement" in its colloquial sense in order to gesture toward the inextricability and co-constitutive relationality of the historical paradigms of literature and liberalism. We do so in recognition of the thoroughly negative connotations that attach to the term in both liberal and literary commitments. Within this definitional tradition, "entanglement" jeopardizes clarity, autonomy, integrity, causality, and beauty and produces embarrassment, ensnarement, confusion, and compromise.[12] We also invoke the meaning of the term in quantum mechanics, which suggests that entanglement is a condition of all interactions and so could hardly be judged either good or bad.[13] From this perspective, literary history and liberalism will not be distinct entities but rather strongly correlated systems that cannot be described or understood separately (i.e., they exist in a quantum state) and so seem to have mysterious causalities – spooky action at a distance – operating between them.[14] Approaching the entanglements of literature and liberalism in this way makes visible their constitutive co-relation without recourse, explicit or implicit, to the interpretive and evaluative norms of either paradigm. Literary history and liberalism as entangled constitute a phenomenon that is different from, and in our minds more interesting than, either concept in isolation. This perspective lets us see literary history and liberalism as sharing an entangled ecology whose boundaries, causalities, and phenomena are not understood or as yet determined. As Karen Barad puts it, "an ethics of entanglement entails possibilities and obligations for reworking the material effects of the past and the future."[15] Viewing literature and liberalism as entangled in this sense has the potential to reframe key distinctions in the literary/liberal nexus – subjects and objects, agents and actions, temporality and effect, matter and meaning, past and present – and to recast key investments of both liberalism and literature: agency, collectivity, judgment, evidence, culture, and disciplinarity itself. In terms of the historical narratives with which we frame this collection, liberalism, literary history, and physics share a parallel history, with key milestones of emergence in the late seventeenth century and key signs of re-imagining in the twenty-first century. The collection is about the first two terms, but physics shadows our investigation of liberalism and literature in the form of entanglement as a trope. We thus deploy this trope – not strictly scientifically but rather colloquially, metaphorically, and tactically – with the aspiration that it can aid in working through the current neoliberal scene of entanglement.

Liberalism and literary history would seem to provide especially unpromising, even counterintuitive ways of addressing the state of English studies within a neoliberal context marked by the apotheosis (or perhaps demise) of the first paradigm and the mothballing of the second. While their entanglement once seemed central to politics and culture, both concepts now appear obsolete. Liberalism's values of individuality, privacy, education, progress, religious toleration, and secularization have lost cultural resonance today, as questions about freedom become ever more exclusively matters for economics. For its part, literary history is arguably the most outmoded among the care-worn methods in English studies. Associated with elitism and tradition and the theories of progress and Eurocentrism that enabled liberalism's worst offences, literary history no longer claims centre stage in English department curricula, and it no longer makes – if it ever did make – heady promises of salutary cultural or political effects. English departments have, since the 1970s, turned to theory, to global literature, and to interdisciplinary inquiry in order to remain relevant. Indeed, during these decades English became that most curious of formations: a complacently disciplinary home for interdisciplinarity in the humanities.

Yet from the current perspective, the interdisciplinary turn has failed in its promise, serving in fact to increase the marginalization of English departments. For while interdisciplinary inquiry has many legitimate academic rationales, including most crucially the critique of disciplinarity as an agent of liberal political theory and practice, the recent interdisciplinification of the humanities has proved compatible with the contemporary university's neoliberal turn, tending to erode the integrity of humanities disciplines and to insinuate neoliberal principles – fungibility, volunteerism, decentralization, outsourcing, accountability, maximization of resources – into the way that scholarly work is conducted and valued. Put another way, an instrumentalized version of interdisciplinarity supplies the lingua franca of the neoliberal university, encouraging a kind of "cruel optimism."[16] English studies in the present moment gives a vivid instance of interdisciplinarity's double bind: a discipline able to absorb or indeed colonize other disciplines, methods, and objects of studies in its bid to compose the ur-modes of humanistic inquiry yet at the same time a discipline bound to the conduct of its campus-wide service function, teaching writing to students so as to inculcate (and monetize) fungible, because translatable, academic skills. Omnivorousness and serviceability read like two sides of the same contemporary coin, precisely because they encapsulate all at once the interdisciplinary ambition and the interdisciplinary subservience (or marginalization) of English studies today.

In proposing entanglement as a means of revivifying the promises of disciplinarity and interdisciplinarity together, we do not seek to recuperate either liberalism or literary history as they have been theorized and practised. We are in no way proposing a return to a notion of the discipline of English studies – based in some nostalgic or romanticizing literary history – as founded on a coherent, let alone privileged, cultural inheritance or on a hegemonic or universal method of critique. We do not advocate a closed, comprehensive, or hegemonic disciplinarity; nor is our purpose to narrate a coherent history of liberalism and literature or to revive some promise within the nexus they have comprised. We have approached the venture tactically, as a version of the type of lateral move associated by Lauren Berlant with the opening of impasse – the counterintuitive engagement with outmoded paradigms supplying, we hope, a means of reframing and re-imagining histories of and in the present differently.[17] So conceived, the project's approach to entanglement presumes that a certain kind of historical anachronism – one that eschews liberal norms of linearity, comprehensiveness, and progress – is not only legitimate but necessary to endeavours in literary history for the twenty-first century. In advocating anachronism and entanglement, we promote a contrapuntal approach to the problem of history, one very much opposed to liberal and literary-historical precepts about the linear, progressive passage or unfolding of time.[18] We propose that critical encounters with episodes from across the history of these now outmoded disciplinary paradigms, encounters that analyse and animate their entanglement, may motivate a constitutively eclectic and resolutely open disciplinarity: an intradisciplinarity, intensive yet expansive. In other words, the project turns on the premise that a disciplinary conversation of the type quite out of favour – grounded, that is, in literary history and disciplinarity but renewed by recognition of entanglement – could illuminate our current cultural moment to surprising, unexpected, and productive effect.

Literary/Liberal Entanglements reflects as it speaks to this confluence of disciplinarity and interdisciplinarity, with its contributors, all affiliated with English departments, exploring intersections among literature, politics, aesthetics, philosophy, sociology, ecology, and mass culture in order to advance at once field-specific and discipline-contesting accounts of the import of liberalism and literary history in the past as in the present – and for the future. Our goal from the outset has been and remains to foster a critical and genealogical reconsideration and reactivation of literary and related aesthetic episodes, practices, and dynamics from liberal modernity's long arc in order to trouble the self-evidence of prevailing narratives of the present era. Hence, we endeavour here to leverage a marginal place of critique based on case studies from the literary-historical provinces of

English studies today, making the risky (but we think successful) bet that scholars of literary culture considering the entanglements of literary history and liberalism – putting their field-specific knowledge in conversation, obvious or oblique, with our contemporary critical moment – can illuminate the long arc of modernity as well as the neoliberal conjuncture more specifically. Investigating major and minor, cherished and abandoned episodes in the estranging entanglements of modern aesthetics and politics, our contributors demonstrate the vivid capacity of literary study writ large to reckon and materialize durative accumulations of history, to provoke into view, by way of attention to diverse cultural events, remnants, and fragments, the contradictory texture and torsion of then-with-now and thereby to produce some unexpected, undeniable histories and historicities of the present.

The Essays

While the following essays contain overlapping lines of inquiry, we have organized them into pairs that orient around a series of terms at the nexus of literary and liberal norms and methods: acting, socializing, discriminating, recounting, and culturing. Each term, in ways that we develop below, serves to put the essays in conversation over key problematics in the literary/liberal entanglement. The terms we have chosen allow us to stage a series of conversations about how liberal commitments and literary representations have engaged with each other in select moments.[19] The pairs of essays tend to take different – at times diametrically opposed – positions on the histories they recount and their relevance for today, and they abjure normative assumptions about the literary/liberal nexus. We offer them, thus, as eclectic and exemplary but not exhaustive encounters with the entanglements of liberalism and literature.

Notwithstanding this diversity of approach and argumentation, the essays do generate a number of interrelated insights about the modes and methods of the literary/liberal entanglement, insights that illuminate just how provocatively complex and productive this entanglement remains. Several of our contributors attend, for example, to genre's capacity to formalize as well as reconceive relations between subjects, objects, and the cultural and political worlds they inhabit; others address the literary facility to mediate, mobilize, or dissipate affect for political purposes; still others focus on narrative in order to explore the entanglement of aspirations, shared by both literature and liberalism, toward political agency and historical truth. All contributors attend, whether explicitly or implicitly, to method itself as a scene of entanglement, both in the past and for the future. Some show how methods of archival investigation require us to attend with care to culture's minor forms and forgotten passages; others use classic modes of literary analysis to locate unseen entanglements at stake in familiar, even canonical literature; still others demonstrate method's persistent entanglement across such spheres as literature, politics, aesthetics, sociology, art, and science. Collectively, these approaches remind us of a telling and tellingly persistent power of literary criticism and cultural study: to help make new worlds in what might otherwise seem to be merely remnants of culture, fossilized culture, or methodological division.

The provocation at stake in the collection's essays issues from their documentation and exploration of the generative capacity of the literary/liberal entanglement. In illuminating this dynamic – the drama of the entanglement of liberalism and literary history – they offer ways to see how the project of literary history could be practised for the future. They remind us to see our neoliberal moment within a much larger history: to refrain from merely bemoaning the eclipse of the humanities by the economy and instead to attend to the possibilities and problems on offer in both our historical context and its historical antecedents. They invite us to speculate that the humanities' aversion to the economic emphasis of neoliberalism is a function of neoliberalism itself, not a critique of it, and to imagine that as scholars of literature, we are not simply consigned to some politically diminished realm of cultural authenticity. Rather, we need to understand the long entanglement of literature and liberalism with the knowledge that its unfolding trajectory remains undetermined.

Acting: Liberal Subjects and Objects

Agency – or what we frame here as the capacity to act and the process of acting – occupies a pivotal position in genealogies of liberalism. Questions and debates in the liberal tradition about individualism, autonomy, liberty, and sovereignty revolve around the distinction between subjects and objects and the prospect of agency as at once given and conundrum. Modern literary movements have likewise tended to foreground agency as topic and problem, as evidenced (to highlight only three of any number of examples) in romanticism's manufacture of expressive individualism, realism's manufacture of psychological interiority, and modernism's manufacture of alienated subjectivity. Paradigms in literary criticism and theory, meanwhile, often foreground agential dynamics and contradictions: for instance, New Criticism's attack on authorial intention, historical materialism's account of interpellation, feminist theory's attention to the personal/political nexus, poststructuralism's insistence on the death of the subject, and reader-response criticism's interest in, well, readers' responses. Probing the fraught dynamics of choice that structure the politics and aesthetics of personhood as articulated in specific literary instances, Jennifer Ashton and Aaron Kunin offer sharply distinct accounts of the significance of acting – of agency and autonomy – within and beyond modernity.

Ashton's "Posthuman Capital, or I ♥ Apocalypse" reads recent American poetry in the context of contemporary political malaise, arguing that the neoliberal present pits liberalism's celebration of self-expression (individual activity as expressive autonomy) against liberalism's demand that citizens make political judgments (the obligation to act). She describes the late capitalist zeitgeist as one in which "liking," as a subset or symptom of the lyric genre in its contemporary manifestation, dominates modes of self-expression and in which political issues are experienced as overwhelming crises that are shared globally yet are resistant to intervention. She sees the current political problems as issuing from and endemic to the cultural alignment of literature and liberalism, whereby literary self-expression siphons political action, ironically, in those moments and genres in which self-expression dominates. In short, the political project of liberalism has foundered precisely because of its relation to the literary project of lyric. Ashton here diagnoses what happens when we try to eliminate subject/object distinctions and embrace "pure contingency": a world where contingent affiliations and "apocalyptic logic" have replaced intention, belief, and attachment and thus a world where utopian political thinking is foreclosed.

In "The Wish to Be an Object," Kunin implies that liberalism has always been wrong about agency: humans do not necessarily seek subjective autonomy – they long instead to become objects. The literary creation of character types epitomizes the replacement, in art, of people with objects and thereby intimates a persistent desire in people to be objectified. Kunin analyses an eclectic array of it-narratives – the autobiographic novels of English writer Denton Welch, the films of Chinese auteur Wong Kar-wai, and the cartoons of American writer Lynda Barry – in order to show that people wish to be characters in the early modern sense. That is, people want to exist and be treated as types, a desire that in liberal modernity can perhaps best be expressed as the desire to become an object: a sofa, a dishtowel, a spoon. Kunin speculates that the very persistence of such desire may make the motives of literary creativity incompatible with the liberal project or, what is more, that literary expressions of character reveal our constitutive incompatibility with liberal models of subjectivity.

Socializing: Aesthetic Autonomies and Collectivities

Liberalism depends upon intertwining notions of the individual and the social. The (individual) freedom from encroachment and the (individual) freedom to participate, however variously contested in their interrelation as facets of liberal philosophy, inform as well as illuminate fully social problems of being and belonging together in secular, capitalist modernity. In the classically liberal variant advanced by John Stuart Mill, liberalism creates conditions of possibility for unlike people to get along. Less prosaically, Ralph Waldo Emerson figures spiritual union – a fully liberal apotheosis – paradoxically, in the self-reliant isolation and atomization of a society's diverse members.[20] Literary aesthetics, meanwhile, offer rich resources for the conception and creation of society, with and against the liberal grain: by envisioning and depicting social worlds; by modelling while also cultivating or educing proper (as well as improper) subjects and subjectivities; by provoking aspiration, desire, and longing; by fostering modes of what Benedict Anderson has taught us to call "horizontal comradeship," modes crucial to the national (but also cosmopolitical) dynamics of imagined community in the modern liberal era.[21] By means of strikingly different cases drawn from the early and middle decades of the twentieth century, Michael Meeuwis and Jonathan Flatley offer quite dissimilar – yet arguably contrapuntal – accounts of a common dynamic: the tremendous capacity of aesthetic practices to mediate, and thereby generate, social relations and collective desires.

In "Full Content: Shaw's Paratexts, Social Liberalism, and Harmonization," Meeuwis compares approaches to harmonization – a theory of sociability that reconciles individual and collective interests by exteriorizing thought and thereby standardizing the understanding of people in society – in the drama of George Bernard Shaw and the philosophy of his frequent political antagonist, the social liberal L.T. Hobhouse. Focusing on the preface and stage directions in *Major Barbara*, Meeuwis shows that the compound form of play-with-paratext supplies the perfect means of harmonizing the thinking of spectator-readers. The experience at issue is intellectual, visual, and ethical all at once; it draws on the combined power of dramatic action and paratextual argumentation to cause audiences to see and to feel – and thereby to participate in – the harmonizing force of socially transformative ideas. Meeuwis's argument, which marks Shaw's unexpected, even counterintuitive alignment with liberal political commitments, concludes by introducing a third figure to the picture: I.A. Richards, whose work played a decisive role in professionalizing literary criticism and whose understanding of literature as a repository of exceptional experience universally available resonates powerfully with the concept of harmonization as theorized by Hobhouse and implemented by Shaw. Situating Richards in this way, Meeuwis thus locates the afterlife of harmonization's practice in the very methods of modern literary criticism.

In "Refreshments of Revolutionary Mood," Flatley considers the significance of militant aesthetic practices for the formation and sustenance of insurgent collectives explicitly opposed to the liberal hegemony that obscures the social relations attending industrial capitalism. He argues that mood – or attunement – supplies our affective orientation to the social worlds we share and helps to reproduce prevailing social relations. Thus changes in mood, and especially the making of what Flatley, adapting Heidegger, calls counter-moods, can help to transform the social as such.[22] Flatley analyses a strike handbill and a film produced in the 1960s by militant African American workers' associations in Detroit. Both the handbill and the film bear out Flatley's supposition that any text aiming to affect its audience has implicit in it a reading of that audience's mood. Yet the mood-work is distinct in each: whereas the film invites us to envision some utopian futurity so as to cultivate an outraged optimism, the handbill – working to refresh revolutionary mood in the midst of proletarian, anti-racist struggle – has no real use for utopian aesthetics. And the difference here will begin to suggest both the urgency of mood-work in any given present and the power and necessity of alternative futures and multiple timescales.

Discriminating: Liberal Ethics and Literary Aesthetics

In the absence of metaphysical or authoritarian foundations for ethics and with its embrace of individuality and diversity, liberalism has been challenged to rationalize the ways that ethical decisions should be made. Aesthetic critique, as a mode of discrimination that mediates interpretation and judgment, has promised to balance the competing demands of liberalism for freedom and justice. Yet to the extent that "discrimination" names not only aesthetic or ethical judgment but also practices of social discrimination, the history of aesthetic critique reveals just how vexed the aspiration toward ethical justification in the liberal/literary-historical trajectory has been. While the relation between liberal ethics and aesthetic engagement has often been posited as analogical or pedagogical (in, for example, Immanuel Kant's influential formulation that aesthetic engagements train us in making moral judgments), in the latter half of the twentieth century, modes of aesthetic critique such as dialectical materialism and poststructuralism ventured a critical (rather than analogical or symbiotic) relationship to liberal politics and subjectivity. From their disparate orientations in literary history, Vivasvan Soni and Heather Love diagnose inadequacies in modes of critique that, because unable to balance empirical and hermeneutic forms of mentation, circumvent either material specificity or human subjectivity. While they imagine very different remediations – Soni calls for a more ends-oriented and conclusive model of judgment whereas Love argues for a non-judgmental/non-heuristic ethic of description – each admonishes literary critics to seek aesthetic critical practices that retain both subjectivity and contingent particularity, therein suggesting a turn toward postdialectical and post-poststructural methods of aesthetic critique for the twenty-first century.

In "Playing at Judgment: Aporias of Liberal Freedom in Kant's *Critique of Judgment*," Soni argues that Kant's theory of judgment – in which moral judgment is based on aesthetic judgment – never actually narrates or explains the final moment of judgment. Judgment, in Soni's reading of Kant, is always deferred, an endless "play" of possible judgments that never resolve. Soni's essay explains why aesthetic judgment, Kant's (and modernity's) solution to the problem of how to make secular judgments, has been and remains deeply vexed. At issue, in Soni's account, is a specific conception of freedom entwining or indeed entangling liberalism and aesthetics: a negative version of freedom as liberation from any orientation toward ends. Yet as Soni demonstrates, such free play works, in Kant's treatment, to render judgment impossible as a very condition of its freedom as such. Soni disputes the emancipatory political potential attributed to play by some commentators and proposes the game instead of play as the model for politics as well as aesthetics, precisely because games require judgment and so offer us freedom as the obligation to discriminate, not as the liberation from discrimination.

In her essay "In Frankenberg's Cafeteria: The Small Worlds of Highsmith's *The Price of Salt*," Love reads the strategies of narration in Patricia Highsmith's *The Price of Salt* as offering a model for contemporary literary criticism that can transcend the division between empirical and hermeneutic epistemologies and ethics. Highsmith's narration demonstrates techniques of observation that are neither scientific nor disciplinary. Rather, they function to show how humans become attached, to objects and to one another, via attention to the material realities and concrete particularities of specific encounters. Love sees Highsmith's techniques as sharing with microsociology a method that literary critics might develop as a means to move beyond ideological critique, to take seriously the social world, in all its subjective, detail-oriented specificity. For Love, this method – at once a practice and an ethic of fidelity, patience, and care – counteracts the universalizing tendency of liberalism. In its place, Love reads Highsmith as upholding the art of the minor, the small, and the insignificant, an art that embraces desire as the means to account for the full range of human social interaction.

Recounting: Literary Evidence and Liberal Narration

The writing of literary history is a place where the entanglement of literature and liberalism is revealed in the tenuous distinctions between evidence and narration and between reality and ideals: where questions of "what counts," in, for example, debates over the canon or balancing minority/majority concerns in democracy, meet technologies of recounting central to the narrative arts and the developmental aspirations of liberalism. This section takes up specific case studies in the nitty-gritty details of how literary history has been written, in Canada and the United States, by way of interrogating whether literary history's commitment to counting and recounting is a cause or effect of the liberal trajectory, whether it is fixed or mutable, and whether and how disciplining the study of literature relates to the formation of liberal national identity. In attending to how the writing of literary history – the determination of what counts and the formation of that value system into narratives of recounting – has related to the nationalist liberal projects of the United States and Canada, Andrea Hasenbank and Jason Potts endeavour to mobilize the literary/liberal entanglement in order to put pressure on fundamental conventions in literary studies. They find in the unsettled relation of these paradigms the means of practising literary history otherwise.

In "The Proletarian Thirties and Canadian Literary History," Hasenbank argues that Canadian liberalism's unique governmental intervention into literary history obscured the history of proletarian texts from the 1930s, either ignoring them altogether or treating them as documentary evidence but not literature. As such, the work of literary history does the work of liberal history, insofar as a radical past, with its challenges to liberalism's narrative of progress, has been forgotten so as to allow literary history to shape the political present and future. Focusing on a particular example drawn from this forgotten radical past, Ronald Liversedge's memoir *Recollections of the On-to-Ottawa Trek*, Hasenbank excavates the remnants, still alive because still entangled, of a literary history at once more radical and more richly rendered. By engaging with such radical texts in material – in addition to generic and nationalist – terms, that is, by accounting for the pluralistic physical and literary experiences constituted by readers and texts, Hasenbank calls for, and models, a literary history for the twenty-first century, one that engages, rather than reifies, the dynamics of the literary/liberal entanglement.

In "The Corporate Reconstruction of American Literary History," Potts excavates American literary history's mediation of the conflict between the liberal ideals of cultural diversity and economic equality. Analysing a selection of late nineteenth-century literary histories in light of Horace Kallen's celebrated essay on the melting pot, Potts argues that these texts privileged cultural identification over economic solidarity, thereby inscribing an early version, heretofore unacknowledged, of corporate liberalism. Thus Potts reveals that certain kinds of cultural identification – with race and region – that might seem to be (or have been seen to be) antagonists to liberal economics are in fact key bulwarks for corporate liberalism. Potts's essay thus finds surprising and unsettling continuities between these early literary historical commitments and contemporary practices of literary history that emphasize subcultural difference, multiculturalism, ethnicity, and regionalism. Like Hasenbank, Potts revisits and thereby re-imagines the future anteriority of actually existing literary histories in ways that intimate how such recounting of national liberal projects might come to matter for the neoliberal present.

Culturing: Economics, Institutions, and the Imagination

A central bifurcation at the heart of the culture of liberalism is the distinction, albeit a frequently false one, between the political or cultural and economic realms. Theorists have produced a bewilderingly complex array of answers to the questions: How are individual, cultural, and economic development and value related? Is it the economy or the individual whose freedom and fulfilment should be prioritized? Are the economy and political ideals of freedom and progress in conflict or mutually reinforcing?[23] Taking on these questions, the final pair of essays excavates two moments in which the economic imperatives motivating work within institutions of liberal capitalism were entangled with the meaning-making (or imaginative) aspects of culture, and they provide surprisingly counterintuitive accounts of the results. Sina Rahmani and Sean McCann offer distinct yet resonant perspectives on the success of the cultures of work in fulfilling or inhibiting the larger cultural and political promises of liberalism: Rahmani finds salutary the possibilities entailed by the imaginary structures of a seemingly exploitative colonial imaginary and administration, while McCann finds insidious the effect of focusing on what can seem (to literary scholars, anyway) uncontroversial narratives of culture and authenticity.

Rahmani's essay "The Empire Digs Back: Kew Gardens, the Assistant for India, and the Problem of Knowledge Production after Empire" explores the history of Kew Gardens in relation to England's colonial project in India and ultimately to India's anti-colonial project. While the empire was not materially coherent, the fiction of Kew as a "world garden" provided an imaginative coherence, one consonant with the liberal values of empire: the free circulation of knowledge and the educative mandate of imperial sovereignty. Rahmani further argues that India's anti-colonial nation-building likewise required an act of the imagination to which Kew was also key, thereby connecting the institutional history of Kew to India's nationalist anti-colonial project. By tracing such links, Rahmani gets at the heart of questions that vex the history of liberalism: how did ideals of freedom and human agency lead to the oppressions of empire, and how did they ultimately become transformed for anti-imperial purposes? Rahmani argues that a version of literary practice – the composing and recomposing powers of fiction – accounts for both these tendencies. In so doing, he shows that Kew's botanical fictions prefigure far better known representations of empire's cultures in colonial literature and postcolonial critique.

McCann's essay "'They Make Their Own Tragedies Too': Harvey Swados and Postwar Liberalism's Discourse of Dependency" explores the concerns of Harvey Swados and other mid-century US writers who, believing that the economic problems of the early twentieth century had been effectively solved by the emergence of a mass society, worried that this mass society was culturally impoverished. These writers believed that the domains of literature and art should address concerns of authenticity, happiness, purpose, and so on. Swados, who narrates the contracted lives of factory workers in short story form, depicts factory work as degrading because it is divorced from a greater purpose, thus participating in his generation's larger critique of liberal capitalism as pitting "authentic" modes of being against economic concerns, which was that generation's characteristic misrecognition of the literary/liberal entanglement. For McCann, we live with the legacy of that earlier moment's prioritization of qualitative over quantitative issues, its formulation of art and literature as at once complements and antidotes to the coercive force of the regimented bureaucratic/technocratic economy. The emphasis on the middle-class value of cultural autonomy over economic justice and the concern for psychological dependency rather than economic inequality in the work of mid-century writers have led inexorably, McCann concludes, to our neoliberal predicament.

NOTES

1 Bensinger, "Amazon Wants to Ship" and "When Drones Aren't Enough." A note on the significance of 1688–9 for the collection: We take this date to be roughly the beginning of liberalism, in all its contradictions, and also as a key milestone in both literary history and – for reasons that become clear in our elaboration of "entanglement" below – modern physics. 1688–9 inspired Locke's *Two Treatises of Government* and "Whig" historiography (a term coined by Herbert Butterfield to refer in a derogatory sense to the way that English historians used 1688–9 to anchor theories of British national destiny) and also, arguably, the beginnings of a theory of literary history (a case that rests, according to Earl Miner, on the late career of John Dryden). The case for a link between these concepts and physics rests on the fact that Isaac Newton's *Principia* was published in 1687.

2 Mark McGurl, "Everything and Less: Fiction in the Age of Amazon."

3 Cherniavsky, "Neocitizenship and Critique," 9. Cherniavsky develops her trenchant account of "neocitizenship" by drawing on analyses of neoliberalism by Foucault, Deleuze, and Hardt.

4 Feher, "Self-Appreciation," 33. In addition to these arguments by Cherniavsky and Feher, see also Timothy Mitchell, who develops the concept of "economentality," arguing that in the mid-twentieth century new "forms of political reason and calculative practice ... formed the

economy as their object and introduced the future into government" ("Economentality," 485); Leerom Medovoi, who finds fungibility at the heart of globalization, arguing that its process "offers a story in which the new world order will culminate, not in an undifferentiated whole, but in an endlessly differentiated circuit of exchangeability" ("Nation, Globe, Hegemony," 169); and Wendy Brown, who parses the importance of "financialized human capital" for neoliberalism, arguing that the project of "*homo oeconomicus*" in the contemporary moment is twofold – "to self-invest in ways that enhance its value or to attract investors through constant attention to its actual or figurative credit rating, and to do this across every sphere of its existence" (*Undoing the Demos*, 33).

5 Cherniavsky traces a similar argument through Deleuze's account of the society of control, observing that he "cites the shift from school-based education to 'perpetual training,' or in the current idiom, lifelong learning" ("Neocitizenship and Critique," 9). It bears emphasizing that the sort of entrepreneurial subjectivity we describe is only one type of subjection under neoliberalism, one that, while formally or in theory universally available, is in practice unevenly distributed (precisely through outlets and institutions such as Amazon or the contemporary university). A fuller account of global neoliberal subjection would in addition need to take stock of forms of precarity and remaindering that serve to manage or govern through neglect vast populations worldwide, populations concentrated in regions familiarly if cumbersomely called the "global south."

6 Literary-critical interest in chronic crises is evidenced in the discipline's percolating engagement with the work of Carl Schmitt, Walter Benjamin, and Giorgio Agamben, which articulates the tendency of liberal versions of sovereignty to presuppose and to promote an ongoing state of emergency or exception. See also Eric Cazdyn's theorization of "the new chronic" (*The Already Dead*, 5), and for a discussion of the neoliberal university's mobilization of the discourse of crisis, see Ramírez and Hyslop-Margison, "Neoliberalism, Universities, and the Discourse of Crisis."
It is by way of debates about chronic crisis that we tend to agree with those commentators – Angela Mitropoulos and David Harvey foremost among them – who read events such as the Brexit triumph and the ascendency of Donald Trump to indicate not so much a break from as a mutation within (an apotheosis or indeed excrescence of) neoliberalism. See Mitropoulos, "'Post-Factual' Readings of Neoliberalism"; Harvey, "Conversation between David Harvey & Evgeny Morozov on Post-Neoliberalism."

7 Much has been written about the neoliberal turn in higher education and its significance for culture, politics, and the production and organization of

knowledge (see, for instance, Frow, "Cultural Studies and the Neoliberal Imagination"; Warner, "Liberalism and the Cultural Studies Imagination: A Comment on John Frow"; Giroux, *Neoliberalism's War on Higher Education;* Lorenz, "If You're So Smart, Why Are You Under Surveillance?"; Newfield, *Unmaking the Public University*). Less has been written about the focus for the present volume: the historical interrelation of liberalism and literary history and the significance of such interrelation for the practice and politics of intellectual work now and in the future.

8 In arguing that race, gender, and sexuality have always been inextricable, via norms of self-regulation, from liberalism, a fact ever more obvious during the last decade, Mitropoulos wryly observes that "it is, of course, far easier to buy into the myth that 'neoliberalism means deregulation or free markets' when one exists on the naturalized because normative side of those demarcations." Mitropoulos, "'Post-Factual' Readings of Neoliberalism," n.p.

9 See Gardiner, "English Literature as Ideology" for a review of the ways that scholars have analysed the "expansion and universalisation of the discipline" of English and the "British state culture" that is its raison d'être (210). In Gardiner's reading, English studies has been marked by "informality, unaccountability, universalism, absorptiveness, and ahistoricism" (210). Gardiner is also useful on how Althusser allows us to see why literature has such an important role in the British context: an unwritten constitution and anti-formalist theory of law meant that literature had a disproportionate "duty to transmit the values of the state as if they were popular, civic, or national" (211). See also Frow for the ways that liberalism functions as an "ethos" rather than a doctrine (in Trilling's terms, an "essential imagination of variousness and possibility") ("Cultural Studies," 424).

10 On the relations between financial and humanistic crisis, see Brown, *Undoing the Demos;* Clover, "Value, Theory, Crisis"; Lye, Newfield, and Vernon, "Humanists and the Public University." On political theology, see Kahn, *The Future of Illusion;* Hammill and Lupton, *Political Theology and Early Modernity*. On republicanism, see Burtt, *Virtue Transformed;* Houston, *Republican Heritage in England and America;* Pocock, *The Machiavellian Moment*. On secularism, see Asad, *Formations of the Secular;* Mahmood, "Religious Reason and Secular Affect"; Pecora, *Secularization and Cultural Criticism;* Taylor, *A Secular Age*. For a defence of the literary/liberal nexus, see Hunt, *Inventing Human Rights;* Nussbaum, *Not for Profit;* Rorty, *Philosophy as Cultural Politics*. For efforts to recover conservative critiques, see During, *Against Democracy;* Perry, *Novel Relations*, and for

rehabilitations, see Anderson, *Bleak Liberalism*; Hadley, *Living Liberalism*; Kahn, *The Future of Illusion*; Lupton, *Thinking with Shakespeare*. On liberal rights, see Agamben, *Homo Sacer* and *State of Exception*; Anker, *Fictions of Dignity*; Bobbio, *Liberalism and Democracy*; Hunt, *Inventing Human Rights*. For monist interventions into liberal paradigms, see Badiou, *Being and Event*; Deleuze, *Difference and Repetition*; Latour, *We Have Never Been Modern*.

11 For a discussion of poesis (work, poetry, making) as an ideal of liberalism, see Kahn, *The Future of Illusion*.

12 *Oxford English Dictionary Online*, s.v. "entanglement," last modified December 2016, accessed 2 March 2017, http://www.oed.com.login.ezproxy.library.ualberta.ca/view/Entry/62785?redirectedFrom=ENTANGLEMENT.

13 Erwin Schrödinger is typically credited with recognizing the centrality of entanglement to quantum physics ("The Present Situation in Quantum Mechanics"). Jason W. Moore has recently deployed the concept of entanglement in his intervention into Marxist debates about ecology and capitalism (*Capitalism in the Web of Life*, 3).

14 The phrase originates with Albert Einstein. For its significance to theories of entanglement, see Barad, *Meeting the Universe Halfway*.

15 Barad, "Nature's Queer Performativity," 47.

16 In Lauren Berlant's definition, cruel optimism "exists when something you desire is actually an obstacle to your flourishing": thus in the contemporary university, widely embraced practices that seem to expand and enliven intellectual possibility actually constrain or undermine such flourishing in the service, instead, of a neoliberal logic of efficiency (Berlant, *Cruel Optimism*, 1).

17 Berlant has illuminated the concept of impasse as not a blockage so much as an indeterminate opening in which the self-evidence of business as usual begins to erode and unexpected, improvisatory modes of thinking and doing become possible and necessary. See Berlant, *Cruel Optimism*, 4–5. Thanks to Darin Barney for his insights into the matter of impasse at the After Oil School workshop, University of Alberta, 19–22 August 2015.

18 In venturing a productive and radical anachronism, we take inspiration from a number of scholars. Victoria Kahn, for example, models in her work a "reverse anachronism" that promotes "a genuine dialogue" between disparate historical periods as a means of rethinking literary-historical methodologies (*Wayward Contracts*, 22). Julia Lupton rethinks liberalism's trajectory as "a resource for unknown futures, unfolding now" (*Thinking with Shakespeare*, 260). We also take seriously the critiques of historical method – by Marxist, postcolonial, and postsecular scholars – that have

illuminated the deep entwining of historical methodologies with liberal, colonial, and capitalist ideologies and practices. Dipesh Chakrabarty, for example, has shown how the anti-colonial heritage involves a critical relationship to developmental or stadial history (*Provincializing Europe*). Also inspirational is Ian Baucom's theorization, in *Specters of the Atlantic,* of anti-progressive history and historiography, which illuminates the pressing and vexed significance of the "what-has-been" in liberalism and literary history for neoliberal "now-being" today (149).

19 These are not the only terms relevant to the histories and entanglements of literature and liberalism. We might have chosen other terms – for example, character, ethics, freedom, or critique – in order to animate the central concepts explored here, and we recognize that the collection treats only indirectly a whole host of other concepts at the heart of the literary/liberal entanglement – for example, property, sovereignty, identity, democracy, publicity, public and private reason, and many others.

20 See Mill, *On Liberty*, xx; Emerson, *Journals and Miscellaneous Notebooks*, 251.

21 Anderson, *Imagined Communities*, 7.

22 See Flatley, "How a Revolutionary Counter-Mood Is Made."

23 John Locke, for example, famously posited private property, which was acquired by labour, as the foundation of the social contract and the possessive individual (*Two Treatises of Government*). Karl Marx, by contrast, found the alienated conditions of labour under nineteenth-century capitalism to be at the heart of social, cultural, and psychological alienation ("Alienation and Social Classes"). In our neoliberal moment, the bifurcation has become yet more stark (or perhaps, as Michel Foucault has suggested, nonexistent), with freedom ascribed to corporate entities that now can have "cultures" of their own (*Society Must Be Defended*). Whether the human capacity to create culture via work is celebrated or denigrated, the question is at the heart of liberal philosophy.

BIBLIOGRAPHY

Agamben, Giorgio. *Homo Sacer: Sovereign Power and Bare Life*. Translated by Daniel Heller-Roazen. Stanford, CA: Stanford University Press, 1998.

– *State of Exception*. Translated by Kevin Attell. Chicago: University of Chicago Press, 2005.

Anderson, Amanda. *Bleak Liberalism*. Chicago: University of Chicago Press, 2016.

Anderson, Benedict. *Imagined Communities: Reflections on the Origin and Spread of Nationalism*. 1983. Rev. ed. London: Verso, 1991.

Anker, Elizabeth S. *Fictions of Dignity: Embodying Human Rights in World Literature*. Ithaca: Cornell University Press, 2012.
Asad, Talal. *Formations of the Secular: Christianity, Islam, Modernity*. Stanford, CA: Stanford University Press, 2003.
Badiou, Alain. *Being and Event*. Translated by Oliver Feltham. London: Continuum, 2007.
Barad, Karen. *Meeting the Universe Halfway: Quantum Physics and the Entanglement of Matter and Meaning*. Durham, NC: Duke University Press, 2007.
– "Nature's Queer Performativity." *Kvinder, Køn & Forskning Nr*. 1–2 (2012): 25–53.
Baucom, Ian. *Specters of the Atlantic: Finance Capital, Slavery, and the Philosophy of History*. Durham, NC: Duke University Press, 2005.
Benjamin, Walter. "Theses on the Philosophy of History." *Illuminations*. Edited and with an introduction by Hannah Arendt. Translated by Harry Zohn, 253–64. New York: Schocken Books, 1968.
Berlant, Lauren. *Cruel Optimism*. Durham, NC: Duke University Press, 2011.
Bensinger, Greg. "Amazon Wants to Ship Your Package Before You Buy It." *Digits* (blog). *Wall Street Journal*. 17 January 2014. http://blogs.wsj.com/digits/2014/01/17/amazon-wants-to-ship-your-package-before-you-buy-it/.
– "When Drones Aren't Enough, Amazon Envisions Trucks with 3D Printers." *Digits* (blog). *Wall Street Journal*. 26 February 2015. http://blogs.wsj.com/digits/2015/02/26/when-drones-arent-enough-amazon-envisions-trucks-with-3d-printers/.
Bobbio, Norberto. *Liberalism and Democracy*. Translated by Martin Ryle and Kate Soper. London: Verso, 2006.
Brown, Wendy. *Undoing the Demos: Neoliberalism's Stealth Revolution*. Cambridge, MA: MIT Press, 2015.
Burtt, Shelley G. *Virtue Transformed: Political Argument in England, 1688–1740*. Cambridge: Cambridge University Press, 2006.
Butterfield, Herbert. *The Whig Interpretation of History*. New York: Norton, 1965.
Cazdyn, Eric. *The Already Dead: The New Time of Politics, Culture, and Illness*. Durham, NC: Duke University Press, 2012.
Chakrabarty, Dipesh. *Provincializing Europe: Postcolonial Thought and Historical Difference*. Princeton, NJ: Princeton University Press, 2007.
Cherniavsky, Eva. "Neocitizenship and Critique." *Social Text* 99 (Summer 2009): 1–23.
Clover, Joshua. "Value, Theory, Crisis." *PMLA: Publications of the Modern Language Association of America* 127, no. 1 (2012): 107–14.

Deleuze, Gilles. *Difference and Repetition*. Translated by Paul Patton. New York: Columbia University Press, 1994.

During, Simon. *Against Democracy: Literary Experience in the Era of Emancipations*. New York: Fordham University Press, 2012.

Einstein, Albert, Boris Podolsky, and Nathan Rosen. "Can Quantum-Mechanical Description of Physical Reality Be Considered Complete?" *Physical Review* 47, no. 10 (May 1935): 777–80.

Emerson, Ralph Waldo. *The Journals and Miscellaneous Notebooks of Ralph Waldo Emerson*. Vol. 2, edited by William H. Gilman and J. E. Parsons. Cambridge, MA: Belknap Press, 1970.

Feher, Michel. "Self-Appreciation; or, The Aspirations of Human Capital." *Public Culture* 21, no. 1 (2009): 21–41.

Flatley, Jonathan. "How a Revolutionary Counter-Mood Is Made." *New Literary History* 43, no. 3 (2012): 503–25.

Foucault, Michel. *Society Must Be Defended: Lectures at the Collège de France, 1975–1976*. Translated by David Macey. New York: Picador, 2003.

Frow, John. "Cultural Studies and the Neoliberal Imagination." *Yale Journal of Criticism* 12, no. 2 (Fall 1999): 423–30.

Gardiner, Michael. "English Literature as Ideology." In *Literature of an Independent England: Revisions of England, Englishness, and English Literature*, edited by Claire Westall and Michael Gardiner, 203–17. New York: Palgrave Macmillan, 2013.

Giroux, Henry A. *Neoliberalism's War on Higher Education*. Chicago: Haymarket Books, 2014.

Hadley, Elaine. *Living Liberalism: Practical Citizenship in Mid-Victorian Britain*. Chicago: University of Chicago Press, 2010.

Hammill, Graham, and Julia Reinhard Lupton, eds. *Political Theology and Early Modernity*. Chicago: University of Chicago Press, 2012.

Hardt, Michael. "The Withering of Civil Society." *Social Text* 45 (1995): 27–44.

Harvey, David. "Conversation between David Harvey & Evgeny Morozov on Post-Neoliberalism, Trump, Infrastructure, Sharing Economy, Smart City." Filmed 14 November 2016. YouTube video, 20:14. Part of the Barcelona Initiative on Technological Sovereignty (BITS). Posted 15 November 2016. http://davidharvey.org/2016/11/video-conversation-between-david-harvey-evgeny-morozov-on-post-neoliberalism-trump-infrastructure-sharing-economy-smart-city/.

Houston, Alan Craig. *Algernon Sidney and the Republican Heritage in England and America*. Princeton, NJ: Princeton University Press, 1991.

Hunt, Lynn. *Inventing Human Rights: A History*. New York: W.W. Norton, 2007.

Kahn, Victoria Ann. *The Future of Illusion: Political Theology and Early Modern Texts*. Chicago: University of Chicago Press, 2013.
– *Wayward Contracts: The Crisis of Political Obligation in England, 1640–1674*. Princeton, NJ: Princeton University Press, 2004.
Kant, Immanuel. *Critique of Judgement*. 1892. Edited by Nicholas Walker and translated by James Creed Meredith. Oxford World's Classics. Oxford: Oxford University Press, 2009.
Latour, Bruno. *We Have Never Been Modern*. Translated by Catherine Porter. Cambridge, MA: Harvard University Press, 1993.
Locke, John. *Two Treatises of Government*. 1690. Edited by Peter Laslett. 3rd ed. Cambridge: Cambridge University Press, 1988.
Lorenz, Chris. "If You're So Smart, Why Are You Under Surveillance? Universities, Neoliberalism, and New Public Management." *Critical Inquiry* 38, no. 3 (2012): 599–629.
Lupton, Julia Reinhard. *Thinking with Shakespeare: Essays on Politics and Life*. Chicago: University of Chicago Press, 2011.
Lye, Colleen, Christopher Newfield, and James Vernon. "Humanists and the Public University." *Representations* 116, no. 1 (2011): 1–18.
Mahmood, Saba. "Religious Reason and Secular Affect: An Incommensurable Divide?" *Critical Inquiry* 35, no. 4 (2009): 836–62.
Marx, Karl. "Alienation and Social Classes." In *The Marx-Engels Reader*, edited by Robert C. Tucker, 133–5. New York: W.W. Norton, 1978.
McGurl, Mark. "Everything and Less: Fiction in the Age of Amazon." *Modern Language Quarterly* 73, no. 3 (2016): 447-71.
Medovoi, Leerom. "Nation, Globe, Hegemony: Post-Fordist Preconditions of the Transnational Turn in American Studies." *Interventions* 7, no. 2 (2005): 162–79.
Mill, John Stuart. *On Liberty and Other Essays*. Edited by John Gray. Oxford World's Classics. Oxford: Oxford University Press, 2008.
Miner, Earl. *Dryden's Poetry*. Bloomington: Indiana University Press, 1967.
Mitchell, Timothy. "Economentality." *Critical Inquiry* 40, no. 4 (2014): 479–507.
Mitropoulos, Angela. "'Post-Factual' Readings of Neoliberalism, Before and After Trump." *Environment and Planning D: Society and Space*. http://societyandspace.org/2016/12/05/post-factual-readings-of-neoliberalism-before-and-after-trump/.
Moore, Jason W. *Capitalism in the Web of Life: Ecology and the Accumulation of Capital*. London: Verso, 2015.
Newfield, Christopher. *Unmaking the Public University*. Cambridge, MA: Harvard University Press, 2011.

Nussbaum, Martha Craven. *Not for Profit: Why Democracy Needs the Humanities*. Public Square Book Series. Princeton, NJ: Princeton University Press, 2010.

Pecora, Vincent P. *Secularization and Cultural Criticism: Religion, Nation, and Modernity*. Religion and Postmodernism. Chicago: University of Chicago Press, 2006.

Perry, Ruth. *Novel Relations: The Transformation of Kinship in English Literature and Culture, 1748–1818*. Cambridge: Cambridge University Press, 2004.

Pocock, J.G.A. *The Machiavellian Moment: Florentine Political Thought and the Atlantic Republican Tradition*. 2nd ed. Princeton, NJ: Princeton University Press, 2003.

– *Political Theology and Early Modernity*. Chicago: University of Chicago Press, 2012.

Ramírez, Andrés, and Emery Hyslop-Margison. "Neoliberalism, Universities and the Discourse of Crisis." *L2 Journal* 7, no. 3 (2015): 167–83.

Rorty, Richard. *Philosophy as Cultural Politics: Philosophical Papers, volume 4*. Cambridge: Cambridge University Press, 2007.

Schrödinger, Erwin. 1935. "The Present Situation in Quantum Mechanics." Translated by John D. Trimmer. *Proceedings of the American Philosophical Society* 124 (1980): 323–38.

Taylor, Charles. *A Secular Age*. Cambridge, MA: Harvard University Press, 2009.

Trilling, Lionel. *The Liberal Imagination: Essays on Literature and Society*. New York: New York Review of Books, 2008.

Warner, Michael. "Liberalism and the Cultural Studies Imagination: A Comment on John Frow." *Yale Journal of Criticism* 12, no. 2 (1999): 431–33.

PART I

Acting: Liberal Subjects and Objects

1 Posthuman Capital, or I ♥ Apocalypse

JENNIFER ASHTON

Marjorie Perloff's 2012 essay "Poetry on the Brink" begins with a question: "What happens to poetry when everybody is a poet?" Rather than suggesting an answer to the question, she gives an extended quotation that paints the conditions under which, if the current trend continues, we might have a world with no more non-poets:

> The colleges and universities that offer graduate degrees in poetry employ about 1,800 faculty members to support the cause. But these are only 177 of the 458 institutions that teach creative writing. Taking those into account, the faculty dedicated to creative writing swells to more than 20,000. All these people must comply with the norms for faculty in those institutions, filing annual reports of their activities, in which the most important component is publication. With that in mind, I don't need to spell out the truly exorbitant numbers involved. In a positive light, it has sanctioned a surfeit of small presses ... to say nothing of all the Web-zines.[1]

This passage happens to have been taken from a lecture by the poet Jed Rasula, but it could just as easily have come from other recent essays making similar claims, which have pegged the current state of affairs in American poetry on its exponential growth in production, whether it's in the number of writing programs and workshops, or print books and journals, or small presses, or webzines and blogs.[2]

Obviously, even a world in which the number of poets has increased exponentially is nevertheless a world in which poets remain a scant minority – hardly one in which "everybody is a poet" or in which there might be no more non-poets. And even if it were such a world, what exactly the threat of such a proliferation would be is not exactly self-evident. It's not obvious, for example, why it should matter that there's more poetry being produced on a daily basis than it's humanly possible to consume – or at least why that should matter for poetry any more than for other products of the culture industry. It's easier to see why a dramatic increase in the number of poets competing for faculty positions might matter, when even recently, at what is arguably the crest of a dramatic increase in the number of creative writing programs, newly minted PhDs have been more likely to wind up in low-paying adjunct positions with little to no benefits or job security than in tenure-track positions with good salaries and benefits. But as poetry has increasingly spoken from the standpoint of crisis, at least since the attacks of 9/11, and, in a much more intensified manner, since the financial collapse of 2008, it has also increasingly spoken from a standpoint in which the nature of the crisis matters less than one's attitude or affect in relation to it – or, to put this slightly differently, in which the crisis itself is a matter of attitude or affect.

We can get a preliminary sense of this turn from an essay by Christopher Nealon, published in 2004, in which expressivity in the form of an affective stance emerges precisely in the context of an apocalyptic standpoint. Nealon introduces a group of younger American poets writing at the turn of the millennium who represent, as he puts it, a "recent affective and strategic shift in American poetry" that "can be described as a shift in attitudes toward the character of late-capitalist totality."[3] The title of Nealon's essay is "Camp Messianism, or, the Hopes of Poetry in Late-Late Capitalism." What it names, Nealon says, is "a kind of camp posture" adopted by "post-Language poets" toward the "'damaged' material life" of "late capitalism."[4] What messianism and, for our purposes, apocalypse have in common is that they both involve the vision of an end time whose defining characteristic is that it is something for which we wait. And thus in good messianist form, the poets Nealon mobilizes for his case "expend their considerable talents on making articulate the ways in which, as they look around, they see *waiting*."[5] Nealon marshals passages from several different poems in quick succession, all intended to exemplify this expectant tendency, and it's worth looking at one of them in particular, from Kevin Davies's 2000 work, *Comp.*:

Every junked
vehicle a
proposition
waiting for

the right rustic
welder
after the war that
never happened
here.[6]

The junked vehicle in Davies obviously indexes the more general state of "damage" that Nealon argues underwrites the poems he writes about. It's also worth pointing out, as Nealon does not, that Davies's lines are especially successful in enacting at the level of their enjambment a precise grammatical allegory for the "messianism" Nealon attributes to them. That is, when Davies uses the line break to suspend the arrival of the noun announced by the indefinite article "a" or the adjective "rustic," or the arrival of the predicate to the subordinate clause announced by the relative pronoun "that," these suspensions force the reader, in effect, to wait. Moreover, as we pass through these momentarily suspended syntactical outcomes to arrive in the present "here," we clearly remain in our unredeemed condition, left with a series of empty representations: a welder yet to materialize and a war that never happened here, both of which are predicated on a proposition with no truth value.

To the extent that these lines by Davies – the last three of which could sustain an essay of their own – index one or another form of withdrawal from the field of representation, they help to clarify what I take to be the apocalyptic stakes in Nealon's term "messianism." That is, the sort of end time that is implicated in both messianism and apocalypse – that for which we must wait – is also that which must remain unrepresented and unrepresentable in any terms given by the present. And insofar as what this messianism requires of us is an attitude – as opposed to, say, some sort of committed action (under the apocalyptic dispensation, how can one know what to commit to?) – a further entailment here is that utopianism turns out to be incompatible with this poetry, as we shall see quite vividly in the case of Juliana Spahr's *this connection of everyone with lungs*. For Nealon, it's the seeming impossibility of utopian ideals that leads to an abandonment of normative claims for the "postures" of "camp." For Spahr, the reduction of "everyone" to their breathing lungs implies a subject position so literalized that even attitudes and postures, much less the kinds of normative claims required for political commitment, become irrelevant. For Spahr, in other words, it's the abandonment of normative claims that, I shall argue, makes utopian ones impossible.

Juliana Spahr's "Poem Written after September 11, 2001," which serves as the opening section of *this connection of everyone with lungs*, is a poem that imagines, in effect, what it looks like when everyone is a poet. The collective subject it envisions is extremely difficult, moreover, to distinguish from the objects it encounters in the world. The poem ends with an elegy for the subject – everyone with lungs – that its title names: "How lovely and how doomed this connection of everyone with lungs."[7] By the time we reach this point in the poem, we have discovered, and the title already gestures in this direction, that the "connection" this line refers to is more physical than spiritual. For one thing, as the anatomical reference of the title implies, the connection is above all a bodily one. But more than that, it is, quite literally, concrete, insofar as we learn that it consists of the physical particles – among other things, of actual concrete – that enter and exit the breathing lungs of the title's subject, "everyone":

> The space of everyone that has just been inside of everyone mixing inside of everyone with nitrogen and oxygen and water vapor and argon and carbon dioxide and suspended dust spores and bacteria mixing inside of everyone with sulfur and sulfuric acid and titanium and nickel and minute silicon particles from pulverized glass and concrete.[8]

As Lisa Siraganian observes in the final chapter of *Modernism's Other Work: The Art Object's Political Life*, which deals in part with Spahr's poem, one of the striking things about the churning cloud of World Trade Center debris that Spahr's poem invokes and that the news footage of 9/11 so spectacularly depicted, was that it continued to drift "for days (if not weeks)."[9] This dispersal of debris is precisely what allows Spahr to attribute what "brings [everyone] together" to the same force that is responsible for its drift: "the physical law of entropy – the expansive force that diffuses everything everywhere over time."[10] Thus, it's through the simultaneity of connection and dispersal that Spahr's poem "dramatizes the political camaraderie emerging immediately after 9/11, when on September 12, 2001, the French newspaper *Le Monde*'s headline proclaimed, 'Nous sommes tous Americains,' a line that became a model to generate other versions, such as the ubiquitous 'We are all New Yorkers' and the decades-old publicity campaign logo 'I ♥ NY,' that took on new meaning after 9/11."[11] Siraganian goes on to suggest just how far the meaning of "I ♥ NY" can travel:

> If we are all New Yorkers because eventually we all breathe some particular bit of New York air, what stops us from being Texans, or Californians, or Afghanis for the very same reason? (I ♥ Kabul.) We are simultaneously everywhere and nowhere ... For Spahr, our inevitable connectedness with other inhalers and exhalers is precisely what makes it impossible to be a people, or simply *persons*. Out of cosmopolitan post-nationalism emerges the impossibility of political subjectivity of any kind, because we become the "lovely" and also the "doomed" citizens of utopia. (I ♥ Utopia.) How exactly the lovely and doomed way of this world might be organized or even lived in [Spahr] leaves unimagined and maybe unimaginable, or at least unsaid.[12]

Siraganian correctly understands that Spahr, despite the fact that the poet does not for a millisecond think of her work as an abandonment of politics, nevertheless subscribes to a logic that entails exactly that, the abandonment of politics.

That is, as soon as Spahr's "utopian" collectivity becomes a function of the mobility of the particles that pass through "everyone with lungs," it becomes, quite literally, a matter of purely contingent causes and effects. We come together for no reason. And it's in giving up reasons that Spahr gives up on the minimum normative grounds for having a politics in the first place, not to mention the imperatives to belief and understanding that go with it.[13] I don't mean here that the people who carried out the attacks on the World Trade Center had no reasons for their actions; what I mean is that once our collective response is literally a function of what we breathe in and out, our reasons have dropped out of the picture. By the same token, however, the term "utopian" starts to look out of place as a description of Spahr's project, for the contingent causes and effects that form "this connection of everyone with lungs" are also an index of the irreducible differences and multiplicity of the bodies in which they occur. Insofar as the collective that Spahr imagines is made up, at any given moment, of all existing subject positions – i.e., "everyone's" – it's not quite right to say that we're "simultaneously everywhere and nowhere." Far from the "non-place" of utopia's Greek etymology to which Siraganian alludes, Spahr's world is all places and nothing less. Because "everybody" also means everywhere, there's no nowhere there.

For this reason it also can't quite be right to say that Spahr gives us the impossibility of political subjectivity, for it's precisely the subjectivity that Spahr gives us, in its radically literalized form – everything is a function of our "inhaling" and "exhaling" – that makes a politics an impossibility. By which I simply mean that it's hard to imagine how a subjectivity originating in our lungs could have a politics at all (if it did, my right lung could only, quite literally, yield a different politics from my left, because it would, quite literally, have a different subject position from the left). The subtitle of this essay, "I ♥ Apocalypse," owes both its form and, in part, the logic it represents, to Siraganian's important analysis of Spahr's moving toxic dust cloud. But "I ♥ Apocalypse" also signals the need for an adjustment, one that we are required to make, I think, especially if we want to locate a project like Spahr's *this connection of everyone with lungs* within other significant poetic developments of the past decade in the United States, particularly within ecopoetics on the one hand and some recent identity-driven poetic projects on the other. The difference in this context between "I ♥ Utopia" and "I ♥ Apocalypse" is the difference between a poetics based on what should be said (a poetics capable of representing, for example, how "our lives might be organized"), and a poetics based on what can only be left unsaid because what "should be" remains unspeakable in any normative terms. As we shall see, moreover, the apocalyptic thinking that underpins ecopoetics turns out to operate as well within a very different poetic discourse following in the wake of 2008, specifically the one dealing with racial identity and "postracial" claims during and following the election of Barack Obama in 2008. What these two apparently unrelated developments have in common is their basis in a commitment to subjecthood as such, and more specifically, to a subjecthood whose political and ethical value is understood as indistinguishable from something like its objecthood.

If, as I'm arguing, "I ♥ Utopia" doesn't quite describe the poetry I'll be discussing below, nothing, in my view, could be more appropriate than the graphic "I ♥" for depicting the kind of subject position that Spahr envisions in *this connection of everyone with lungs* – that is, for depicting a subject that consists, as "everyone" does for Spahr, in purely contingent affiliations. Which is to say that the glass and concrete particles that enter everyone's lungs and connect everyone to everyone else don't mean anything by their attachments, any more than anyone can mean anything by breathing them in. In reducing the totality of the world to nothing but material causes and effects, Spahr transforms a world structured politically into a world structured purely contingently – despite the fact that mixed in with those material causes and effects are political ones. But the fact that the material and the political coincide does not make them equivalent or interchangeable.

Moreover, if, after all, the logo "I ♥" is an emblematic token of the type that is self-expression as such, at the same time it's an emblem for the contingent affiliations of the market – I buy what I'm sold – delivered in the guise of individual self-expression – I buy what "I ♥." Given that the literal medium in which the contingent affiliations that connect everyone occur is the breath – a trope, I scarcely need to point out, with long-standing ties to poetic utterance in general and to lyric in particular – in finding ourselves squarely in the terrain of the breath in *this connection of everyone with lungs*, we find ourselves not just in the terrain of, say, air quality, but also that of the lyric subject. When everyone, and, for that matter, everything, consists of purely contingent material connections with other ones and things – as is clearly the case in Spahr's poem and as will turn out to be even more vividly the case in some of the most radical claims of the movement that goes by the name of ecopoetics – what remains for poetry, and what passes for politics in it, is essentially an attitude or inclination toward those relations. Which is to say it isn't an intention or belief about a given state of affairs. If the world as it's organized by our lungs somehow counts as having a politics, it's a politics that could never count as right or wrong.

Ecologically conscious art produced around the time that the United States Environmental Protection Agency was founded (1970), when "ecology" would become a regular lesson topic in public school classrooms, represented simultaneously a means of refusing the increasingly evident market systems by which artistic careers were made and art was bought and sold and a means of consciousness-raising about the increasingly catastrophic effects of human industry on all forms of life.[14]

At the same time, the ecological movement that came to be known as "deep ecology" was building on the work of the Norwegian philosopher Arne Naess. Naess argued that most ecological initiatives were limited by a fundamental anthropocentrism – we try to control air pollution to keep our lungs healthy; we preserve the nature around a river to keep our water safe to drink. What this anthropocentrism entails, Naess argued, is a failure to recognize the value that mountains, rivers, oceans, plants, and animals have in themselves and for one another, independent of anything humans see in them or would seek to gain from them. A properly ethical relation to nature, Naess argued, meant treating nature as if it had the same rights and value as a person.[15] Thus deep ecology also gave us a world in which, as the philosopher Tom Regan put it in his foundational 1981 essay, "The Nature and Possibility of an Environmental Ethic," "the class of those beings which have moral standing includes but is larger than the class of conscious beings – that is, all conscious beings and some nonconscious beings must be held to have moral standing."[16] That is, a mountain or a stream could be imagined to have the same rights as any legal subject, as Christopher Stone had argued a decade earlier in his 1972 "Should Trees Have Standing?," and as cases such as *Fisher v. Lowe* argued before the Michigan Court of Appeals in 1983 (Justice Gillis famously began his decision with a poem: "We thought that we would never see / A suit to compensate a tree").[17] The very recent turn ecology has taken toward the philosophy of object-oriented ontology (OOO) has given us a different world. What differentiates deep ecology from object-oriented ecology is that object-oriented ontology argues that the mistake we make in anthropomorphizing nature is not the mistake of believing that plants and rocks are really subjects just like us, when they aren't, but the mistake of believing that humans are subjects, when we aren't. If deep ecology sought to extend the ontology of persons to objects, the application of object-oriented ontology to ecology is a means of extending the ontology of objects to persons. And if we put this in terms of ecopoetics, what this means is that the poetics of the subject position is replaced by a poetics of the object position. As we shall see, however, the poetics of the object position turns out to work just like the recent poetics of the subject position that I've been discussing, and its politics – or, as I will argue, its debilitation of politics – is the same.[18]

The philosopher Graham Harman gives a concise illustration of how object-oriented ontology works, and he does so by borrowing a well-known hammer from the philosopher Martin Heidegger. "Heidegger radicalized phenomenology," Harman writes,

> by noting that most of our contact with entities *does not* occur in the manner of having them present before the mind. Quite the contrary. When using a hammer, for instance, I am focused on the building project currently underway, and I am probably taking the hammer for granted. Unless the hammer is too heavy or too slippery, or unless it breaks, I tend not to notice it at all ... Heidegger's tools always remain hidden from the mind, just like Kant's things-in-themselves. In Heidegger's terminology, they "withdraw" (*entziehen*) from all access: they remain veiled, concealed, or

> hidden. But real objects must also have individual features, since otherwise all things would be interchangeable.... The broken hammer alludes to the inscrutable reality of hammer-being lying behind the accessible theoretical, practical, or perceptual qualities of the hammer. The reason for calling this relation one of "allusion" is that it can only hint at the reality of the hammer without ever making it directly present to the mind.[19]

It's easy to see in this account how the human subject's understanding of her relation to the hammer – the point of view that, when translated into ecology, becomes our anthropocentrism – reveals itself to be a blind spot even when we believe it. Any given quality that may come to light about the hammer – as our relation to it changes when it goes from pounding a nail to breaking – for Harman points only to the infinite other qualities of the hammer that it has in reality but that cannot reveal themselves to us under any circumstances. From the perspective of the subject who uses the hammer, the world is permanently apocalyptic. Which is just to say that the revelation of the hammer's "true" nature, like that of every object (and this category, for Harman's purposes, includes the hammer user herself) is on the one hand perpetually immanent and on the other perpetually on the horizon, unavailable in any given present.

But this is only half of the story. What Harman and others committed to this metaphysics understand as its crucial turn – that is, what they think makes this an object-oriented ontology and not a subject-oriented one – is that the relation the hammer, as subject, has to the object using it is understood to have exactly the same apocalyptic structure as the relation we have to it. For Harman, whenever one entity stands in relation to another, which is to say, at each and every moment of its existence (for it always stands in relation to something), an infinite variety of qualities that the object possesses in reality remain withdrawn with respect to its relation to any given other object. The utility for ecology of this perpetual withdrawal from any positive grounds for ontology is that it looks like a solution – indeed, more than a solution, a nullification – with respect to the problem of anthropocentrism. To ecocritics like Timothy Morton, object-oriented ontology offers a logic whereby our tendency to anthropomorphize represents a structure of being that also belongs to everything else: "Just as I fail to avoid anthropomorphizing everything, so all entities whatsoever constantly translate other objects into their own terms. My back maps out a small backpomorphic slice of this tree that I'm leaning on. The strings of the wind harp stringpomorphize the wind. The wind windpomorphizes the temperature differentials between the mountains and the flat land … If everything is itselfpomorphizing everything else, anthropomorphism is not as big a deal as some ecological criticism thinks."[20] We can begin to see here why it's called "object-oriented ontology." Every object is always oriented toward some other or others, and for every object, the object toward which it orients itself is, as I've already suggested, both expressing itself and withdrawn. At the same time, because, as Harman puts it, "staring at a hammer does not exhaust its depths," the object is never fully present in its perpetually changing orientation toward other objects.[21] Yet it is at all moments fully what it is; what it fully is is just eternally "withdrawn." This condition produces what Morton calls the constitutive contradiction of object-oriented ontology: "objects are *themselves* (withdrawal) and *not themselves* (appearance) at the very same time. This means not only that objects are one thing to themselves and another to others, but that objects are also one thing to themselves and *another thing to themselves*, all at once."[22]

In an earlier work, *The Ecological Thought*, Morton gives this same contradiction a different name: "dark ecology." An obvious play on "deep ecology," "dark ecology" imagines not just plants and animals but everything, including ourselves, as irreducibly "other," "a multitude," Morton says, "of entangled strange strangers."[23] Thus "dark ecology" corrects what Morton thinks is mistaken in deep ecology – thinking of rocks or trees as having the same standing as persons, i.e., treating them as if they were like us, when, as Morton argues, the only thing we share is our irreducible estrangement.[24] For Morton, what makes all of us and everything surrounding us "strange strangers" is that we remain forever "dark" to one other. At this point we can also see the degree to which Morton's ecological critique looks exactly like an identity critique of a very familiar kind; indeed, Morton's 2010 essay "Queer Ecology" adheres precisely to the script of "dark ecology."[25] If deep ecology was ecology's civil rights movement, dark ecology is its queer theory.

We can begin to see just how closely the memes of dark ecology and queer theory resemble one another when Morton elaborates on the concept of the "strange stranger":

> According to prevailing ideologies, we must become, or be thought of as, like "animals" (biocentrism), or they should become, or be thought of as, like us (anthropocentrism). Neither choice is satisfactory. There is no way to maintain the strangeness of things … We should instead explore the

> paradoxes and fissures of identity *within* "human" and "animal." Instead of "animal," I use *strange stranger*. This stranger isn't just strange. She, or he, or it – can we tell? how? – is strangely strange. Their strangeness itself is strange. We can never absolutely figure them out. If we could, then all we would have is a ready-made box to put them in, and we would just be looking at the box, not at the strange strangers.[26]

To paraphrase the passage by Harman that I quoted earlier: staring at a stranger does not exhaust her/his/its depths. And just as in the case of the inexhaustible depths of Harman's hammer, Morton suggests that whatever perception or understanding we settle on in trying to figure out a stranger will inevitably force some other aspect of the stranger to withdraw from view. On the one hand, it would seem, all we have is all identity all the time. We can't avoid our knowing looks. On the other hand, any given stranger has no identity because any identity we give to it is not what it is. We can't know any stranger – and by extension, anyone or anything – by our knowing looks. But because everything is expressing the truth of itself at all moments, we are in the midst of a constant revelation that we haven't got the eyes to see.

"What if," Morton writes, "[ecological] disaster isn't an imminent cataclysm but has already occurred? What if this is how it looks? … There is no beyond, no depth, and no comforting background. No Being, only beings."[27] Being unable to know the future is one thing, but Morton suggests that we also cannot recognize the past – that is, because we cannot fully apprehend any given object, we cannot fully apprehend the myriad effects of objects coming into contact with and affecting one another and the multiple facets of beings that every such contact produces. Thus the apocalyptic logic of infinitely plural but infinitely withdrawn being by which we cannot know the future or recognize the past is exactly the same logic, I will argue, according to which "dark ecology" so seamlessly transitions into a "queer ecology" and more broadly into something like an ecology of identity. We can see this logic clearly if we consider the ecocritical theory we've been discussing in the context of some very recent poetry and theory situated around black identity in the African American literary tradition.

Fred Moten's 2003 *In the Break: The Aesthetics of the Black Radical Tradition* argues that black experience resides in an "unbridgeable break," or, as he also puts it, "in the cut": "Blackness is … [an] improvisational immanence – where untraceable, anoriginal rootedness and unenclosed, disclosing outness converge, where that convergence is articulation by and through an infinitesimal and unbridgeable break."[28] To illustrate this "unbridgeable break" or "cut," Moten turns to such examples as the jazz performances of Cecil Taylor and Eric Dolphy, the poetry of Amiri Baraka and Nathaniel Mackey, and the performance art of Adrian Piper, among others. But it's in Moten's use of Piper's work in particular that we can see how close the concept of "the cut" comes to the "paradoxes and fissures of identity" that Morton refers to in his elaboration of "strange strangeness."

To get at this "strange strangeness," we can begin with Piper's *Untitled Performance for Max's Kansas City*, in which the artist, wearing blindfold, gloves, and tape over her ears and mouth, circulated among the art-goers at a gallery exhibition. Piper explains her objectives for the performance as follows:

> To even walk into Max's was to be absorbed into the collective Art Self-Conscious Consciousness, either as object or as collaborator. I didn't want to be absorbed as a collaborator, because that would mean having my own consciousness co-opted and modified by that of others: It would mean allowing my consciousness to be influenced by their perceptions of art, and exposing my perceptions of art to their consciousness, and I didn't want that. I have always had a very strong individualistic streak. My solution was to privatize my own consciousness as much as possible, by depriving it of sensory input from that environment; to isolate it from all tactile, aural, and visual feedback. In doing so I presented myself as a silent, secret, passive object, seemingly ready to be absorbed into their consciousness as an object ... My objecthood became my subjecthood.[29]

Here, Piper's "subjecthood" emerges in the interstices – in what Moten calls the "cut" – between her own presence to herself and her exposure to the perceptions of the surrounding spectators. The objecthood that the spectators see is, as Morton might put it, a "ready-made box."[30] Piper constructs the situation so that the spectators' perception of her ("the objecthood that the spectators see") is unavailable to her own perception as a subject, rendering the "subjecthood" that her "objecthood became" "withdrawn" in Harman's Heideggerian terms, both to the spectators and to herself.

We can recall that among Harman's synonyms for "withdrawn" is "veiled," and the "break" or "cut" into which black subjectivity withdraws is perhaps fully legible only in the context of a barely veiled source, this famous passage from W.E.B. Du Bois's *Souls of Black Folk*:

> The Negro is a sort of seventh son, born with a veil, and gifted with second-sight in this American world – a world which yields him no true

> self-consciousness, but only lets him see himself through the revelation of the other world. It is a peculiar sensation, this double consciousness, this sense of always looking at one's self through the eyes of others.[31]

Obviously the Jim Crow conditions under which Du Bois wrote these words were different in substantial ways from the conditions being interrogated by the twenty-first-century poets I want to turn to now. But for both these poets and for the ecocritics I've been discussing, the logic of double-consciousness imagined by Du Bois yields an apocalyptic identity: the prospect of revelation is embodied in objecthood, and objecthood is embodied in a subject that is perpetually withdrawn.

Douglas Kearney's 2009 *The Black Automaton* includes a series of graphic poems that bear the title "Black Automaton" with varying additions. Here's "The Black Automaton in de Despair ub Existence #2: Our New Day Begun."[32]

THE BLACK AUTOMATON IN DE DESPAIR UB EXISTENCE #2: OUR NEW DAY BEGUN

(in the cut)

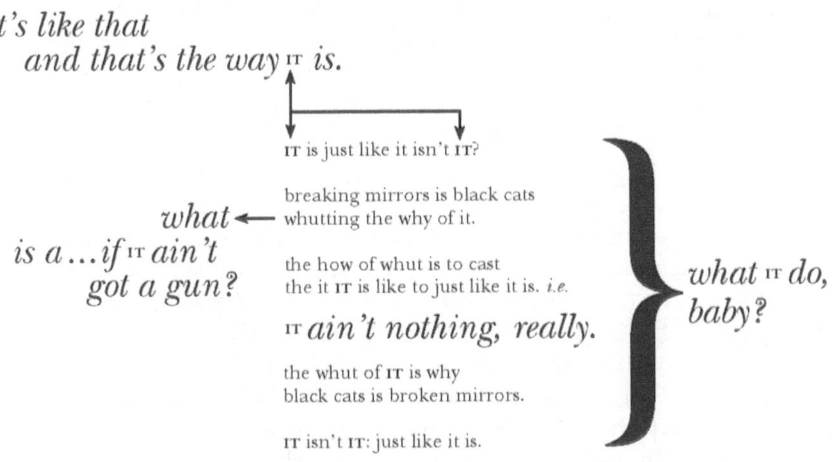

so sun down to sun up/run up with [ITS] *gun up*

.../all day. e'ey day.

Figure 1.1. "The Black Automaton in de Despair ub Existence #2: Our New Day Begun." Reprinted by permission of Fence Books and the author.

What we see in the very first section of text in Kearney's poem is a grammatical enactment of something like Du Bois's imagination of the objectified black subject.[33] The very first word of the poem – "it's" (a contraction of the subject "it" and its "be"-ing) – immediately points us elsewhere. We go looking for the referent of "it," and rather than finding it we get instead a concatenation of shifters and displacements. We're not told what "it is," but we move instead to what "it's like," and then we find a further doubling of "it" into its lower-case and upper-case incarnations. "It" moves through the poem as two.

The poem also enacts something very similar to what we've seen in Morton's explanation of "strange strangeness" in that if we follow the typical reading habit of moving left to right and top to bottom in Kearney's poem, our starting point is from the claim that "it is like" something. We move from there to the suggestion that blackness has no likeness, for the reflective apparatus for producing one is inoperative so that "breaking mirrors is black cats / whutting the why of it." That phrase then appears again, but as a distorted reflection of itself, in "the whut of IT is why / black cats is broken mirrors." From there, not only is there no likeness (or at best a distorted one), but we move to the implication that "IT" is not even self-identical. "IT" is its own strange stranger.

In this poem, it's also important to register, in the tiny letters at the top (the only ones in parentheses), the direct reference to Fred Moten's phrase "in the cut." The "gun" in "begun" gestures to the allusion with the bracket symbol, and the phrase simultaneously reads as a distillation or outcome of "gun." So how do we understand the "gun" that enters the poem in "begun" and then detaches itself as "a gun" in the second two portions of text that start at the far left side of the page? If we keep in mind the graphic connection between "gun" and "in the cut" as we move to the first recurrence of "gun," we can see that the "thats" that we also began with in the poem have now given way to "whats." Here in "what / is a … if IT ain't / got a gun," we have another allusion, this time to a popular hip-hop song from the nineties, "What?," by A Tribe Called Quest. The actual line from the song is "what is a what if you ain't got a gun."[34] Once again we're in the world of shifters, and Kearney has even shifted the "you" from the original song to the "IT" of the poem. We can say that the pronoun "what" is anchored by a referent – namely the pronoun "it" – but the "IT" here not only has no discernible referent (unless we count the "you" in the original song); whatever referent it might have within the poem is occluded by an ellipsis (and even if we trace the elided material to its source, we find ourselves back where we started: with "what"). By the end of the poem (if we're following the left-to-right, top-to-bottom conventions of reading), the "IT" is delivered to us in brackets – which, while they are not identical in appearance to the parentheses around "in the cut" at the top of the page (everything in the poem "shifts"), remind us of the parenthetical gesture as such (they are, as it were, a parenthesis within a parenthesis), and now the "it" or "what" is something that moves "with [ITS] gun up." The gun, the thing that appears "in the cut" now looks as though it functions precisely as a sort of shield or wall – it is, like Du Bois's "veil" of "second sight," the thing that keeps "what it is" both present and withdrawn. Like the subject positions of object-oriented ontology's objects, the answer to what "IT" is in Kearney's poem is either a case of mistaken identity ("IT is just like it") or a revelation that would be tantamount to death. The fugitive subject is an apocalyptic subject.

The opening poem of Evie Shockley's 2011 *The New Black*, "my last modernist poem #4 (or, re-re-birth of a nation)," begins with the figure of a "clean-cut man" in whom "some see … the end of race," echoing the common and much criticized notion of a "postracial" America that circulated during the 2008 presidential campaign of Barack Obama:

  a clean-cut man brings a brown blackness
to a dream-carved, unprecedented
  place. some see in this the end of race,

like the end of a race that begins
  with a gun: a finish(ed) line we might
finally limp across. for others,

  this miracle marks an end like year's
end, the kind that whips around again
  and again: an end that is chilling,
with a lethal spring coiled in the snow.

---

ask lazarus about miracles:
the hard part comes afterwards. he stepped
into the reconstruction of his
life, knowing what would come, but not how.[35]

"The end of race" quickly morphs into "a race" (with its electoral associations), one that "begins with a gun." Even as the line evokes the non-violent gunshot that marks the start of a footrace around a track, it simultaneously gestures toward the violence of racial oppression in the United States through the title's reference to the 1915 D.W. Griffith film *Birth of a Nation* (and by extension toward the latter's scenes of election-day violence against blacks). Metonymies of that history follow in the form of the "whip" and the "coiled" spring, evocative of the slave owner's tool for punishment and the lyncher's rope. The allusion to the circular shape of the "race"-track in the year that "whips around again" and the "coiled" form of "spring" contributes to the sense of false hope, in that "limp[ing] across the finish line" is just to be back where one started – every sign of progress, of crossing over into a new era (emancipation, civil rights legislation, the election of a black president) points back to a history that can only repeat itself. The poem's eschatological ending – our eyes must literally cross a line to witness the "miracle" beyond it – brings no new construction, but a "reconstruction." And it's perfectly apocalyptic – it's an ending we "know will come," but "how" remains unrevealed. In this world of "reconstruction," we know the future and the past the way we know other beings – all we can see are the effects of the past, and the inevitable causes of the future, without ever understanding "how." Or, for that matter, why. That is, Shockley's decision to conclude the poem with "how" keeps the world of the poem in the register of causes and effects and not of reasons. How history will happen hovers on the messianic horizon, but the reasons why it happens remain outside the frame altogether. Or, to put the point more succinctly, history is only what happens.

I want to return now to what we might say is the basic state of affairs at the heart of object-oriented ontology. Both subjects and objects exist as things that, as Morton puts it, "happen" to other things: "A guitar just is what happened to some wood, which just is what happened to a tree."[36] We're also in a world that looks a lot like Juliana Spahr's post-9/11 universe of floating debris in *this connection of everyone with lungs*, but it ought to be more than a little disconcerting to think about what this entails for the apocalyptic repurposing of Du Boisian double consciousness that we've seen in recent poetic form. If we position blackness (or queerness or any identity) within the frame of object-oriented ontology, blackness becomes what "happens" to a subject to render it an object. The problem with the orientation of recent poetry around the black "object," I would argue, is not so much that blackness looks like a contingent effect (which it obviously in some basic sense is) whose history haunts it like some Derridean spectre (history becomes, as Moten puts it, its "untraceable, anoriginal" cause) but that the embrace of that pure contingency starts to look like a politics, and not just a poetics, of contingency as well.

Of course, if a guitar, to stick with Morton's analogy, is fundamentally understood as an "effect" of "wood," what it is is importantly not a function of what, say, the guitar-maker meant to make, any more than, to extend this to subjects again, Spahr imagines the "connection of everyone with lungs" could be a function of what anyone might mean to do in relation to anyone else or believe about organizing the world in which we exist as both subjects and objects. When the interconnected entities of the world, including all of us and our bodies and all the things we take as subjects and objects, collide, in the imagination of both recent poetry and object-oriented ontology, nobody can mean anything by it. In this light, Spahr's post-9/11 world, but also the critique of postrace claims following the 2008 election, now starts to look no less like an object-oriented world than a subject-oriented one. And as we've already seen, the object-oriented world has no trouble looking like a subject-oriented one: "Freud," Timothy Morton reminds us, "argues that the ego is just the record of 'abandoned object cathexes.' What if we inverted this phrase, and assert that the form of objects is their ego? If ego is objectlike, then the inverse applies."[37] If the form of an object is its ego, we haven't had far to go for the objects of object-oriented ontology to look exactly like subjects, and apparently what these subjects are doing in their infinite, unknowable orientations is expressing themselves. At this point it should hardly come as a surprise that for Morton what also happens when objects express themselves is that everything – or, we might as well say, everyone – is a poem: "Paper can tear. Ink can spill. Lines of poetry can burst asunder. Trees can be pulped to form paper and wind harps."[38] Whether or not we think that we "shall never see / A poem as lovely as a tree," what must we think has happened to the poem, when it's literally the expression of a tree?[39] We have a poem that "should not mean, / But be."[40]

The world of the poem (or object – or subject) that should not mean but be is a world in which the being of everyone and everything is just what "happened" – it's all cause and effect all the time. It's Spahr's and Morton's worlds alike. And it makes no difference whether we think that the "being" "happened" to a subject or an object. We're all, of course, free to enjoy the poems of that world, the poems that should not mean but be. But because they cannot mean, we cannot understand them, and because we can't understand them, what draws us to them is simply a matter of contingent affiliation. When politics, too, becomes a matter of orientation rather than understanding (much less conviction), we basically have a politics of liking things. Or maybe we should say we have a politics of affect. Or why not just "I ♥ the market"? (to paraphrase the writing that was on the wall in June of 2008, when Barack Obama told the viewers of CNBC, "I love the market!").[41]

NOTES

1 Jed Rasula, quoted in Perloff, "Poetry on the Brink," 60.
2 See Dworkin, "Seja Marginal." See also Lazer, "American Poetry."
3 Nealon, "Camp Messianism," 588.
4 Ibid., 579.
5 Ibid., 588.
6 Davies, *Comp.*, 61. Cited in ibid., 582.
7 Spahr, *this connection*, 10.
8 Ibid., 9–10.
9 Siraganian, *Modernism's Other Work*, 172.
10 Ibid.
11 Ibid. In the weeks and months following the violent murders at the offices of the French magazine of political satire *Charlie Hebdo*, the portability of the slogan was made all the more evident in public responses to the attacks as "Je suis Charlie" demonstrations and vigils took place worldwide.
12 Ibid., 173.
13 The question of the relative weight of causes of actions versus reasons for actions – and, for that matter, the very question of what counts as an action – are of course the subjects of long-standing philosophical debate. Davidson's "Actions, Reasons, and Causes" in *The Journal of Philosophy* and Anscombe's *Intention* are foundational in their disagreement over whether reasons can be considered the same as causes. For Davidson the answer is yes; for Anscombe, it's no. My argument here, however, does not require settling the question, insofar as neither Davidson nor Anscombe's arguments would understand our lungs to have reasons for breathing. Moreover, the fact that for Spahr the lungs of "everyone" are doing the breathing doesn't grant to our breathing reasons it never could have had in the first place. "Everyone" may breathe the literal, material effects caused by the World Trade Center attacks, but the fact that those causes affect our

breathing collectively – indeed, that they affect anyone's breathing at all – does not entail any reasons for "everyone," much less anyone, to choose one politics as opposed to another. I have argued elsewhere not only that reasons and causes are categorically distinct, but that politics and aesthetics alike become incoherent without the distinction. In "Authorial Inattention," I make this argument specifically with respect to literary meaning. In "Two Problems with a Neuroaesthetic Theory of Interpretation," I make this argument with respect to aesthetic interpretation and the work of art more generally. And in "Poetry and the Price of Milk," I use Bertolt Brecht, Gertrude Stein, and Denis Diderot to make this argument with respect to the relationship between politics and the work of art as such.

14 Examples of such art include the first "Earth Works" exhibit, featuring artists like Robert Smithson, Michael Heizer, and Walter De Maria, that took place at Dwan Gallery in New York in 1968 and explicitly "ecological" poetry like Gary Snyder's *Turtle Island* (1974), which earned the Pulitzer Prize.

15 In their 1984 "Platform Principles of the Deep Ecology Movement," Naess and George Sessions begin with the principles that "the well-being and flourishing of human and nonhuman Life on Earth have value in themselves (synonyms: intrinsic value, inherent value)" and that "these values are independent of the usefulness of the nonhuman world for human purposes" (see *Deep Ecology Movement*, 49).

16 Regan, "Nature and Possibility of an Environmental Ethics," 20.

17 Stone, "Should Trees Have Standing?"; *Fisher v. Lowe*, 122. I owe this connection to Walter Benn Michaels's "Prehistoricism" chapter in *Shape of the Signifier*, 118–19.

18 Object-oriented ontology is just one instance of this development. Differently clothed versions of exactly the same logic can be found in Bennett, *Vibrant Matter*; Chen, *Animacies*; and Best and Marcus, "Surface Reading." To encapsulate this tendency, I would point to what Heather Love (summarizing Best and Marcus) understands as the need for "a stance of political and epistemological humility" ("Safe," 171). What such a stance embodies is a general animus against normative claims of any kind – that is, against what would seem to be a minimum requirement for a politics that might convince more than one person.

19 Harman, "Well-Wrought Broken Hammer," 186–7.

20 Morton, "Object-Oriented Defense of Poetry," 207.

21 Harman, "Well-Wrought Broken Hammer," 186.

22 Morton, "Object-Oriented Defense of Poetry," 210.

23 Morton, *Ecological Thought*, 15.

24 I would just add to this that Morton's estrangement, like the World Trade Center debris that passes through everyone's lungs in Spahr, is likewise always contingent and accidental.
25 Morton, "Queer Ecology."
26 Morton, *Ecological Thought*, 41.
27 Ibid., 119.
28 Moten, *In the Break*, 255.
29 Piper, *Out of Order, Out of Sight*, 27.
30 Morton, *Ecological Thought*, 41.
31 Du Bois, "Souls of Black Folk," 364.
32 Kearney, *Black Automaton*, 75.
33 Anthony Reed, whose terrific *Freedom Time: The Poetics and Politics of Black Experimental Writing* had not yet appeared when I originally wrote this essay (or I would have tried to address his argument for the "postlyric" status of Kearney's work at greater length), also reads *The Black Automaton* in light of Du Bois: "Kearney … returns us to a Du Boisian question of speaking in a socially stratified context where what one says is always already mediated by a set of racial scripts and norms, where one's speech is always at once singular and exemplary" (*Freedom*, 99). But saying that *The Black Automaton* animates something like Du Bois's imagination of double consciousness is also a way of saying that Du Bois might not recognize the intended import of his analysis of black subjectivity in the subsequent critical and aesthetic uses to which it has been put. For a devastating survey of the afterlife of double consciousness – long after the concept had ceased to be of use to Du Bois's own political thinking – see Adolph Reed, "Du Bois's 'Double Consciousness'" and "From Historiography to Class Ideology." As Reed argues, the concept may have lost its utility early on for Du Bois, but "the black middle-class appropriation of the double-consciousness trope" in the present has served to ground not just identity but class consciousness as well. In this capacity, Reed explains, "the ambivalence bemoaned by contemporary petit black bourgeois sufferers is conceptually quite similar to the old fretting about the threat of overcivilization – an ailment that simultaneously certifies elevated class standing and elicits sympathy for suffering. Double consciousness, therefore, is the neurasthenia of the black professional-managerial class at the end of the twentieth century" ("From Historiography to Class Ideology," 176).

My argument at the end of this essay is partly intended to suggest that the logic of double-consciousness has not deviated from this class project.
34 A Tribe Called Quest, "What?" As the notes to Kearney's book make clear, the poem contains other allusions to hip-hop music, which unfortunately it is not within the scope of this project to address: "'THE BLACK AUTOMATON IN DE DESPAIR OF EXISTENCE #2: OUR NEW DAY

BEGUN' uses Run DMC, 'It's Like That'; Q-Tip (A Tribe Called Quest), 'What?!'; Paul Wall, 'Grillz'; Prodigy (Mobb Deep), 'Shook Ones Part 2'; Mack 10, 'Hoo Bangin' (WSCG Style)'; and Peaches (featured with Outkast), 'Peaches Intro.'" Kearney, *The Black Automaton*, 193. It is striking that Kearney adds an exclamation point to the title of the Tribe Called Quest song, perhaps meant to evoke LeRoi Jones's "How You Sound?!!"

35 Shockley, *New Black*, 1.

36 Morton, "Object-Oriented Defense of Poetry," 218.

37 Ibid., 220.

38 Ibid., 222. The analogy here between the expressive object/subject would come as no surprise to a poet like the modernist Laura (Riding) Jackson, who renounced poetry mid-career (in the late thirties) precisely because she understood its sensuous properties – the emphasis on the aural and visual features of the poem – as giving the poem over to the individual and idiosyncratic perceptions of the reader, and thus as giving up on anything like the normative possibilities of meaning and truth. She explains the basis of her renunciation in a preface to a 1970 edition of her poems. The preface (along with the one she wrote for the original 1938 collection of her poetry) can be found in the appendices to *The Poems of Laura Riding*.

39 Kilmer, "Trees," 160.

40 MacLeish, "Ars Poetica," 126–7.

41 For a transcript of the interview, see Bauble, "CNBC Exclusive."

BIBLIOGRAPHY

Anscombe, G.E.M. *Intention*. Oxford: Blackwell, 1963.

Ashton, Jennifer. "Authorial Inattention: Donald Davidson's Literalism, Jorie Graham's Materialism, and Cognitive Science's Embodied Minds." In *From Modernism to Postmodernism: American Poetry and Theory in the Twentieth Century*, 146–76. Cambridge: Cambridge University Press, 2005.

– "Poetry and the Price of Milk." *nonsite.org* 10 (September 2013). http://nonsite.org/article/poetry-and-the-price-of-milk.

– "Two Problems with a Neuroaesthetic Theory of Interpretation." *nonsite.org* 2 (June 2012). http://nonsite.org/issues/issue-2/two-problems-with-a-neuroaesthetic-theory-of-interpretation.

A Tribe Called Quest. "What?" On *The Low End Theory*. Zomba Recording, 1991.

Bauble, Jennifer. "CNBC's Chief Washington Correspondent John Harwood Sits Down with Presidential Candidate Senator Barack Obama (Transcript Included)." News release. *CNBC*. June 10, 2008. http://www.cnbc.com/id/25084346#.

Bennett, Jane. *Vibrant Matter: A Political Ecology of Things*. Durham, NC: Duke University Press, 2010.

Best, Stephen, and Sharon Marcus. "Surface Reading." *Representations* 108, no. 1 (2009): 1–21.

Chen, Mel Y. *Animacies: Biopolitics, Racial Mattering, and Queer Affect*. Durham, NC: Duke University Press, 2012.

Davidson, Donald. "Actions, Reasons, and Causes." *Journal of Philosophy* 60, no. 23 (1963): 685–700.

Davies, Kevin. *Comp*. Washington, DC: Edge Books, 2000.

Du Bois, W.E.B. "The Souls of Black Folk." In *Du Bois: Writings*, 357–548. New York: Library of America, 1987.

Dworkin, Craig. "Seja Marginal." In *The Consequences of Innovation: 21st Century Poetics*, 7–24. New York: Roof Books, 2008.

"Earth Works" exhibit. New York: Dwan Gallery, 1968.

Fisher v. Lowe, 122 Mich.App. 418, 333 N.W.2d 67 (1983).

Harman, Graham. "The Well-Wrought Broken Hammer: Object-Oriented Literary Criticism." *New Literary History* 43, no. 2 (2012): 183–203.

Jackson, Laura (Riding). *Laura Riding: A Newly Revised Edition of the 1938/1989 Collection*, edited by Mark Jacobs. New York: Persea Books, 2001.

– *Laura Riding: Selected Poems in Five Sets*. New York: Persea Books, 1970.

Kilmer, Joyce. "Trees." *Poetry: A Magazine of Verse* 2, no. 5 (August 1913): 160.

Kearney, Douglas. *The Black Automaton*. Albany, NY: Fence Books, 2009.

Lazer, Hank. "American Poetry and Its Institutions." In *The Cambridge Companion to American Poetry since 1945*, edited by Jennifer Ashton, 158–72. Cambridge: Cambridge University Press, 2013.

Love, Heather. "Safe." *American Literary History* 25, no. 1 (2012): 164–75.

MacLeish, Archibald. "Ars Poetica." *Poetry: A Magazine of Verse* 28, no. 3 (June 1926): 126–7.

Michaels, Walter Benn. "Prehistoricism." In *The Shape of the Signifier*, 82–128. Princeton, NJ: Princeton University Press, 2005.

Moten, Fred. *In the Break: The Aesthetics of the Black Radical Tradition*. Minneapolis: University of Minnesota Press, 2003.

Morton, Timothy. *The Ecological Thought*. Cambridge, MA: Harvard University Press, 2010.

– "An Object-Oriented Defense of Poetry." *New Literary History* 43, no. 2 (2010): 205–24.

– "Queer Ecology." *PMLA* 125, no. 2 (2010): 273–82.

Naess, Arne, and George Sessions. "Platform Principles of the Deep Ecology Movement." In *The Deep Ecology Movement: An Introductory Anthology*, edited by Alan Drengson and Yuichi Inoue, 49–53. Berkeley, CA: North Atlantic Books, 1995.

Nealon, Christopher. "Camp Messianism, or, the Hopes of Poetry in Late-Late Capitalism." *American Literature* 76, no. 3 (September 2004): 579–602.

Perloff, Marjorie. "Poetry on the Brink: Reinventing the Lyric." *Boston Review* 37, no. 3 (May/June 2012): 60–9.

Piper, Adrian. *Out of Order, Out of Sight*. Vol .1, *Selected Writings in Meta-Art 1968–1992*. Cambridge, MA: MIT Press, 1999.

Reed, Adolph L. "Du Bois's 'Double Consciousness': Race and Gender in Progressive-Era American Thought." In *W.E.B. Du Bois and American Political Thought: Fabianism and the Color Line*, 93–126. New York: Oxford University Press, 1997.

– "From Historiography to Class Ideology." In *W.E.B. Du Bois and American Political Thought: Fabianism and the Color Line*, 163–76. New York: Oxford University Press, 1997.

Reed, Anthony. *Freedom Time: The Poetics and Politics of Black Experimental Writing*. Baltimore: Johns Hopkins University Press, 2014.

Regan, Tom. "The Nature and Possibility of an Environmental Ethic." *Environmental Ethics* 3, no. 1 (1981): 19–34.

Shockley, Evie. *The New Black*. Middletown, CT: Wesleyan University Press, 2011.

Siraganian, Lisa. *Modernism's Other Work: The Art Object's Political Life*. Oxford: Oxford University Press, 2012.

Snyder, Gary. *Turtle Island*. New York: New Directions, 1974.

Spahr, Juliana. *this connection of everyone with lungs*. Berkeley: University of California Press, 2005.

Stone, Christopher. "Should Trees Have Standing? Toward Legal Rights for Natural Objects." *Southern California Law Review* 45 (1972): 450–87.

2 The Wish to Be an Object

AARON KUNIN

How do you talk to a dishtowel?

> –I told you to stop crying. How long are you going to cry? You have to be strong. You're so limp and shapeless, look at you. I'll help you. [Wrings dishtowel three times.] There. Isn't that more comfy?

Cop 663 uses a special tone in this scene from Wong Kar-wai's film *Chungking Express*. This is not the cool, polite voice that he uses when ordering coffee, or the doubtful tone that creeps into his voice when he flirts with the woman who pours his coffee. Nor is this the private voice of his numerous voiceovers, where he narrates his actions and thoughts to himself.

In the conversation with the towel, the twang that Cop 663 puts at the end of each phrase may be a feature of Cantonese pronunciation. In Cantonese, words have their tones built in, and someone who does not speak the language would be a fool to try to distinguish the part of tone that belongs to pronunciation from the part that belongs to the speaker's attitude. The folly of trying to decipher tone in a foreign language, particularly one in which diction governs tone, puts me not in the position of the cop but rather that of his towel, which, like me, does not speak Cantonese. My original mistake in identifying myself with the human figure rather than the cleaning utensil tells me something, finally, about the cop's attitude. Maybe this is a way of talking to someone who does not speak your language. You might use a similar cadence when talking to an infant or a pet, for example.

Or a big white teddy bear. The teddy bear is a toy, and when Cop 663 talks to it, he is playing with it. Because he uses the same tone with the other sad things in his apartment, we might identify that tone, provisionally, as a playful one. The other things are useful household objects. But Cop 663 isn't using them to dry the dishes, to clean or clothe his body, or for any other practical purpose. He uses them as toys too.

How do you talk to a towel? No one has to be told. Every child knows. You talk to your towel in the same voice that you use to talk to your doll.

When you play with a toy, what happens, according to the cartoonist Lynda Barry, is that it lives. "There is something brought alive during play, and this something, when played with, seems to play back."[1] This means that play does not always succeed. Sometimes you play with a toy that does not come to life. For Barry, there is nothing ambiguous about the distinction between failed play and successful play: "A fake imaginary friend is still you. A real imaginary friend feels like someone else."[2]

Barry extends D.W. Winnicott's insight in *Playing and Reality* that toys are points of contact, transitions, between inside and outside. Although playing uses psychic material from inside the person, and although it may project this material onto the toy, it can't happen at all unless there is something that isn't inside. Does play occur inside the person or outside? Winnicott approaches this question on practically every page of his book, but he declines to give an answer more detailed than "neither inside nor outside."[3] In fact, he adds, the success of play may depend on not disturbing or resolving the paradox: "Of the transitional object it can be said that it is a matter of agreement between us and the baby that we will never ask the question: 'Did you conceive of this or was it presented to you from without?' The important point is that no decision on this point is expected. The question is not to be formulated."[4] Thus almost anything can be used as a toy, as long as it is "neither inside nor outside" the person.[5]

Does the towel live? Does it play back? Maybe not. It would be easy to say that the towel is merely an extension of Cop 663 rather than a real imaginary friend. The things in the apartment aren't lonely. They don't miss the flight attendant who used to live there, because she wasn't their girlfriend. They never had a girlfriend. The cop misses the flight attendant, projects the feeling onto his apartment, and, in a nightly bedtime ritual, comforts himself with the alibi that he is comforting them. Just as in a dream, every object in the apartment is a version of the cop. He might as well be talking to his image in a mirror. The toy merely provides a convenient receptacle for his feelings, allowing him to say things that would be too painful if he thought he were talking only to himself.

Cop 663 would disagree with this interpretation. For one thing, he isn't talking to a mirror image. The bar of soap looks nothing like him. Further, he has different words of advice for different objects, and his observations are specific to their careers. The bar of soap gradually loses its substance. The towel absorbs and releases water. Each object misses the flight attendant in its own way. Tony Leung, the actor who plays the cop, makes a space for these unique responses in his delivery. I mean, he doesn't give them time to say anything – why should he, since they don't speak his language? But he does pause and give them room to do the kinds of things that towels do, like flop on the counter and release a few drops of water.

For a moment, at the start of the scene, Cop 663 might be addressing his routines to himself. When he says, "You've lost a lot of weight, you know," the screen shows a dark wall in his apartment. Then the camera pans left to reveal that he is talking to the depleted bar of soap that he holds in his hand. By recording the soap's reaction, the camerawork objectively confirms the cop's sense that he is talking to something that not only might receive the communication but might also answer him. The cinematographer Christopher Doyle, in whose Hong Kong apartment this scene was shot – and whose personal hand soap, I imagine, Cop 663 might be addressing – also seems to think that the objects in the household have responses and that film can capture them.

The towel is alone on screen three times: at the start of the shot, as it weeps; when it flops on the counter; and when it hangs in the window. It probably has more screen time than the face and soulful eyes of the handsome male lead. The exchange with the shirt is a shot/reverse-shot setup: first Cop 663 addresses the shirt in a close-up, then the shirt, alone on the screen, appears to meet his gaze without saying anything. The scene culminates in a master shot that finally brings the cop and shirt together over an ironing board – not to maintain the shirt's creases, but to heat it up, compensating for the warm body of the woman who used to wear it.

Some viewers will insist that these seeming toys are mere props, extensions of Cop 663, in a different sense. Doesn't he anthropomorphize them? It is true that the teddy bear has a number of key features in common with the human body, that the soap and the towel are designed to accommodate the human hand, and that the shirt alludes to the torso that it used to clothe. It is also true that all of these objects are products of human civilization. But these references to human form are how the dolls and utensils were designed, not assumptions that the cop is projecting onto them. If the things have been anthropomorphized, this process occurred long ago, in their production.

Maybe, by focusing on the relationship between the cop and the towel, I'm missing the point. Even if the cop isn't imposing human form on the towel, the film might be. I don't think so. In general, in a film, it's easy to tell whether something has human form or not. If a human actor were cast in the role of the towel, that would give the towel human form. Instead the towel is played by a towel or a reasonable approximation. This towel may even be ragged from use in the cinematographer's kitchen.

It would make sense to say that the cop anthropomorphizes the towel only if you think that the human mind alone is capable of retaining the image of an absent person. But I don't think that. To those who say that regardless of whether a towel can miss a person, the towel in question, surely, does not miss the person in question, I would point out that the same can be said, with equal justice, of the actor Tony Leung. I would add that the towel is better equipped to cry on demand, whenever the scene happens to require it, than most human actors.

For Leung, this scene is a performance of play. Not being an expert on play like Barry or Winnicott, I am not qualified to evaluate the success or failure of his playfulness. What I study is character. I have argued elsewhere that the truth of character becomes visible in a performance of performance – one in which either several actors play one character, or one actor plays several characters. The following scene is an example of the former. Not, however, for Leung. For the towel, rather.

> –You know, I have to tell you, you've totally changed. You can't just change personality like that. Her walking out is no excuse. I want you to think about that.
>
> [Voiceover.] It was a relief when I saw it crying. It may look different on the outside, but it's still true to itself. It's still a very emotional towel.

This scene helps to clarify what it means for an object such as a towel to be a character. The towel does not have to be an agent or have human form or emotional depth. (Whether you agree or disagree with Cop 663 that the towel does have emotional depth is not important.) For the performance of character, the key word in "still a very emotional towel" is not "emotional" but "still." What makes the towel a character is the fact that it remains "true to itself" even after it has been replaced by a different object. Cop 663 views two towels as a single object because they are playing the same character.

There is no confusion here. Viewers of the film see two towels and one character. The cop sees exactly the same thing. We would see the same thing if the second towel were played by another object, such as a Coke can (with condensation on the outside to represent tears), or by a human being, such as Maggie Cheung.

There has never been any confusion regarding the performances in Buñuel's *That Obscure Object of Desire* either. Some viewers have proposed dubious interpretations of this film; they see, for example, Angela Molina and Carole Bouquet as sensual and frigid, respectively. Or they see other patterns in which the two performers represent different aspects of the character Conchita. However, no viewer has ever proposed that they are two different characters.

Buñuel himself was almost surprised to discover "that audiences have accepted the constant change of actresses ... So you see that cinema is like a kind of hypnosis. There is no way you could confuse the two women in real life; they look very different."[6] Buñuel thought that his film put viewers in a trance, subjecting them to the same obsessions as the lovestruck Matteo. I have a different explanation: character type. The character Conchita collects many different examples. The fact that two women play Conchita in this film is not different from the fact that another woman plays Conchita in the 1929 film *La femme et le pantin*, or that the same character also appears in the novel by Pierre Louÿs on which the two films are based. The extravagant rule that Buñuel's production exploits has as its basis the character's collection of examples.

If *Chungking Express* suggests that we apply the same typologies to the things we use in daily life, where a certain blindness to the home environment allows us to replace worn-out objects with new ones that we treat with total familiarity, it goes a step further still and suggests that we do the same thing with people in romantic relationships.

> –I've become more observant. I notice things I used to take for granted. The taste of sardines, for instance.

The scene in which Cop 663 discovers a new vitality in the things in his apartment is open to an ironic reading. Sardines taste different to him because they are not sardines but swordfish: Faye, the woman who serves his coffee at Midnight Express, has been breaking into the apartment during the day and switching the labels on all the canned goods. She has also replaced many of the worn-out utensils with new ones. Cop 663 attributes the changes that he observes to a new stage in the grieving process that the apartment is going through. What looks to him like a relation to his ex-girlfriend is actually a relation to the woman who is going to be his girlfriend, and whom he is going to treat in exactly the same way. In a scene near the end of the film, he massages her legs, just as he used to do for his ex-girlfriend after a hard day at work, remarking in a voiceover that this is a part of a woman's body that he especially likes. She, for her part, will get a new job as a flight attendant, the same job held by the ex-girlfriend.

The characters treat each other as types, as does the film. Cop 663 is known only by his number in the Hong Kong police force, which suggests a typology of profession: he and Cop 223 are examples of the same type. Other character names suggest a similar typology: for example, Cop 223 considers asking out a woman who works at Midnight Express who has the same name as his ex-girlfriend May; the name of her successor working at the counter of Midnight Express is a rhyme, Faye.

The lesson is clear. In erotic life, as in home life, people make use of types, and are even attracted to types. The "gift of the magi" is real. It happens all the time: consciously or not, people accommodate each another by exchanging and diminishing the qualities to which they are adapting, until the original qualities are gone and only the adaptations remain.

This insight from *Chungking Express* suggests in turn a new, although no less dubious, interpretation of *That Obscure Object of Desire*. Isn't this the story of serial monogamy, which is a kind of polygamy? I have argued that *That Obscure Object* owes its intelligibility to typologies of character. It should additionally be intelligible to anyone who has spoken the same words to different lovers, taken different lovers to the same place, told them the same stories, had the same kind of sex. Or anyone who has accidentally used the name of an old lover for a current one.

Maybe it's just me? But I doubt it. I think that I am talking about a basic human desire. Hitchcock thought so too, which is why he celebrated the logic of this desire in a film, *Vertigo*. Turning people into objects is one of the powers of art, and one of the reasons why we make art. No one says you have to like this desire, any more than you have to like art. Even more interesting is the other side, the wish to be an object. The latter desire is a real human possibility, although perhaps not as basic as the former.

What about Faye? In her seduction of Cop 663, she deploys the powers of cuteness, among which are indirection and cunning. But how can I be certain that seduction is Faye's intended goal? Maybe, by entering the cop's apartment while he is away, she is practising a kind of flirtation that would deny anything so deep as an erotic relationship. Or maybe she wants to fast-forward to a point in the relationship where he would take her for granted and she would enjoy the closeness (or blindness) of the utensils that he lives with.[7]

Here is a paradox worthy of Winnicott. Although Faye seems to embody the spirit of play, she does not seem to be playing with these utensils on her visits to the apartment. She isn't even using the Mary Poppins method of turning dreary chores into a game. No, she's cleaning the things. Like in a hotel, where cleaning the room means replacing the sheets, towels, and soaps with different sheets, towels, and soaps.

Winnicott's writing is useful for identifying instances of playing, but less useful for identifying activities that are not instances of playing. He sometimes says that all cultural activity is play. He sometimes seems to think that any relationship is a kind of play – when wind blows through the curtains, he says the wind is playing with the curtains.[8] Perhaps playing was Winnicott's method of analysis. Certainly playing is what he did when he met with the children who were his patients. But at this point in my account, I need to reintroduce some distinctions that Winnicott, in his effort to maintain a strong middle ground between inside and outside, is reluctant to make.

In the captions to her cartoon "Magic Lanterns," Barry follows Winnicott in expanding the field of play to include all cultural activities: "How does a story come so alive? ... When we finish a good book, why do we hold it in both hands and gaze at it as if it were somehow alive? What happened to my yellow blanket?"[9] Drawing a cartoon history of the loss of a transitional object, a yellow blanket, from her early childhood, Barry seems to treat the story she tells as the same kind of object. She does not use Winnicott's term, but, as Hillary Chute has shown, the piece is an extended meditation on his ideas about playing.[10] However, the exclusion of his term may be deliberate, because it does not accurately describe what Barry does in her cartoons.

There is already a suggestion of something added to Winnicott in Barry's impatience with "fake imaginary friends" as opposed to real ones. The difference between real and fake imaginary friends – a difference between playing and playing at playing? – is obvious to Barry but would not be to Winnicott. The difference becomes crystal clear in "Magic Lanterns," which is only incidentally about her lost yellow blanket and predominantly concerned with a stuffed panda toy that she picks up in an airport and imagines as the precious lost transitional object of some child.

> –You're throwing this out?
> –You want it?
> –It should go to lost and found.
> –They only gonna toss it. Airport's too big to keep everything. Some kid's gonna cry tonight.[11]

When Barry plays with her blanket, it's neither inside nor outside. When she saves another child's toy from the trash, the toy is unambiguously outside. When she draws a cartoon story about her blanket and the other child's toy and sends it into the world, the cartoon is definitely outside.

Similarly, Lewis Carroll liked playing with young girls, and he also wrote two novels for a particular girl. These activities were not unrelated, but the novels have a frame that makes them the product of a very different kind of activity. They are works of art, and therefore outside.

In 2013, I went to the Museum of Childhood in East London to look at the eighteenth-century dollhouse restored by Denton Welch in the 1940s. The funny thing about the Museum of Childhood is that people bring their children there. The displays are uneasily addressed to an audience that might include adult patrons and children. But the children have little interest in some of the displays, particularly of the museum's older holdings. They might like to play with some of the toys, but they don't particularly want to look at toys that they can't play with. They don't even want to play with the eighteenth-century toys, which don't look like toys to them. But I didn't go there to play, and I don't usually want to get too close to pieces in museums. I was doing research.

What was Welch doing with the old dollhouse? Not playing with dolls. But not studying it either. He did some things that were kind of like playing. For example, he slowly filled the house with toy furniture and miniature cups and dishes. At one point he wrote in his journal that "slowly the house is coming to life again,"[12] just as Barry would say. Some of what he did sounds like the work of scholars in museums – stripping the outer layer of paint to reveal older painted lines that represented brickwork and trying to match the rooms to period-correct furnishings. Welch himself seems to have been at a loss to account for the motives behind his activity, mainly repeating the word "again" as though going in circles: "I suddenly had a passion for it again, unaccountable, unless it was just looking at it in its ruined condition and seeing again how lovely it could be."[13] A purely aesthetic motive: wanting to see the house lovely rather than ruined.

Welch was doing with the dollhouse the same thing that he does with the bottles, combs, and other handheld things that are, along with himself, the main and recurring characters in his books. In a scene that recurs in all three of his novels, the protagonist drinks tea in an institutional setting such as a hospital, hotel, or school and notices that some beautiful old pieces of silverware have been incorporated into the regular rotation for everyday use. The following is taken from his first novel, *Maiden Voyage*:

> I stopped at the table and looked down. Most of the things were electroplate but two spoons had caught my eyes.... They had large hall-marks on the thin part of the stem and I knew that they were early Georgian. They belonged to Sister, I supposed, and had got muddled with the others. I thought how easy it would be to steal them. I would like to have had them for myself very much.[14]

What is he looking for? Not something to sweeten his tea. The spoons themselves fix his attention. He examines the pieces and learns everything about them. He is able to read the marks that announce their age, manufacture, and provenance. He also guesses the identity of the current owner and why the valuable pieces are on the table with the ordinary ones.

The climax of this scene is the imagined act of taking the spoons. The fantasy of stealing could be described as a temptation, but the narrator might not think that it would be wrong. Stealing the spoons might be better for the spoons. In another scene, touring the home of the Duke of Devonshire, he is offended by a guide who asks that he "not touch the things" and nurses his wounded pride with the reflection "I could appreciate and take care of the things in the room better than the whole lot of them put together."[15] At least, unlike Sister, he isn't going to lose track of the spoons.

There is a surprise at the end of the passage. "I would like," the narrator says, "to have had them for myself."[16] He does not say, "I would have liked." He still wants them! In narrating this scene, he reaches back through memory and longs to hold them. The tone suggests regret for not taking them when he had the chance. That is the meaning of the last sentence: he would like to have stolen them very much.

Welch wanted them so much that he wrote about them in several places. Here is a version of the same scene from his second novel, *In Youth Is Pleasure*:

> Orvil remembered with pleasure the low dining-room in the desolate house … the kitchen cups large as babies' chambers, and the thin delicate old spoons quite lost in their rude saucers.
>
> Orvil remembered the spoons particularly, for they were beautiful early-Victorian ones with bowls shaped like scallop-shells and crests on the handles. How he wanted one of the spoons! But he had not the strength of mind to steal the one which lay so near in his saucer.[17]

This passage delivers some of the "pleasure" advertised in the title. For once the word is not used ironically; Orvil experiences pleasure in remembering a set of Victorian spoons, mixed with regret for not stealing a spoon. Here the act of theft is not even implicitly criminalized but fully heroized. Only a kind of moral weakness stops Orvil from seizing the opportunity: he lacks "strength of mind," which means that he is not attentive enough to see that he could steal a spoon, not clever enough to plan the theft, or not courageous enough to carry it out.

By this point, you will not be surprised to learn that Welch actually stole some spoons. He writes about doing so in a journal of a walking tour in Sussex. In a youth hostel, another traveller steals the spoon that Welch had previously stolen at school, "the George IV spoon with the Prince of Wales feathers on it, which I had found amongst the greasy base-metal cutlery at school, and which I had appropriated to myself with such satisfaction."[18] Later, at a different hostel, he steals someone else's spoon as compensation: "I found a silver spoon there. It seemed to be sent specially to compensate me for the one I'd lost at Midhurst."[19] What makes the spoon a character is not the detail and the sensitivity of the descriptions, but the substitution. Various pieces of silverware play the singular role of "spoon." Welch replaces the spoon with a different object and treats it as the same object.

I'm isolating the spoons because they are a theme in Welch's writing. But I could do similar work with other things, even bits of detritus. In *Maiden Voyage*, the protagonist spies on a man waiting for his lover and notices him throwing his cigarette "impatiently, so that it fell like a small rocket."[20] Later he returns to the same spot and finds "the shape their two bodies had made in the snow" and "the sickly, yellow patch of his cigarette,"[21] the sodden remains of which he gathers and saves. In his journals, after a picnic with Eric Oliver, he writes about the eggshells left on the ground, and two months later, he takes Oliver back to the same spot in the forest to view "those blessed eggshells lying there still."[22]

My examples have been taken indiscriminately from Welch's journals and novels. The fictional status of the novels is not easy to determine. At best, the fictional guise is thin. *In Youth Is Pleasure* was to have been subtitled "A Fragment of Life Story with Changed Names." The printed book finally did not carry this subtitle, only because the publisher feared lawsuits.[23] Like Barry, Welch is an artist who champions imagination but works entirely from memory. As though the work of imagination were not to add new objects to the world but to invest existing objects with fantasy and anxiety, so that "the best tea-table" becomes "endowed with nightmare possibilities," in the words of Auden's review of *Maiden Voyage*.[24]

Or perhaps the fictional element in Welch's novels is the uncanny knowledge of other minds that the narrator consistently has. The attribute of heightened sensitivity gives these books, which are essentially first-person memoirs, the traditional advantage of third-person novels: no private thoughts. Perhaps this feature fictionalizes the memoirs enough to turn them into novels. However, Welch's knowledge of other minds may not have been a fiction. So skilled was Welch at reading minds that, according to Eric Oliver, "the only way of keeping a secret from him (and even that was not always effective) was to force oneself to think only of other matters in his presence."[25]

No writing by Welch, fictional or nonfictional, includes an indifferent object. In his review, Auden describes the unrelieved differentiation of each object as a "Hitchcock lighting" effect under which "both people and things stand out with startling and sinister sharpness."[26] The spoons reward attention with pleasure, but everything else on the tea table demands the same attention. The narrator of *Voyage* notices the modern plated pieces as well as the solid silver eighteenth-century spoons, and Orvil in *Pleasure* can't help noticing the "rude saucers" since they practically swallow the "thin delicate old spoons."[27] Even the "hateful" school uniform attracts a special kind of attention: "Although I had always hated their tightness and blackness, I had never felt so conscious of myself as I had in them. To wear clothes you hate makes you concentrate inside yourself."[28]

Welch's readers have proposed two psychological explanations for this obsessive sensitivity. Both explanations replace the things with a person. Either Welch's attention to things compensates for the early loss of his mother, or it registers the fragility of his injured body.[29] Why does the narrator of *Voyage* take such an interest in pieces of silverware? "Because they were my mother's," obviously, and "if she were alive, she'd give them all to me!"[30] Why do the opening pages of *A Voice Through a Cloud* linger over the "creamy-white ivory comb" that has been "wrapped … up carefully … and stowed" in a travelling case?[31] Why, when the narrator stops for tea on the road, do the decayed or absent "beautiful little brass handles" on the windows of the tea shop seem to him emblems of "universal damage and loss"?[32] Because a car is about to run into him, leading to spinal tuberculosis and years of suffering.

Both explanations are obviously true, but insufficient. Note that the narrator does not say, "If Mother were alive, I wouldn't need the silverware!" He wants his mother to be alive, and he also wants the silver. It is not as clear that he even wants his father to be alive. In an astonishing journal entry that records the news of his father's death, he speculates about items that he might inherit and is careful to state that he wants his father's cufflinks "chiefly for what they are and only a very little because they were his."[33] Anyone else would be careful to say the opposite.

No one else in Welch's books is like Welch. For the waiter at the hotel, for the sister in the infirmary, the place settings are "whole 'nests' of forks and spoons … melted together."[34] One spoon is as good as another if you are looking for an instrument to stir milk and sugar into your tea. The narrators in the novels are frequently shocked by the failures of their companions to recognize that they are in the presence of rare beauty: "'I thought that there was nothing you would like.' I was startled. I had never been in a house where I had liked so much."[35] "I thought nobody could miss such obvious beauty."[36] In journal entries, Welch characterizes the neglect of old things as "another form of cruelty" and the human agents of this cruelty as themselves degraded to a bad form of objecthood, lacking the human features of "eyes, nose, mouth, ears, limbs. They are trunks of wood always repudiating; although they have *already* been deprived of all sense and movement."[37]

At the same time, Welch doesn't seem to enjoy the effects of his greater sensitivity. Unlike Barry, if he had a choice, he would not give life to inanimate matter. "I have had the horrible sensation that the tables, chairs, lamps and confusion of books near me were writhing into life."[38] Similarly, Orvil in *Youth* resents the "evil souls" of "the wardrobe, the chest of drawers," and "the chairs ... even the eiderdown stored evil knowledge."[39] His sensitivity gives life to the things, but he would rather be insensible among inanimate things. Elsewhere he complains about conventions of speech that attribute human qualities, such as gender, to things, "calling an inanimate object, like a boat or a car, 'she.'"[40] The root of his dislike for this language, which he puzzlingly calls "vulgar," appears to be a helpless sense of the vividness of conventional phrases: "Hackneyed images and proverbs have always had the power to jump suddenly alive for me. There is a click and I see the needle in the bottle of hay, the stupid one crying over the spilt milk, the stitch in time saving nine."[41]

You get a different sense of what the things mean to Welch from passages where he imagines what it would be like to be an ordinary household object whose usefulness is taken for granted and whose other qualities barely register. In fact, he consistently discovers, this condition of objecthood would be desirable but impossible to experience. His term for this condition from which consciousness has been deleted, for this "never-happening happening," is acceptance: "His pleasure lay chiefly in the fact that the man seemed to have accepted him as completely as the tables and chairs in the hut."[42] "I suppose deep down she accepted me placidly, did not necessarily understand, yet did not question; so this acceptance flowed out to me and I was warmed."[43] It might be bad for you to take things for granted, but it might not be so bad to be taken for granted. How pleasant, how warm it would be to be ordinary. To be accepted without question, to be used without attention. To be acceptable.

Welch's sensitivity is automatic. He can't turn it off. One name for this condition of total, excruciating awareness might be grief; another might be stupid physical pain; a third might be art. From this point of view, the opposing condition of indifference (to put it negatively) or comfort (to put it positively) looks increasingly alluring. It looks like the cure to his spinal injury, the end of mourning and of his career as an artist: "One day you will want dullness and no help from outside – for only in dullness can your heart and mind grow."[44] The condition of objecthood is impossible for Welch, the one thing he can't have, but at the same time utterly desirable. That is the best explanation for his sensitivity to things. He is waiting for them to recede into the background. He is waiting to follow them.

I propose to call the stories that I have been discussing – Wong Kar-wai's film, Barry's cartoon, Welch's novels – it-narratives. Critics recently invented this term to classify a genre in the early European novel in which ordinary household objects such as shoes, corkscrews, wheels, and coins are heroes and tell their own stories. In current usage, the name of this genre has several problems. For one thing, it is supposed to name an eighteenth-century genre, but it is a new term, not in use in the eighteenth century. The neutrality of "it" is a problem in that the objects at the centre of the stories, although they have no sexual parts, usually have a gender. A shoe, for example, is usually masculine or feminine. "Narrative" is a problem in that these novels foreground setting at the expense of action and causation. The narratives, such as they are, tend to be circular rather than linear.

The term has some virtues insofar as the same problems are often built into the eighteenth-century novels we now call it-narratives. In Crébillon's *The Sofa*, the narrative element threatens to undo the work of objectification. The sofa tells its own story and positively enjoys its contact with persons; he (for this sofa is occupied by a masculine soul) even communicates his love to a particular person: "My soul transferred itself to the padding, and so close to Zeinida's mouth that at length it succeeded in adhering wholly to it."[45] Crébillon gets around the problem through metempsychosis. The narrator, a man, was a sofa in a previous existence, which a god mysteriously allows him to recall. In this way, "narrative" is in a relation of productive tension with "it."

Critics have suggested numerous ingenious explanations for the existence of this genre, finding in it-narratives allegories of reification (Lynch), imperialism (Festa), and slavery (Lamb). My interpretation of Welch's tortured relationship with silverware suggests a different reading. What if these books are about exactly what they say they are about? That is to say, an impossible desire to delete consciousness and recede into the background, like a sofa cushion.

Readers in the eighteenth century understood Crébillon's novel as a work of pornography whose final perversion was to describe itself, with a mixture of irony and hypocrisy, as a "moral tale." In *Les liaisons dangereuses*, the presence of this moral tale is a motif on the bookshelves of various characters, who use it to inspire themselves or corrupt younger readers. The conceit of the amorous sofa provides the inspiration for Valmont's virtuoso letter with double meanings, which he writes to seduce its addressee, but while using the back of a different sexual partner as a writing desk.[46] (This letter may be, indirectly, Crébillon's most important contribution to literature.) In this scene, Crébillon's novel inspires its readers to imitate its exact mode of intimate relation. The meaning of the book, for Valmont and Émilie, is that it would be fun to be a writing desk or to treat another person as a writing desk.

In the twentieth century, *The Sofa* may have also inspired Edogawa Rampo's story "The Human Chair," in which a carpenter makes a superlatively comfortable chair and spends several years living inside it. The key to this story is the multiplication of motives. Why does the narrator conceal himself in the chair he has made? Here are some of his explanations.

Because he is hideously ugly, "ugly beyond description," and can hope for no other mode of human contact.[47]

Because he is so proud of his work that he can't bear to part with it.

Because he wants to possess the chair himself, but he can't, and living inside the chair is a dismal compromise. "At first, no doubt, the idea found its seed in my secret yearning to keep the chair for myself. Realizing, however, that this was totally out of the question, I next longed to accompany the chair wherever it went."[48]

Because he wants to hide in the western-style hotel and steal jewels from the guests. "You may already have guessed long ago," he presumes, that theft was his motive all along.[49]

Because he enjoys physical contact with people who sit in the chair.

Because he especially enjoys the different weights and smells of the bodies, "the feel of flesh, the sound of the voice, and body odor."[50] (Note that this part of the story is indifferent to the sexes of the people sitting in the chair. This "love in a chair" is a sexual preference in that it's sexually gratifying, but not a preference for one of the sexes. It's more like a preference in the sense that a chair has human scale and prefers the bodies for which it was designed.)

Because he prefers the extraordinary bodies of foreign dancers. "On this occasion, instead of my carnal instincts being aroused, I simply felt like a gifted artist being caressed by the magic wand of a fairy."[51]

Because, in a fit of nationalism, he wants a Japanese body to sit in the chair: "As a Japanese, I really craved a lover of my own kind."[52]

The narrator, the human chair, is as ingenious in proposing motives as critics have been in their interpretations of it-narratives. These are all good things to want, and the narrator clearly wants them. But the most eloquent passages in the story are the ones where the narrator does not offer a motive but describes what it feels like to live in the chair.

> I felt that I had buried myself in a lonely grave. Upon careful reflection I realized that it was indeed a grave. As soon as I entered the chair I was

> swallowed up by complete darkness, and to everyone else in the world I no longer existed!
>
> ...
>
> What was it about this mystic hole that fascinated me so? I somehow felt like an animal living in a totally new world.[53]

(Scenes in which a man seals himself inside a piece of furniture and experiences unanticipated joy seem to have a special meaning for Rampo, and recur in his fiction. Compare "The Apparition of Osei," where the hero climbs inside a bridal chest: "The pitch-black confines of the chest, which smelled strongly of camphor, were strangely comfortable. Kakutaro was suddenly overcome with fond memories of his childhood.")[54]

"The Human Chair" is finally about what happens in the story: wanting to be a chair, while at the same time retaining human consciousness, and thus adding experience to the chair's existence. Rampo wrote an essay on this subject later in his career, where he considers the wish to be an inanimate object as a subcategory of a universal human desire for transformation. "Under the right conditions, human beings will even want to become wooden planks."[55]

It would be moving too quickly to identify this wish with masochism, although there is probably an element of that in the stories by Rampo and Crébillon. (Perhaps masochism should be understood in an almost philosophical sense, and restricted to pain experienced as pleasure, but the term is commonly used to refer to eroticized humiliation.) In masochism, the fantasy is simple abuse: treating a human being as an object. It is ritualistic degradation, as in Sade, where the libertines use their victims as tables or candelabra, and in Sacher-Masoch, where Wanda uses Gregor as a footstool. In the latter scene, dehumanization becomes contractual, as Deleuze observes.[56] In both scenes, there is a pretence of forgetting that the object is a human being. The lure, potentially on both sides, is the violation of the categorical imperative. Neither sadist nor masochist ever forgets that it's wrong to treat someone as a means, not an end. And that imperative, always in the foreground, is what makes the scene sexy.

Now imagine that part of this transaction is unknown. (The distinction may seem unremarkable or academic, but not it if the quality of your sexual experience depends on it.) Imagine, for example, Wanda resting her foot on Gregor's body without first addressing him as a footstool. To call someone a footstool is not the same as treating a person as a footstool, since ordinarily it isn't necessary to have conversations with the furniture. The contractual relationship couldn't be sustained, or would become an obstacle, if Gregor wanted to be a useful household object (in other words, to disappear) and Wanda actually forgot about his existence as she relaxed. This is more or less the kind of scene that Crébillon and Rampo describe.

Now imagine that the transaction is unknown on both sides. The concepts of sadism and masochism become inadequate at this point, as both person and object disappear into habitual existence. Neither person nor object has any awareness; the most intense feeling that such a scene could generate is comfort. Pornography also becomes an inadequate term, insofar as a description of such a scene would be innocuous. A person lounging on a sofa. This is the impossible desire that Welch calls "acceptance."

There are not many pornographic images that would answer to such a description, but there is a market for them and a subgenre called "forniphilia." Jeff Gord, who maintained the website "House of Gord" until his recent death, specialized in this subgenre. His vision of the human body is as spectacular and thorough in its commitment to objectification as Busby Berkeley's. He defines forniphilia as "the ultimate in artistic expression" because it uses "the ultimate material."[57] By this he means that he uses women's bodies as furniture (chairs, lamps, chandeliers, hood ornaments) and takes pictures of them. Because he uses real bodies and never forgets it, Gord's work should properly be called sadism. His work is instructive in that it shows how difficult the approach to objecthood would be for most persons and what existence is really like for most objects.

The longest and most instructive page on his website is a list of admonitions addressed to readers who think they would like to try using living human bodies as materials for art.[58] Plaster, he warns, should be used with caution:

> I have seen plaster molds so hot that they were steaming and could not be touched without asbestos gloves. Think about that before you pour it around the woman you love.

Urethane foam is a volatile material:

> NEVER, EVER, get this stuff around the head region unless you wanna loose your loved one.

Indifference can be simulated in play but is forbidden in fact:

> NEVER leave an inverted person gagged. In fact, NEVER leave them anyway.

The care that people require when they are used as furniture is a strange reminder of the care they ordinarily require in human society, as well as the care that furniture requires if you don't want it to go completely to hell. Furniture can take care of itself, and is superior to human furniture, only to this extent: it is in no danger of suffocating if you leave it alone. Otherwise, just like a human body, a piece of furniture will fall apart if you concentrate too much weight on its back. If it falls over, furniture has no way of protecting itself, just like a human body.

However, as Gord writes, this defencelessness, this need for protection, makes furniture "not an object of ridicule, but an object of immense power."[59] In fact, we do not treat furniture with contempt. Instead we take care of it, arrange it, cover it, clean it. Or (better) we aren't supposed to treat furniture with contempt. No doubt we *do* sometimes talk to furniture.

NOTES

1 Barry, *What It Is*, 51.
2 Ibid., 199.
3 Winnicott, *Playing and Reality*, 129.
4 Ibid., 17.
5 Ibid., 129.
6 Buñuel, *Objects of Desire*, 226.
7 On flirtation, see Moi, *Simone de Beauvoir*, 145–67. For the suggestion that being taken for granted is the best kind of love, see François, "Virgil and the Missing of Love in Hardy's *Poems of 1912–13*."
8 Winnicott, *Playing and Reality*, 132.
9 Barry, "Magic Lanterns," 154.
10 Chute, *Graphic Women*, 127.
11 Barry, "Magic Lanterns," 155.
12 Welch, *Journals*, 26 March, 1945.
13 Ibid.
14 Welch, *Maiden Voyage*, 38.

15 Ibid., 55.
16 Ibid.
17 Welch, *In Youth Is Pleasure*, 14–15.
18 Welch, "I Left My Grandfather's House," 167.
19 Ibid., 214.
20 Welch, *Maiden Voyage*, 96.
21 Ibid.
22 Welch, *Journals*, 2 April, 1944.
23 De-la-Noy, *Denton Welch*, 47.
24 Auden, *Prose*, 252.
25 Welch, *Last Sheaf*, 7.
26 Auden, *Prose*, 252.
27 Welch, *In Youth Is Pleasure*, 10.
28 Welch, *Maiden Voyage*, 74.
29 Michael De-la-Noy's critical biography develops both explanations fully. For a different view of the influence of Welch's accident on his development as a writer, see Waters, *Role Models*, 178–84.
30 Welch, *Maiden Voyage*, 280.
31 Welch, *Voice Through a Cloud*, 9.
32 Ibid.
33 Welch, *Journals*, 7 December, 1942.
34 Welch, *Journals*, 13 November, 1942.
35 Welch, *Maiden Voyage*, 94.
36 Ibid., 133.
37 Welch, *Journals*, 31 January, 1946.
38 Welch, *Journals*, 28 January, 1947.
39 Welch, *In Youth Is Pleasure*, 144.
40 Welch, *Journals*, 7 December, 1942.
41 Welch, *Voice Through a Cloud*, 212.
42 Welch, *In Youth Is Pleasure*, 117.
43 Welch, *Voice Through a Cloud*, 171.
44 Ibid., 139.
45 Crébillon, *The Sofa*, 275.
46 Laclos, *Les liaisons dangereuses*, letter XLVIII.
47 Rampo, *Japanese Tales*, 31.
48 Ibid., 34.
49 Ibid., 35.
50 Ibid., 38.
51 Ibid., 40.
52 Ibid., 16.

53 Ibid., 35, 37.
54 Rampo, *Edogawa Rampo Reader*, 23.
55 Ibid., 214.
56 Deleuze, *Masochism*, 91–102.
57 Gord, "Forniphilia."
58 Ibid.
59 Ibid.

BIBLIOGRAPHY

Auden, W.H. *Prose: 1939–1948*. Vol. 2 of *The Complete Works of W.H. Auden*, edited by Edward Mendelson. Princeton: Princeton University Press, 2002.

Barry, Lynda. "Magic Lanterns." In *One! Hundred! Demons!* Seattle: Sasquatch Books, 2002.

– *What It Is*. Montreal: Drawn and Quarterly, 2008.

Buñuel, Luis, José de la Colina, and Tomás Pérez Turrent. *Objects of Desire: Conversations with Luis Buñuel*. Edited and translated by Paul Lenti. New York: Marsilio, 1993.

Chungking Express. Directed by Wong Kar-wai. Hong Kong: Jet Tone Production, 1994. DVD.

Chute, Hillary. *Graphic Women: Life Narrative and Contemporary Comics*. New York: Columbia University Press, 2010.

Crébillon fils, Claude Prosper Jolyot de. *The Sofa: A Moral Tale*. Translated by Bonamy Dobrée. London: Routledge, 1927.

De-la-Noy, Michael. *Denton Welch: The Making of a Writer*. New York: Penguin, 1987.

Deleuze, Gilles. *Masochism: Coldness and Cruelty*. Translated by Jean McNeil. New York: Zone Books, 1989.

Festa, Lynn. *Sentimental Figures of Empire in Eighteenth-Century Britain and France*. Baltimore: Johns Hopkins University Press, 2006.

François, Anne-Lise. "'Not Thinking of You as Left Behind': Virgil and the Missing of Love in Hardy's *Poems of 1912–13*." *ELH* 75, no. 1 (2008): 63–88.

Gord, Jeff. "Forniphilia." *House of Gord*. Accessed 13 March 2014. http://www.houseofgord.com/forniphilia-human-furniture.

Laclos, Choderlos. *Les liaisons dangereuses*. Edited by René Pomeau. Paris: Flammarion, 1964.

Lamb, Jonathan. *The Things Things Say*. Princeton: Princeton University Press, 2011.

Lynch, Deidre Shauna. *The Economy of Character: Novels, Market Culture, and the Business of Inner Meaning*. Chicago: University of Chicago Press, 1998.
Moi, Toril. *Simone de Beauvoir: The Making of an Intellectual Woman*. 2nd ed. New York: Oxford University Press, 2008.
Rampo, Edogawa. *The Edogawa Rampo Reader*. Translated by Seth Jacobowitz. Fukuoka: Kurodahan Press, 2008.
– *Japanese Tales of Mystery and Imagination*. Translated by James B. Harris. Boston: Tuttle, 1956.
That Obscure Object of Desire. Directed by Luis Buñuel. France: Greenwich Film Productions, 1977. DVD.
Vertigo. Directed by Alfred Hitchcock. United States: Alfred J. Hitchcock Productions, 1958. DVD.
Waters, John. *Role Models*. New York: Farrar, Straus and Giroux, 2010.
Welch, Denton. "I Left My Grandfather's House." In *In Youth Is Pleasure*. Cambridge: Exact Change, 1994.
– *In Youth Is Pleasure*. New York: L.B. Fischer, 1946.
– *The Journals of Denton Welch*. Edited by Michael De-la-Noy. New York: E.P. Dutton, 1986.
– *A Last Sheaf*. Edited by Eric Oliver. London: John Lehmann, 1951.
– *Maiden Voyage*. New York: E.P. Dutton, 1968.
– *A Voice Through a Cloud*. New York: E.P. Dutton, 1966.
Winnicott, D.W. *Playing and Reality*. London: Routledge, 2005.

PART II

Socializing: Aesthetic Autonomies and Collectivities

3 Full Content: Shaw's Paratexts, Social Liberalism, and Harmonization

MICHAEL MEEUWIS

Writing in 1919, the American dramatic critic Archibald Henderson describes the experience created by the printed drama of George Bernard Shaw: "The aim of [Shaw's] new technic," he notes, "is to create a perfectly objective illusion for the picture-frame stage, imaginatively for the reader as well as actually for the spectator."[1] Henderson gestures toward a tendency in Shaw's own writing to tightly control how readers would construct the world of the play in their own minds.[2] Shaw, indeed, is one of the writers credited by Martin Puchner with extending the descriptive reach of stage directions.[3] My essay demonstrates the role of the so-called social liberalism of the 1900s and 1910s in this innovation, using Shaw to explore this liberalism's role in the history of literature more generally. Shaw may have been an avowed enemy of many tenets of contemporary liberal philosophy. This essay argues, however, that in a way similar to social liberalism, Shaw's writing encourages the mass of individuals to standardize how they think. After detailing the specific ways in which Shaw channels this dimension of social liberalism in *Major Barbara* (1907), I turn in my conclusion to briefly consider the influence of its treatment of social liberalism on the writing of I.A. Richards and – through him – the foundation of twentieth-century literary studies more generally.

Shaw's paratextual materials – stage directions and prefaces – incite a process that is similar to an underappreciated aspect of contemporaneous political and cultural theory: specifically, the concept of *harmonization*. This idea was promoted by L.T. Hobhouse, the most important of the so-called social liberals of the 1900s and 1910s. Social liberalism holds that individual freedoms should be accommodated to the good of society as a whole and that individuals need to be guided to think in harmony with the rest of the population. To this end, harmonization suggested that in an ideal society, the elements of mental life – impressions, opinions, and ideas – could be shared among the whole of the population. In this paper, I examine how Shaw's innovative use of paratexts encouraged this popular sharing of objects of thought. My reading reveals Shaw as closer to this thread of political thought than his antiliberal stance might lead us to believe. Indeed, Shaw provides what Hobhouse's theory mostly does not: a concrete mechanism for harmonizing thought among wide populations.

The idea of harmonization, conversely, makes a stated ambition of Shaw's printed drama seem more historically plausible – and, indeed, shows how this strain of liberalism influenced stage directions as we now think of them. Shaw claims in his prefaces that his drama will create a standardized virtual performance space in the minds of its readers. My essay explores the process through which this occurs. I begin with an idea from performance practitioners Tim Etchells, Gabriella Giannachi, and Nick Kaye. When watching a performance, they note, audiences generally display a tendency "to fill absence[s]": to try to make sense of unexplained elements that appear in performance.[4] This is also true, I suggest, within the virtual performance spaces Shaw's plays create in the minds of their readers. Characters in Shaw's plays often express philosophies that they do not fully expound. For example, the anarchist would-be social reformer Jack Tanner in *Man and Superman* (1903) has published a "Revolutionist's Handbook," whose ideas are briefly mentioned by characters onstage; the full text of this handbook is included within Shaw's edition of the play. Prompted to respond to the absences within virtual performances, as Etchells et al. suggest they might, audiences are guided toward Shaw's explanatory paratexts.

Why include full explication only in the paratext – why not, in other words, simply have a character explain these philosophies within the play? There is of course the matter of dramatic expediency. (Few wish Shaw's plays talkier.) Reading Shaw alongside Hobhouse's contemporary theories, however, provides us with other reasons for these deferred explications. Shaw's paratexts involve the reader in what Hobhouse terms "the development of [a] human faculty in orderly co-operation": that is, the ability to think in harmony with others.[5] These plays encourage readerly cooperation with the terms of the paratext. To produce a vision of society, readers think using the terms that Shaw has provided for them.

This mechanism in Shaw's plays is a literary instantiation of what Hobhouse suggests harmonization could achieve: an "awakening of the imagination" toward the "common good."[6] Even Shaw's supermen – his energetic elites, whose selfish desires overwhelm those of weaker characters – work at the behest of an aggregate, guiding human power, which Shaw terms the "Life Force." Both writers claim that mass mental life should be harmonized to the common good – even if for Shaw this common good might appear to be mass selfishness. Shaw, additionally, furnishes what Hobhouse's *Liberalism* seems to necessitate, but not describe: some agent to concretely direct how others think.

Shaw and Hobhouse spent much of their careers in political disagreement. Early in his career, Hobhouse was close to the Fabian Society, of which Shaw was a prominent member, but broke with the organization – and, particularly, with its authoritarian and pro-imperial views – around the time of the 1900 publication of *Fabianism and the Empire*.[7] This disagreement, however, masks the extent to which both writers believe that human beings have an innate tendency toward harmonious mental standardization, which government policy should promote and which literary works could encourage.

When Shaw imagines his printed drama achieving social change by influencing his readers, he describes a process that fulfils Hobhouse's description of the standardization of thinking. Conversely, when Hobhouse imagines a socially influential author, that figure sounds like Shaw: someone who can encourage this kind of standardization within the minds of his readers. In demonstrating this similarity between these seeming political enemies, I show how harmonization deserves wider consideration in the study of the literature of the period: to put it another way, that social liberalism's call for the standardization of thought influenced even writers advancing avowedly anti-liberal ends.

I examine how Shaw's plays-with-prefaces guide the reader into harmonizing their thinking. Reading *Major Barbara*, I show how Shaw's text demonstrates harmonization on two interrelated levels: as a process dramatized within the play and as a process that the play encourages in its readers. First, Shaw uses the specific form of the debate-play to show his ideas entering the society – and the resistance they experienced from conventional society. The arms-merchant hero of *Major Barbara*, Andrew Undershaft, acts within the play as an agent of harmonization by causing other characters within the play, including the classics scholar Adolphus Cusins, to freely standardize their beliefs to his own. Undershaft's belief that society advances when individuals follow their strongest desires regardless of social convention reflects Hobhouse's belief in the total compatibility of the good of the individual and of the society. Although for Hobhouse the ideal individual is selfless, and for Undershaft selfish, both figures speak to social liberalism's faith in the existence of a "common good" – and in the compatibility of individual and collective ends within this common good.

Second, Shaw uses his paratexts to manifest a more direct form of harmonization, specifically within the reader's mind as it creates the world of the play in the reader's imagination. This process begins with an absence in the script of the play itself. Undershaft presents his ideology as something that he does not fully explain or comprehend, calling himself instead a "mystic."[8] Shaw takes advantage of a philosophical dialogue's ability to show ideas entering the world, specifically as characters convince other characters that they are right. Shaw innovates within this form, however, by leaving a final explanation of the play's ideas out of the play itself, but including it in the paratext. The absence of explanation within the play engages the reader's curiosity, directing them to consider Shaw's preface. The preface, in turn, explains this absence: Undershaft is the "instrument of a Will or Life Force which uses him for purposes wider than his own."[9] So the play encourages readers to harmonize to Shaw's own beliefs by completing the play's reality, in their own minds, through the playwright's paratextual instructions concerning not only the visual appearance of the characters but also the ethical values that they present.

In particular, I want to examine how Shaw's form of harmonization makes use of the visual register that Henderson finds in his work. Shaw uses this visual register in a way that typifies harmonization's *exteriorization of thought*, its account of thinking as a social process. Jock Macleod reminds us that "many of the intellectuals" associated with social liberalism "were also deeply concerned with literary culture" and specifically "its function in the modern world."[10] I conclude by showing how this claim to literature's social effect registered in the formation of literary studies, linking Shaw and Hobhouse's accounts of thought's exteriorization to I.A. Richards's 1929 *Principles of Literary Criticism*. By briefly sketching Shaw's affinities with Richards's text, which is foundational to the academic study of literature, I invite a wider consideration of social liberalism's role in literary history.

Hobhouse and Harmonization

C.M. Griffin notes that *harmony*, and the related process of harmonization, only "came ... to be regarded as a political principle" in the nineteenth century.[11] The principle sought to reconcile "a plurality of social and economic interests ... indicating a belief in the spontaneity or 'naturalness' of such a reconciliation."[12] Unlike Darwinian theories of progress, however, harmony emphasized cooperation rather than competition: what is best for one individual does not come at the expense of another. As Haia Shpayer-Makov notes, harmonization resonated with the culture more generally, in which "a certain shift away from laissez-faire individualism and a growing acceptance of state authority and its ability to contribute to the common good was evident in liberal thought and in the policies of the various governments in power."[13]

Hobhouse describes harmonization in his 1911 *Liberalism*. A partial restatement of earlier liberal ideals, *Liberalism* continues what David Lloyd and Paul Thomas call the project of "ethical training devoted to the 'educing' of the citizen from the human being."[14] *Liberalism* does so via an equation of individual and collective interest that typifies social liberalism. The text asserts that individual "self-interest" and communal "public interests" are entirely compatible: "Self-interest, if enlightened and unfettered, will, in short, lead [the individual] to conduct coincident with public interest. There is, in this sense, a natural harmony between the individual and society."[15] Understanding how Hobhouse arrives at this premise means understanding his account of mental life, what he terms "thought." A defining difference between social liberalism and the mid-century liberalism of figures like J.S. Mill is social liberalism's emphasis on the exteriorization of thought. Hobhouse writes that "liberty of thought is of very little avail without liberty to exchange thoughts – since thought is mainly a social product."[16] The mental life of humans, in Hobhouse's account, is primarily public: that is, its objects are primarily exchangeable with others. It is for this reason that "the 'inward' life," he writes, "will seek to express itself in outward acts."[17] Because humans are social animals, we learn how to think – even in our most private moments – in tandem with others. The contents of "thought" are mostly drawn from, and then cycle back into, society: specifically, from and back into society's store of thoughts held in "common."

The "common good" also centres Hobhouse's definition of the individual's "freedom." His specific definition of "Liberalism" calls it the "belief that society can safely be founded" on the "self-directing power of personality"; he equates self-direction with community direction.[18] For Hobhouse, our thoughts are never fully our own. Instead, we draw our objects of thought from society. As a result, humans are innately predisposed to develop in mutual harmony. As Stefan Collini writes, Hobhouse "implicitly restrict[s] self-development to those activities which not only do not conflict with, but actually stimulate, the development of others."[19] Since thinking occurs in tandem with others, true self-development – premised on thinking – is a process whose content must move freely between the self and others.

Hobhouse, to this end, redefines certain terms associated with liberal individualism – "will," "personality" – in a way that makes the individual good and the social good entirely compatible. As he writes, "to teach … man to discipline himself … is to foster the development of will, of personality, of self control, or whatever we please to call that central harmonizing power which makes us capable of directing our own lives."[20] Humans are always socialized, as it is through language and concepts learned from society that we make sense of ourselves as individuals. So, it is a "central harmonizing power" that allows us to "direct[] our own lives." Because humans are innately prone to harmony with a common good, the best way for individuals to develop is to work together toward that common good. As Peter Weiler notes, "Hobhouse failed to give serious consideration to the possibility that there was a fundamental conflict of interest within society that could not be healed by a common adherence to the ideal of Humanity."[21] In other words, Hobhouse did not acknowledge that there might be ultimately conflicting individual interests within society.

"Freedom," variously defined, centres the liberal tradition. The kind of freedom that primarily interests Hobhouse is what he terms "social freedom": any "freedom that can be enjoyed by all the members of a community, and … the freedom to choose among those lines of activity which do not involve injury to others."[22] Hobhouse equates social development and self-development. Following one's "self-interest, if enlightened and unfettered, will … lead" the individual "to conduct coincident with public interest."[23] Government's role was thus to make people enlightened. As Weiler writes, one significant purpose of government in Hobhouse's view was to make individuals aware of this innate tendency toward the pursuit of self-interest, such that the "mutual realization" of the "development of both the individual and society … would be consciously controlled as man came to understand the direction of progress and was able to manipulate society accordingly."[24] So government would work to promote within the individual an awareness of how society should progress: specifically, an awareness of the compatibility of their own interests with those of their community.

Shaw's writing can help us to see how compatible with the social ends of literature Hobhouse's early work is. Although Hobhouse does not mention literature specifically in *Liberalism*, literature's ability to entice individuals to think in particular ways – to construct mental worlds, to feel sympathy for characters within those worlds – and ultimately its ability to produce better citizens suggests the ways that it could further this governmental mission. Hobhouse's account of the harmonization and exteriorization of thought elucidates what Shaw sets out to do: show the operation of a social law within the diegesis of the plays themselves, then articulate this social law within the prefaces and paratexts, raising the awareness of their readers.

Both writers believe in an overarching force directing human society and in the importance of communicating that force to the widest possible audience. Hobhouse approaches the compatibility of the interests of the individual and society from the perspective of selflessness, Shaw from that of selfishness. Yet each ultimately says that what is best for the individual is also what is best for society. Their faith in this compatibility involves a theory of progress: that is, an account of how an abstract force leads to improvements in human life and society. In *Liberalism*, Hobhouse describes "a natural harmony between the individual and society."[25] Hobhouse's later works would describe this developing harmony as caused by "orthogenic evolution": a universal tendency toward improvement, realized in the harmony of individual and group interests.[26] Because of this force harmonizing the individual's development, "men's interests" – that is, the individual needs of the population as a whole – are not "fundamentally at odds" with the needs of society.[27] Instead, Hobhouse holds that certain laws of development are objectively true for all individuals and that individuals made aware of these laws – that is, made aware that their self-interest is also the communal interest – will go on to benefit both themselves and the whole of society. This is the "spontaneity" that Griffin notes. It is not that harmonization will happen without anyone prompting it to but rather that it will be spontaneously recognized as right once that process is started by an adequately enlightened individual.

Hobhouse asserts that a small part of the population will desire to work toward the common interest and that the mass of the population is primed to receive this instruction. In *Liberalism*, for example, he relies on a "rare" group of individuals, possessed of a "wholehearted absorption in public interests," to work on behalf of the majority: "the democrat is well aware that it is the remnant which saves the people."[28] However, Hobhouse's theories are rarely accompanied by practical systems of implementation for best effecting this progress. What is this remnant actually to do? The clearest answer seems to be something like awareness-raising among an amenable population, performed in the name of the "human faculty in orderly co-operation."[29] This awareness-raising seeks, specifically, to engage the "imagination": to make individuals imagine their needs as in concert with those of others. For Hobhouse, the "mass" is not equipped, mentally, to govern themselves, but is able to recognize good governance and agree to follow it. "The masses who spend their toilsome days in mine or factory struggling for bread have not their heads for ever filled with the complex details of international policy or industry law"; indeed, "to expect this would be absurd."[30] Yet Hobhouse does "expect them to respond and assent to the things that make for the moral and material welfare of the country": to react, spontaneously and favourably, when the "remnant" acts in their interest.[31]

This occasion has strong affinities, as we will see, with Shaw's account of speaking to his own audience. Shaw frames his characters onstage as being aware to varying extents of the truths that his paratexts clarify. For example, Undershaft has an understanding (if an incomplete one) of a social truth, around which he has organized his factory. His workers do not seem to understand this truth. Yet they happily work within the factory, which organizes their natures to best mutual benefit. Shaw's readers are placed at a higher level even than Undershaft, being given the full details of the theory that Undershaft only implicitly grasps.

That Shaw's system allows for full awareness in some and partial awareness in others marks a key difference between his theory and Hobhouse's. Hobhouse objected to the Fabian promotion of "bureaucratic rule by the specially trained expert," who would act in the best interest of the masses but without making any attempt to influence or even acknowledge their views.[32] In contrast to what the Fabians proposed, Hobhouse writes that government "must engage the efforts and respond to the genuine desires not of a handful of superior beings, but of great masses of men."[33] The Fabians preferred rule by experts and were happy for cognition, and for full awareness, to be distributed unevenly through society. Hobhouse, by contrast, gestures toward a more delegated structure of awareness and "engagement." As he does not set out many concrete proposals for governance, however, what "engage" could mean is vague: a proposition, perhaps, to stir the minds of these "masses," but one given without any definite means of doing so. In the next section, I explore how Shaw theorizes his own form of engagement by harmonizing the readers of his plays into agreement with his theories.

Shaw's Plays: Harmonization in Print vs. Performance

Shaw first gives an example of the particular form through which his engagement with harmonization will take place in the introduction to his 1898 collection *Plays Unpleasant*, which comprises a series of plays accompanied by extensive prefaces and stage directions. These paratexts respond, in this collection, to the very particular problem of being something like an avant-garde playwright in turn-of-the-century Britain. Victorian plays were strictly censored by the Lord Chamberlain's office. Further, as Tracy Davis describes, the Victorian theatre industry actively embraced this strict censorship, benefiting from the imprimatur of respectability that this regulation gave.[34] Because Shaw's plays would be either banned or not produced, he had to choose non-performative venues to reach a wide audience. As a result, "by the turn of the century many more had probably read the plays and their ... prefaces than had ever attended the scattered performances of his works."[35]

Needing to address audiences through print, however, was also an opportunity, as these paratexts allowed Shaw to guide the imaginations of those reading his plays in a way that would be impossible at a live theatrical event. The *Plays Unpleasant* introduction announces the collection as nothing less than "the institution of a new art."[36] This art form will provide the "full content" of these plays.[37] By "full content," Shaw indicates a concept with affinities to harmonization: specifically, to harmonization's focus on the exteriorization of thought. In Shaw's plays, this exteriorization often takes the form of the sort of visual information that was best included in paratexts, which could direct the visual sense of both the reader and (perhaps less forcefully) the director. As we will see, giving the reader the "full content" involves telling them how to think: both about what the play's visual world looks like but also about the ethical dimension of that world. So, accepting the paratext's ethical vision means agreeing to an extent with Shaw's social philosophy, at least insofar as one constructs within one's mind the visual-and-ethical world of his plays. Further, this social philosophy, like the ideas Hobhouse proposes, frames itself as reconciling the interests of the individual and of society.

As far as I can tell, Shaw does not use the word "harmony" in precisely Hobhouse's sense in his theatrical writing. Nevertheless, ideas like harmonization – particularly its engagement with the imagination and its exteriorization of thought – inform his writing. Shaw often standardizes the imagination through visual descriptions that also carry ethical significance. In a letter from 1888, he writes:

> I hardly ever go to the theatre here, but I enjoy reading a play now and then in the evening; and as I have a powerful imagination where anything dramatic is concerned, I can see everything that is really natural, authentic, and credible happening before my eyes. The reading of a play produces almost the same effect as its performance.[38]

This paragraph not only describes Shaw's reading, but also sets out how Shaw's drama will function for his own readers. Shaw, first, conflates the virtual visual world of the play-in-reading and the real world. The ambiguity in "everything that is really natural, authentic, and credible" – is this taking place within the play, or in the world more generally? – suggests that the standard for both is the same: plays could induce experiences similar to seeing things in real life. One whose "imagination" is touched in this way has a specifically visual experience: one that occurs "before [their] eyes." This experience is also "natural, authentic, and credible": that is, an experience in which visual experience and ethical assessment are linked. Ethical thinking has in this way, to use Hobhouse's term, exteriorized.

Shaw grounds his authority in the *Plays Unpleasant* preface, and the paratextual "art form" that it introduced, on this visual sense. Hobhouse's idea of the exteriorization of thought helps us to understand this visuality as literal rather than figurative. Shaw is aware of the truths about human life because he "simply understood life differently from the average respectable man," owing to his "power of seeing things accurately."[39] Shaw does not frame himself here as reflective or interiorized. The truest aspects of "life" are those that instead have an exteriorized, visual register; it is those that he perceives more accurately than the "average … man."

Vision makes Shaw like a member of Hobhouse's elite "remnant": someone whose "wholehearted absorption in public interests" leaves him better able to note the laws truly underlying human behaviour.[40] Shaw's self-attribution of remarkable powers of sight, which remains consistent throughout this preface, is how he explains this "absorption" in himself: he sees society clearly, so he is constantly absorbed – enveloped – in ideas that would help others to live better. This emphasis specifically on sight reflects Hobhouse's "'inward' life … express[ing] itself in outward acts": that is, a belief that the most important trends in mass mental life manifest themselves in exteriorized form.[41]

Shaw ascribes to himself the specifically governmental role of consciousness-raising Hobhouse gives to his "remnant": a role in which one contributes to the pool of ideas available to a society that freely listens to him. "The classes," Shaw notes, "eagerly read my essays: the masses patiently listened to my harangues."[42] Shaw saw these "masses" as willing to cooperate in an orderly fashion, to listen patiently to his ideas. Yet what his essays and public speeches lacked was what he could provide through paratext-accompanied plays: specifically, a simultaneously visual and ethical experience for his readers like that which he had described in his 1888 letter.

Also like Hobhouse, Shaw describes himself as a social scientist: one able to observe daily life and perceive certain truths operating within it. Shaw specifically frames his drama, when being read, as able to communicate these truths. In the *Plays Unpleasant* introduction, he writes: "What would we not give for the copy of Hamlet used by Shakespear at rehearsal, with the original stage business scrawled by the prompter's pencil? … It is for want of this elaboration that Shakespear, unsurpassed as poet … has left us no intellectually coherent drama, and could not afford to pursue a genuinely scientific method in his studies."[43] "Stage business" refers to the exterior parts of the performance: bodies, sets, and so forth. It is these exterior elements that, in this account, allow drama to be sociological "science": that is, one that includes both an account of how things are and assessments about those things. Shaw writes to a time that believed that sociology could be fully a "science of the living together," an account of social laws every bit as rigorous as, say, the laws of physics.[44] Calling for a "scientific method" was a claim to objectivity, asserting that the drama could demonstrate objective truths about society if accompanied by the exteriorized elements of the "stage business."

Shaw tells the drama to enact the sort of awareness-raising that Hobhouse calls on government to perform. Hobhouse describes his ideal citizens in the way that Shaw describes himself: as constantly confronted by the exterior truths of social life. His elites, those who work to influence the lives of others, are pressed at on all sides by exterior notions: they experience a "wholehearted absorption" in the social world, as "common interests envelop their life and thought."[45] Hobhouse is, again, vague on precisely how the government these elites participate in will work – except insofar as it will engage the "imagination" of the population, tuning this mass "imagination" in such a way that it will harmoniously perceive the existence of a "common good" through thinking in unison.

In Shaw, a standardized visual register is an important component of this thinking in unison via the consideration of exteriorized, objective truths. Shaw's plays, as he claims, will "force the spectator to face unpleasant facts" about human behaviour.[46] Addressing readers rather than theatregoers as his primary audience, Shaw asserts that these readers will experience in their minds a virtual visual space that is similar to the "natural, authentic, and credible" vision that he himself described in his letter. That is, these plays will, through the visual register implied by "spectator," communicate ethical truths.

The spread of ethical truths does not occur so cleanly within the plays themselves. In many of Shaw's plays, one character champions the ideas put forward in the preface. This "hero," as Shaw writes in the preface to *Pygmalion* (1912), attempts to act as a "reformer" of his society.[47] Gareth Griffith writes that "one figure" often "dominates the plays and prefaces: the free-thinking progressive, the realist who can see life for what it is."[48] This figure's "free-thinking" means both thinking outside of a set of false truths imposed by society and recognizing an alternate set of "irresistible" truths that stand ready to change society through this figure's influence.[49] These "irresistible" truths are, however, hindered by social conventions. So, this "hero" does not necessarily create social revolution but rather may convince certain other characters to change their minds.

Indeed, these heroic characters do not even fully comprehend the ideas that the preface presents, as we shall see in the case of Andrew Undershaft. Instead it is in the preface that these ideas are articulated most completely; indeed, their incomplete appearance within the play leads the curious reader back to the authority of the preface. This process of directing curiosity is analogous to Hobhouse's direction of the individual's will – that key term from mid-century liberalism – toward agreeing with communal values. Shaw implicitly regards his audiences as Hobhouse regards the "mass": inclined to look to elites to provide guidance regarding how to think and amenable to this guidance in furnishing the contents of their own minds.

Undershaft's arms manufactory at Perivale St Andrews, which enriches the lives of workmen and bosses alike, is a fulfilment of the Life Force as set out in the preface: it gives its workers an opportunity to make money and live comfortable lives. The workers, however, do not fully appreciate what is going on. As Hobhouse suggests, the "toilsome" mass requires an elite to direct their thinking for them. When asked how he maintains the factory's "discipline," Undershaft replies:

> I dont. They do. You see, the one thing Jones wont stand is any rebellion from the man under him, or any assertion of social equality between the wife of the man with 4 shillings a week less than himself, and Mrs Jones! Of course they all rebel against me, theoretically. Practically, every man of them keeps the man just below him in his place ... The men snub the boys and order them about; the carmen snub the sweepers; the artisans snub the unskilled laborers; the foremen drive and bully both the laborers and artisans ... The result is a colossal profit, which comes to me.[50]

Undershaft claims to have noticed an objective truth: that humans desire hierarchy and are strongly self-interested. In turn, he has created a mechanism, the social organization of his factory, that induces others to live according to this truth. This produces the factory and the model city that houses its workers – both of which create a space that is orderly and salubrious. Sustaining the city shows that individual and communal interests are not "fundamentally at odds," as harmonization suggests. In Hobhouse's terms, the "genuine desires" of Undershaft's workers are being met by the social arrangement of his factory. What is best for each individual involved is best for every other individual – even if some individuals, particularly the industrialist Undershaft, receive an unequal share of the benefits.

How do we move from the organization of a factory to the organization of a country – the level of organization that Hobhouse addresses? Like Hobhouse in his theorization of harmony, Shaw in his prefaces states that certain values will benefit everyone in a society. Undershaft's "conduct," the preface maintains, his desire to make money regardless of ethics, "stands the Kantian test."[51] That is, for Shaw, society would benefit if everyone acted as Undershaft does, fulfilling the terms of the categorical imperative. Shaw also reflects Hobhouse's ideas in disregarding the possibility for private ends ultimately at odds with one another. Instead, as harmonization proposes, this universal value – the self-fulfilment that the Life Force calls for, which all will believe in if awakened to it – will in turn benefit society as a whole. The preface to *Major Barbara* calls Undershaft "a man who has become intellectually and spiritually as well as practically conscious of the irresistible natural truth which we all abhor and repudiate: to wit ... that our first duty, to which every other consideration should be sacrificed, is not to be poor."[52] The preface sets out what "nature" is, in this case a "truth" about behaviour, which if followed will benefit society. If "the great mass of men" were to "act and believe ... as Undershaft acts and believes, the immediate result would be a revolution of incalculable beneficence."[53] This "revolution" comes about through selfishness rather than through the selflessness Hobhouse proposes; yet for both writers, successful behaviour is judged in terms of its benefit for the "common good."

If in Hobhouse it is unclear how much the "mass" should know about the social arrangements undertaken on their behalf, in Shaw the masses are explicitly kept in the dark. Undershaft's workers do not seem aware of the principle that they embody; they act for the Life Force without knowing that this is what they are doing. Nevertheless, this arrangement resembles harmonization's assertion that individual interests are compatible with the common good. Undershaft's workers "respond and assent to the things that make for the moral and material welfare of the country," as Hobhouse suggests.[54] Here, however, they do so merely for selfish reasons. They do not have to understand that the Life Force betters everyone in order to follow it; social benefit is at the conscious level simply an unintended consequence of their actions. So, Undershaft, this play's incarnation of the Shavian superman, does not necessarily promote free thinking in others. Rather, he compels others to act in the way that is best for society without knowing that this is what they are doing. The character who understands the most efficient social truths will create organizations, like the arms manufactory, that benefit all who work for them. Shaw's paratexts explain everything to the reader, who is placed in the flattering position of understanding the characters better than they understand themselves.

The position offered to the reader of paratexts is in this sense different to that offered to the audience of Shaw's plays in performance. In the play's second act, the eponymous Barbara Undershaft's belief in the Salvation Army's charitable work is systematically dismantled. Charity, as the preface and Undershaft alike maintain, keeps the poor in poverty. In performance, nevertheless, Undershaft is one of many voices. One argument in favour of charity is presented by Peter Shirley, an "honest poor man" turned out of his job once his actual age is discovered.[55] The audience's experience of Shirley marks a defining difference between *Major Barbara* as a hybrid playtext and as a performed piece. Whenever I have seen *Major Barbara* onstage, as in the 2008 National Theatre production, Shirley's self-description ("I'm not an old man, I'm ony [*sic*] 46 ... and now am I to be thrown into the gutter and my job given to a young man") evokes sympathy and, through it, this character's right to charity.[56] The preface, in contrast, contradicts this sympathetic connection made possible by performance. It tells us outright that "the misery of the world is due to the fact that the great mass of men act and believe as Peter Shirley acts and believes."[57] The preface calls Shirley's ethics, his desire to remain "what we call the honest poor man,"[58] a failure because they would not benefit the common good if taken as a universal principle.

This moment also presents a difference between Shaw's plays in reading and Shaw's plays in performance. Human performers may compel audience sympathy. A body on stage will make us notice it, and a particular actor may leverage this innate capacity in order to further their character's agenda. In performance, then, the audience's sympathies might well fail the "Kantian test." We might sympathize with characters whose ideas do not represent a universal ideal of conduct because we find an actor portraying them uniquely compelling. The paratext, more completely under Shaw's control, can correct for the inherent vagaries of the relationship between a live actor and an audience. The preface enshrines the claim that "the greatest of our evils, and the worst of our crimes is poverty" – that following the Life Force out of poverty reflects a truth about human behaviour – as analogous to a physical law within the world of the play. The play read via the paratext limits and even corrects our sympathy for Peter Shirley in a way that performance does not.

And yet, Undershaft does not fully comprehend the truths that he espouses. Shaw's heroic characters, those who represent the values of his prefaces, are also the most incomplete characters in his plays. That is, they are incomplete without a guiding paratext to fill in what they stand for: for example, to provide the link between Shaw's theory of the Life Force and Undershaft's limited articulation of this theory.

Undershaft will explain his social philosophy voluminously; however, he also asserts a "mystic" element to the beliefs that he follows.[59] Espousing a truth he does not fully understand makes Undershaft an ideal figure for the particular form of the paratextually directed playscript: he provides an "absence" that engages the reader's curiosity, but this absence is always presented alongside a paratext that directs – we might say harmonizes – that curiosity. He, too, would need to read the preface in order to figure out the Life Force toward which his beliefs ultimately direct him. There, Undershaft might be surprised to learn that the capitalism for which he stands is not the fullest fulfilment of Shaw's particular understanding of socialized values. Nevertheless, Shaw depicts Undershaft's views as a further step toward realizing the Life Force than mere charity would permit.

Because he embodies the preface's ideas, even if he does not fully understand them, Undershaft is the centre of harmonization in *Major Barbara*. He is "irresistible": to the workmen because he forcefully embodies a truth that enables self-actualization and to the reader because he presents an intriguing "absence" that directs them to the paratext. The stage directions note that Undershaft is *"on the surface, a stoutish, easygoing elderly man."*[60] As the reader is invited to consider the visual – what Undershaft looks like – the play also suggests that this visual "surface" requires further explanation. Beneath this surface, the stage directions tell us, are *"formidable reserves of power, both bodily and mental,"* which reside in a *"capacious chest and long head."*[61] Yet what this capacity contains – what the "formidable reserves of power" are – is not clarified within the play.

Instead, the preface completes Undershaft for the reader. Indeed, it knows Undershaft better than he himself does. This is particularly true when Undershaft describes his beliefs as a form of finally unknowable mysticism:

> CUSINS. … You do not drive this place: it drives you. And what drives the place?
> UNDERSHAFT *(enigmatically)*. A will of which I am a part.[62]

In this case, the *Major Barbara* introduction clarifies that Undershaft "is only the instrument of a Will or Life Force which uses him for purposes wider than his own."[63] In this way, Shaw's plays use potential confusion – these ideas present in the plays but not fully explained by them – in order to engage the reader's curiosity, directing them toward the preface. Tracy Davis writes that Shaw's plays in performance might have been intended to produce "a stupid (or stupefied) public": to potentially confuse their audience on certain points.[64] These explanatory paratexts aided in the making of Shaw the celebrity, providing an acknowledged place where audiences could find out more about his theories.

And these theories were very much stamped with the "Shaw" brand. Ultimately, no author can completely control how a reader interprets a text. Shaw could not prevent a reader from – to use Leah Price's terms – skimming through his introductions, or indeed skipping them altogether.[65] However, Shaw's decisions regarding the production of the text reflect an unusual desire to attempt to exercise influence over the reader. Certainly Shaw's plays were to be read with his own celebrity in mind. In his introduction to the *Fabian Essays in Socialism* (1889), Shaw had written that "metropolitan readers" had the "advantage of … getting face to face with the writers, stripping the veil of print from their personality."[66] This immediate presence of the author was obviously not possible through a print text. Yet this relationship between absence and paratextual explanation was a concrete device designed to direct the reader back toward the "personality" – manifested in the paratexts – that had created it. While no character in *Major Barbara* says anything as explicit as "I'm a disciple of Bernard Shaw," as does a character in *The Doctor's Dilemma* (1906), a variety of devices within the play gesture toward the writer behind it: toward, as Katherine Kelly writes, "fashioning" an "authorial persona" that would come across in the reading of the play.[67]

Like orthogenic evolution, Shaw's theory of the Life Force held that a universal force directed human evolution toward its highest potential.[68] Both of these theories argued for the existence of certain common values toward which humanity would in time become harmonized. The play may be performed without further clarification of these values. The question of "what drives the place" – a homophone for Shaw's *plays* more generally – might, in performance, be interpreted very differently. The "will" Undershaft refers to might be interpreted as the local organization giving shape to the play's production – the stage manager or designer, say. The preface, however, provides another definition of the "will" to the reader. So Undershaft acts in accordance with Shaw's theories, but understands them only implicitly. Shaw's audiences are given incomplete explanations of his theories; Shaw's readers, in contrast, find such explications near at hand.

Visual description within Shaw's stage directions exteriorize the ethical truths that Undershaft's factory embodies – but the most direct account of these truths is available only to the play's readers who can read these stage directions. The arms manufactory at Perivale St Andrews, the organization that Undershaft has set up to direct his workers to realize the Life Force (even if he himself does not fully understand this term), is described in the stage directions as *"beautifully situated and beautiful in itself."*[69] This equation of explosives with beauty is, on its own terms, objective: no individual viewer is named, so all are implied. This beauty is ethical as well as aesthetic: *"The best view,"* the stage direction notes, *"is obtained from the crest of a slope about half a mile to the east, where the high explosives are dealt with."*[70] The "best view" of the manufactory, the reader is informed, is that from the location of the "high explosives" that the factory sells in the name of amoral capital acquisition. This stage direction expresses the play's central ethical message – that the resistance to poverty is the highest moral good – in aesthetic terms. This is another potential disjunction between what the stage direction indicates to the reader and what scenery might connote to an audience of the play in performance. This installation of the means of violent death within an English landscape would seem to present a powerful discord – as, in performance, placing the manufactory onstage might. As in the case of Peter Shirley, however, the preface corrals this discord, even gaining energy from overcoming it in the name of a higher morality.

The paratext's opinions are not entirely absent from the play itself, however. Within the play's diegesis, various audience surrogates confirm this reading. When he sees it, Cusins describes the city – "Everything perfect! wonderful! real!" – in terms that echo not only the stage directions' instruction of how to view the scene but also Shaw's own description of the "natural, authentic, and credible" stage illusion he experiences when reading plays.[71] Cusins's statement that this scene is "real" suggests that he has come around to the "truth" about the amoral acquisition of capital that the preface proposes. He can see the manufactory, and its surrounding town, in the way that the preface suggests the audience should view it: as a mixed visual and ethical milieu, a spectacle confirming this particular account of human nature.

Also, these readers can observe the play's characters grappling with their lack of knowledge. Undershaft's ideas may be based in the "irresistible" idea of the Life Force; several of the play's characters nevertheless resist him, because social conventions hold them back. For example, Undershaft finds that he is unable to successfully describe the ideals he stands for to his estranged wife, Lady Britomart:

> UNDERSHAFT. ... *I* was an east ender. I moralized and starved until one day I swore that I would be a full-fed free man at all costs ... I was a dangerous man until I had my will: now I am a useful, beneficent, kindly person. That is the history of most self-made millionaires, I fancy. When it is the history of every Englishman we shall have an England worth living in.
>
> LADY BRITOMART. Stop making speeches, Andrew. This is not the place for them.
>
> UNDERSHAFT *(punctured).* My dear: I have no other means of conveying my ideas.[72]

Undershaft may be able to create the factory, putting his "ideas" into practice. He laments that he has a difficult time communicating his ideas, as such, to others – a difficulty that Lady Britomart confirms. As Griffith writes, one "aspect to Shaw's thought ... viewed the public realm as a place of discourse not science, presenting opportunities for self-discovery and collective agency, a forum for the search for rational consensus through argument and debate."[73] This "search," however, indicates that these truths may not actually be found by the characters onstage. Noting that Undershaft has been "punctured," the stage directions confirm that harmonization may have a difficult time occurring within this domestic setting. Puncturing implies a loss of inflation, and so of interior completeness, within the world of the play's dialogue.

This process of harmonization that takes place between the play and the reader is also not wholly absent within the play itself. This moment of conversion, though, leads to a character's conversion to a creed he, too, does not fully understand. The classics professor Cusins is converted to Undershaft's capitalist philosophy – and, through it, to an early form of the philosophy of the Life Force. This philosophy undergirds capitalist self-interest but will also in some more complete form eventually supplant capitalism. Cusins typifies harmonization in framing self-interest as, finally, a tool that will promote the interests of the society as a whole:

> CUSINS. You cannot have power for good without having power for evil too. Even mother's milk nourishes murderers as well as heroes. This power which only tears men's bodies to pieces has never been so horribly

> abused as the intellectual power, the imaginative power, the poetic, religious power that can enslave men's souls. As a teacher of Greek I gave the intellectual man weapons against the common man. I now want to give the common man weapons against the intellectual man. I love the common people. I want to arm them against the lawyers, the doctors, the priests, the literary men, the professors, the artists, and the politicians, who, once in authority, are more dangerous, disastrous and tyrannical of all the fools, rascals, and impostors. I want a power simple enough for common men to use, yet strong enough to force the intellectual oligarchy to use its genius for the *general good*.[74]

Cusins here reflects that general trend of the 1900s to adapt the earlier concepts of liberalism into a more explicitly socialized form. "Genius" was Mill's term for that mental distinction that made an individual an elite: one who was allowed to think freely, and whose thinking in turn should be followed by others. Cusins claims that "genius" must work for the "general good": Hobhouse's term.

The broad outlines of Cusins's thought, as expressed in this speech, present a theory with strong affinities to harmonization. However, this speech is also quite confused – a confusion that, in presenting an idea that is not fully defined, is like Undershaft's description of his "mysticism." Again, the reader of the paratext has access to information that would clarify the situation of characters within the play, if they too had access to it; the reader therefore becomes like one of both Shaw and Hobhouse's elites, able to articulate social processes whose participants lack this fuller awareness. What Cusins proposes is not fully articulated but rather riddled with unresolved contradictions and paradoxes: "weapons" but also "love"; a "democratic" force nevertheless responsive to the "genius" of an "oligarchy." The vagueness of this speech, then, potentially has the same effect as the vagueness of Undershaft's assertion of "mysticism," directing readers to an explanatory preface by stating an idea that is incomplete within the play itself. The paratext-guided play allowed *Major Barbara* to both direct the reader to certain "scientific" truths and to dramatize the slow spread of these truths through a population.

Afterword: A Long Afterlife for Literary Harmonization

Harmonization would have a long influence over twentieth-century literary practice. Despite his capacious self-regard as a singular social prophet, Shaw was far from alone in his belief in the power of an author to encourage mental harmony through literary texts. In fact, in his 1915 book *The World in Conflict*, Hobhouse offers an account of how literature should induce harmonization that is remarkably similar to what Shaw's plays propose. Hobhouse's thought is thus more like Shaw's in this last decade of his career, particularly because the events of the First World War shook Hobhouse's belief in the inevitability of orthogenic evolution. This later writing shows a shift in his faith in the spread of harmonizing tendencies: as Griffin writes, "harmony, [Hobhouse] now asserts, is not 'given' as an attribute of reality, but rather it must be imposed upon experience through an act of purposive will."[75] Hobhouse had come around to a Shaw-like belief that a strong figure was required to organize and induce harmonization in others. The exemplary figure that Hobhouse chooses is in fact George Eliot, whom he casts as a proto-sociologist: "George Eliot, in reality, has one theme throughout her stories. Her method is wholly scientific in spirit. It is a repeated attempt to show in the concrete case, how the wheels of life turn."[76] Eliot grasps certain objective social truths, then communicates them to readers. However, Hobhouse provides no mechanism through which this transfer might happen. In contrast, as I have shown, Shaw frames his stage directions as able to do precisely this: induce a particular population to think in a particular, standardized way.

Stage directions were not the only twentieth-century attempt to standardize the mental experience of literature. Indeed, social liberalism has a role to play within our understanding of literary studies more generally. However we might contest the precise degree of its influence, the work of I.A. Richards has been indisputably influential over the professionalization of literary criticism.[77] Richards, in *Principles of Literary Criticism* (1924), calls literature a unitary "storehouse of recorded values," capable of presenting certain similar experiences to similar minds across time. Richards reflects and repeats harmonization's socialization of thought.[78] He qualifies this statement with a greater acknowledgment of the possibility of "eccentric experience": that is, things felt or perceived by individuals that could not be felt by others.[79] Such experience is, however, unusual. Richards describes the "vast majority" of mental activity, and the literature that communicates it, as "common to all men."[80] "We," he writes, in a phrase that could have appeared in Hobhouse's description of the exchange of thoughts, "are social beings and accustomed to communication from infancy … The very structure of our minds is largely determined by the fact that man has been engaged in communicating for so many hundreds of thousands of years."[81]

I do not want to overextend the similarities between Richards, Shaw, and Hobhouse. Richards is not, for example, a straightforward proponent of the visual experiences that Shaw proposes. He attacks the "assumption … that all attentive and sensitive readers will experience the same images," calling it what he terms "such ignorance … too crude, too hasty, and too superficial" for "the present day."[82] Yet Richards also discusses the existence of what he terms "tied images," noting that – even if not *fully* standardized – "visual sensations of words do not commonly occur by themselves. They have certain regular companions so closely tied to them as to be only with difficulty disconnected."[83] Richards is in fact concerned in *Practical Criticism* with the question of which elements of poetry depend on evoking harmonized experiences and which occur differently in the minds of different readers.

Indeed, despite his condemnation of this visual tendency, Richards is particularly close to Shaw, and to harmonization, when he describes this "storehouse" of experience, which "spring[s] from and perpetuate[s] hours in the lives of exceptional people, when their control and command of experience is at its highest, hours when the varying possibilities of existence are most clearly seen."[84] That is, "exceptional" people have the same experiences that are available to all individuals, but do so with greater intensity than normal. Richards writes that literature is a way for a wider population to access these exceptional individuals' version of experience – in effect, to harmonize with them. Shaw's theory of the Life Force, too, tells the "exceptional" to follow their appetites for "experience," which will in turn enrich the "storehouse" of what humans can experience.

Richards attests to an interest in concepts like harmonization extending into the 1920s and 1930s. Full consideration of his theories' interplay with social liberalism, in particular the complex debt both owe to contemporary neuroscience, lies outside of the scope of this essay. I hope, nevertheless, that this consideration of Shaw's literary instantiation of ideas like Hobhouse's might begin a wider conversation about social liberalism's influence over the literary culture of its period – and, through Richards, over the field of literary studies.

NOTES

1 Henderson, *Changing Drama*, 247.

2 Martin Meisel notes how Shaw's innovative stage directions provided the equivalent of the "practical aspects" of stage directions for readers who

could not attend productions of his plays. In Meisel's account, Shaw's playtexts filled in "the descriptive, atmospheric, and even symbolic characterization of the projected scene" for these readers. Meisel, *How Plays Work*, 6.

3 Puchner, *Stage Fright*, 67.
4 Etchells, Giannachi, and Kaye, "Looking Back," 185.
5 Hobhouse, *Democracy and Reaction*, 51–2.
6 Hobhouse, *Liberalism*, 69.
7 Hobhouse and Shaw would quarrel directly in the pages of the *Nation* in May of 1913 regarding the issue of a guaranteed wage. For a summary of this debate, see Collini, *Liberalism and Sociology*, 134–6.
8 Shaw, *Major Barbara*, 88.
9 Ibid., 22.
10 Macleod, *Literature, Journalism, and the Vocabularies of Liberalism*, 1.
11 Griffin, "L.T. Hobhouse," 648.
12 Ibid.
13 Shpayer-Makov, *Ascent of the Detective*, 269.
14 Lloyd and Thomas, *Culture and the State*, 7.
15 Hobhouse, *Liberalism*, 28.
16 Ibid., 13. I have discussed this passage elsewhere; see Meeuwis, "Representative Government."
17 Hobhouse, *Liberalism*, 71.
18 Ibid., 59.
19 Collini, *Liberalism and Sociology*, 127.
20 Hobhouse, *Liberalism*, 59.
21 Weiler, "New Liberalism of L.T. Hobhouse," 157.
22 Hobhouse, *Liberalism*, 44.
23 Ibid., 28.
24 Weiler, "New Liberalism of L.T. Hobhouse," 149.
25 Hobhouse, *Liberalism*, 28.
26 For an account of Hobhouse's understanding of evolutionary theory, see Collini, *Liberalism and Sociology*, 171–208.
27 Weiler, "New Liberalism of L.T. Hobhouse," 152.
28 Hobhouse, "Liberalism," 111.
29 Hobhouse, *Democracy and Reaction*, 62.
30 Hobhouse, *Liberalism*, 111.
31 Ibid.
32 Collini, *Liberalism and Sociology*, 77.
33 Hobhouse, *Liberalism*, 84.
34 Davis, *Economics of the British Stage*, 82.
35 Griffith, *Socialism and Superior Brains*, 14.

36 Shaw, *Plays Unpleasant*, 24. I have retained the original – and unusual – orthography present in Shaw's original texts.
37 Ibid.
38 Quoted in Henderson, *Changing Drama*, 237.
39 Shaw, *Plays Unpleasant*, 7, 8.
40 Hobhouse, *Liberalism*, 111.
41 Ibid., 71.
42 Shaw, *Plays Unpleasant*, 10.
43 Ibid., 22.
44 For an account of the scientificity of early-century social science, see Latour, *Reassembling the Social*, 2. Latour notes that this belief marks a shift from our own day: "The virtues that we are prepared nowadays to grant the scientific and technical enterprises bear little relation with what the founders of the social sciences had in mind when they invented their disciplines" (2).
45 Hobhouse, *Liberalism*, 111.
46 Shaw, *Plays Unpleasant*, 25.
47 Shaw, *Pygmalion*, 3.
48 Griffith, *Socialism and Superior Brains*, 3.
49 Shaw, *Major Barbara*, 15.
50 Ibid., 127.
51 Ibid., 19.
52 Ibid., 15.
53 Ibid., 19.
54 Hobhouse, *Liberalism*, 111.
55 Shaw, *Major Barbara*, 19.
56 Ibid., 78.
57 Ibid., 19.
58 Ibid.
59 Ibid., 88.
60 Ibid., 65.
61 Ibid., 66.
62 Ibid., 139.
63 Ibid., 22.
64 Davis, *George Bernard Shaw*, 73.
65 Price, *The Anthology*, 9.
66 Shaw, "Introduction," iii.
67 Shaw, *Doctor's Dilemma*, 152; Kelly, "Imprinting the Stage," 26.
68 Fully describing Shaw's theory of the Life Force, and its role within his thought, lies outside of the scope of this essay. See instead Smith, *Bishop of Everywhere.*

69 Shaw, *Major Barbara*, 129.
70 Ibid.
71 Ibid.
72 Ibid., 143.
73 Griffith, *Socialism and Superior Brains*, 6.
74 Shaw, *Major Barbara*, 150 (my emphasis).
75 Griffin, "L.T. Hobhouse," 653.
76 Hobhouse, *World in Conflict*, 15.
77 For a discussion of Richards's place in the development of the profession, see Joshua Gang, "Behaviorism," 3.
78 Richards, *Principles of Literary Criticism*, 27.
79 Ibid., 181.
80 Ibid., 177.
81 Ibid., 20.
82 Ibid., 111.
83 Ibid., 108.
84 Ibid., 27.

BIBLIOGRAPHY

Collini, Stephan. *Liberalism and Sociology*. Cambridge: Cambridge University Press, 1979.

Davis, Tracy. *George Bernard Shaw and the Socialist Theatre*. London: Greenwood Press, 1994.

– *The Economics of the British Stage, 1800–1914*. Cambridge: Cambridge University Press, 2000.

Eliot, George. *Middlemarch*. Edited by David Carroll. Oxford's World's Classics. Oxford: Oxford University Press, 2008.

Etchells, Tim, Gabriella Giannachi, and Nick Kaye. "Looking Back: A Conversation about Presence, 2006." In *Archaeologies of Presence*, edited by Giannachi, Kaye, and Shanks, 183–95. Milton Park: Routledge, 2012.

Gang, Joshua, "Behaviorism and the Beginnings of Close Reading." *ELH* 78, no. 1 (2011): 1–25.

Griffin, C.M. "L.T. Hobhouse and the Idea of Harmony." *Journal of the History of Ideas* 35, no. 4 (1974): 647–61.

Griffith, Gareth. *Socialism and Superior Brains*. Milton Park: Routledge, 1993.

Henderson, Archibald. *The Changing Drama*. Cincinnati: Stewart and Kid, 1919.

Hobhouse, L.T. *Democracy and Reaction*. London: T. Fisher Unwin, 1904.

– *Liberalism*. In *Liberalism and Other Writings*, edited by James Meadowcroft, 3–120. Cambridge: Cambridge University Press, 2012.
– *The World in Conflict*. London: T. Fisher Unwin, 1915.
Kelly, Katharine. "Imprinting the Stage." In *The Cambridge Companion to George Bernard Shaw*, edited by Christopher Innes, 25–54. Cambridge: Cambridge University Press, 1998.
Latour, Bruno. *Reassembling the Social: An Introduction to Actor-Network-Theory*. Oxford: Oxford University Press, 2005.
Lloyd, David, and Paul Thomas. *Culture and the State*. New York: Routledge, 1998.
Macleod, Jock. *Literature, Journalism, and the Vocabularies and Liberalism*. Baskingstoke: Palgrave Macmillan, 2013.
Meeuwis, Michael. "Representative Government: The 'Problem Play,' Quotidian Culture, and the Making of Social Liberalism." *ELH* 80, no. 4 (2013): 1093–120.
Meisel, Martin. *How Plays Work: Reading and Performance*. Oxford: Oxford University Press, 2007.
Price, Leah. *The Anthology and the Rise of the Novel*. Cambridge: Cambridge University Press, 2000.
Puchner, Martin. *Stage Fright: Modernism, Anti-Theatricality, and Drama*. Baltimore: Johns Hopkins University Press, 2002.
Richards, I.A. *Principles of Literary Criticism*. London: Routledge, 2001.
Shaw, Bernard. *The Doctor's Dilemma*, edited by Dan Lawrence. London: Penguin, 1998.
– Introduction to *Fabian Essays in Socialism*, edited by Bernard Shaw, iii–iv. London: Fabian Society, 1899.
– *Major Barbara*. London: Penguin, 1960.
– *Plays Unpleasant*, edited by Dan Lawrence. London: Penguin, 2000.
– *Pygmalion*, edited by Dan Lawrence. London: Penguin, 2003.
Shpayer-Makov, Haia. *The Ascent of the Detective*. Oxford: Oxford University Press, 2011.
Smith, Warren Sylvester. *Bishop of Everywhere: Bernard Shaw and the Life Force*. University Park, PA: Penn State University Press, 1982.
Weiler, Peter. "The New Liberalism of L.T. Hobhouse." *Victorian Studies* 16, no. 2 (1972): 141–61.

4 Refreshments of Revolutionary Mood

JONATHAN FLATLEY

I am the kind of person, and maybe you are as well, for whom not being depressed by the current political situation in the United States presents itself as a real task, one for which I need a set of tactics.[1] What does one do, after all, with the feelings of rage and despair at the ongoing, constant, murderous police hostility to black lives? How can one relate to the complete triumph of corruption in what the newspapers call "politics"? And the newly arctic winters in America's Midwest (where I live) are certainly depressing enough in themselves, even without the sense that these new weather patterns are merely the tip of the climate change iceberg. It is difficult to escape the sense that the US electoral system is itself irredeemably broken (if it ever did work). After the retreat of the Occupy movement from Wall Street and other common spaces, there appears to be no viable political force actually attending to or concerned with our shared, common existence, no force that is even trying to stand up to defend the earth and the people on it from the interests of wealth.

Speaking more locally, which is to say of our so-called profession as university teachers and researchers in the humanities, it has also become quite clear that the relentless attack on any value not immediately serving the accumulation and circulation of capital – for instance, the value of culture or knowledge or even sleep (as Jonathan Crary has recently detailed)[2] – has come with new aggression to the sphere of university education, most especially public higher education.[3] In fact, I would not be surprised were Michigan's Republican governor to announce a proposal to dramatically cut funding to Wayne State University (where I teach), which would be met with enthusiastic approval by the Republican legislature, with special negative attention given to the professors and graduate students engaged in research that does not immediately translate into something valued by the "business community," or into "innovation" that is useful for "economic growth." In Wisconsin and North Carolina, at the moment of this essay's composition (spring 2015), proposals along these lines are being actively entertained, and it appears that in Wisconsin tenure has been effectively abolished.[4] The utter collapse of the job market for PhDs, which it seems to me nobody has really figured out how to address or absorb, makes the already grim situation of graduate students and adjunct teachers even more punishing than it already was. Although I am buoyed by recent strikes and efforts to organize, I must admit that I am not at all optimistic about our (I mean those of us who work in universities) collective resistance to these attacks on our working conditions and indeed our livelihood itself, which would require much broader solidarity than has so far been felt or made.

This is all to say that the whole enterprise of higher education and the intellectual life it has made possible seems increasingly precarious. Even though I have a good job and tenure, I feel vulnerable and anxious. While I know that my anxiety is not just personal, that its origin is systemic, and that this mood of anxiety is surely shared (and it is shared not only in the university professions, and not only on Facebook), this anxiety has not found a way to be transformed into or taken up by a political collective and a political project. I feel the absence of a collectivity to oppose these developments and the vulnerability that is their product. And without such a collectivity, the feeling of vulnerability is left to reverberate in my own "personal" situation, shaping the quality and rhythm of my daily concerns, amplifying, for instance, my worries about the always already late everything (book manuscript, essay, reader's report, papers to grade), or sharpening my resentment and deepening my despondence about the latest disregard for my working conditions from the departmental or university administration.

In such situations, where the profit motive is asserting itself with new aggression as the only possible value in a way that poses a direct threat on a number of fronts, it seems especially helpful to recall that it is in fact true that from time to time, variously abused, alienated, and depressed persons manage to come together in solidarity to make energetic, hopeful, and demanding collectives, which then engage in transformative political action. In an earlier essay ("How a Revolutionary Counter-Mood Is Made," 2012), I suggested that such moments of revolutionary organization work, when they do work, through the transformation of a collective *mood*. In some moods collective political action might not even enter one's consciousness except perhaps as a dream, or as something impossible, futile, silly, or obscure. But, then, something happens and one is attuned to a different world, a different way of being with others; friends and enemies are newly visible, and organized political resistance all of a sudden seems obvious, achievable, and vital.

Yet even in those instances when a self-aware, interested, revolutionary class-for-itself forms, another problem quickly presents itself. How does such a collective sustain and refresh itself? How can a revolutionary counter-mood, once awakened, be maintained and directed? Working through the process of political struggle once the collective has come into being presents a problem of a different order and kind. The tactics and principles that may have worked for the initial formation may not necessarily hold for this next stage. It is the possible differences between the task of awakening a collective revolutionary counter-mood and the problem of sustaining and refreshing that mood that I want to focus on in this essay. In focusing on this set of issues, I mean to suggest the present value of an archive of non-liberal, anti-capitalist projects and the collective subjectivities they bring into being. Insofar as agitational and propagandistic aesthetic modes play a central role in this archive, it may also require that we reorient our ideas about reading and about what counts as literature and aesthetic experience.

In the "Revolutionary Counter-Mood" essay, which focused on the problem of revolutionary collective formation, I followed a case made by Lenin in "What Is to Be Done?" and examined a particular kind of reading experience – reading descriptions of the mistreatment of other persons in a shopfloor newspaper – and the key role it played in the successful organizing done by the Dodge Revolutionary Union Movement (or DRUM) at the Dodge Main plant near Detroit in 1968. The formation of DRUM was led by a group of black radicals, including General Baker (who worked at the factory), John Watson, Luke Tripp, Kenneth Cockrel Sr, and Mike Hamlin, who had seen during the insurrection in the summer of 1967 that a potentially revolutionary collective existed. Their first move upon making this realization, one inspired by a reading of Lenin, was to start a newspaper: *Inner City Voice*. The work of putting together this weekly newspaper gave the group a way of working, thinking, and being together and allowed them to articulate a particular political position and the availability of a group politically and organizationally committed to that position. Thus, when an opportunity for the organization of workers and political action arose, as it did after a wildcat strike at the Dodge Main factory on May 2, 1968, they were ready to seize it. They quickly organized the factory with the aid of a weekly shopfloor newspaper, *drum*, creating a model that was then adopted in other factories, which later came together to form the League of Revolutionary Black Workers.[5] What role did the newspaper play in this organization of a revolutionary collective? How did it work to shift the collective mood?

As we know, for Lenin, the creation of a revolutionary collective required the representation of a group to itself: without the capacity for collective self-representation, collective self-consciousness was understood to be impossible, and collective action was thus limited to spontaneous, unplanned uprisings. Lenin's solution to this problem (represented by Marx as the transformation of a class-*in*-itself to a class-*for*-itself) was the vanguard party, which would engage in this work of representation through a variety of means, none more significant than the party newspaper, which must first of all publish "exposures" that describe abuses of power and the suffering they cause.[6]

Such exposures offer a solution to one of the persistent problems the party faces in organizing a revolutionary class: the fact that workers tolerate surprising amounts of abuse. They seem unmoved by their own misfortune. However, upon reading about the mistreatment of *others*, Lenin writes, "the most backward worker will understand, *or will feel*, that the students and religious sects, the peasant and the writer are being abused and outraged by those same dark forces that are oppressing and crushing him at every step of his life."[7] As for the spectator at a tragedy (at least as Plato presents it in Book X of the *Republic*), here too the feeling that one has not permitted oneself to have about one's own life comes into being in relation to someone else's suffering, as if the feeling requires imitability and plurality to come into being at all.[8] And then once this feeling of being part of a collectivity, of sharing an experience of oppression and an oppressor, has come into existence, it leads to what Lenin calls "an irresistible desire to react," a desire that brings with it, moreover, a knowledge of *how* to respond: "He will know how to hoot the censors one day, on another day to demonstrate outside the house of a governor who has brutally suppressed a peasant uprising," and so on.[9] This knowledge arises *from* the feeling, without reflection or theorization, as if it were already there, a kind of "unthought known" itself present in this new way of being-with-others. We might be surprised by Lenin's emphasis on the primacy of feeling and on what is essentially an aesthetic experience: the desire for action and the knowledge of how to act arise directly from the *feeling* produced by an experience of reading. This means that the problem of worker mobilization, Lenin suggests, is not one of false consciousness; it is not primarily ideological. Lenin does not call for the party to explain the evils of capitalism, convince workers that they are exploited, or sing of the future glories of communist society. Instead, the Communist Party must transform workers' feeling by presenting clear, unvarnished descriptions of the suffering of other persons in analogous situations.

Inasmuch as mood, for Martin Heidegger, is the overall atmosphere or medium in or through which our thinking, doing, and acting occurs, a way of being that shapes our thoughts, our will, and our particular affective attachments to particular objects, it is a concept that helps us to explain the sudden shift into a new way of seeing the world, a new way of affecting and being affected that Lenin describes. Crucially, for Heidegger, *Stimmung*, which might also be translated as *attunement* (and which has a musical connotation) establishes the conditions for our encounter with the world *before* cognition and volition.[10] Although our moods often escape notice, it is only through mood and by way of mood that we encounter the world: "*The mood has already disclosed, in every case, Being-in-the-world as a whole, and makes it possible first of all to direct one-self towards something.*"[11] Mood discloses the world in the sense that it is the situated directionality of our openness to the world; as such it shapes the totality of things that we see and that can "matter" to us. As Charles Guignon put it, "moods enable us to focus our attention and orient ourselves," and as such they themselves exert a very broad but foundational form of judgment.[12] In this sense, one's mood also sets the situation in which one's particular affects come into being, allowing certain affects, which are more punctual and more object oriented than moods, to attach to certain objects, while foreclosing other affective attachments and relations.[13] (Here, I use "affect" to refer to those feelings that are about something in particular or which pertain to a particular encounter, while moods are about everything in general.) Heidegger writes that *Stimmung* is the "melody" that "does not merely hover over" our being but that "sets the tone for such being, i.e., attunes and determines the manner and way [*Art und Wie*]" of that being.[14]

Heidegger is emphatic in arguing that mood is not a "psychological" concept (which is true, of course, for all the concepts in his resolutely anti-Cartesian project). A mood is not something there "inside" us; indeed, a mood "comes neither from 'outside' nor from 'inside', but arises out of Being-in-the-world, as a way of such Being."[15] Even as we "feel" them on a subjective, emotional level, moods belong to a shared, public world. They are fundamentally collective. More precisely, inasmuch as "being" is for Heidegger necessarily also a "being-with" others (as it is being-in-a-world), then we might say that mood is the "way" of this with, the form that our *with-ness* takes. As such, moods are also historical: they arise from and shape our relation to a given historical moment. "People make their own moods but they don't make them just as they please," Ben Highmore and Jenny Bourne Taylor put it in their recasting of a famous sentence: "They do not make them under circumstances chosen by themselves, but under circumstances directly encountered, given and transmitted from the past."[16] To that we might add that we are limited by the given moods in circulation at a given historical moment. "We live the mood-worlds we've inherited." *Stimmung* is the way we encounter the historical situation into which we have been "thrown"; moods locate and orient us in our particular, situated position in the world. "Being in a mood brings being to its 'there.'"[17]

Insofar as *Stimmung* is a historical form that orients us in a specific world, a collective mode that is felt on an intimate and individual level even as it is not "psychological," and a key player in the psychic life of power, it is analogous to Althusser's conception of ideology. If ideology in Althusser's account "represents the Imaginary Relationship of individuals to their real conditions of existence," if it is the way that we make sense of our relationship to an essentially non-meaningful world and our place in it, then *Stimmung* is how we are affectively oriented in that world.[18] Like the weather, it shapes how we approach the world, what we care about, what we ignore, what we are ashamed of or anxious about, whom we see as possible friends and who appears as foe, and whom we pay no attention to at all. And if, for Althusser, the reproduction of the relations of production is secured in large part by way of ideology, I think we can say that those relations are also reproduced by way of a set of dominant moods. A given social order needs certain things to "matter" and certain other things to escape notice, just as much as it needs a set of ideologies and interpellated subjects in order to manage a population and secure its own reproduction. Challenging a social order thus requires that different moods be awakened. Thus, for instance, we might see the Black Lives Matter movement as an effort to change the collective *Stimmung*, to awaken a new *with-ness*, which would alter what matters and how it matters.

In a provocative 2014 text called "We Are All Very Anxious," the Institute for Precarious Consciousness, a radical political collective out of the UK, argues that "each phase of capitalism has a particular affect which holds it together" and that the affect that holds this post-Fordist precarious moment of capitalism together is anxiety.[19] Previous moments were organized by misery (industrial capitalism) and boredom (Fordist consumer capitalism). Even if I think that it is likely that this anxiety has been mixed with misery and boredom rather than replacing them (so that one is miserable about one's anxiety, or bored of it), I appreciate their attempt to think about the production of certain affects – ones that structure our daily concerns and preoccupations – as a control mechanism as important as ideology in reproducing the relations of production. The periodizing argument is important for the Institute for Precarious Consciousness because it helps them to understand why current modes of resistance have not been working: the problem is that they have been keyed to boredom rather than anxiety. That is, these modes of resistance are based on bad readings of what I have been calling mood (but what they call the dominant affect). So what they do is to set out to read the current mood so as to figure out how to resist it. In their attempt to map out the affective terrain of the post-Fordist moment, they are of course not alone and enter into an implicit conversation with the work of Arlie Hochschild, Gilles Deleuze, Paolo Virno, Lauren Berlant, Sianne Ngai, Ann Cvetkovich, and others.[20] What distinguishes their project is their praxis-oriented insistence that any successful political strategy must first of all have a correct reading of this dominant affect or mood and of how it shapes everyday collective modes of concern, attention, and togetherness. Toward this end, they offer a brief but incisive description of the ways that variously structuring elements of everyday life such as debt, the constant demand to be in communication, the surveillance of the security state and social media alike, police violence, job insecurity, and affective labour together produce a feeling of insecurity, a sense of precarity, which "differs from misery in that the necessities of life are not simply absent. They are available, but withheld conditionally."[21] This feeling is exhausting; it makes political resistance difficult. And as long as we relate to these feelings as psychological concerns, so long as we do not have a critical language for connecting them to the social order, these negative feelings appear primarily as personal failings: I just need to be better organized, more confident, less negative, more effectively medicated, etc.

Unlike the Institute for Precarious Consciousness, Heidegger is not especially concerned to use the concept of mood to think about the politics of control and the politics of resistance (as we know, thinking explicitly about politics was not Heidegger's strong point), but that does not mean we cannot use the concept to do that thinking. Of particular interest for such a project is the idea of the "counter-mood." As we are never outside of ideology, so too are we never not in some mood or another. Moods do, however, shift and change, and indeed Heidegger asserts that the only way we can "master" mood is by way of what he calls "counter-moods." While Heidegger does not directly explain how we awaken counter-moods, he does suggest that one of our best resources in this thinking remains Aristotle's *Rhetoric*, which he calls "the first systematic hermeneutic of the everydayness of Being with one another."[22] Aristotle's *Rhetoric*, as we know, offers a still useful definition of emotion (or affect, depending on the translation): "The Emotions are all those feelings that so change men as to affect their judgments, and that are also attended by pain or pleasure. Such are anger, pity, fear and the like, with their opposites."[23] The concept of emotion is useful for Aristotle not in the context of a "psychology" but precisely in relation to the question of how we affect each other, how our ways of being together affect our judgment; being affected changes what matters to us. Aristotle examines the various emotions and presents a series of hypotheses about how to produce them in different particular audiences and in different situations. Heidegger implies that Aristotle is concerned here with the *Stimmungen* of these different audiences, and what he provides are readings of these moods, these situations, these ways of being together that the successful speaker or political organizer must be able to read. "It is into such a mood and out of such a mood that the orator speaks. He must understand the possibilities of moods in order to rouse them and guide them aright."[24] The successful speaker needs to be able to understand not only the possibility of moods in general but also the particular mood of this "they" and the possible moods that they might be moved into.

The effective and affecting orator or political agitator must be able to scan the rhythms and keys attuning a collective in order to crystallize and direct the moods they find there in manifestoes, slogans, newspapers, or handbills. Indeed, it may well be that implicit in the form of *any* given text (not just agitational ones) that seeks to affect its audiences is a theory of the mood of its readers, a "reading" of that mood. Here, I want to "read for mood" by reading that reading, recreating the implicit theory of the reader's mood – as itself a historical mode of attunement – embedded in the agitational textual practices of DRUM and the League of Revolutionary Black Workers.

In the "Revolutionary Counter-Mood" essay, in order to examine a concrete instance of a counter-mood being awakened, I analyse one particular story from the *drum* newspaper in some detail, making the case that its relatively flat and descriptive – its "factographic" – focus on a series of actions and behaviours directs the reader away from immediately recognizing the event and instead encourages the reader to stay close to the patterns of intensity, escalation, and punctuation that comprise the particular shape and rhythm of the event and the bodies involved in it. It is these patterns and this rhythm, I think, that facilitate what Daniel Stern calls an "affective attunement," his term for the way that people share affective states. In *The Interpersonal World of the Infant*, Stern examines the ways that parents share affective states with infants and finds that parents accomplish this attunement by performing "some behavior that is not a strict imitation but nonetheless corresponds in some way to the infant's overt behavior."[25] So, in one instance "the intensity level and duration of the girl's voice is matched by the mother's body movements."[26] That is, the mother engages in an activity that is not identical to the infant's but similar to it, a similarity that is marked by way of a translation between modes or senses, from sound to movement, by way of "amodal" characteristics such as intensity, shape, or rhythm. In this way, Stern writes, "what is being matched is not the other person's behavior *per se*, but rather some aspect of the behavior that reflects the person's feeling state."[27] It is the translation across the senses that does the work of communicating that the *feeling* (and not just the behaviour) is shared. While the infants Stern examined usually took no apparent notice of attunement behaviours on the part of the mother, when the mother abruptly *stopped* these behaviours or *failed* to match the child's intensity or rhythm, the infant interrupted its activities, often displaying confusion or uncertainty. Without the sharing of an affect, the infant suspends the behaviour, unsure of how to continue, as if affects *require* a plural existence, a sense of being shared, in order to come into being at all (a phenomenon that appears to be observable in various aesthetic experiences, such as tragedy or the readings of the "exposures" that Lenin discussed and *drum* published).

Stern also calls these amodal characteristics (primarily intensity, shape, and rhythm) through which we share affects "vitality affects," and later, "forms of vitality." He is referring to things such as "the force, speed, and flow of a gesture; the timing and stress of a spoken phrase or even a word; the way one breaks into a smile or the time course of decomposing the smile; the manner of shifting position in a chair; the time course of lifting the eyebrows when interested and the duration of their lift; the shift and flight of a gaze; and the rush or tumble of thoughts."[28] That is, he is concerned with the *how* of bodily activity, the "forms of feeling," a phrase Stern borrows from Susanne Langer.[29] I argue that what Stern calls affective attunement, itself a *way* of being with another, is one way that we can awaken a counter-mood, a different way of being with others.

As we know, and as Stern reminds us, affective attunement takes place not only between parent and infant; it is a constant, ongoing process in nearly any form of social interaction. Between two people, the process may be easier to observe, and easier to manage (even if it occurs mostly unconsciously), than it is among a large collective or between the leaders and the members of a large group. In the "Revolutionary Counter-Mood." essay, I argue through a reading of the *drum* newspaper that agitational texts can awaken counter-moods by way of formal elements that create a point or site where readers or audiences can engage in affective attunement by matching and sharing forms of vitality. In that newspaper, as I mentioned, it was detailed descriptions of racist behaviour by bosses at the factory that provided such a site, that allowed readers to feel as if they shared with someone else an experience of the particular racism practised in the factory.

In what follows, I want to return to the problem I started with above by examining attempts by DRUM and the League of Revolutionary Black Workers, after the initial formation, to direct the way that they were with-each-other, to reanimate the shifting aesthetic of their with-ness, to keep it oriented toward the solidarity of that collectivity as such, and to keep that collective moving toward a particular goal. That DRUM and the League were indeed concerned to maintain a sense of orientation toward a praxis after DRUM's initial formation is suggested by the wide range of activities they initiated, which included, in addition to the continued emphasis on the newsletter, pressing both the United Automobile Workers (UAW) and company management with a series of demands; a boycott of racist bars; various rallies; wildcat strikes; involvement in electoral politics; community organizing; the exploration of national and even international expansion; and film-making.[30]

The significance of DRUM's initial achievement was immediately confirmed and amplified by the emergence over the following weeks and months of other RUM groups at factories around Detroit and indeed throughout the country. These included ELRUM, at the Eldon Avenue Gear and Axle Plant, FRUM (for Ford workers), UPRUM (among UPS workers), HRUM (hospital workers), and a range of others.[31] DRUM clearly had spoken to the mood of exploited and angry black workers across different work contexts. The Dodge Main plant in Hamtramck, where DRUM formed, remained a centre of gravity, but ELRUM was also very active, organizing a number of rallies and wildcat strikes in their struggle with factory management and the UAW over working conditions. In June 1969, the different RUMs decided to come together to form the League of Revolutionary Black Workers. The twists and turns of the League's very compelling history can be found in the excellent histories by Dan Georgakas and Marvin Surkin, James Geschwender, Muhammad Ahmad, and Heather Thompson. The League dissolved in 1971 when several members resigned for a complex set of reasons, including internal differences about ideology and tactics that had intensified in response to a range of pressures and concrete problems, such as lack of resources to support strikers. Some members wanted to focus on the expansion of the League into a national and even international organization and into alliance with other radical groups, while others argued for a continued focus on the point of production as their real source of power.

In order to see how DRUM and then the League engaged in the project of mobilizing and refreshing the mood of the newly formed collective, I will examine two texts that represent distinct attempts to move a collective and to affect the political mood. The first of these is a handbill calling for a strike. The second is the well-known film *Finally Got the News*, which the League made in 1969 and 1970, in collaboration with the radical film collective Newsreel. The questions I am bringing to these two texts are: What understandings of everyday being-with-one-another are at work here? How does each of these texts itself appear to be operating within and speaking to an already existing *Stimmung*, which is to say, a way that people are with each other? Where in these texts do we find sites for attunement along the lines of what Stern calls vitality affects, those affects that translate across senses by way of rhythm, shape, and intensity? What theory of the mood of their audience can we read in these texts?

racism / strike / refreshments

At the beginning of July 1968, DRUM planned a rally across the street from the plant, which led to a collective presentation of a number of demands to the UAW Local 3. The following day there was another strike.[32] This strike was not a spontaneous reaction to a speed-up on the assembly line (as the May strike had been) but an actualization of DRUM's power as a collective. It communicated to Chrysler and the UAW and in a self-conscious way to the workers themselves that a collective now existed that was capable of self-representation and planned actions, none more important than the withholding of their labour, which caused an immediate, significant, and direct loss of profit for Chrysler and showed that the UAW no longer represented the black auto workers, both in the sense that they could no longer "speak for" them and in the sense that they no longer understood or responded to their interests.

Among the materials General Baker donated to the Reuther archives at Wayne State University, one may find a well-handled, undated handbill calling for black workers to strike, which may have been part of the agitational materials for this July 1968 strike.[33] Inasmuch as this linguistically and graphically rich document addresses black workers in a Detroit factory in the months after the formation of DRUM, it offers a concrete example of how the mood of the RUM members might have been directed toward a particular action once the collective had been formed and of how the attunement of affects were part of that direction.

In viewing the handbill, one might first notice certain elements of the shape and placement of the text, such as the split between the larger text on the top two-thirds of the page, printed in a sans serif typeface, with no punctuation or capitalization, and the bottom third of the page, where capital letters return in a smaller brush script typeface that imitates handwriting. This graphic division corresponds to the distinction between two different rhetorical modes. The larger text at the top of page begins, grammatically speaking, in the imperative mood, offering a series of two instructions or commands: "strike your / blow against / racism"; "do your part." The following statements *could* be read as commands, but they might also be descriptive in nature (a double sense I will return to below): "no work today" can be read as "(do) no work today" or "(there is) no work today"; "blackworkers / strike" could be instructing black workers to strike, or it could be saying that what black workers do is strike. The bottom of the page shifts into an indicative mood rendering an observation – "Only Racist Honkies & Uncle

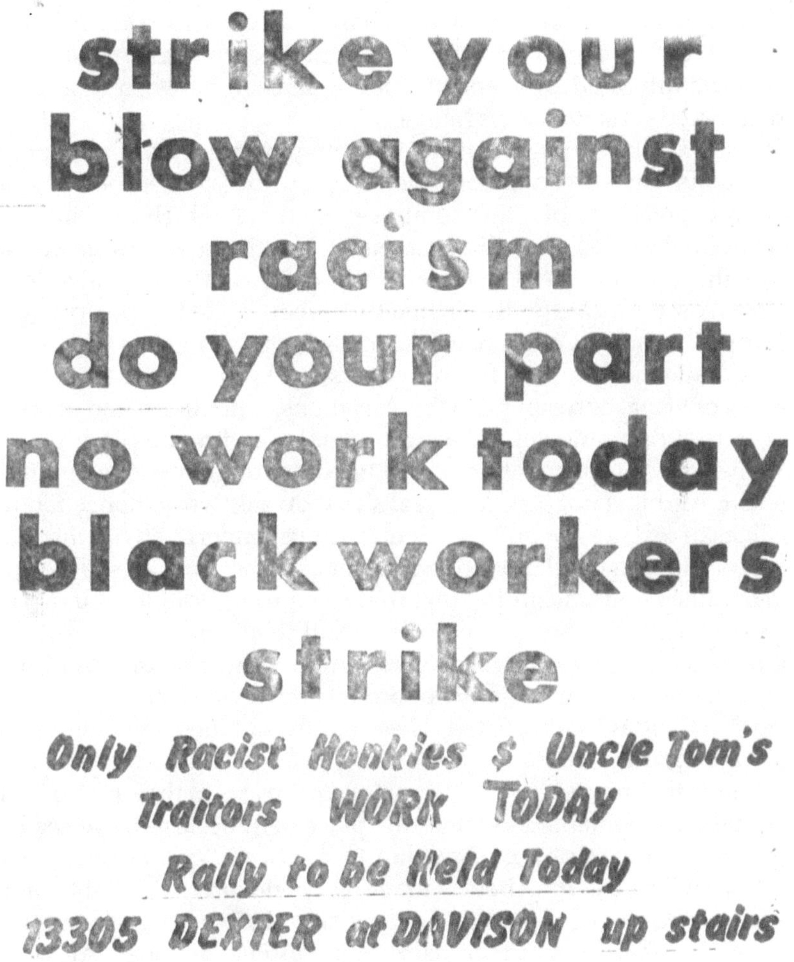

strike your
blow against
racism
do your part
no work today
black workers
strike

Only Racist Honkies $ Uncle Tom's
Traitors WORK TODAY
Rally to be Held Today
13305 DEXTER at DAVISON up stairs
refreshments

Figure 4.1. Strike handbill. Courtesy of Walter P. Reuther Library, Archives of Labor and Urban Affairs, Wayne State University.

Tom's / Traitors WORK TODAY" – and then key information: "Rally to be Held Today"; "13305 DEXTER at DAVISON up stairs"; "refreshments." Taken together, the direct, urgent appeal to participate in an inherently engaging event and the strong distinction between friend (black workers) and enemy (racism, Racist Honkies, and Uncle Tom's Traitors) makes this an affectively charged document.[34] Yet I think its affective force is also a product of the document's dynamic and complex structure of address and the subtle tension between its semiotic function and its status as an image.

We see a printed page, but then we may notice that in its typography, layout, and organization this body of text evokes the irregularity and expressivity of a text composed by hand, which may interrupt our habitual modes of reading. Consider, for instance, how line breaks shape the visual form of the centre-aligned text. These breaks do not seem to communicate pauses in breath, as they might in a poem; instead they open up what Walter Benjamin calls "graphic regions of ... eccentric figurativeness."[35] This figurativeness works through the creation of a series of visual correspondences, variations, repetitions, and contrasts that introduce a range of ordering principles and modes of apprehension that may supplement or exceed the other more literal meanings of the text. And it is not just line breaks that do this work; notice too that the lines of text are not quite straight, various letters subtly rising, veering, and slipping in relation to each other, and that one can see the faint, uneven lines underneath the text that seem to indicate cuts in a piece of paper that were then pasted or set. And then observe that the spacing between and within words varies from word to word and line to line, a characteristic especially apparent when a word (such as "strike," "your," or "today") is repeated. These features of the text offer not only regions of figurativeness; they also serve as mimetic traces of the bodies and hands that placed these letters on the page and of the situations and material environments in which this placement occurred. We see here a "grain" of the graphic design akin to Barthes's "grain of the voice," the place where a certain bodily materiality and affective vitality enters and also exceeds the page.[36] In their consideration of textual irregularities clearly made by a human hand, Russian Futurist poets Alexander Kruchonykh and Velimir Khlebnikov argue that letters are like bodies and that writing, like dance, can function as a bodily mechanism for affective attunement. "Our mood," they write, "alters our handwriting as we write," and this mood is conveyed to the reader "independently of the words."[37]

The graphic designers Experimental Jetset make the case that such overt displays of madeness mark a properly socialist design. Echoing Marx's comments in the *Economic and Philosophic Manuscripts of 1844*, they suggest that reminding the reader that "a piece of printed matter

Figure 4.2. Still, *Finally Got the News.*

is above all a human-made construction" helps to create the sense of "a material environment that is not only shaped by humans, but that can also be changed by humans."[38] Certainly, this handbill announces that it is not the reified product of wage labour. Instead of moving from worker to employer in exchange for wages, it passes from hand to hand, like the *drum* newsletters in this image for the film *Finally Got the News.*

By announcing its madeness so clearly, it not only indicates the exigency surrounding its likely hurried production. It also allows the person handing this piece of printed paper out and the person taking it to see and feel there a confirmation of the human capacity to imitate, engage with, and make things in the world. One is thereby relieved of what Marx calls the stupidity that comes with relating to objects as private property, in which we think that a thing is ours only when we *own* or use it.[39] Instead, this handbill presents itself as a way to be with other people. Its being is itself social.[40]

Look, for example, at the first "your" of the handbill in relation to the second. Does this first one seem a bit more spacious, the *y* and the *r* floating a bit on the edges of the word? Likewise, when one compares the "strike" that begins the text with the one that ends this larger body of text, one might notice that a small fissure opens between the *r* and the *i* at the word's centre and that the *e* seems to float away just a bit at the word's edge. By contrast, the final strike is more tightly configured, the letters getting closer together at the end, even as the *s* at the beginning hangs noticeably lower. These seem to be indications of the kind of compositional idiosyncrasies that mood might affect and on which our imaginative and innervative interpretations might batten.

Walter Benjamin suggests that handwriting is dream-like: when writing, one's hand produces "picture puzzles – that the unconscious of the writer conceals [there]."[41] The hand creates those similarities that un-innervated affects need to come into being. At work here is a creative mimetic faculty, Benjamin's term for the human capacity to perceive and produce similarity (as distinct from sameness or identity). These similarities are, as Benjamin puts it, "non-sensuous": they are not obvious or literal; they cross from one sense to another. And, just as the activity of writing may be a mimetic practice that may allow certain affects to come into being, so too the scene of *reading* such letter forms and textual composition creates sites of imaginative imitation that may allow readers' affects to come into being as we dwell on a particular word's alignment or a letter's slanted curve, or perceive a certain rhythm to the spacing between and among words as if they were bodies dancing on a stage.

The result of the coexistence of the words and their irregular forms – the "grain" that may invite affective attunement – is not that the image of the text gives us a clearer sense of its meaning. Instead, an internal fissure opens in the document.[42] This fissure offers a space for the reader to step into the text; it encourages the reader to "read into" the handbill, precisely to the extent that the sign is no longer transparent in its meaning. One apprehends the traces of hands, bodies, and their feelings as one perceives the document. Our sense of what the letters "mean" is inextricable from unconscious suppositions or guesses about who placed these letters and composed these lines on the page, what mood they might have been in, and how this mood may have affected how its composition mattered to them. Such speculation means the reader must create or project that person or persons behind the text, to imagine the world they see and feel in a kind of "mutual reflexive substitution."[43] Such instances of reading into, as we know, may be especially electric sites of affective charge. Like the scene of therapy, they encourage us to transfer affects from our own past onto the present, a sharing of those affects with the person whose image we imagine by way of the vital forms on the page that we read into.[44] In these ways, the handbill text, here, presents a puzzle that encourages our imitative, affectively charged reading into it.

Of course, this attuned reading is not made in a textually neutral setting, but one shaped by the specific language of the text, one that reminds readers of racism and the battle against it and asks its addressees to collectively engage in a specific, risky, confrontational act. It should be no surprise, then, that the forms of feeling that we find in letters and lines here also direct us toward the handbill's specific language. The irregularities in the words "your" and "strike" that I mentioned above thus not only invite affective attunement but also focus attention on the repetition of these keywords and the different meanings circulating through them. In this way, the handbill is inviting attunement and then also telling us some things about the nature of this attunement and of the collective that the handbill seeks to thereby refresh and direct, narrating, as it were, the production of its own collective addressee.

So, for instance, that "your" is repeated and varied in its presentation suggests the complexity of the addressee here. In each case – "strike your / blow against / racism" and "do your part" – the referent of the pronoun could be singular or plural. The dual meaning is most clear in the first occurrence, but "do your part" is too a call for both individual and collective action. "Do your part" suggests that each person must strike (doing her or his part) for the strike to happen but then also that the strike itself, with everyone acting together in solidarity, is also "doing a part" in the broader struggle against racism and capitalism. It makes sense, too, to subtly emphasize that the addressee here is both singular and plural since this is in fact how power functions in a striking collective. Insofar as the strike does not happen unless there is solidarity, the plurality of the striking subject is essential and fundamental to the strike's being. In the strike power is not additive: it is not as if each worker individually possesses some power that is then added together to make a greater power. The singular power of each worker depends essentially on it being at the same time plurally exercised. Being-many-together is, in the case of the strike, constitutive. At the same time, the solidarity of the striking collective does not imply an undistinguished mass. This being together also implies a certain spacing, as communication and sharing require a multiplicity of distinct positions: each "you" must "do your part."[45]

One might notice that the only word that appears three times in the document – "today" – is also the occasion for its only handwritten letter. If one examines the *T* in the "TODAY" of "Traitors WORK TODAY," one sees that it is different from the other upper-case *T*'s, of which there are several. Was this letter somehow forgotten or cut off or damaged? And why this *T*? Whatever the reason, the fact that this letterform was hand composed clearly communicates the urgency of the document's production and distribution: there was no time to find another *T*, because this handbill had to be printed *today*. The handbill's "today" communicates that DRUM's "we" is operating according to a collectively made and interruptible temporality, one distinct from the time of production, work shifts, and assembly line speed-ups. In the strike, this "we" needs and thus makes its own "today."[46]

Part of the peculiar temporality of the document is generated by its structure of address. That is, the handbill is telling its readers to do something and also describing a series of acts or events that will happen: "only Racist Honkies and Uncle Tom's Traitors" work today; rally to be held today; there will be refreshments. But there will be a rally and no black workers working *only* if the handbill's addressees make those things happen; they alone can make these statements true.[47] The text is like a performative utterance that does not *yet* have the institutional context to make the performative utterance "do" what it says it is doing. But by making its meaning and status contingent on the behaviour of its readers, the text emphasizes that the readers of the handbill *do* have that power.

The repetition of the word "strike," the first and last word of the upper body of text, also seems to make reference to this self-constituting capacity of the striking collective. In the first case ("strike your / blow against / racism"), the meaning may be a bit unexpected, since this "strike" is a transitive verb, active and violent, something one does with one's arm and hand. One of course also strikes a drum, and although the DRUM here is not *being* struck but is striking, in striking it is also self-reflexively creating itself as a collective through its refusal to work. "In order to say 'we,' one must present the 'here and now' of this 'we,'" Jean-Luc Nancy writes.[48] The self-constituting strike is necessarily punctual; its rhythm and intensity attune a collective to itself. As John Mowitt suggests, even if strikes are not musical events, "their complex and irreducibly percussive character cannot be separated from the broad practices of musicking that both constitute and exceed them."[49] In its reference to the hand-powered strike, the handbill is reminding us that even if it may seem to be only negative in quality – a refusal of work, work's absence, a withholding of one's labour – the collective strike is an act with its own percussive force. The repetition of the word "strike" reminds the reader that the punctual withdrawal from work is also, at the same time, a blow against racism.

That racism and capital, together, constitute the target here and the occasion for the collective being called into action may also be seen in the way the handbill describes the striking subject: "blackworkers / strike." It appears that "blackworkers" is here rendered as a single word, suggesting that "black" is not a racial identity, a characteristic or attribute, that could be *applied* to some of the workers. Instead "blackworkers" names the class brought into being by the alliance between racism and capitalism; as such this class may entail a distinct way of being with its own situations and attunements.[50]

This sense of the relational, oppositional quality of the black worker is underscored by the description, at the bottom of the page, of the black workers' enemies on this day: "Only Racist Honkies & Uncle Tom's Traitors WORK TODAY." At first, this statement might seem to be a simple oppositional mode of identity politics. However, upon reflection, one sees that being a Racist Honky or Uncle Tom's Traitor is defined in relation to work and the willingness to strike: if you are working today, then that is what you are, precisely as a function of your presence at work.[51] Correspondingly, not working, not doing your part, implicitly removes you from these categories. In fact, the black worker, here, is itself a mode of being brought into existence by the strike itself: "blackworkers strike." That is, as I suggested above, the phrase might be understood as descriptive as well as imperative: striking is what black workers do.[52]

The significance of the class relations here being redefined and enacted is deepened when we notice that what, at first glance, when reading for sense, is seen as an ampersand bringing together the Racist and the Traitor is in fact a dollar sign. The enemies of the striking black workers are allied by way of the articulative, associative power of money. If, as Marx famously notes in the *Grundrisse*, "Where money is not itself the community [*Gemeinwesen*], it must dissolve the community,"[53] then DRUM, here, is indicating its opposition to this dissolution, its invention of another form and way of being, one that comes into being in the strike itself. As Antonio Negri remarks, "Communism begins to take shape when the proletarian takes it as her objective to reappropriate the *Gemeinwesen*, the community, to turn it into the order of a new society."[54]

The attempt to both attune to and direct the mood of the plurality brought into being here is also subtly indicated by the three single words that are permitted to occupy a line on their own and that occupy the space in the centre of the page: "racism" and "strike" on the top of the page and then "refreshments" at the very bottom. In a fairly evident way, the first two of these words might be considered the central concepts of the handbill: racism is what is here opposed, and the strike is the action being taken against it. What about "refreshments," floating there at the bottom of the page, without a sentence containing it? To be sure, the suggestion that there will be something to drink is clear enough. But in being associated by its position on the page with racism and strike, we might say that a kind of narrative of optimism is suggested as well, perhaps: from racism, to strike, to refreshments. We start with the shared situation of racism, which brings black workers together in solidarity to strike, and this solidarity not only clears a space for one to enjoy refreshments but is itself refreshing, in the sense of starting anew, gaining fresh energy. The plural power of the black workers' way of being with one another is here being refreshed. Thus, the "refreshments" at the bottom of the page may also be something like the handbill's (sub)title, commenting, as it does, on one of the functions of the event of the strike and of the handbill itself. An elsewhere and a different temporality opposed to the racist plant is offered here, one where there will at least be drinks but where there may also be refreshments of the way that members of the group enjoying those drinks are with each other. "Refreshments" here names a way for the collective of bodies to be with each other. Like "strike your blow," it also focuses attention on the bodiliness of revolutionary action, a body that needs rest and refreshment. "The collective is a body, too," Benjamin notes.[55] "Refreshments" communicates an optimism connected to the power of a collective body and to the pleasures and rewards of feeling connected to a collective body.

Thus, in its modest, local optimism, one that attaches not only to the possibility of a drink and a break but also to the promise of the sociality, conviviality, and solidarity produced by this collective of black workers, this handbill reads the *Stimmung* it seeks to direct. It is no longer enough only to awaken the sense of collectivity; this collectivity must now continue to be rewarding and refreshing in itself and for itself. And it must seek and find encounters with affective objects that increase its "power of acting," which is another way of saying its collective joy, as Gilles Deleuze points out in his reading of Spinoza.[56]

Its own feeling of itself as a collective must itself become one of these force-increasing objects of affective attachment. The collective needs to be interested in the feeling of collectivity-in-action. The mood here is self-referential in that its optimism is not about a future pictured by an aesthetic or political narrative – but about attachment to the solidarity of black workers brought about by the very action the handbill calls for. As the just-in-time handwritten *T* in "Today" suggests, this is an optimism whose temporality is not organized by the forward motion through progressive time. Instead, this is an optimism squarely oriented toward today.[57]

Getting the News

In 1969 and 1970, in collaboration with members of the leftist film collective Newsreel, the League of Revolutionary Black Workers made the film *Finally Got the News*.[58] The title of the film is borrowed from one of the chants – "FINALLY GOT THE NEWS HOW YOUR DUES ARE BEING USED" – that can be heard, called out from off-screen by General Baker, to move marching demonstrators. This chant refers to the racism of the UAW, an organization that not only failed to represent the interests of black workers but indeed paid the local police to harass them. (As another slogan chanted by the off-screen Baker tells it: "UAW MEANS YOU AIN'T WHITE.") Through interviews with the members of the movement, footage shot in the auto plants, and depictions of leafleting and picketing actions, *Finally Got the News* presents the League's analysis of capitalism and the place of black workers therein, as well as documenting the League's formation, its fight against institutional racism within the unions, and its efforts to build an independent, revolutionary black labour organization that could represent and respond to the interests of black workers. In taking its title from Baker's off-screen voice, the film not only obliquely recognizes Baker's role in the formation of the League (and his desire to avoid public attention) but also points to one of the film's most striking formal features, its use of sound and voice, which are often in various interesting forms of tension with the film's images (something I will return to below).[59]

The film's title also refers to the fact of the news *being gotten* – that is, it refers to the central organizational and agitational function of the weekly newsletter *drum* itself, which had, indeed, been reporting the news of how union dues were being spent. In several scenes, the film shows us the production and distribution of *drum* and other printed matter. We see workers being handed newsletters at the factory gates (Figure 4.2, above), printers printing, women laying out text, and various printed materials (including some in Arabic, for the many Arabic-speaking workers in the Detroit area). The acts of producing, giving, and getting the news are presented as the League's foundational organizational move.

However, in considering the film's prioritization of print, one may be struck by the film's somewhat awkward promotion of the virtues of another medium. As a viewer of the film, one cannot help but realize that one is not (*qua* film viewer) experiencing what is presented as the League's most consequential agitational and representational work. Why do we a need a film to tell us about the importance of print? What did the League hope to achieve by expanding into the film medium?

In fact, it appears that the League was divided on this issue. Some members, especially those focused on shopfloor organizing, were less than enthusiastic about making a film, never mind having a film made *about* them by white outsiders with no direct knowledge or experience of their struggle. For other members of the League, especially John Watson (who delivers an extremely lucid lecture on the centrality of black labour in the history of capitalism after the film's opening montage), expansion into a different medium promised different – cross-class, national, and international – audiences and alliances. The League made a gamble that the wider circulation of the revolutionary mood that had been awakened in Detroit might also refresh and strengthen that mood. Most concretely, wider support from a broader public might help the League defend itself against pressure from the local police, the FBI, the UAW, and the auto industry, who all had far greater material and ideological resources than the League.

Inasmuch as the Newsreel collective sought, like the League, to create alternative ways to make and get the news, the new Detroit chapter of this loose film collective made sense as a collaborator. Formed by a group of around thirty mostly white film-makers at Jonas Mekas's Film-Makers Coop in New York City at the end of 1967, Newsreel wanted to make films that would "provide an alternative to the limited and biased coverage of television news," which did not represent "any event that suggests the changes and redefinitions taking place in America today, or that underlines the necessity for such changes."[60] In order to challenge this paradigm, Newsreel "formed an organization that serve[d] the needs of people who want to get hold of news that is relevant to their own activity and thought." They also wanted to change distribution and screening practices, providing "information on how to project films in nontheatrical settings – on the sides of buildings, etc. We hope that whoever receives our films will show them to other local groups as well, thus creating an expanding distribution network."[61] And they hoped to stimulate the creation of similar Newsreel groups around the country in a loose-knit network.

In their aesthetic orientation, Newsreel drew on a tradition of radical documentary going back to early Soviet film-maker Dziga Vertov; they understood themselves to be challenging audiences. According to one member, they wanted to "make films that unnerve, that shake assumptions, that threaten, that ... explode like grenades in peoples' faces or open minds like a good can opener."[62] They sought to make "a form of propaganda that polarizes, angers, excites, for the purpose of discussion." Thus, in contrast to the agitational modes of the *drum* newsletters and the strike handbill (in which black workers straightforwardly addressed black workers in their given situations in an effort to produce collective solidarity), Newsreel championed an aesthetic that sought to shock a presumably bourgeois audience accustomed to watching the evening news on television. However, black factory workers in Detroit, already alienated in many important respects from dominant ideological forms, did not necessarily need such defamiliarization, especially if they already understood themselves to be engaged in revolutionary struggle. Instead, as I suggested in my reading of the strike handbill, they needed a way to continue to find their existence and action as a collective compelling, necessary, and joyful. If Newsreel's emphasis on alternative ways of making and receiving the news did match up with some of the League's goals, its aesthetic, which drew on an avant-garde tradition and was thus more challenging but also more critically recognizable and prestigious, was nonetheless a departure from the form of the League's other agitational work.

For their part, the Detroit Newsreel group expressed a desire to adapt to the local situation (although they arrived in Detroit more ideologically compelled by the confrontational politics modelled by the Panthers and the Weathermen), and they did adapt organizationally, ideologically, and aesthetically. As part of their project "to develop films as a medium of radical self-expression by working people," they hoped that this production "would be used as a film skills workshop for local movement people, and as the organizing framework of an independent Detroit Newsreel."[63] Thus, with the energetic participation of John Watson, the League engaged in a collaboration with Detroit Newsreel, punctuated by the League's seizure of cameras and other equipment (after a disagreement about speaker's fees that Newsreel had given to visiting Black Panthers although they had been claiming poverty in their collaboration with the League). Even though Detroit Newsreel as a collective then dissolved, some of its members (the ones credited with directing the film: Stewart Bird, Rene Lichtman, and Peter Gessner) agreed to help complete work on the film. John Watson took the occasion to start a film production company, Black Star Productions, which along with Black Star Publishing made up something like a media wing of the League. Several League members were trained in film-making skills, and in fact, this film is unique in Newsreel's body of work in that the "subjects" of the film were also centrally involved in its production.

A fundraising letter from Black Star Productions gives us a sense of how the League may have been thinking about the function and value of the film. The letter states that "the potential audience for the film will include existing national and international distribution networks, as well as the possibilities of educational television, broad community screenings, schools, colleges, and union caucuses. It will have an immediate and direct use as an organizing tool in the League's day-to-day work."[64]

That is, the League had ambitious hopes that the film could serve an educational or propagandistic function for a wide audience in multiple settings, and *also* have a direct organizing function. Both of these impulses can be seen in the film's representations of the newspaper and the print medium.

The film's representations of the news and of the importance of the print medium in the delivery of the news may function like a lesson in "how to begin," the title of the short text by Lenin advising prospective revolutionaries to start a newspaper as their first move. Indeed, Watson credits a group reading of "How to Begin" with inspiring the founding of the newspaper *Inner City Voice* by Watson, Baker, Mike Hamlin, Luke Tripp, and Ken Cockrel after the 1967 insurrection.[65] And as Lenin had suggested, this newspaper did in fact create a division of labour, an organizational continuity, and a way of working together among the group of revolutionaries who would then form DRUM and the League. Like the Lenin text, *Finally Got the News* is a film about how to make a revolutionary collective and a revolutionary mood. It describes a concrete situation and history, it lays out a position and a strategy, and it represents a particular mode of feeling that might motivate others, including students and workers, to do their own revolutionary work. In this way it solicits a mimetic response: "this is what we did and it

preview of black workers' film

SPECIAL SHOWING OF A FILM-IN-PROGRESS ABOUT BLACK WORKERS AND THE AUTO INDUSTRY

PRODUCED IN COOPERATION WITH THE CENTRAL STAFF OF THE LEAGUE OF REVOLUTIONARY BLACK WORKERS

We feel the history of black workers, consistently slighted or distorted by the priorities of the established media, needs to reach a wide audience. This film-in-progress, running approximately 60 minutes, has been drawn from some 10 hours of material filmed over the last 6 months in Detroit. Its central focus is The League of Revolutionary Black Workers, the nature of racism and exploitation in modern industrial society and the forms of organization now emerging for black self-determination and liberation. The filming has been undertaken by three film-makers originally from New York, in association and co-operation with the League. They are Stewart Bird, Peter Gessner, and Rene Lichtman; their combined film experience has included work with "Newsreel" and other independent radical film projects, such as Time of the Locust, one of the first anti-war Vietnam films to be produced in this country.

The potential audience for the film will include existing national and international distribution networks, as well as the possibilities of educational television, broad community screenings, schools, colleges and union caucuses. It will have an immediate and direct use as an organizing tool in the League's day-to-day work. We project that the film will be available for distribution within one month.

The film is presently in its last stages of production. In order to reach completion, certain final technical steps remain, and these are costly. Sound equalization and mixing, final negative and laboratory work remain to be done, which when combined with outstanding debts, amount to approximately $1500. Given the nature of the film, traditional sources of financial support such as foundations etc. are not open to us at this point. We are asking for any financial support you can make available to the completion of this important project.

I wish to become a supporter of The League of Revolutionary Black Workers' Film Project

Name ______________ Amount ______________

Address ______________

______________ ______________ signature

Telephone ______________

Figure 4.3. Fundraising letter. Courtesy of Walter P. Reuther Library, Archives of Labor and Urban Affairs, Wayne State University.

might work for you too." But, insofar as it does not seek to move people to immediate action, it is not itself agitational like *drum* or the strike handbill; it is propagandistic and educational.

At the same time, the film's emphasis on the newspaper also appears to indicate its desire to remediate print, to translate the organizational and agitational function of the shopfloor newsletter into the medium of film.[66] As the fundraising letter suggests, the film seeks to "have an immediate and direct use as an organizing tool in the League's day to day work." That is, the film not only describes and represents the importance of the newspaper; I think it also intends to extend, expand, and amplify the League's agitational and organizational efforts into a national or even international context. These more ambitious hopes, not unjustified by what Mike Hamlin called their early "dizzying success" in organizing RUMs in multiple factories, are represented, for instance, in this undated flyer depicting League member Ron March calling for people to prepare for the "National-Black Strike."[67]

However, on a basic level, the film medium resisted this remediation. Where the distribution of the newspaper itself served an organizational purpose with *drum*, allowing workers to make contact with each other in the actual passing of newsletter from hand to hand, distribution and screening presented real difficulties for the film's use as an organizational tool. A film cannot be distributed in the way that a shopfloor newspaper can. It cannot slip into a pocket (as we see being done in the film) to be read surreptitiously at lunch or, later, at home, in little snippets of time. Seeing a film requires that a block of time be set aside; there also has to be a place to screen the film. Workers are busy, and they are tired at the end of their long shifts of compulsory overtime. The film circulated in the alternative, often informal, distribution networks that Newsreel had relied on. As is suggested in this flyer announcing its first screening at Wayne State University, along with the film *Battle of Algiers* (a compelling pairing to be sure), the film found audiences among radical students and intellectuals who were already inclined to see experimental political films.

Had the League itself not dissolved less than a year after *Finally Got the News* was finished, in part as a result of the very same ideological and tactical differences that surrounded its making, the film may have ended up serving different functions. For the most part, the League's way of being together that the film described no longer existed by the time the film was shown.[68] This means that, despite the film's status as a political film *par excellence*, it did not succeed in refreshing or renewing

drum

VOL. 2 NO. 1 DODGE REVOLUTIONARY UNION MOVEMENT.

Prepare for the

National-Black Strike!!

Figure 4.4. National Black Strike. Courtesy of Walter P. Reuther Library, Archives of Labor and Urban Affairs, Wayne State University.

Figure 4.5. Flyer for film. Courtesy of Walter P. Reuther Library, Archives of Labor and Urban Affairs, Wayne State University.

the revolutionary mood at the moment. What the film does quite compellingly do, however, is represent the *desire* for (which is also to say the felt absence of) the refreshment and expansion of a collective revolutionary mood.

That mood is represented and addressed in a number of places in the film, nowhere better than in a scene about fifteen minutes in, one generally recognized to be a high point, and the focus of at least two other readings of the film.[69] The scene is part of a (several-minute) juxtaposition of the working conditions of workers and management. First, we see remarkable images of workers on the line in the factory and hear descriptions of the dangers of this work environment (fires, chains snapping), the injuries they cause, and the indifference of management and the union to both. Then, as we see a sequence of shots of offices and office workers, we hear a searing critique of capital delivered by an off-screen voice. We have not yet seen him in the film, but the unidentified voice belongs to Ken Cockrel, a member of the League's central committee. Here is the entirety of his speech:

> They give you little bullshit amounts of money for working, wages and so forth and then they steal all that shit back from you in terms of where they got this whole other thing set up, this whole credit gimmick society, man. Consumer credit: buy shit, buy shit, on credit. He gives you a little bit of shit to cool your ass out and then steals all that shit back. With shit called *interest*. The price of money. Motherfuckers are non-producing, non-existing, you know, industry, you know, motherfuckers who deal with paper.
>
> There's a cat who will stand up and say to you he's in mining. And he sits in an office on the 199th floor in some motherfucking building on Wall Street and he's in mining. And he has papers, certificates, which are embroidered and shit, you know. Stocks, bonds, debentures, obligations, you know. He's in "mining."
>
> He ends up on Wall Street and his fingernails ain't been dirty in his motherfucking life. He went to Philips Andover or Exeter. He went to Harvard, he went to Yale, he went to the Wharton School of Business and he's in "*mining*"?
>
> And the motherfuckers who deal with intangibles are the motherfuckers who are rewarded in this society, the more abstract and intangible your shit is, i.e. stocks. What is stock? A stock certificate is evidence of ownership in something that's real. *Ownership*. He owns and controls and therefore receives, you know, the benefit from. That's what they call profit.
>
> He's fucking with stuff in Bolivia, he's fucking with shit in Chile, he's Kennecott. He's Anaconda. He's United Fruit. He's in *mining*. He's in *what*? He ain't never in his life produced shit. Investment bankers, stockbrokers, insurance men – it's motherfuckers who don't do nothing.
>
> We see that this whole society, man, exists, and rests upon workers, and that this whole motherfucking society controlled by this ruling clique is *parasitic, vulturistic, cannibalistic* and it's sucking and destroying, man, the life of motherfucking workers and we have to stop it because it's *evil*.

Every time I hear this speech, I am impressed by the economy and lucidity of Cockrel's full-blown critique of capital, a critique that, in its attention to the "motherfuckers who deal with intangibles" and to the "credit gimmick society," that is, to the role of finance and credit, remains remarkably relevant.[70] In addition to the compelling nature of the speech's content, the listener here, I think, cannot but be impressed with the "scorching irony … blasting reproach [and] withering sarcasm" (to borrow from Frederick Douglass[71]) that Cockrel brings to his case for the evil of capitalism – parasitic, vulturistic, cannibalistic – and cannot but sense his rage at a system that is not only unjust but absurdly, *ridiculously* unjust. In order to underscore this absurdity, Cockrel focuses his speech on the figure of "a cat who will stand up and say to you he's in mining" even though "his fingernails ain't been dirty in his motherfucking life" and "he ain't never in his life produced shit." Instead of work and production, being "in mining" means *ownership*, for this "motherfucker who deals with intangibles" sits as far away as possible from the dirty mines "on the 199th floor." Ownership, Cockrel reminds us, means controlling and benefiting from the labour of workers, a relationship and process fetishistically hidden by papers "with embroidery and shit."

In accounting for the power of this voice, it is significant, as Fred Moten notes in his brilliant reading of the film, that it is here unidentified and unlocated; we do not see the body that produces it. That is, it belongs to the zone of what Michel Chion has called the *acousmetre*, his name for these off-screen voices that hover in an uncertain space neither clearly inside nor outside the film.[72] The acousmetric voice has a peculiar authority by way of its disembodiedness, Chion writes; it appears to know everything and see everything. Indeed, even though this voice is not exactly narrating the sequence of shots, there are a series of correspondences between the voice's commentary and what we see: at the end of the sequence, we realize/discern that this critique of the credit gimmick society has been delivered as we look around the central office building of the Ford Motor Credit Company; as we hear Cockrel's critique of consumer credit, we are shown cars one might purchase with credit on display in the lobby; as we hear about the "motherfuckers who deal with paper," we see paper on a desk and look over the shoulder of a man looking through papers. With the voice's discourse on abstraction and then ownership, the camera shows us a view of the abstract signs of both economic and political authority – the Ford flag and the US flag flying outside together, one right above the other. At one point a Brink's truck drives by out front. The voice is not *commenting* on the images so much as it is directing our vision to show us what it knows.

And just as in the classical scene of psychoanalysis, the absence of the analyst's face before our eyes forces us to imagine their expressions by way of their voice and thus to engage in an imaginative imitation that promotes the transference of our own affects from the past onto that voice, so too, here, Cockrel's disembodied voice aids in our feelingful, innervative imagination as we connect the vitality of the voice with its critique of capital. The absence of a visible body allows us to imagine the speaking body and face that will allow for our own critical-political feelings to emerge by way of transference. Further amplifying and extending the affective power of this voice, its will to produce "live intensities and desires that make messages affectively immediate, seductive, and binding" (to appropriate an evocative phrase from Lauren Berlant[73]), is the fact that even as this voice is visually disembodied, it is at the same time intensely aurally embodied. This voice is filled with what Barthes calls grain, the traces of its bodily origins, which are also the forms of vitality that Daniel Stern sees as the basic mechanisms of affective attunement. Listen, in Cockrel's speech, to the whole "prosody of speech consisting of melody, stress, volume modulation, vocal tension,"[74] the varied rhythms of his slowed-down, lowered pronunciation of "insurance men" or his repeated, overcareful enunciation of "own-er-ship." Perhaps most noticeable, however, as Moten points out, is Cockrel's *falsetto* and its punctuating veerings and word-bends. Moten makes the case that what may appear to be a narrative of defeat becomes a projection of victory by way of a "kind of potential energy" that we find in this vital sound irreducible to meaning.[75]

This sound provides us with an image, as Moten puts it, of "how the world would be that cuts and augments the form of the description of how fucked up the world was then and is now."[76] That is, Cockrel is on the one hand describing why and how the world is so fucked up; he is breaking down a theory of the exploitative and evil nature of capital and identifying the class enemy. At the same time, he is performing a kind of freedom from that world in his soaring fugitive falsetto, where he explores, Moten argues, what Nathaniel Mackey calls a "redemptive, unworded realm – a meta-word, if you will."[77] And a "new word, new world," Mackey notes: these new words bring into being a new world precisely inasmuch as they perform a different way of being with one another. Cockrel brings into being this different way of being with others – and of being-with-us, his audience – not just in the falsetto but also in the force and confidence of his biting sarcasm, in all the ways that he indicates that his mood may be a way of finding himself in the "there" determined by the credit gimmick society but that that mood itself is not determined or limited by that society or by the ruling clique that runs it. Cockrel's voice comes from a way of being with others that opposes that clique and escapes and exceeds its sovereignty.

Walter Benjamin once noted that "the existence of the classless society cannot be thought at the same time that the struggle for it is thought."[78] In other words, as a task, utopian thinking about what the classless society will be like is fundamentally distinct from thinking about how to struggle against the current order of capitalist society right now. I think that Benjamin was right to distinguish these two tasks as belonging to separate registers. But I think it is the combination of these non-synchronous tasks, and the non-synchronous *feelings* that go with them, in the film's form that gives this aesthetic performance its particular power. In articulating the asynchronous together, Cockrel does something here that the African American musical tradition has always been good at doing. I am thinking of how Frederick Douglass noted that the slaves would sing "the most pathetic sentiment in the most rapturous tone, and the most rapturous sentiment in the most pathetic tone."[79] In this way the struggle for freedom and the existence and feeling of freedom manage to coexist, but in a necessary tension with each other.

We might also discern an image of this other world and a narrative of the refreshment needed to get there in the arc traced out by Cockrel's use of the word "motherfucker" in this speech. Like many profane words – "goddamn," "shit," "fuck," "bullshit" – "motherfucker" here is a highly charged locus of vitality affect.[80] Indeed, sometimes such words seem to *primarily* serve the function of being a place where various forms of affect – sound that exceeds meaning – can come into being by way of pitch, duration, emphasis, glottal pressure, breath. Take a look at the speech again, attending to all the uses of "motherfucker" and "motherfucking." Note how all the uses until the last ones more or less seem to convey the sense of "an unpleasant, difficult, formidable, or oppressive thing, situation, place, or person" (to quote from the not unhelpful *Oxford English Dictionary*). But then right at the end, "motherfucking" modifies workers – and then the meaning shifts, but in an ambiguous, indeed dialectical way. To the extent that workers are oppressed by a "whole motherfucking society" that is "*parasitic, vulturistic, cannibalistic*," controlled by a ruling clique made up of the "motherfuckers who deal with intangibles" and are rewarded for doing so, to that extent, these workers are at the same time themselves (from the point of view of the ruling clique) the locus of formidable and difficult revolutionary power. As such they are also "strong and admirable," two other meanings the *OED* indexes. Or, to borrow from Langston Hughes: they are "black, beaten, but unbeatable."[81]

I think Cockrel's semi-optimistic narrative and the vital connection to things being another way that we hear in the musicality of Cockrel's speech together express what Berlant calls a "desire for the political," which she characterizes in the powerful final paragraph of *Cruel Optimism*: "The energy that generates this sustaining commitment to the work of undoing a world while making one *requires* fantasy to motor programs of action, to distort the present on behalf of what the present can become. It requires a surrealistic affectsphere to counter the one that already exists, enabling a confrontation with the fact that any action of making a claim on the present involves bruising processes of detachment from anchors in the world, along with optimistic projections of a world that is worth our attachment to it."[82] I see Berlant to be describing an aesthetic logic similar to the one Moten sees in *Finally Got the News*. The aesthetic can itself create a space for different affective attachments, an affectsphere (what I am calling a mood) – some transformed version of the present that we can attach to instead of the present world – so that we can survive our detachment from objects in this world and be hopeful about trying to make another. Cockrel's (well-nigh surrealistic) new words create a new world, and indeed the world occupied by that voice *is* a world I want to inhabit; I can feel its distortion of this world, I can sense the freedom it promises from the cannibalistic vulturistic parasitic credit gimmick society. Being-with that voice, speaking and singing along with it, occupying that non-existent world for a minute makes it easier to imagine the possibility of another world and makes it less depressing to come back to the one I live in every day. The optimism here is not the cruel optimism that Berlant describes: it is not an optimism that attaches us to the ideological forms that also prevent us from flourishing. It is closer to the utopian thought that José Muñoz describes in *Cruising Utopia*: we find here the anticipation of what he calls a "restructured sociality,"[83] one where we all can laugh at the ridiculous injustice and stupidity and poverty of the concept and practice of *ownership*.

However, in thinking about the potentially political effects of this aesthetic, I think it is valuable to remember how this aesthetic mode, and the mood it addresses, is distinct from that of the *drum* newsletters (and the exposures that Lenin calls for in "What Is to Be Done?") that succeeded in organizing the workers in the factory and making DRUM possible. There, instead of a distortion of the present world, we find a direct, flat description of it, of the fucked-up things that have happened to other people like its readers, and nary an optimistic or utopian note. Those factographic newspapers prepare the place for a different kind of aesthetic experience than the one at work in Cockrel's speech and theorize a different set of readers with a different mood, ones who do not need optimism so much as collectivity and solidarity. Those texts work by pluralizing an experience of racial capitalism that had until then simmered in isolated resentment in order to awaken a revolutionary counter-mood.

The renewal and refreshment of revolutionary mood does not require a surrealistic affectsphere. A collective in the midst of a struggle that already feels real and urgent instead needs ways to make the attachment to colleagues and coworkers, comrades in strike and struggle compelling, urgent, and joyful in the here and now. This may be why the newsletters and handbills that were successful in organizing and agitating at that moment do not move us all these years later; they are speaking about a different "Today."

Finally Got the News is involved in a different task, and one that is more familiar. In its anticipation of another world, the film addresses an audience that is looking to the future, one that already feels the absence of revolutionary mood, one that *needs* a future to look to. Even as we see how this may not serve the agitational or organizational function the League may have hoped for, I think we must nonetheless be grateful for it, because it is a future we need too. That is, the film's form addresses an audience that is alienated and anxious, an audience that is looking for a way to manage to not be completely depressed or incapacitated by politically depressing situations. Which is why I like it so much.

NOTES

The author would like to thank Andrew Anastasi, Danielle Aubert, Lauren Berlant, Daphne Brooks, Gregg Bordowitz, Marie Buck, Rita Felski, Rod Ferguson, Susan Fraiman, Phillip Harper, Eric Lott, Kathryne Lindberg, Heather Love, Janet Lyon, Crystal Parikh, and Ken Warren for conversation, encouragement, and feedback. Special gratitude to Lara Cohen, Tavia Nyong'o, and the editors of this volume for reading earlier drafts of this essay and offering suggestions and advice that substantially improved it.

1 And this was written well before Donald Trump was elected!

2 I am thinking of Jonathan Crary's *24/7: Terminal Capitalism and the Ends of Sleep.*

3 While the dramatic cuts to funding for public colleges and universities affect the profession as a whole, private universities seem to increasingly have a different set of problems and anxieties related to their dependence on the beneficence of the one percent and the extremely high tuition their students must pay. See Newfield, *Unmaking the Modern University*.
4 In following the developments in Wisconsin, I have relied on the excellent blogs by Richard Grusin (*Ragman's Circles*) and Nick Fleisher (*Language Politics*).
5 See Flatley, "Revolutionary Counter-Mood." Over the next few pages, I summarize the arguments and concepts presented there. For historical accounts of the origins of DRUM and the League, see Ahmad, *We Will Return in the Whirlwind*, 237–86; Geschwender, *Class, Race, and Worker Insurgency*; Georgakas and Surkin, *Detroit: I Do Mind Dying*; Thompson, *Whose Detroit?*, especially 71–127. For the political and ideological positions of DRUM and the League, see first the writings by League members, especially Jacobs and Wellman, "An Interview with Ken Cockrel and Mike Hamlin"; Watson, "Black Editor: An Interview"; Cockrel, "From Repression to Revolution." See also Mike Hamlin and General Baker interviews in *Detroit Lives*, 85–8, 305–13; and Wooten, "Why I Joined DRUM" (one of a series of articles originally published in the 15 February and 18 March 1969 issues of the *Guardian*, which was an independent radical newsweekly).
6 Lenin, "What Is to Be Done?" 43.
7 Ibid.
8 I am thinking in particular of the description of tragedy in book 10 of Plato's *Republic*.
9 Lenin, "What Is to Be Done?" 43.
10 "Ontologically mood [*Stimmung*] is a primordial kind of Being for Dasein, in which Dasein is disclosed to itself *prior* to all cognition and volition, and *beyond* their range of disclosure." Heidegger, *Being and Time*, 175.
11 Ibid., 176 (italics in original). I rely on both this translation and the newer Stambaugh translation (Albany: SUNY Press, 1996). But unless otherwise noted, references are to the Macquarrie and Robinson text. In the German edition (Tubingen: Niemeyer, 1979), pages of which are referenced in both English translations, the primary discussion of *Stimmung* is on pages 134–40. The best overall account of *Stimmung* in Heidegger can be found in Guignon, "Moods in Heidegger's *Being and Time*." See also Dreyfus, *Being-in-the-World*, especially 168–83; Gumbrecht, *Atmosphere, Mood, Stimmung*; Flatley, *Affective Mapping*, especially 19–24, 109–13.
12 Guignon, "Moods in Heidegger's *Being and Time*," 237.

13 Heidegger writes: "Under the strongest pressure and resistance, nothing like an affect would come about, and the resistance itself would remain essentially undiscovered, if Being-in-the-world, with its state-of-mind [Befindlichkeit], had not already submitted itself [sich schon angewiesen] to having entities within-the-world 'matter' to it in a way which its moods have outlined in advance." *Being and Time*, 177.

14 Heidegger, *Fundamental Concepts of Metaphysics*, 67. As what sets the tone, perhaps melody is the wrong musical metaphor here, since melody stands out from the background; *Stimmung* perhaps is more like the key, major or minor, that is more or less invisible but establishes what sounds good or right. Thanks to Tavia Nyong'o for pointing this out.

15 Heidegger, *Being and Time*, 176.

16 This quote and the next one from Highmore and Taylor, "Introducing Mood Work," 8.

17 Heidegger, *Being and Time*, Stambaugh translation, 127.

18 Althusser quote from "Ideology and Ideological State Apparatuses," 162. I realize that this paragraph is a very brief sketch of what would have to be a much more substantial discussion to adequately examine the analogy between *Stimmung* and ideology.

19 Institute for Precarious Consciousness, "We Are All Very Anxious."

20 See Deleuze, "Postscript on the Societies of Control," which seems to resonate with (and perhaps to have influenced) this text. Lauren Berlant provides a great riff on Deleuze's short piece, writing of all the pressures and demands that never stop in the just-in-time economy, that "pressured affectsphere of entrepreneurial subjectivity" where "more and more, even when asleep, one is never closed for business." Berlant, "On Persistence," 34. See also Hochschild, *The Managed Heart*; Ngai, *Our Aesthetic Categories*; Virno, *A Grammar of the Multitude*; Cvetkovich, *Depression: A Public Feeling*.

21 Institute for Precarious Consciousness, "We Are All Very Anxious."

22 Heidegger, *Being and Time*, 178.

23 Aristotle, *Basic Works*, 1380.

24 Heidegger, *Being and Time*, 178.

25 Stern, *Interpersonal World of the Infant*, 139.

26 Ibid., 141.

27 Ibid., 142.

28 Stern, *Forms of Vitality*, 6.

29 Ibid., 81.

30 Throughout the twists and turns of organization and activity, the newspaper as a form remained a centre of organizational activity. After the formation of DRUM, the *Inner City Voice* remained a strong voice in

support of the RUMs and the League. In 1969, John Watson was elected to the editorship of the Wayne State newspaper, the *South End*, which he turned into a League organ.

31 See the accounts in Georgakas and Surkin, Geschwender, and Thompson of the various RUMs and the formation of the League.

32 See Geschwender, *Class, Race, and Worker Insurgency*, 92–3, and Georgakas and Surkin, *Detroit: I Do Mind Dying*, 38–9, for an account of this strike.

33 For accounts of both the May strike and the July strike, see Georgakas and Surkin and Geschwender. It is also possible that this handbill (which can also be found in the Kenneth V. and Sheila M. Cockrel Collection) was part of the agitational material for an ELRUM (based at the Eldon Avenue Axle Plant) wildcat strike in 1969.

34 In its emphasis on the present moment, on a clear enemy, and a Manichean worldview, the handbill participates in the agitational rhetoric of the manifesto as outlined by Janet Lyon in *Manifestoes*.

35 Benjamin, "One Way Street," 456.

36 Barthes, *Image-Music-Text*, 179–89.

37 In their 1913 manifesto. See Khlebnikov, "The Letter as Such," 121–2. Experimental Jetset make a similar observation, remarking that "a sheet of paper" may be a "stage for graphic actors (letters, pictures) to act on" ("Socialism as Graphic Language," 122), though it is Brecht and the estrangement effect that they are referring to.

38 Experimental Jetset, "Socialism as Graphic Language," 121.

39 "Private property has made us so stupid and one-sided that an object is only *ours* when we have it – when it exists for us as capital, or when it is directly possessed, eaten, drunk, worn, inhabited, etc., – in short when it is *used* by us." Marx, "Economic and Philosophic Manuscripts of 1844," 87.

40 For a different take on the politics of design, see Jacques Rancière's suggestion that "by drawing lines, arranging words or distributing surfaces, one also designs divisions of communal space." He sees graphic design as a "certain configuration of what can be seen and what can be thought." At a certain level of abstraction, this is correct, but I think it is insufficiently attentive to the specific mediation of print and to the modes of production and distribution specific to it in particular historical settings. Rancière, "Surface of Design," 91.

41 Benjamin, "Doctrine of the Similar," 697.

42 Benjamin would say that phenomena of the past are "saved through the exhibition of the fissure within them." "N," 473.

43 Paul de Man, "Autobiography as De-Facement," 70.

44 Freud first confronted the phenomenon of transference in the infamous case of Dora. See Freud, *Dora*, especially page 138. Noticing intense, seemingly unmotivated appearances of both positive and negative affects during analysis, Freud came to realize that his patients were "transferring" feelings from past objects onto the person of the analyst, substituting the analyst for the past object on the basis of some real or imagined similarity. See also Freud, "Dynamics of the Transference" and "Further Recommendations."

45 Jean-Luc Nancy emphasizes this point in *Being Singular Plural.* See also Benjamin's suggestion that the "the loosening of the proletarian masses is the work of solidarity," involving an abolition of the "opposition between individual and mass." "Work of Art," 129n24.

46 I am thinking here of the arguments about messianic time made by Benjamin in "On the Concept of History," 389–400.

47 Part of the force of the document and its reference to today is generated by its performative mode. Janet Lyon makes a similar case about the manifesto, which can be performative in two senses: in the linguistic sense, "by implying a priori assent, it forecasts the unified class that it invokes; and in Judith Butler's sense, it produces a flexibly scripted *faux* identity for workers and non-workers uniting under hortatory radicalism." *Manifestoes*, 29.

48 Nancy, *Being Singular Plural*, 65.

49 See Mowitt, *Percussion*, 104.

50 On "racial capitalism," see Robinson, *Black Marxism.*

51 The attack on what DRUM called "Tomism" was a central aspect of DRUM's ideology and rhetoric. The second issue of the *drum* newsletter focused on an extensive analysis of Tomism in the factory and a naming of specific persons and their behaviour.

52 It may be worth emphasizing that the blackness of the blackworker here should be understood neither as an identity or an essence nor as reducible to the racism or racial capitalism that, in some senses, brought it into existence. Although racism aided by and in the service of capital is the occasion for the collective of the blackworkers to be asserted, the blackness thereby invoked exceeds and overruns the occasion for its being asserted. Following Fred Moten and Nahum Chandler, I would suggest that this blackness itself is fugitive in its being; it is foundationally "more" than any given identity meaning or ontology.

53 Marx, *Grundrisse*, 224.

54 Negri, "Communism."

55 Benjamin, "Surrealism," 217.

56 For Deleuze, to be affected is to have one's capacities altered, even slightly, and we are more or less constantly being affected in one way or another. Thus, as we move through the world, our affect is defined by "a melodic line of continuous variation." In fact, this melodic line "is what it means to exist." Deleuze explains that on this line constituted by affect, "Spinoza will assign two poles: joy-sadness, which for him will be the fundamental passions. Sadness will be any passion whatsoever which involves a diminution of my power of acting, and joy will be any passion involving an increase in my power of acting." See Deleuze, "Spinoza: 24/01/1978," *Les Cours de Gilles Deleuze*.

57 My thinking here has been influenced by Michael Snediker's *Queer Optimism*, which makes the case for an optimism oriented toward the present rather than the future, and Lauren Berlant's *Cruel Optimism*, which argues that all affective attachments are optimistic. I will return to Berlant below. I am also thinking of Benjamin's reflections on homogeneous time in relation to messianic time in his "On the Concept of History."

58 *Finally Got the News* was directed by Stewart Bird, Rene Lichtman, and Peter Gessner in 1970.

59 The heterogeneous soundtrack draws, for instance, upon an original blues addressed to an assembly line foreman (by Joe L. Carter, a Ford worker, composer, and musician), an amateur bluegrass guitar riff on a white worker's porch, free jazz, African drumming around the plant, the sound of the sped-up assembly line, and a medley of picketers' chants, including the staccato "Be Mad! Be Mad! Be Mad! You Can't Do Anything If You Ain't Mad."

60 This quote and the next one from Mekas, *Movie Journal*, 305. Newsreel made films about strikes, protests, movements that were not represented anywhere in "the news." Garbage collectors striking, anti-war protests and Columbia University, the Black Panthers, and the destruction of the neighbourhood that became Lincoln Center were all subjects of early Newsreel films.

61 Mekas, quoting from statement by Newsreel, *Movie Journal*, 306.

62 This quote and the next one from Kramer, "Newsreel," 46. As Michael Renov notes, Kramer was one of many members of the group who were "college-educated white males, verbal, assertive, confident, with access to funding sources both personal and institutional." "Newsreel: Old and New," 25.

63 "Newsreel Detroit Project," Walter P. Reuther Library, Wayne State University.

64 "Preview of Black Workers' Film," fundraising letter, Walter P. Reuther Library

65 See my "Revolutionary Counter-Mood" on this; see also Watson, "Black Editor: An Interview."
66 On remediation, see Bolter and Grusin, *Remediation: Understanding New Media.*
67 On dizzying success, see Mike Hamlin's statements in Georgakas and Surkin, 228. The problem of dealing with success and with the expansion into a national context is the line Fredric Jameson follows up on in his "Cognitive Mapping" essay, where he makes the case that the League could not expand the model that had worked at the level of the factory and the city (for which they had a cognitive map) to the national and international context. Jameson, "Cognitive Mapping," in *Jameson Reader*, 277–87.
68 For accounts of the breakup of the League, see Hamlin's statements in Georgakis and Surkin; Ahmad, *We Will Return in the Whirlwind;* Geschwender, *Class, Race, and Worker Insurgency.*
69 See Moten, *In the Break*; Adamson, "Labor, Finance, and Counterrevolution."
70 On this relevance, see Adamson.
71 Douglass, "What to the Slave Is the Fourth of July?," in *Narrative of the Life of Frederick Douglass*, 144.
72 Chion, *Voice in Cinema.*
73 Berlant, *Cruel Optimism*, 224.
74 Stern, *Forms of Vitality*, 122.
75 Moten, *In the Break*, 221.
76 Ibid., 224.
77 Mackey, *Bedouin Hornbook*, 51–2. Cited by Moten, *In the Break*, 194.
78 Paralipomena to Benjamin, "On the Concept of History," 407.
79 Douglass, *Narrative of the Life of Frederick Douglass*, 46.
80 See Daphne Brooks on Nina Simone's "Mississippi Goddamn" in Brooks, "Nina Simone's Triple Play," 176–97.
81 Hughes, "Songs Called the Blues," *Collected Works of Langston Hughes*, vol. 9, 212–13.
82 Berlant, *Cruel Optimism*, 263.
83 Muñoz, *Cruising Utopia*, 7.

BIBLIOGRAPHY

Adamson, Morgan. "Labor, Finance, and Counterrevolution: *Finally Got the News* at the End of the Short American Century." *South Atlantic Quarterly* 111, no. 4 (Fall 2012): 803–23.

Ahmad, Muhammad. *We Will Return in the Whirlwind: Black Radical Organizations 1960–1975*. Chicago: Charles H. Kerr, 2007.

Althusser, Louis. "Ideology and Ideological State Apparatuses (Notes toward an Investigation)." In *Lenin and Philosophy and Other Essays*, translated by Ben Brewster. New York: Monthly Review Press, 1971.

Aristotle. *The Basic Works of Aristotle*. Edited by Richard McKeon. New York: Random House, 1941.

Baker, General. "General Baker" (interview). By Robert Mast. In *Detroit Lives*, edited by Robert Mast, 305–13. Philadelphia: Temple University Press, 1994.

Barthes, Roland. *Image-Music-Text*. Translated by Stephen Heath. New York: Hill and Wang, 1978.

Benjamin, Walter. "Doctrine of the Similar." In *Walter Benjamin: Selected Writings*. Vol. 2, *1927–1934*. Cambridge, MA: Harvard University Press, 1999.

– "N." In *The Arcades Project* [N9, 4]. Cambridge, MA: Harvard University Press, 2002.

– "On the Concept of History." In *Walter Benjamin: Selected Writings*. Vol. 4, *1938–1940*, 389–400. Cambridge, MA: Harvard University Press, 2003.

– "One Way Street." In *Walter Benjamin: Selected Writings*. Vol. 1, *1913–1926*, edited by Marcus Bullock and Michael W. Jennings, 444–88. Cambridge, MA: Harvard University Press, 1996.

– "Surrealism: The Last Snapshot of the European Intelligentsia." In *Walter Benjamin: Selected Writings*. Vol. 2, *1927–1934*. Cambridge, MA: Harvard University Press, 1999.

– "The Work of Art in the Age of Its Technological Reproducibility: Second Version." In *Walter Benjamin: Selected Writings*. Vol. 3, *1935–1938*. Cambridge, MA: Harvard University Press, 2002.

Berlant, Lauren. *Cruel Optimism*. Durham: Duke University Press, 2011.

– "On Persistence." *Social Text* 32, no. 4/121 (2014): 33–7.

Bolter, Jay David, and Richard Grusin. *Remediation: Understanding New Media*. Cambridge: MIT Press, 1999.

Brooks, Daphne. "Nina Simone's Triple Play." *Callaloo* 34, no. 1 (Winter 2011): 176–97.

Chion, Michel. *The Voice in Cinema*. Translated by Claudia Gorbman. New York: Columbia University Press, 1999.

Cockrel, Kenneth V. "From Repression to Revolution." *Radical America* 5, no. 2 (March/April 1971): 81–9.

Crary, Jonathan. *24/7: Terminal Capitalism and the Ends of Sleep*. New York: Verso Books, 2013.

Cvetkovich, Ann. *Depression: A Public Feeling*. Durham: Duke University Press, 2012.

Deleuze, Gilles. "Postscript on the Societies of Control." *October* 59 (1992): 3–7.
– "Spinoza: 24/01/1978." *Les Cours de Gilles Deleuze*. Translated by Timothy Murray. http://deleuzelectures.blogspot.com/2007/02/on-spinoza.html.
de Man, Paul. "Autobiography as De-Facement." In *The Rhetoric of Romanticism*, 67–81. New York: Columbia University Press, 1984.
Douglass, Frederick. *Narrative of the Life of Frederick Douglass, An American Slave, Written by Himself*, edited with an introduction by David W. Blight. Boston: Bedford, 1993.
– "What to the Slave Is the Fourth of July?" In *Narrative of the Life of Frederick Douglass, An American Slave, Written by Himself*, edited with an introduction by David W. Blight, 141–5. Boston: Bedford, 1993.
Dreyfus, Hubert L. *Being-in-the-World: A Commentary on Heidegger's "Being and Time," Division I*. Cambridge: MIT Press, 1991.
Experimental Jetset. "Socialism as Graphic Language: Ettore Vitale." In *The Italian Avant-Garde: 1968–1976*, edited by Alex Coles, 119–26. Berlin: Sternberg Press, 2013.
Finally Got the News. Directed by Stewart Bird, Rene Lichtman, and Peter Gessner. Detroit: Black Star Productions, 1970.
Flatley, Jonathan. *Affective Mapping: Melancholia and the Politics of Modernism*. Cambridge, MA: Harvard University Press, 2008.
– "How a Revolutionary Counter-Mood Is Made." *New Literary History* 43, no. 3 (2012): 503–25.
Fleisher, Nick. *Language Politics* (blog). http://languagepolitics.org.
Freud, Sigmund. *Dora: An Analysis of a Case of Hysteria*. Edited by Philip Rieff. New York: Collier Books, 1963.
– "The Dynamics of the Transference." 1912. In *Therapy and Technique*, edited by Philip Rieff, 105–15. New York: Collier Books, 1963.
– "Further Recommendations in the Technique of Psychoanalysis: Recollection, Repetition and Working-Through." 1914. In *Therapy and Technique*, edited by Philip Rieff, 157–66. New York: Collier Books, 1963.
– *The Interpretation of Dreams*. Translated and edited by James Strachey. New York: Avon, 1965.
Georgakas, Dan, and Marvin Surkin. *Detroit: I Do Mind Dying: A Study in Urban Revolution*. Cambridge: South End Press, 1998.
Geschwender, James A. *Class, Race, and Worker Insurgency: The League of Revolutionary Black Workers*. Cambridge: Cambridge University Press, 1977.
Glaberman, Martin. "Survey Detroit." *International Socialism* 1, no. 36 (April/May 1969): 8–9.
Grusin, Richard. *Ragman's Circles* (blog). https://ragmanscircles.wordpress.com.

Guignon, Charles. "Moods in Heidegger's *Being and Time*." In *What Is an Emotion? Classic Readings in Philosophical Psychology*, edited by Cheshire Calhoun and Robert C. Solomon, 230–43. New York: Oxford University Press, 1984.

Gumbrecht, Hans Ulrich. *Atmosphere, Mood, Stimmung: On a Hidden Potential of Literature*. Stanford: Stanford University Press, 2012.

Haar, Michel. "The Primacy of Stimmung over Dasein's Bodiliness." In *Heidegger and the Grounds of the History of Being*, translated by Reginald Lilly, 34–46. Bloomington: Indiana University Press, 1993.

Hamlin, Mike. "Mike Hamlin" (interview). By Robert Mast. In *Detroit Lives*, edited by Robert Mast, 85–8. Philadelphia: Temple University Press, 1994.

Heidegger, Martin. *Being and Time*. Translated by John Macquarrie and Edward Robinson. San Francisco: Harper & Row, 1962.

– *Being and Time*. Translated by Jean Stambaugh. Albany: SUNY Press, 1996.

– *The Fundamental Concepts of Metaphysics: World, Finitude, Solitude*. Translated by William McNeill and Nicholas Walker. Bloomington: Indiana University Press, 2001.

Highmore, Ben, and Jenny Bourne Taylor. "Introducing Mood Work." *New Formations* 82 (2014): 5–12.

Hochschild, Arlie. *The Managed Heart: Commercialization of Human Feeling*. Los Angeles: University of California Press, 1983.

Hughes, Langston. "Songs Called the Blues." *Phylon* 2 (Summer 1941). Reprinted in *Collected Works of Langston Hughes*. Vol. 9, *Essays on Art, Race, Politics, and World Affairs*, edited by Christopher De Santis, 212–15. Columbia: University of Missouri Press, 2002.

Institute for Precarious Consciousness. "We Are All Very Anxious." *Plan C* (blog). April 4, 2014. http://www.weareplanc.org/blog/we-are-all-very-anxious/.

Jacobs, Jim, and David Wellman. "An Interview with Ken Cockrel and Mike Hamlin of the League of Revolutionary Black Workers." *Leviathan* 2, no. 2 (1970). Reprinted in *Our Thing Is DRUM!* Detroit: Black Star Printing, 1970.

Jameson, Fredric. "Cognitive Mapping." In *Marxism and the Interpretation of Culture*, edited by Lawrence Grossberg and Cary Nelson, 347–60. Urbana: University of Illinois Press, 1988. Reprinted in *The Jameson Reader*, edited by Michael Hardt and Kathi Weeks, 277–87. New York: Blackwell, 2000.

Khlebnikov, Velimir. "The Letter as Such." In *The King of Time: Selected Writings of the Russian Futurian*, translated by Paul Schmidt, edited by Charlotte Douglas, 121–22. Cambridge, MA: Harvard University Press, 1985.

Kramer, Robert. "Newsreel." *Film Quarterly* 22, no. 2 (1968–9): 43–8.

Lenin, Vladimir Ilyich. "What Is to Be Done? Burning Questions of Our Movement." In *The Lenin Anthology*, edited by Robert Tucker, 12–114. New York: Norton, 1975.

Lyon, Janet. *Manifestoes: Provocations of the Modern*. Ithaca: Cornell University Press, 1999.

Mackey, Nathaniel. *The Bedouin Hornbook*. Callaloo Fiction Series. Lexington: University Press of Kentucky, 1986.

Marx, Karl. "Economic and Philosophic Manuscripts of 1844." In *The Marx-Engels Reader*, 2nd ed., edited by Robert C. Tucker. New York: Norton, 1978.

– *Grundrisse: Foundations of the Critique of Political Economy*. Translated by Martin Nicolaus. New York: Vintage Books, 1973.

Mowitt, John. *Percussion: Drumming, Beating, Striking*. Durham: Duke University Press, 2002.

Mekas, Jonas. *Movie Journal: The Rise of a New American Cinema 1959–1971*. New York: Collier Books, 1971.

Moten, Fred. *In the Break: The Aesthetics of the Black Radical Tradition*. Minneapolis: University of Minnesota Press, 2003.

Muñoz, José Esteban. *Cruising Utopia: The Then and There of Queer Futurity*. New York: New York University Press, 2009.

Nancy, Jean-Luc. *Being Singular Plural*. Translated by Robert Richardson and Anne O'Byrne. Stanford: Stanford University Press, 2000.

Negri, Antonio. "Communism: Some Thoughts on the Concept and Practice." Lecture at Birkbeck, University of London, March 2009. http://www.generation-online.org/p/fp_negri21.htm.

Newfield, Christopher. *Unmaking the Modern University: The Forty-Year Assault on the Middle Class*. Cambridge, MA: Harvard University Press, 2011.

"Newsreel Detroit Project." n.d. Glaberman Archives. Walter P. Reuther Library, Wayne State University.

Ngai, Sianne. *Our Aesthetic Categories*. Cambridge, MA: Harvard University Press, 2012.

Rancière, Jacques. "The Surface of Design." In *The Future of the Image*, translated by Gregory Elliott, 91–107. New York: Verso Books, 2007.

Renov, Michael. "Newsreel: Old and New – Towards an Historical Profile." *Film Quarterly* 41, no. 1 (Autumn 1987): 20–33.

Robinson, Cedric. *Black Marxism: The Making of the Black Radical Tradition*. London: Zed Books, 1983.

Snediker, Michael. *Queer Optimism: Lyric Personhood and Other Felicitous Persuasions*. Minneapolis: University of Minnesota Press, 2008.

Stern, Daniel. *Forms of Vitality: Exploring Dynamic Experience in Psychology and the Arts, Psychotherapy, and Development*. New York: Oxford University Press, 2010.

– *The Interpersonal World of the Infant*. New York: Basic Books, 1985.
Thompson, Heather Ann. *Whose Detroit? Politics, Labor, and Race in a Modern American City*. Ithaca: Cornell University Press, 2001.
Virno, Paulo. *A Grammar of the Multitude*. Los Angeles: Semiotext(e), 2004.
Watson, John. "Black Editor: An Interview." *Radical America* 2, no. 4 (July/August 1968): 30–8.
Wooten, Chuck. "Why I Joined DRUM." In *Black Workers in Revolt: How Detroit's New Black Revolutionary Workers Are Changing the Face of American Trade Unionism*, edited by Robert Dudnick. Detroit: Radical Education Project, n.d.

PART III

Discriminating: Liberal Ethics and Literary Aesthetics

5 Playing at Judgment: Aporias of Liberal Freedom in Kant's *Critique of Judgment*

VIVASVAN SONI

There are few places where the entanglement of literary history and liberal history is more apparent than in Kant's *Critique of Judgment*. When it established the aesthetic as an autonomous domain, the third *Critique* made the case for an interpretive relation to aesthetic objects that is largely still ours, namely the commitment to a certain formal open-endedness of interpretation that becomes apparent in the "free play" of the understanding and imagination. This refusal of closure or conceptual determination in aesthetic interpretation, implied by the free play of the faculties, would be difficult if not impossible to gainsay today. At the same time, the third *Critique* is a profoundly political text, indeed the most political of Kant's three critiques, as Hannah Arendt long ago recognized.[1] But although for Arendt the third *Critique* holds out the promise of a praxis of judgment that is very nearly an antidote to liberalism, I would suggest that the concepts of freedom, autonomy, and community at the heart of the *Critique of Judgment* are deployed in fundamentally liberal ways. I have argued elsewhere that the community of aesthetic judgment underlying the third *Critique* has the structure of what Jean-Luc Nancy calls an "inoperative community," a community with no communal essence whatsoever, the form of community that one might argue is peculiar to liberal polities.[2] Whether we grant this or not, it is fair to say that the third *Critique* wrestles with one of the fundamental problems of liberalism, namely how, given the radical autonomy of judging subjects, it is possible to discover a sense of something shared or common, a *sensus communis*. But it is not a coincidence that the *Critique* addresses questions concerning both liberalism and the literary at the same time. These questions are deeply entangled in this text. If the structural open-endedness of the interpretive horizon produced by

Kant's notion of the aesthetic paves the way to an infinite conversation, a conversation that can never properly conclude, then this is precisely the accusation that critics like Leo Strauss and Carl Schmitt have levelled at liberalism, namely that it engages in an infinite conversation that goes nowhere, that is incapable of providing a ground for decision.[3] Literary and aesthetic conversations, on this view, would model the failed conversations of liberal politics: incessant chatter that serves only to defer the moment of judgment.[4]

It should be evident, from this high-altitude synopsis, that there is hardly another text in which issues of liberalism and the literary or aesthetic are more closely entwined through the possibility of their mutual evasion of judgment. It is to this nexus of problems that I want to turn my attention in this essay, especially with regard to the question of how the *Critique of Judgment* conceives of its central concept: judgment. Commentators have noted that the third *Critique* identifies a new class of judgments – "reflecting" rather than "determining" judgments – that demand a suppleness of mind and go beyond the rote application of rules. But will we find in these the promise of an aesthetico-political practice of judgment attuned to contingency and the condition of plurality, a practice that can serve as a remedy to liberalism's putative allergy to judgment, as Arendt and Linda Zerilli believe?[5] Or will the text expose the problematic co-implication of literary and liberal history in their mutual discomfort with judgment?[6]

Before we proceed further in this venture, it is worth pausing to make sure that we are not imposing a set of anachronistic concerns on Kant's text. At first sight, it must seem strange to expect the aesthetic to do all this work with respect to a liberal politics that may not even have existed yet.[7] But if, for a moment, we set aside fraught words like "liberalism," it is clear that the aesthetic emerges in response to a set of simultaneously epistemological and political dilemmas in the eighteenth century. The aesthetic as such, it must be remembered, is not a perennial philosophical concern, but a discursive configuration that is distinctive to the period. We tend to locate its inception with Kant, with only a nod to a few inadequate precursors, because it is with him that aesthetics famously becomes an autonomous discourse.[8] But to begin the story with him is to begin it too late, because by the time of the *Critique of Judgment*, many of the *reasons* for the emergence of aesthetics had been concealed or were only poorly understood. I prefer to think of the aesthetic as a response, inadequate at best, to a set of problems concerning human motivation that arise within Lockean empiricism.

In the revised version of book 2, chapter 21 of the *Essay Concerning Human Understanding*, Locke claims to have discovered a new account of motivation, one that relies only on the immediacy of desire, not on some abstract notion of the "good" for the sake of which we act.[9] As compelling as such an account might seem, it generated at least three problems with significant political import. First, because we only ever act in response to our desires, to some "uneasiness" or discomfort as Locke puts it, the possibility of a disinterested action, that is to say an action undertaken for reasons other than self-interest, becomes impossible to conceive. Second, on this model, actions are not construed as oriented toward particular ends, but driven forward by impulsions whose goals might be inapparent or even non-existent. Finally, if the impulse of desire is determinative of motivation in the last instance, then there is no place allowed to judgment in the formation of resolutions.

Early aesthetic thought, whose first inklings can be found in Addison, Steele, Shaftesbury, and Hutcheson, attempts to respond to this constellation of problems, particularly the first two. Aesthetic perception, in this tradition, is thought to be the exemplary instance of a capacity for disinterested contemplation, because the pleasure it gives responds to no particular desire, need, or discomfort.[10] Moreover, specific aesthetic experiences orient us toward ends that cannot be supplied from within the empiricist framework: beauty orients us to sexual reproduction or the pursuit of wealth; sublimity to the contemplation of god; and novelty to curiosity and the pursuit of knowledge.[11] In other words, in its earliest incarnations, the aesthetic is demonstrably an attempt to solve a set of problems that arise within empiricist discourse about motivation. But it is significant that in these early forms, the solution does not proceed by restoring the role of judgment. For Shaftesbury, the *sensus communis* is as primordial an instinct as self-interest: he calls it the "*herding* Principle."[12] And Hutcheson believes that aesthetic perception takes place by way of an aesthetic sense rather than a practice of judgment, an internal sense that is entirely analogous to the five outward senses.[13]

With this long view on empiricism and aesthetics, the political character of Kant's intervention and the magnitude of the claims he makes for the faculty of judgment are unmistakable. The eighteenth-century aesthetic tradition, in its response to empiricist dilemmas, had largely avoided the language of judgment in favour of "taste," with a few notable exceptions such as Locke and Rousseau, but Kant accords judgment pride of place in the solution to these dilemmas.[14] Judgment becomes the key to solving the problems of aesthetic and political thought earlier in the century. Most significantly, Kant tells us that "**taste** is the faculty for judging an object [*Geschmack ist das Beurteilungsvermögen eines Gegenstandes*] … through a satisfaction or dissatisfaction **without any interest**."[15] The capacity for disinterested contemplation that we discover in the aesthetic must not be mistaken for uninterested, unenthusiastic, or disengaged contemplation. That which pleases without interest means, in this context, that which gives us pleasure even though we have no stake in it, even though we do not expect to derive any profit from it, even though we do not care about it for selfish or self-interested reasons. Its pleasure arrives unexpectedly and improbably, almost as if for no reason at all, surprising us by its grace.

Out of context, the project to establish a capacity for disinterested contemplation and judgment might appear to be a solipsistic one. But in the terms of the period, its import is openly and immediately political. The empiricist model of subjectivity developed by Locke had offered a reductive account of motivation, in which the capacity for disinterested motivation had become all but inexplicable. When radicalized by Mandeville's hermeneutics of suspicion, the task becomes one of explaining (away) any seemingly disinterested or altruistic behaviour by finding its springs in self-interest.[16] If we have not found such an explanation, the theory goes, it is only because we have not looked hard enough. The political consequences of this model were clear from the beginning. If individuals are motivated only by their self-interest, it is impossible to conceive a polity of citizens who care for the commonweal, or *res publica*. The only way of coordinating these interests, then, is by giving them free rein in a market, where they check themselves immanently.[17] It is no coincidence that we witness, throughout this period, from Mandeville and Smith to Schiller and Hegel the emergence of a dialectical and agonistic social theory, in which providential outcomes are the result of an immanent and conflictual market logic. Judgment, if there is any, is an emergent property of a market, not the result of any individual's cogitation and deliberation. Against this discourse, however, aesthetic theory sets out to establish that we have the capacity to reflect, contemplate, and resolve in ways that are not governed by self-interest. Shaftesbury's essay "*Sensus Communis*" takes itself to be refuting Hobbes's interest-driven and contractual model of sociality by discovering in aesthetic experience the possibility of a disinterested pleasure. The political significance of the aesthetic concept of *sensus communis* is openly remarked on by Shaftesbury. Thus, when Kant defines beautiful objects as those that engender a pleasure without interest, when he declares that in aesthetic judgments we speak with a universal voice or give evidence of a *sensus communis*, he is taking sides in an urgent and highly charged political debate, and doing so not just symbolically or allegorically, as though the aesthetic were a cover for politics, but quite directly. One of his most promising innovations, in this regard, is to secure the possibility for disinterest through the labour of judgment rather than through a moral sense or altruistic instinct. *The capacity for judgment opens the way to a politics that would be something other than the anarchy of the market.*

There are a number of other aspects to the concept of judgment Kant develops that promise not only to resolve earlier problems with judgment and to revalorize judgment as a cognitive capacity, but also to establish it as what Arendt calls "the most political of man's mental abilities."[18] These have been well described by Arendt and Zerilli, among others, so I will not spend much time rehearsing them, but it is important to recall, if only briefly, what the third *Critique* promised not only for Kant's generation but also for our own. Foremost among these aspects is Kant's identification of a whole new class of judgments, what he calls "reflecting" judgments as opposed to "determining" judgments.[19] Determining judgments are those in which a rule is given, and the act of judgment involves applying this rule to a particular instance. Reflecting judgments are those in which I am confronted with the particular, and I have to find the rule of which it is the example. Because rules are not given in advance in a reflecting judgment, these judgments are attuned to contingency and particularity. They cannot involve the application of any straightforward algorithmic technique to make the judgment, since the rule is not known but has to be discovered. From an ethical perspective, we might say that reflecting judgments are about the process of *forming* rather than imposing norms. It is reflecting judgments that are judgments in the fullest sense of the word, because they do not involve a simple implementation of rational calculation.[20] They require a different kind of cognitive process, one not reducible to a computational rationality. We have to exercise our judgment rather than simply reasoning through a problem. For Kant, aesthetic judgments are the exemplary instance of these unusual and difficult kinds of judgment.[21]

A second important aspect of Kantian aesthetic judgments is that they are autonomous,[22] and they also require that we respect the autonomy of others' aesthetic judgments.[23] For Kant, most judgments are not autonomous, because the materials and rules for understanding them are given from outside, but aesthetic judgments demonstrate the possibility for the exercise of judgment that is not unduly influenced by extrinsic factors. They serve as a model for autonomous judging, that is to say a judgment exercised in freedom. The political valence of autonomous judgment should be clear, particularly in the reciprocity of respect demanded by competing aesthetic judgments. Something like an ideal democratic polity is at stake in the possibility of such autonomous judgments.[24]

Finally, as in the earlier aesthetic tradition, and its response to empiricism, Kantian aesthetic judgments are concerned with the problem of how we relate to ends. However, unlike the earlier tradition, Kant's reconceived aesthetic judgments do not straightforwardly restore a relationship to ends-oriented thinking. Kant tells us that "**beauty** is the form of the **purposiveness** of an object, insofar as it is perceived in it **without representation of an end**"[25] – purposiveness without purpose, as it is sometimes translated. I will return to this aspect later, but it is important to situate Kant's complicated efforts to restore an ends-oriented thinking within a longer tradition, as I have above, in which this was one of the most important tasks performed by aesthetic thought, namely to invest a world stripped of ends with purposes again.

In short, the *Critique of Judgment* promises a rich and robust account of the faculty of judgment, preserving all the interesting features of judgment that make it a distinctive cognitive faculty not reducible to reasoning, willing, desiring, or opining. And it makes these promises as no other text in the history of philosophy has done. It is not surprising, then, that such large claims can be made on behalf of this text as a key resource for thinking about judgment. As Arendt says: "Not till Kant's *Critique of Judgment* did this faculty become a major topic of a major thinker"; "behind taste, a favorite topic of the whole eighteenth century, Kant had discovered an entirely new human faculty, namely, judgment."[26] Nor is it any wonder that when contemporary thinkers want to theorize the operation of judgment, they turn to the third *Critique* before all else.[27] It is on this text, it seems, that we must stake our hopes for a viable account of judgment or none at all.

What, then, if it should turn out that Kantian aesthetic judgments are not judgments at all but a recipe for the systematic and perpetual evasion of judgment? And how could it be that this massively obvious fact about the third *Critique* is rarely noted by those who turn to it for their accounts of political and aesthetic judgment?[28] I say "massively obvious fact" because it is not a secret truth of the critique that will require an inordinate hermeneutic labour to discover; it is, rather, a characteristic gesture of many of the distinctive arguments the critique makes about the nature of aesthetic judgments, beginning with its very first pages. Allow me to describe some of the key ways in which judgment is avoided in the critique, and you will see that all I am doing is describing the structure of aesthetic "judgments." Aesthetic judgment is not, as Christoph Menke has recently argued, "reluctant taste," judgment that hates itself or judgment with a bad conscience.[29] That is too generous a description. It is judgment that refuses to judge, or what we might call, to echo a Kantian formulation, judgmentness without judgment.

Let us begin by noting that, on the face of it, some kind of judgment does in fact take place when I claim, for example, that "this flower is beautiful" and expect or require that everyone will agree with me. The statement "this flower is beautiful" has the formal structure of a judgment. It is the possibility and meaning of such judgments that the critique is at pains to elucidate. So, what, according to the critique, do I mean when I declare that an object is beautiful? Paradoxically, nearly the first gesture that the critique makes is to claim that I am not making a judgment about the *object* at all. When I say "this flower is beautiful," I am saying nothing meaningful or substantive about the flower itself. Kant's remarkable account of judgment is achieved at the price of distracting us from the object, indeed of radically suspending judgment with regard to the object.[30] The shift away from the object is established in the first sentence of the critique and is one of its most distinctive contributions: "In order to decide [*unterscheiden* – distinguish] whether or not something is beautiful, we do not relate the representation by means of the understanding to the object for cognition [*auf das Objekt zum Erkenntnisse*], but rather relate it by means of the imagination … to the subject [*auf das Subjekt*] and its feeling of pleasure or displeasure."[31] Turning judgment away from the object does not imply that there is no relation to the object in a judgment of beauty. If the relation to the object were completely severed, all that would be left would be "a merely subjective play of the powers of representation."[32] The form of the object, the representation we have of it, generates aesthetic reflection in some inexplicable fashion. This allows us to speak, and even to speak with some right, *as though* beauty were a property of the object, even though it is not. Strictly speaking, the judgment of beauty does not refer to the object, though it is provoked by it. The judgment of beauty takes the object as its occasion, but the object is not really its concern.[33]

Here, then, is a first, momentous evasion of judgment: aesthetic judgment suspends judgment with regard to the very object it claims to be making a judgment about. It couches its claim as a judgment about the object, but closer investigation reveals that *nothing* is being said about the object at all. Instead, aesthetic judgment turns the subject back on itself, to reflect on the unusual state of its own cognitive faculties. This flight into self-reflexivity is one of the most characteristic ways that the critique avoids judgment.[34] Aesthetic reflecting judgments had held out the promise of an encounter with the contingency and heterogeneity of the world, because rather than imposing normative categories on the world by starting with the rule and subsuming the particular under it, they were supposed to engage with the particularity of the object and immerse themselves in the specificity of a situation or context before making a judgment. The subject would reach out toward the world and touch upon it gently, rather than dictating to the world in advance the ordered forms in which it must present itself. Instead, when confronted with this situation in which it is not allowed to judge using pregiven rules, the subject takes flight from the world, seeking refuge in a solipsistic reflection on its own powers rather than confronting the world in its heterogeneity.

However, we need not despair just yet. We can cling to the fact that some judgment has still taken place, even though it might not have been a judgment about the object as we expected. The judgment that "this object is beautiful" may tell us nothing about the object in question, but it still appears to have some content. It is, for Kant, not a judgment that the object possesses a certain property ("beauty") but rather a judgment about the condition the subject's cognitive apparatus finds itself in when perceiving a particular object. This characteristic condition is what Kant terms "the free play of the imagination and the understanding."[35] Now, I want to argue that the free play of the faculties Kant describes is nothing but a pleasurable suspension of judgment. After all, when the imagination and understanding enter into a *fixed* and determinate relationship, this is precisely a moment of judgment. Free play is when the mind finds itself in "neutral" (a degree zero of cognition, as it were), recognizing in the interplay between understanding and imagination its *capacity* to judge but not fixing this relation in a determinate judgment:[36] "The animation of both faculties (the imagination and the understanding) to an activity that is indeterminate but yet, through the stimulus of the given representation, in unison, namely that which belongs to a cognition in general, is the sensation whose universal communicability is postulated by the judgment of taste."[37] Kant is explicit that the "judgment of taste" must not issue in an actual judgment; to discover a rule under which to subsume the aesthetic object (such as "unity in variety," "symmetry," "harmony," "perfection," etc.) would be to arrest the specifically aesthetic experience of free play by a judgment that yields some knowledge about the object.[38] Schiller's "translation" of Kantian aesthetics makes the necessary suspension of judgment even clearer: "If, after enjoyment of this kind, we find ourselves disposed to prefer some one particular mode of feeling or action, but unfitted or disinclined for another, this may serve as infallible proof that we have not had a *purely aesthetic* experience."[39] In other words, in a Kantian aesthetic "judgment," the judging subject turns inward on itself – when it recognizes its inability to make a judgment about the object – and reflects on the state of its cognitive faculties. What it discovers, then, is that this inability to judge constitutes the pleasurable free play of its cognitive faculties, which it then feels authorized to impute to everyone. Instead of attributing a particular property to an object, a judgment of beauty requires that everyone will experience the same *inability* to judge when confronted by this object and that the specific nature of this inability (the free play of the faculties, rather than simply confusion or the failure to cognize the object adequately) will be pleasurable in the same way for all of us.

Here, then, is a second, systematic failure of judgment in the aesthetic experience. The first was the turn away from the object toward the subject. But we still held out hope that the judgment made some claim about the state of the subject's cognitive faculties. Indeed, it does make the distinctive and unusual claim that the cognitive faculties of the understanding and imagination are in free play. In a way, what we discover in aesthetic experience is our capacity for freedom, for allowing our faculties to engage in play without being determined by the constraints of the world, autonomy in a word, and in fact, this was precisely the bridging function that the third *Critique* was supposed to play between the other two critiques. In judgments about the beautiful, the autonomy of judgment is achieved only when we experience the beautiful object as resisting our judgment. When we judge our faculties to be in free play in an aesthetic judgment, we are simply acknowledging that we have been unable to judge the object. Aesthetic judgment is a judgment that we have failed to come to a judgment and that this failure is *constitutive* of the experience of beauty itself.

The loss of the object of judgment and the suspension of judgment in free play are only two symptoms of the problems generated by Kant's approach to recuperating autonomous judgment. Another is the nagging suspicion that there may not be a *process* of judgment involved in a so-called aesthetic judgment. If judgment is fundamentally an act of cognitive mediation, and mediation takes time, it is far from clear that there is any time for this mediation in an experience of the beautiful. Kant sometimes insists that the beautiful pleases immediately (*unmittelbar* – without mediation), since it proceeds without the mediation of any concepts.[40] In this he resembles Hutcheson, for whom the immediacy of the perception of beauty elides judgment: "The judgment of taste must rest on a mere sensation."[41] It would be more appropriate to say that we "sense" or "intuit" beauty rather than judge it.[42] But in a section that Kant introduces as "the key to the critique of taste," he argues that a feeling of universal communicability must precede and even generate the feeling of pleasure we take in the object.[43] If this is the case, then there is mediation after all. Presumably an act of judgment is required in order for us to be able to recognize and distinguish a state of universal communicability and its ability to produce pleasure in us. As Dieter Henrich astutely points out: "The feeling has to be such that there can be no doubt the aesthetic attitude has occurred. Otherwise a distinctively aesthetic judgment could not be based upon it, let alone a judgment claiming universal agreement."[44] But because everything depends on a feeling or sensation, the necessary judgment lies beyond the limit of articulation, although this is where the difficult work of judgment is most called for. A place for judgment does open up here – especially if, despite some indications, the feeling of pleasure is not immediate – but it is more a placeholder than a viable account of judgment.

Another way of putting the problem would be this. It is imperative for Kant that the pleasure of aesthetic experience *follow* on the judgment of taste, because if the pleasure preceded the judgment, then the judgment would have been determined by the pleasure and not made freely. But the judgment, if it is not to be empty, has to be a judgment about *something*, and that something, we have seen, is the free play of faculties. So we make a judgment that our faculties are in free play, and a certain pleasure follows from this recognition. The problem is that Kant describes the free play of the faculties in terms that make it nearly indistinguishable from pleasure itself. The free play of the faculties, even before we make any judgment about it, produces an enlivening sensation; it heightens our sense of being alive, and in it, we even "feel our freedom," to use Linda Zerilli's language.[45] Kant speaks of the "animation (*Belebung*) of both faculties" and the "facilitated play of both powers of the mind ... enlivened (*belebten*) through mutual agreement."[46] Now, it is not simply that this language of animation and enlivening vaguely resembles something we might want to call pleasure. As the editors point out, Kant often "explained pleasure as the feeling of the promotion of life and displeasure as the feeling of a hindrance to life."[47] Thus, the feeling of the free play of the faculties, prior to the judgment of taste, is indistinguishable from pleasure, a pleasure at feeling ourselves alive and free.[48]

Here, then, is a third problem for judgment in the experience of the aesthetic. Although the judgment of taste has to precede the feeling of pleasure if it is to be made freely and not be determined by a feeling, it turns out that that which it passes judgment on is a pleasure that must precede it, threatening to undermine the freedom with which the judgment is made. Kant's language about the immediacy of pleasure in aesthetic experience confirms this danger, since the immediacy of pleasure risks eliding the practice of mediation that is integral to any work of judgment.

A final symptom of the difficulties Kant encounters in theorizing judgment: I have said that judgment concerns our relation to ends, meanings, and purposes, and the *Critique of Judgment* is undoubtedly Kant's effort to reintroduce concerns about purposes and final causes into a world that has otherwise been stripped of them. But in relation to judgments about beauty, the difficulty with Kant's strategy is apparent in his third definition of the beautiful as "the form of the **purposiveness** of an object, insofar as it is perceived in it **without representation of an end**."[49] Beautiful objects are those that appear as though they have a purpose, but we must not be able to specify (judge) such a purpose or we would put an end to the free play of faculties that is the hallmark of the experience of beauty. Put differently, we might say that beautiful objects remind us of our lost relation to purposes and ends produced by the crisis of judgment, without being able to restore our orientation toward ends.[50] In a natural world disenchanted by the laws of physics, and a moral world subjected to the rigorous discipline of the categorical imperative, beautiful objects – by their uselessness, their failure to signify,[51] their very insignificance – provoke an intuition that purpose is ours to make, even as they mock as naive and unaesthetic any effort to specify those ends and purposes concretely. They invite us to imaginatively enter a world animated, through constitutive acts of judgment, by our own purposes and ends, and then slam the door in our faces when we try! Aesthetic objects do not restore our capacity for judging in relation to ends or provide a privileged sited for the exercise of judgment. Rather, aesthetic cognition, the last potential refuge for judgment, reveals only our failure or inability to judge.

Here, then, is a fourth way in which the critique deepens the crisis of judgment rather than offering to lead us beyond its impasses. From Locke's account of vision to the aesthetic conceptions of Shaftesbury, judgment was required both to constitute ends and to enable the further work of judgment in relation to those constituted ends. By insisting that aesthetic judgment concerns a purposiveness without purpose, a goal-directedness that must never harden into an actual goal for fear of destroying the aesthetic experience, Kant makes the aesthetic into an experimental site where we may play at purpose, at judging purposes or feeling purposive. But this play must not ever become serious or result in the orientation toward specific ends. On Kant's view, to posit purpose, which is one of the tasks of judgment, is not to recognize beauty but to annihilate it. There is only beauty as long as we find ourselves on the brink of judgment, without ever taking the leap to resolve on some meaning or course of action. When we stop playing on the brink, or dancing on the edge of the precipice, when we finally judge or make a determination, we surrender nothing less than our freedom.

We have now tracked the systematic evasion or suspension of judgment that constitutes what Kant calls the judgment of taste, supposedly the freest kind of judgment we are able to make. In a Kantian aesthetic judgment, we find a radical suspension of judgment masquerading as the exercise of autonomous judgment. This is no lapse or oversight, but characteristic of the very structure of aesthetic judgment in its most essential features, so much so that we should really speak of an aesthetic experience *rather than* an aesthetic judgment, an aesthetic experience whose defining quality is the experience of the recognition of my inability to judge in the face of the beautiful object. But if this is the case, then a significant puzzle remains, and it is to this puzzle that we must now turn our attention. Why is it that a text that had promised to establish the radical autonomy of judgment, its distinctiveness and irreducibility as a cognitive faculty, its remarkable capacity to bridge between the phenomenal and noumenal realms – why is it that this text takes as its exemplary instance of the practice of judgment a kind of judgment that is better described as a reflection on the failure of judgment? There must be something important at stake for Kant to risk ruining the project this way, as though he had said: I will show you how judgment can achieve all these remarkable things, but only on the condition that you promise to refrain from judging.

I believe something very important indeed is at stake in Kant's otherwise incomprehensible decision to rewrite judgment as the suspension of judgment, namely freedom itself. Or at least a certain conception of freedom that I will hazard to call liberal. Given his understanding of freedom, Kant can construe an act of judgment only as a loss or sacrifice of freedom rather than the fulfilment of freedom. Judgment, on this view, means determination, constraint, limitation, and the closing off of possibilities and potentials. In order to remain free, then, one must refrain from judging, and it is this freedom that aesthetic judgment preserves and affirms in the free play of faculties. Kant's recourse to the idea of "free play," his characterization of the aesthetic attitude as one in which the mental faculties find themselves in free play, is not an accident or a felicitous metaphor: free play (only later will we be able to specify precisely the meaning of this term) names the kind of activity that most exhibits the qualities of freedom Kant prizes. And free play, we will find, is perhaps the only conceivable *activity* that can be undertaken without judgment; indeed, it *requires* the suspension of judgment in order to remain free; free play, almost by definition, is only free as long as the work of judgment does not intervene; it preserves its freedom by structuring itself in such a way as to inoculate us against the possibility of making judgments.

Our task is now clear. First, we must explore the extent to which freedom is at stake in Kant's account of aesthetic judgments, showing that liberal and aesthetic history are irreducibly intertwined through a shared conception of freedom. We must also be clear about the *type* of freedom aesthetic judgments exemplify. Second, we must understand how play, especially the peculiar activity called "free play," exhibits the features of freedom most salient to Kant. Third, we must explain why free play, as a condition of its freedom, renders judgment impossible. Only once we have made apparent how Kant's conception of freedom, realized as free play, requires the suspension of judgment will we be able to envision an alternative form of activity to free play, in which the work of judgment is the very manifestation and exercise of freedom rather than its betrayal.

Freedom's relationship to beauty in the third *Critique* is multifaceted and discloses itself in various ways. But it cannot be primarily the kind of freedom that is the concern of the second *Critique* and its conception of the moral law, namely freedom as autonomy or the capacity for self-legislation. That republican conception of freedom as giving the law to oneself – now deeply unfamiliar and counterintuitive to us – is precisely the one whose demise I am obliquely tracking here, and I will be defending *some* version of it in my own account of judgment. In the third *Critique,* Kant helps us understand one of the reasons why this conception of freedom has so fallen out of favour. The self-binding or self-constraint involved in giving oneself the law is easily misconstrued as a form of unfreedom, and this has been perhaps the strongest objection to it ever since: "For where the moral law speaks there is, objectively, no longer any free choice with regard to what is to be done."[52] I cannot respond to this objection now; my response will emerge as I outline an alternative to Kant's conception of free play below. For the moment, it is sufficient to note that some other conception of freedom must be at work in the third *Critique,* a freedom envisioned as more primordial than obedience to the moral law because it is a precondition of our capacity to obey any law whatsoever.

Freedom insinuates itself into nearly every aspect of aesthetic judgment, especially in the "Analytic of the Beautiful." No doubt the different senses of freedom in the "Analytic" are interconnected. I will not be concerned to disentangle them here. For my purposes, it is sufficient to recognize how much a certain constellation of freedoms guides Kant's conceptualization of beauty. At least three of the four "moments" of the judgment of taste that comprise the "Analytic" concern freedom in some fundamental way. The definition of the beautiful inferred from the third moment states that "**beauty** is the form of the **purposiveness** [*Form der Zweckmäßigkeit*] of an object, insofar as it is perceived in it **without representation of an end** [*ohne Vorstellung eines Zwecks*]."[53] This means that the beautiful object is *freed* from any orientation to a specific end. Even if the object does have such an end (Kant's example is the sexual organs of plants), we do not consider it when we make a judgment that the object is beautiful. Beauty is not the perfection of an object according to some standard of what it should be like but rather a liberation from teleological orientation altogether while nevertheless preserving the appearance of purposiveness or design.[54] To interpret "without" in the above definition as code for freedom may seem like overreach, but the language of freedom is Kant's. The kind of beauty that rigorously conforms to this definition Kant calls "free beauty [*freie Schönheit*]," and its freedom arises from that fact that it refuses to be subordinated to any conception of its end or purpose.[55] Freedom is a freedom *from* orientation toward any ends, not a freedom *in order to attain* particular ends: "Many birds (the parrot, the hummingbird, the bird of paradise) and a host of marine crustaceans are beauties in themselves, which are not attached to a determinate object in accordance with concepts regarding its end, but are free and please for themselves."[56] This is one of the reasons why natural objects are easier to judge as beautiful: they have not in any obvious way been intentionally created for a purpose. In the realm of human creations, it is those objects that "signify nothing [*bedeuten nichts*]," as Kant says,[57] that appear to exhibit no purpose even though they seem purposive, that can most easily be judged beautiful: wallpaper and musical fantasias.[58] If we judge an aesthetic object against some prior notion of what its purpose should be, we fail to make a pure aesthetic judgment because we restrict "the imagination, which is as it were *at play* in the observation of the shape [*die Freiheit der Einbildungskraft, die in Beobachtung der Gestalt gleichsam spielt*]."[59] The mere fact of being oriented toward a particular end is viewed as a restriction ("*eingeschränkt werden würde*"), a constraint on the imagination's freedom, a position that would be unthinkable to Aristotle, for example, for whom freedom was only meaningful in relation to the ends one might want to attain. Freedom is thus indubitably at issue in the third moment, and the meaning of freedom is liberation from any teleological orientation whatsoever. (Of course, it remains unclear what it would mean to *judge* an object at all in the absence of such an orientation, hinting at the problem Kant faces in conceiving aesthetic perception as a form of judgment. What judgment are we making here? Do we judge that the object – wallpaper, for example – has no purpose and therefore cannot be judged by us?) From the third moment, one can deduce that Kant's theory would not be hospitable to neoclassical conceptions of beauty that specify rules, however vague, that beautiful objects must satisfy (perfection, symmetry, harmony, unity in variety). There is a constitutively *anti-normative* tenor to Kant's aesthetic, since beautiful objects resist conforming to any conception of what they ought to be: free beauty "presupposes no concept of what the object ought to be [*setzt keinen Begriff von dem voraus, was der Gegenstand sein soll*]."[60] Freedom is as much a freedom from normative constraint as it is from ends-orientation. The refusal of rules and norms will become important below as we try to understand what Kant means by "free play."

Freedom is just as clearly at issue in the definition of the beautiful inferred from the first moment of the judgment of taste: "**Taste** is the faculty for judging an object or a kind of representation through a satisfaction or dissatisfaction **without any interest** [*ohne alles Interesse*]."[61] Once again, we are confronted by a "without" that signifies freedom, in this case freedom from desire or interest. Kant contrasts the disinterested satisfaction we take in beauty with two other kinds of satisfaction. The first is the kind of satisfaction we find in merely agreeable things. These things arbitrarily gratify the senses of this or that person, without our feeling compelled to claim that they should please everyone. For example, I may like the flavour of sugar while you prefer the taste of vinegar. The second is the kind of satisfaction we take in things that are (morally) good. In this case, we expect everyone to agree with our assessment, but this expectation has an objective basis unlike the case of the aesthetic, where the expectation of agreement can only be subjectively grounded. According to Kant, our liking for the agreeable and the good is connected with the *existence* of the objects they are associated with: we desire the agreeable or the good object.[62] The beautiful object, by contrast, pleases us simply by virtue of its form. We do not desire to consume it or to make it real; contemplation alone suffices. Aesthetic disinterest does not mean that we are uninterested by or emotionally disconnected from the object; the pleasure we take in the aesthetic object can be every bit as real and intense as the interested pleasures of the agreeable and the good. It means only that the pleasure is not connected to desire, that attention to aesthetic form is enough. Although the notion of aesthetic disinterest has been much maligned, it is important to securing the possibility of judgment both in the eighteenth century and beyond. Unlike Locke or Mandeville, for whom any judgment was simply conditioned by desire or self-interest, Kant discovers in the aesthetic the possibility for a judgment that is not merely a reflex of desire or interest. Such a judgment can still involve narrative commitments and an emotional orientation, but the cognitive work of judgment is not simply determined, short-circuited, or replaced by desire. It remains to be undertaken. Something like Kant's account of disinterest is essential to any theory of judgment, or else every putative judgment would just be a mask for some desire or interest, as the hermeneutics of suspicion claims. Disinterest names the capacity for self-transcendence that we see in Shaftesbury's "Soliloquy," the possibility for a buffer between desire and the determination of will, where the mediation of judgment takes place. If there is a problem with Kant's theory, it lies not in the aspiration to disinterest, but rather in the worry that disinterest as Kant conceives it can be secured only by refraining from judgment altogether.[63]

An aesthetic judgment, then, is undoubtedly *free* from interest in a loose sense, since it is without interest. But we must again wonder whether we are reading too much into this moment when we burden it with a strong discourse of freedom. However, here as elsewhere, the language of freedom is Kant's:

> Among all these three kinds of satisfaction only that of the taste for the beautiful is a disinterested and **free** satisfaction [*ein uninterresiertes und freies Wohlgefallen*]; for no interest, neither that of the senses nor that of reason, extorts approval ... An object of inclination and one that is imposed upon us by a law of reason for the sake of desire leave us no freedom [*lassen uns keine Freiheit*] to make anything into an object of pleasure ourselves. All interest presupposes a need or produces one; and as a determining ground of approval it no longer leaves the judgment on the object free [*läßt es das Urteil über den Gegenstand nicht mehr frei sein*].[64]

Aesthetic judgment is free judgment because it is not determined by some need or compulsion (and let us recall that it is precisely this freedom from determination, this refusal of a mechanical or algorithmic determination of judgment, that has drawn me and many others to Kant's account of aesthetic judgment). What is distinctive about an aesthetic judgment is that it frees us from the strictures of desire, that it exhibits the freedom of judgment as no other kind of judgment does. Aesthetic experience is perhaps best described as a free encounter with the sensible given in its alterity.[65]

I have so far explored the freedom implied in the first and third moments of the "Analytic of the Beautiful." Before I turn to the second moment and the free play of the faculties so characteristic of Kant's conception of aesthetic judgment, I want to note briefly a few other ways in which freedom manifests itself in the experience of beauty. First, my judgment about the beauty of an object, to be pure, cannot be coerced by the judgment of others. Although the aesthetic judgments of others demand or require the agreement of everyone,[66] my agreement or assent cannot be compelled.[67] I must judge the object for myself each time, freely. The community of aesthetic judgment is a community of autonomously judging subjects. Second, when making aesthetic judgments, the imagination must also be considered as free without being anarchic: "If one draws the conclusion from the above analyses, it turns out that everything flows from the concept of taste as a faculty for judging an object in relation to the **free lawfulness** of the imagination [*die freie Gesetzmäßigkeit der Einbildungskraft*]."[68] In an aesthetic judgment, the imagination ranges freely without being subjected to any law, but it nevertheless behaves lawfully, *as if* it were subjected to a law. It exhibits "a lawfulness without law."[69] In other words, freedom permeates nearly every aspect of aesthetic experience, as though the judgment of taste were uniquely revelatory of freedom, and in particular our freedom of judgment. The kind of freedom at issue here is not so much indeterminate as it is an experience of *determinability*: we recognize our *capacity* to determine the supersensible, thereby bridging between the determinacy of the phenomenal world and the indeterminacy of the noumenal world (a different kind of freedom). Aesthetic experience shows that we are able to act morally – shows us our freedom, in other words – without determining us toward any particular moral action. It is precisely this freedom at the heart of Kantian aesthetic experience that Schiller brings to light so well in his *Letters on the Aesthetic Education of Man*.

The freedom I most want to focus on here, however, is the freedom implied in the second moment of aesthetic judgment, not only because it is arguably the most central to Kant's account and the one that since Schiller has most influentially shaped our perceptions of the aesthetic, but also because I believe it can best elucidate the type of freedom Kant means to secure with aesthetic experience. As before, the definition of the beautiful that follows from the second moment appears innocuous and unburdened by anything so weighty as freedom: "That is **beautiful** which pleases universally without a concept [*ohne Begriff*]."[70] But we know by now to suspect that the "without" harbours the force of freedom: in the third *Critique*, freedom is without. Kant's discussion of the second moment confirms our suspicions. This time, however, it is not simply that the beautiful object is free from conceptual determination. Kant gives a more specific sense to this freedom when he observes that the freedom from conceptual determination in the beautiful results in the free play of the faculties: "The powers of cognition that are set into play [*ins Spiel gesetzt werden*] by this representation are hereby in a free play [*sind hiebei in einem freien Spiele*], since no determinate concept restricts [*einschränkt*] them to a particular rule of cognition."[71] Above, we have explored the precise technical meaning of this free play as a suspension of judgment. But now I want to pursue a different line of questioning. What does Kant mean by "play" here? Is it simply a felicitous metaphor that has captured the imagination of subsequent aesthetic thinkers, from Schiller and Morris to Huizinga and Victor Turner? Or is there a deeper significance to the evocation of play in the text, though Kant does not thematize it? How might play epitomize the freedom of beauty, and what might that teach us about its relationship to judgment?[72] In what sense might play be said to be free, especially since Kant seems to imply that there are kinds of play that are not free? It is not difficult to intuit what Kant means by the "free play of the imagination and the understanding," but addressing these questions will yield some unexpected insights about play and freedom and their relation to judgment.

Given the technical precision of Kant's language and his passion for definitions, it is disconcerting that he does not explain what is entailed by the metaphorics of play, and that he uncharacteristically resorts to other metaphorical language to describe the effects of free play, such as animation and enlivening, in this all-important section that he calls the "key to the critique of taste [*der Schlüssel zur Kritik des Geschmacks*]."[73] Yet there is no need to be mystified; one can easily guess at his meaning. At a first level, the "free play" of the faculties means simply that the cognitive powers of the imagination and understanding are not locked into a determinate relationship with one another. Rather than the gears of the mental apparatus meshing tightly, there is some "play" or "give" in the system.[74] The parts of the machine can move freely in relation to one another: the mind is in neutral, as I argued earlier. Although this explanation is sufficient to grasp Kant's metaphor, it relies on a colloquial and rather marginal sense of the word "play." One suspects that Kant means a good deal more when he describes the relation of the faculties as one of "free play." In aesthetic experience, it is as though we approach the world and even cognition itself playfully. We apprehend the beautiful object with the joy and delight of a child at play, thrilled by the activity of our own contemplation for no more reason than kittens have when they take delight in tussling with each other. We are engaged by the world, even enraptured by it, but simply for its own sake, without the usual purposes or interests that make our relationship to the world anything but playful: knowledge, consumption, moral action. For a brief moment, as we contemplate a beautiful object, we have the exhilarating sense that the world is our playground, that we can gambol in it freely, without being tied to the concerns that ordinarily burden our understanding of it. We soak in our representations of the world joyously, convinced that they have meaning, but without worrying about what exactly they might mean. In aesthetic contemplation, it feels as though the mind sets aside the serious work of cognition and allows itself to play imaginatively and delightedly with its representations. It is no wonder, then, that Schiller spoke of a "play drive" as a fundamental orientation to the world when popularizing Kant's aesthetics.[75]

I have described Kantian aesthetic experience loosely and analogically as playful. But I want to make a stronger and more precise claim, that the activity involved in aesthetic perception *is* play at its purest. As a form of activity, it exhibits many of the salient characteristics of play and may even be the activity that comes closest to being pure play, if there is such a thing. When Kant describes the relationship of the faculties as one of free play, he is not importing a metaphor from a different domain (the anthropology of childhood) to understand aesthetic experience. Rather, it is as though he is trying to grasp the essence and distinctiveness of play through his account of the aesthetic and to grasp the aesthetic as the essence of play. As activities, aesthetic appreciation and free play are nearly indistinguishable.

What characterizes play as an activity? The freedom of play tends to be viewed as one of its indispensable distinguishing characteristics. If I am made to play under some kind of compulsion, I may go through the outward motions of playing, but I cannot actually be said to be playing. Just as I cannot be forced to make an aesthetic judgment based on the perceptions of others but must recognize the object as beautiful for myself, so I cannot be forced to play without destroying the playfulness of the play experience. I must consent to play, or else I am not playing at all, even though I may be doing something that looks like play:[76] "Play is superfluous … Play can be deferred or suspended at any time. It is never imposed by physical necessity or moral duty. It is never a task. It is done at leisure, during 'free time' … Here, then, we have the first main characteristic of play: that it is free, is in fact freedom."[77] Playing is not just performing a set of actions, but doing so in an attitude of playfulness.[78] Indispensable to this attitude is that I do not play out of some sense of need, compulsion, or obligation, which makes playfulness resemble closely the Kantian aesthetic attitude of disinterest or freedom from interest. To say I play freely, it would seem, is very nearly a tautology. Given that play epitomizes free activity, it is not surprising that Kant reaches intuitively for the language of play to grasp the freedom so integral to aesthetic cognition.

However, play is free not only in the sense of being undertaken voluntarily, but also in a number of the more precise, technical senses we found in aesthetic judgment. Indeed, the extent to which play recapitulates the diverse array of freedoms found in the Kantian aesthetic is striking. Let us trace the most important of these. We judge aesthetic objects as though they are liberated from the constraint of having to serve particular ends. They appear to be designed, intentional, purposive, and yet they are without a specifiable purpose. Play is precisely the activity that models this purposiveness without purpose. Play activity is certainly intentional, organized, purposive. It is directed toward something, toward sustaining play itself. And yet play has no discernible purpose beyond play. It is, in the larger context of a life, without a point, and indeed it must be in order to qualify as play: "Playfulness frees us from the dictates of purpose through the carnivalesque inheritance of play. Through playful appropriation, we bring freedom to a context."[79] We are supposed to indulge in play for its own sake, just as we appreciate art for its own sake. And conversely, when games are perceived as morally threatening, it is often for the same reason, that they usurp our purposive orientation for pointless activity. "Stop playing (or leave aside the arts) and do something useful," might be the rebuke that accompanies this attitude. If the activity of play seems to be useless or without a point, this is also what allows it to become exemplary of non-instrumental forms of action.[80] Play's resistance to instrumentalization arises partly because of the absence of a purpose to guide its activity. At its most general, instrumental thought is characterized by a coordination of means to end, so without a specified end in view, it is impossible for play to be instrumental, though it can always be instrumentalized for external ends such as commercial gain. But play is non-instrumental in the more precise Kantian sense that we noted above: it offers a satisfaction unconnected with interest. Fun is vital to the play experience, but it is not an enjoyment that derives from knowledge, consumption, or bringing the good into existence. Play is exemplary of activity that is disinterested, that desires nothing beyond itself.[81] Another way of describing the anti-instrumentality of play, though this is not the same thing, would be to say that play is autotelic.[82] It is its own end, or has its own end within it, rather than having an end imposed on it from elsewhere, just like aesthetic cognition is an activity that, because it is disinterested, is its own end.[83]

I noted earlier that Kantian aesthetics tends to construe freedom as a freedom from norms. Because there is no concept to which the beautiful object must correspond, no rules or standards can serve as a measure for beauty, and aesthetic production must not be governed by a set of pregiven norms. The beautiful object is not a sensuous manifestation of perfection, harmony, symmetry, or any of the other criteria that traditionally served to define beauty.[84] This is one of the reasons why, for Kant, there cannot be a metaphysics corresponding to the third *Critique* as there is for each of the other two. There is no doctrine of the beautiful because the beautiful, by its very definition, resists doctrinal specification.[85] Kant famously marks the turn away from neoclassical aesthetics and its rule-bound or norm-governed vision of art. After Kant, from romanticism to modernism and beyond, it becomes almost commonplace to view the aesthetic object as that which challenges, resists, undermines, or unsettles previous norms or rules of art, leading to an endless logic of novelty and disruption in aesthetic production. As soon as the refusal of norms guides aesthetic production, novelty becomes the only enduring criterion, the value without value against which aesthetic objects are to be judged.

Likewise, play, even though it can be highly structured and organized, is often valued for its potential to challenge, disrupt, and unsettle norms.[86] Because play is by its nature free, it is often thought to be at odds with the rules that constitute it,[87] and a playful attitude is not one of subservience to rules but one that ironizes, reworks, or even undermines the rules. For Sicart, "players of a game are playful when they consciously manipulate the relative rigidity of the system."[88] There is similarly a strongly anti-normative cast to Turner's conception of play as it manifests itself in liminal and liminoid spaces, producing novelty, liberating human potentials, and unsettling fixed structures through ludic recombination.[89] Freedom here is nearly indistinguishable from the refusal of normative constraint, and this freedom comes into view only through play.[90] Play, then, inasmuch as it is the paradigm of free behaviour that can serve to challenge norms, is an especially apt description of the cognitive activity underlying Kantian aesthetic perception. Play is not simply a metaphor or analogy deployed from another domain of human activity in order to elucidate our rarified experience of beauty. Rather, it would be more appropriate to say that the activity of aesthetic cognition exhibits or instantiates play in its purest form. In Kant's view, we are never more at play than when we are looking at a beautiful object. The freedom of play is the gift of beauty.

The reader will have noticed that my presentation of play is somewhat strained, opening itself to a number of objections and counterexamples. This is perhaps clearest when I describe the anti-normative character of play, since it is obvious that so many games are rule-bound and fit the anti-normative characterization only awkwardly, or when I vacillate about whether play is autotelic or purposive without purpose, since so many games clearly have goals and purposes. The account of play I have given is not wrong exactly, but it represents one particular tendency within the literature on play, namely the desire to find and value in play precisely the kind of anti-instrumental freedom that Kant describes in the third *Critique*, the understanding of freedom that we have more or less inherited. It will be easiest to grasp what might be inadequate about this conception of freedom if we ask ourselves again, after all this discussion of play as the paradigm for the activity of aesthetic cognition: What does Kant mean by play? What kind of game might he have in mind when he speaks of the "free play" of the faculties? Is there a game that satisfies all the requirements of free play enumerated above? Would we even know how to play it?

These questions bring us to a surprising realization. Even though the activity of aesthetic perception may be the purest form of play, *there is in fact no game that can satisfy the stringent requirements of free play*, if by "game" we mean a structured form of play with rules and objectives, the kind of play we most often indulge in and are most likely to call to mind when speaking about playing.[91] There are many reasons for this. While games may not be purposive within the larger context of human life, they have objectives. As soon as there is a purpose, even one that is purely internal to the game and without import for the rest of life, then the activity of playing the game becomes purposive. I want to score points or keep the ball in the air as long as possible or checkmate the king. Games may give us exemplary instances of autotelic activity, but this activity is purposive *with* a purpose, not merely "as if purposive," as required by Kant's definition of purposiveness without purpose. By the same logic, as soon as there is a goal to the game, playing it cannot be said to be disinterested in Kant's sense. Our activity aims at bringing about a "good," albeit one that is defined only by the arbitrary stipulations of the game. Indeed, games combine, in a surprising way, the interested pleasures of the agreeable and the good, since games have an internal standard of excellence (akin to morality) but one that is entirely arbitrary and can make no universal claims on anyone beyond the community of those who play (akin to the sensory pleasures of the agreeable).[92] Similarly, if a game acquires its structure, cohesion, and even identity only by the rules that define it, then playing a game must involve a voluntary subservience to the norms that make the game what it is. Even the cheat acknowledges these norms and appears to abide by them, while exploiting the difficulties of enforcement for advantage. Only the spoilsport – the one who refuses to play and whose refusal exposes the fictionality of the game – escapes the normative constraint of the rules. They can do this by simply granting no authority to the normative claims embedded within the rules.[93]

I appear to have contradicted myself. First, I argued that play offered the exemplary instantiation of the freedom characteristic of aesthetic cognition: play is voluntary, purposive without purpose, anti-instrumental, anti-normative. Then I showed that no game could satisfy the requirements of "free play" as Kant understands it. Games, insofar as they are defined by their rules and objectives, are characterized by constraint, normativity, and purpose-driven activity, the antithesis of the freedom that exhibits itself in aesthetic experience. But there is no contradiction here. I have simply exploited an oddity of English in order to highlight a conceptual distinction that is often elided but crucial for understanding what Kant means by "free play." In English, even though one can speak of "playing a game," one can also readily draw a *distinction* between play and games. However, the distinction, though perhaps easier to make in English than, say, German or French (*das Spiel/spielen, le jeu/jouer*), is not just an artefact of language; it is conceptual rather than merely linguistic.[94] Games and free or pure play are both activities that fall within the broader rubric of play, and both are studied together in the literature on play. They are voluntary activities undertaken for fun, outside the normal instrumental pressures of ordinary life. From this perspective, they are both free activities. But games are structured by a more or less explicit set of rules and objectives, whereas play is a free-form, loosely structured activity usually not directed to discernible ends at all, other than the fun of playing itself. It is precisely play in this latter sense *and not games* that Kant must mean when he describes the activity of the faculties as "free play." To understand why, it is necessary to explore the distinction between games and play more fully.

One can easily find examples of games. Think of chess, tennis, bridge, or the many video games that have so suddenly come to pervade our youth culture.[95] It is much more difficult if not impossible to find examples of what we might call "pure play," play that has not been structured into some form of game with rules, objectives, and norms. If we try to imagine what such play could be, it would have to be something like children running around a playground for the sheer joy of it, before that running has been structured into even the most rudimentary game, like tag, before they're even aware that they're running "for" joy. Or we might imagine young animals tussling with each other for sheer pleasure, simply indulging in the activity with no other end in view and no rules to bind them.[96] These are the kinds of activities, barely imaginable as they are, that qualify as "free play" in Kant's sense; no other kind of activity that I know meets the stringent criteria required for something to count as free play, not even games. Above all, if we are looking for an activity that is purposive without purpose, then pure play is nearly the only kind of activity that fits this description. As an activity, it is undoubtedly purposive, but since we have posited that this play has no structure or goal, it is just as clearly without purpose. Animals wrestling or children running are the cinematic equivalent of Kant's wallpaper, arabesques, and musical fantasias, lines and patterns that whirl around without end, signifying nothing.[97] Similarly, such play, by definition, makes no normative claims on its participants; it instantiates, as nothing else could, the kind of activity that has been radically freed from norms. There are no rules to play by in this play that is before or beyond games. There is no "should" to running around playfully on a playground. Finally, such play can be described as disinterested, as the playing of games cannot, because it is not interested in bringing about some good, discovering some knowledge, or consuming any object. Only this elusive ideal of pure play, the merest activity of playing without any aim or purpose whatsoever – not tagging someone out or capturing the king in chess or scoring points in a basketball game – only this play without games can model for us the activity of the cognitive faculties when they are in "free play." Or, given the difficulty of imagining such play in its pure form, perhaps we should say that aesthetic cognition gives us the only example, the inimitable example, of pure free play, the untainted activity of playing before it has been organized into anything like a game.

It is not by accident that we reach for the example of children when trying to imagine Kant's elusive ideal of free play. Of course, play in the broad sense (encompassing both games and pure play) is usually associated with children and childhood. Children play games, just as they engage in free play. But adults play games too. What is much harder to picture is an adult engaging in pure play. Because pure play is possible only in the absence of any structure or organization, it requires us to postulate a form of free and purposive activity that precedes the trappings of culture, and perhaps even the advent of language. Otherwise, it is difficult to avoid at least some minimal organization of activity.

Children, in this imagined schema, are able to play purely only before culture and language have taken hold; they play purely only as long as they have not learned any games.[98] It is the youngest children, in their most unorganized forms of activity, that give us some insight into the possibility of free play. One can thus detect a latent Rousseauvianism in Kant's idealization of free play as the paradigmatic instance of free activity. It is almost as though aesthetic cognition allows us a return, in a purer way, to a childlike encounter with the givenness of the world, before cultural mediation had contaminated the view with the structures, goals, and norms that we associate with ordinary life. Children play at those rare and unimaginable moments when their activity is not directed toward any ends, before they have internalized any social norms, and they remain free only for as long as they can do so. It is not the transition from play to work, then, that would signal maturation and the acquisition of culture.[99] Rather, internal to the broader rubric of playing, it is the transition from pure play to games that marks very precisely the "fall" into culture.[100]

Thus, although the notion of "free play" is hardly elaborated in the third *Critique*, its underlying structure can be gleaned from the other claims Kant makes about aesthetic judgments: free play is the rudimentary play of children before it has been organized into any form of game. Not only does this idealized "free play" govern Kant's understanding of the activity of aesthetic perception, but it would not be difficult to show that something like this idea of play as the paradigm of free activity has guided radical political imaginaries of many different stripes since Kant, from Schiller's use of play to conceive an unalienated relation to the state and Morris's utopian dream of unalienated playful labour to Huizinga's deployment of play as a counter to Schmitt's conception of politics and Derrida's portrayal of play and the dance as figures of emancipation.[101] This vision of play – so temptingly radical in its conception of freedom – appears elusive, even impossible, yet if it holds out the promise of a freedom more profound than anything else we can imagine, why should we not pursue it with all the resources at our disposal? If play is the model for a free, unalienated, non-instrumental, joyful engagement with social life, why should it not serve as the foundation of our utopian aspirations, as it so often has? The problem is not, as one might suspect, that this vision is impossible, that it cannot be achieved in practice or is forever receding, that its freedom is too unworldly, ethereal, or elusive for practical purposes. Although it is true that this freedom is difficult to achieve in its purity, the free play of children approximates it well enough to serve as a model. If this vision of freedom is the wrong one for politics, it is for a different set of reasons entirely. Anyone who has watched children engaging in such play for any length of time knows that unstructured play that has not been organized into a game cannot hold our interest for long; it is not just disinterested but uninteresting. As essential as child's play is for the development of children (and there can be no doubt about this),[102] it is intensely boring to watch and frustrating to engage in, since there seems to be nothing to do or no point to doing it. If this is what it means to be free, why would we even want it? Lest it be thought that I am simply not creative enough to imagine the uses to which such freedom can be put, let me remind the reader that this freedom is only free *because and for as long as* it refuses to be directed toward any ends. That is the meaning of freedom as it is conceived here, and the notion of free play, play without purpose or end, was constructed precisely to give body to this ideal of freedom. Above all, there is no better way to understand why Kant's notion of aesthetic perception demands the complete suspension of judgment than to concretize this activity as free or pure play. Since this playful activity is playful but without purpose or orientation, there are simply no judgments to be made. If you are just running around on a playground having fun, what judgments could you be called on to make? What would necessitate or require judgment? What would you judge about, and what ends would you judge your activity in relation to? All you have to do is enjoy, indulge, appreciate. Pure play is the model for purposive activity purged of judgment.[103] Conceiving activity as free play makes judgment impossible not by forbidding or disallowing it but by making sure that there is no call to judge. Only free play allows us to imagine a kind of activity radically freed from the need for judgment. On this model, freedom and judgment are not complementary but antithetical to one another. Freedom is not the enabling condition of judgment, and judgment is not the fulfilment of freedom. Rather, freedom can lie only in the complete suspension of judgment. As soon as we introduce judgment, purpose, and orientation, freedom itself will have been lost. This freedom can be instantiated by the free play of children for as long as they refuse the rules and objectives that both require and give salience to judgment. Freedom can be enjoyed, appreciated, indulged in for its own sake, but it cannot be determined or actualized through judgment. It is this freedom that is flamboyantly on display in aesthetic judgment, a freedom that is free only as long as it commits itself to no purpose or objective whatsoever. It is a freedom that preserves itself as pure potentiality, refusing to actualize itself for fear of compromising its essence as freedom. On this conception, as soon as children begin to play a game that has objectives and calls on them to make judgments, they have surrendered their freedom for bondage to rules and purposes. *Now, it is precisely to avoid such an untenable consequence – namely, the equation of judgment and ends-orientation with unfreedom – that we need a conception of freedom that is not allergic to judgment but embraces it.* Freedom conceived as free play must not be allowed to serve as a foundation for a liberal, emancipatory, or radical politics, since it can never amount to more than the mind-numbing utopia of children running around on a playground.

I have judged the playing of children rather harshly. But much of what I say about the lack of interest in children's games can be confirmed by scholarship on play. Huizinga's study purports to begin where the play of animals and children leaves off,[104] and Elias, Garfield, and Gutschera explain that they will "exclude the games without formal rules that very small children play (e.g., 'playing house' or swinging)."[105] The reason for the exclusion is undoubtedly that there is very little one can say about such play, just as there is little interpretation to be done in the case of Kant's wallpaper and flowers. Since pure play has almost no structure and by definition is without a purpose, one cannot search for strategies of play or modes of judgment. Any description of such play is likely to amount to a literary version of Kant's arabesques or musical fantasias. It is not surprising, then, that writing on play, when it chooses examples, tends to focus on games rather than the free play of children. *And yet, paradoxically, the underlying conceptuality that guides its valorization of play tends to be the notion of "free play" in the Kantian sense,* along with the freedom from purpose, anti-normativity, disinterest, and anti-instrumentality that accompanies it. The idealized conception of the free play of children more or less explicitly shapes the understanding of play and the terms in which it is valued, even though games are the focus of the studies and these only awkwardly fit the description of free play. Thus, Huizinga explicitly declares that "child-play possesses the play-form in its veriest essence, and most purely," even as he begins his study where child's play leaves off.[106] It is this peculiarity of scholarship on play – its simultaneous idealization and bracketing of child's play – that allowed me to use it to elucidate Kant's conception of free play, even though this literature mostly discusses games, which cannot be assimilated to the underlying notion of free play. Even though Huizinga and others are aware of the distinctiveness of child's play and its difference from games, that distinction tends to get elided to the extent that games are grasped through the framing conceptuality of free play, which is inadequate to them in important ways.[107] By and large, it is games, not "free play," that are interesting to us, and they demand a different mode of accounting than the logic of "free play" we have uncovered in the third *Critique*.

The alternative to "free play," then, and its rendering impossible of any practice of judgment as a condition of freedom should not be some austere and puritanical notion of work as ends-oriented activity. We need to envision a form of activity that combines the relevant freedoms of play with the ends-orientation characteristic of work, instead of being forced to choose between these, so that judgment can be free and yet directed toward ends. Kant's conception of free play excludes from consideration all games that posit any purpose or objective, *but what if it is precisely games and not play that offer us the paradigm for a freedom that is not allergic to judgment?* Unlike free play – where judgment is rendered impossible, where it does not even make sense to speak in terms of judgments – games of a certain complexity, with their rules and objectives, generate what we might call "structures of judgment" or heuristics,[108] at the same time as playing a game is always something one does freely if it is still to be called "playing." There is no reason to think that operating within a structure of judgment is determined or unfree simply because objectives and constraints on how to achieve those objectives have been specified in advance. Properly considered, freedom is at stake in multiple ways when we engage in the activity of playing games. There is the freedom to make the rules of the game, and the freedom involved in assenting to play. There is the freedom to change the rules of the game. But most importantly, and internal to the game, there is the freedom to choose strategies to achieve the objectives of the game, as long as the game is sufficiently complex that there can be reasonable disagreement about the most appropriate way to reach the goals of the game.[109] Games require us to make judgments with a view to the end, but that does not make them unfree, because they do not *dictate* the judgments we must make. The freedom to make judgments is meaningful only insofar as we choose to realize it in the making of a decision. The one who refuses to make judgments for fear of compromising their freedom is less the aesthete engaging in free play than the spoilsport who refuses to play the game. But of course, that is a game they can always choose to play.

Rules specify the conditions and constraints under which judgment must be exercised, while objectives specify the ends toward which judgment must be oriented. Neither determines in advance the means to the end. Rather than constraining one's freedom, they give judgment its meaning, orientation, and purpose. Without rules and objectives, there is no conceivable point to engaging in judgment. It is precisely the task of judgment to discern the appropriate means to the end within the constraints of the rules of the game.[110] Think once again of tennis or chess. The rules for the game are rather simple and easy to teach, and the objectives clear and well defined. There are rote techniques one can be taught to improve one's game (openings or endgame techniques in chess, the various strokes in tennis). But ultimately, learning to play the game well requires the development of good judgment that cannot be taught but only learned by playing the game over many years.[111] Every move in the game requires the exercise of judgment about the appropriate strategy, the psychology of one's opponent, one's situation in the narrative arc of the game, the "feel" of the board or court, and the style of play best suited to one's temperament. Unlike free play, whose value lies in the complete freedom from judgment it makes possible, the fun and challenge of playing a game lies in the exercise of judgment founded on long experience, not in the withholding or avoidance of judgment. Indeed, just as free play makes judgment inconceivable within its space, it is impossible to imagine how one could play a game like tennis or chess *without* using one's judgment. When we say of someone who is playing a game like this that they have no judgment, we mean that they judge poorly, not that they play without judgment. To refuse to judge altogether would be to refuse to play the game. If we want to imagine a model of judgment freed from the usual pejorative connotations of judging such as condemnation, prejudice, discrimination, and above all the constriction of freedom and possibility, we should look to the experience of playing games. A phenomenology of game-playing has much to teach us about the value and necessity of judgment, its freedom, its orientation toward ends, the importance of experience for judgment, and ultimately how we learn to judge and how we develop habits of judgment.

I have been arguing that the logic of "free play" in Kant's text and the underlying notion of freedom to which it gives expression help us understand how and why aesthetic "judgment" so assiduously avoids any judgment. If Kant's text is symptomatic of a wider allergy to judgment that characterizes a variety of contemporary aesthetic and political formations,[112] then what I am suggesting here is that modelling our understanding of freedom on the freedom to *create and play* games rather than on the indeterminate freedom found in "free play" can teach us how to restore a robust understanding of judgment to our aesthetic and our political practices, ensuring that we recognize judgment as indispensable for the actualization of freedom rather than as a lamentable limitation, abdication, or even betrayal of our freedom.

NOTES

1 See Arendt, *Lectures on Kant's Political Philosophy*.
2 See Soni, "Communal Narcosis."
3 See Schmitt, *Crisis of Parliamentary Democracy*; Strauss, *Natural Right and History*, 6.
4 On the importance of this open-ended hermeneutic mode for constituting a middle-class subjectivity in the Romantic period, see Pfau, *Wordsworth's Profession*.
5 See Arendt, *Lectures on Kant's Political Philosophy*; Zerilli, "'We Feel Our Freedom'" and "Democratic Theory of Judgment."
6 I will not be taking up the problem of historicism explicitly, but a number of theorists have made the case that certain forms of historicism elide judgment. See Pfau, *Minding the Modern*, 35–52; Arendt, *Lectures on Kant's Political Philosophy*, 5; Arendt, *On Revolution*, 40–52; Strauss, *Natural Right and History*; Berlin, "Historical Inevitability."
7 See especially Pocock, *Machiavellian Moment*.
8 But for a thoroughgoing account of the German rationalist tradition of aesthetics before Kant, see Beiser, *Diotima's Children*.
9 See Locke, *Essay Concerning Human Understanding*, 233.
10 See Shaftesbury, "*Sensus Communis*."
11 Addison and Steele, *Spectator* 413, 720–1; Hutcheson, *Inquiry*, 46–60, 76, 79. For a detailed account of debates in the period about the argument from design and the purposiveness of nature, and especially Kant's innovations in this regard, see Loesberg, *Return to Aesthetics*, 14–73. See also Zuckert, *Kant on Beauty and Biology*, 36, 79.
12 Shaftesbury, "*Sensus Communis*," 70.
13 Hutcheson, *Inquiry*, 8–9, 23–4.
14 See Arendt, *Lectures on Kant's Political Philosophy*, 4, 10.
15 Kant, *Critique of Judgment*, 5: 211. Hereafter abbreviated *CJ* and cited by the pagination of the standard German edition of Kant's works (volume

and page number) provided in the margins of the Cambridge edition. The German is supplied from Kant, *Werke*. All boldface type is in the original.

16 See Soni, "Can Aesthetics Overcome Instrumental Reason?"

17 Sandel documents the persistence of such arguments today. See Sandel, *What Money Can't Buy*.

18 Arendt, "Thinking and Moral Considerations," 188.

19 Kant, *CJ*, 5: 179.

20 Kant, "First Introduction," in *CJ*, 20: 211.

21 Against those who find the question of reflective judgment tangential to the *Critique* and those who see little in common between aesthetic and teleological judgments, Ginsborg, Pippin, and Zuckert have argued for the unity of the third *Critique*'s project. See Ginsborg, "Reflective Judgment and Taste"; Pippin, "Significance of Taste"; Zuckert, *Kant on Beauty and Biology*.

22 Kant, *CJ*, 5: 185–6; "First Introduction" in *CJ*, 20: 225.

23 Kant, *CJ*, 5: 215.

24 See Soni, "Communal Narcosis."

25 Kant, *CJ*, 5: 236.

26 Arendt, *Lectures on Kant's Political Philosophy*, 4, 10.

27 See, for example, Zerilli, "Toward a Democratic Theory of Freedom"; Makkreel, *Imagination and Interpretation in Kant*, 4–5, 128, 154, 167, 170; Zuckert, *Kant on Beauty and Biology*, 11. Even Longuenesse's study, which is largely concerned with judgment in the first *Critique*, makes the reflective judgments of the third *Critique* central to her account (*Kant and the Capacity to Judge*, 112, 163–4).

28 Longuenesse, who has given us the most detailed and sustained account of Kant's complex thinking about judgment, makes the point forthrightly, though she does not dwell on it. For her, reflective judgments, which are first identified as such in the third *Critique*, are already at work in the first *Critique*, in combination with determinative judgments. What distinguishes the judgments discussed in the third *Critique* is that they are *merely* reflective, without any determinative component (*Kant and the Capacity to Judge*, 163–4). About these, she says: "What makes judgments *merely* reflective is that in them, the effort of the activity of judgment to form concepts *fails*" (164). Although other commentators are not as explicit about the failure of judgment in aesthetic perception, they invariably point to the inconclusiveness and indeterminacy that characterize aesthetic judgment. See Pippin, "Significance of Taste," 554, 556; Burnham, *Kant's Philosophies of Judgment*, 154, 160, 165; Ginsborg, "Aesthetic Judging," 169; Zuckert, *Kant on Beauty and Biology*, 66. Failure is more often associated

with the sublime than the beautiful. See Burnham, *Kant's Philosophies of Judgment*, 193; de Man, *Aesthetic Ideology*, 75.

29 Menke, "Aesthetic Practice."

30 Kant's insight about the inward turn involved in aesthetic experience is confirmed by Starr's recent neuroscientific experiments (*Feeling Beauty*). She has discovered that the default mode network – the part of the brain most involved with our sense of self and inwardness, with "self-referential thought" and "'internal modes of cognition'" (62) – is surprisingly engaged in the most intense aesthetic experiences (57–62, 65). Her descriptions even point to the suspension of judgment involved in aesthetic perception: "Powerful aesthetic experience makes us return to that state of watchful waiting characteristic of core consciousness" (66).

31 Kant, *CJ*, 5: 203.

32 Ibid., 238.

33 See Zuckert, *Kant on Beauty and Biology*, 3. Carnes argues that the turn away from the object is a feature of eighteenth-century aesthetics more generally. See Carnes, *Beauty*, 19, 22.

34 See Soni, "Introduction," 278–9.

35 Kant, *CJ*, 5: 218.

36 Although she does not use Kant's notion of "free play," Starr's neuroscientific research appears to confirm the idea of aesthetic perception as a zero degree of cognition (*Feeling Beauty*, 59, 66). See also Makkreel, *Imagination and Interpretation in Kant*, 62, 95; Allison's description of free play, quoted in Ginsborg, "Aesthetic Judging," 169.

37 Kant, *CJ*, 5: 219.

38 Ibid., 237.

39 Schiller, *Letters*, 149.

40 Kant, *CJ*, 5: 208; 5: 285; see also "First Introduction" in *CJ*, 20: 224.

41 Kant, *CJ*, 5: 287.

42 See Pippin, "Significance of Taste," 568.

43 Kant, *CJ*, section 9, 5: 216-19; see also "First Introduction," 20: 224–5. On the question of how pleasure relates to judgment in aesthetic cognition, see especially Ginsborg, "Aesthetic Judging"; Pippin, "Significance of Taste." There is significant debate on this question. Ginsborg explains that Guyer and Allison view aesthetic pleasure as preceding judgment ("Aesthetic Judging," 166). She and Aquila argue that the pleasure and judgment are simultaneous, even indistinguishable ("Aesthetic Judging," 166, 175; "Reflective Judgment and Taste," 73–4). See also Burnham, *Kant's Philosophies of Judgment*, 174. While acknowledging the temptation to see aesthetic pleasure as immediate, Pippin makes a strong case for the

coherence of Kant's claim that pleasure follows judgment and explains how it is possible to make sense of this position ("Significance of Taste," 260). See also Makkreel's complex description of what happens during free play (*Imagination and Interpretation in Kant*, 56).

44 Henrich, *Aesthetic Judgment*, 42.

45 See Zerilli, "'We Feel Our Freedom,'" 177. Zerilli's essay reconstructs Arendt's incomplete account of judgment. Although I am sympathetic to many aspects of this account, Arendt's reliance on Kant means that she replicates a number of the problems I am diagnosing here, in particular the retreat into self-reflexivity (164), the loss of an orientation toward ends (174, 177), and the loss of the object of judgment (175).

46 Kant, *CJ*, 5: 219. Both Burnham and Makkreel argue that the language of life in the third *Critique* is not merely metaphorical but conceptually significant for the argument. See Burnham, *Kant's Philosophies of Judgment*, 149–203; Makkreel, *Imagination and Interpretation in Kant*, 88–107. Indeed, for Makkreel, "aesthetic harmony is the feeling of life at its purest" (92), and "the idea of life does play a transcendental role in Kant's aesthetics" (106).

47 Kant, *CJ*, page 361, note 24. See also Makkreel, *Imagination and Interpretation in Kant*, 91.

48 Pippin notes the tendency to read the free play of the faculties this way, but argues against this position ("Significance of Taste," 561). However, even if Pippin's interpretation is correct, the suspension of judgment in aesthetic cognition is apparent in other ways that Pippin grants (554, 556).

49 Kant, *CJ*, 5: 236.

50 A number of commentators have argued that a key contribution of the third *Critique* is to show how we find our orientation in the world, both practical and existential, prior to any epistemological investigation. See Pippin, "Significance of Taste," 569; Zuckert, *Kant on Beauty and Biology*, 12, 14; Makkreel, *Imagination and Interpretation in Kant*, 159; Burnham, *Kant's Philosophies of Judgment*, 28, 41. I am sympathetic to these almost Heideggerian interpretations of the task of the *Critique*. However, if the failure or suspension of judgment in aesthetic perception is as radical as I suggest, then one must wonder whether the project can succeed and whether the orientation provided amounts to any orientation at all or rather a recognition of radical disorientation. This would seem to be confirmed in the descriptions that suggest that we are being oriented to an open and indeterminate future (which, I would add, *must* not acquire determinacy if our judgments are to remain pure). See Zuckert, *Kant on Beauty and Biology*, 10, 16; Burnham, *Kant's Philosophies of Judgment*, 146,

154, 165; Makkreel, *Imagination and Interpretation in Kant*, 153, 169. Derrida ("Economimesis," 14) and Loesberg (*Return to Aesthetics*, 112) make similar points.

51 Kant, *CJ*, 5: 207; 5: 229.

52 Ibid., 210.

53 Ibid., 236.

54 On this question, see Loesberg, *Return to Aesthetics*, 51, 65; Zuckert, *Kant on Beauty and Biology*, 17, 36–42, 85.

55 Kant, *CJ*, 5: 229.

56 Ibid. Makkreel prefers the example of crystals (*Imagination and Interpretation in Kant*, 64). See also Loesberg, *Return to Aesthetics*, 105.

57 Kant, *CJ*, 5: 229.

58 On this point, see Loesberg, *Return to Aesthetics*, 67–8.

59 Kant, *CJ*, 5: 230, my emphasis.

60 Ibid., 229.

61 Ibid., 211.

62 See Loesberg, *Return to Aesthetics*, 75, 91; Makkreel, *Imagination and Interpretation in Kant*, 91.

63 For a recent critique of aesthetic disinterest (and functionalism in aesthetics), see Carnes, *Beauty*, 45–60. She offers the theological categories of fittingness and gratuity in their stead.

64 Kant, *CJ*, 5: 210.

65 On the way that reflection can stage an encounter with the sensible given, see Burnham, *Kant's Philosophies of Judgment*, 82–3, 108. But for him, the sublime is the site of this encounter (203). See also de Man, *Aesthetic Ideology*, 80–2, 88–9. He similarly locates the encounter with materiality in the sublime. One might also deduce this point from Longuenesse in *Kant and the Capacity to Judge*. Her study is mostly concerned with judgment in the first *Critique*, and particularly the importance of the logical forms of judgment for the deduction of the categories. For her, judgment is about how the discursive forms of the understanding can be brought to the sensible given (79, 106, 107–30). But since we know this process fails in merely reflective judgments (164), we must be left with a primordial encounter with the sensible given.

66 Kant, *CJ*, 5: 216.

67 Ibid., 215.

68 Ibid., 240.

69 Ibid., 241.

70 Ibid., 219.

71 Ibid., 217.

72 Murdoch observes the link between the freedom of beauty and the freedom of play in Kant (*Existentialists and Mystics*, 209).

73 Kant, *CJ*, 5: 216.

74 On this meaning of play and its association with freedom, see Caillois, *Man, Play and Games*, 8.

75 Schiller, *Letters*, 127. For scholars of play like Huizinga (*Homo Ludens*), Turner (*From Ritual to Theatre*), and Sicart (*Play Matters*), more important than individual games is the attitude of playfulness, which orients us to the world. As I noted above, contemporary scholars also view Kant's third *Critique* as concerned with the problem of existential orientation, revealing the deep shared concerns of play and aesthetics.

76 As the language of consent shows, play can model in microcosm the problems of the social contract and what it means to participate in a political community. Although much work has been done to "politicize" the aesthetic, it is explicit in Shaftesbury and Schiller (and very nearly so in Kant) that play and the aesthetic are understood as solutions to the aporias of foundation in the social contract. See Shaftesbury, "*Sensus Communis*," 69; Schiller, *Letters*, 90–1. See also Arendt, *Lectures on Kant's Political Philosophy*.

77 Huizinga, *Homo Ludens*, 8; see also 3, 7, 28, 132; Turner, *From Ritual to Theater*, 33–4, 37; Caillois, *Man, Play and Games*, 6–8; Sicart, *Play Matters*, 18, 30, 72; Brown, *Play*, 18.

78 Sicart (*Play Matters*, 19–34) and Brown (*Play*, 123–55) both observe that it is possible to be playful even while working.

79 Sicart, *Play Matters*, 29; see also Huizinga, *Homo Ludens*, 17, 19, 49; Brown, *Play*, 8, 17, 60. Brown speaks of the "apparent purposelessness" of play (17) and recognizes that there may be a purpose to play even when it appears to be without purpose (29). Below, I will insist on a more rigorous distinction between purposive and purposeless play, but for now, it is sufficient to acknowledge the commonplace view of play as purposive without purpose.

80 See Sicart, *Play Matters*, 5; Brown, *Play*, 7. Once again, I will qualify this position significantly below.

81 See Huizinga, *Homo Ludens*, 9; Caillois, *Man, Play and Games*, 9; Turner, *From Ritual to Theater*, 37.

82 See Huizinga, *Homo Ludens*, 28, 211; Sicart, *Play Matters*, 16; Turner, *From Ritual to Theater*, 56–8.

83 Although reductive evolutionary approaches to aesthetics often seek a purpose for aesthetic perception, thereby re-instrumentalizing it, Starr argues forcefully for a non-instrumental understanding of the aesthetic, even from a neuroscientific perspective (*Feeling Beauty*, 50).

84 However, given this, it is remarkable the extent to which the language of neoclassical aesthetics resurfaces in relation to Kant's aesthetics. It is not simply that Kant characterizes the free play of the faculties as a harmony; rather, for a number of commentators, the notion of "unity in variety," which for Beiser is the key formula of neoclassical and rationalist aesthetics (*Diotima's Children*, 8), characterizes the operation of Kantian aesthetic perception. See Zuckert, *Kant on Beauty and Biology*, 5, 11, 21, 51, 85; Longuenesse, *Kant and the Capacity to Judge*, 30; Makkreel, *Imagination and Interpretation in Kant*, 5, 75.
85 See Zuckert, *Kant on Beauty and Biology*, 2.
86 Once again, this position will have to be significantly qualified below.
87 See Turner, *From Ritual to Theater*, 37; Caillois, *Man, Play and Games*, 8; Huizinga, *Homo Ludens*, 22; Galloway, *Gaming*, 27; Brown, *Play*, 193.
88 Sicart, *Play Matters*, 23.
89 See Turner, *From Ritual to Theater*, 44.
90 See Brown, *Play*, 18.
91 Galloway defines a game as "an activity defined by rules in which players try to reach some sort of goal" (*Gaming*, 1). However, Elias, Garfield, and Gutschera are critical of the notion that a game can be reduced to its rules, and give an important role to agential features of a game, qualities that depend on the community of players (*Characteristics of Games*, 71–4).
92 However, one could make the case that, within a gaming community, judgments about the pleasure of a particular game or the beauty of a certain play have the same aspiration to universality as Kantian aesthetic judgments.
93 Huizinga, *Homo Ludens*, 11; Caillois, *Man, Play and Games*, 7.
94 Huizinga's account suggests that the distinction between play and games may be operative in other languages too (*Homo Ludens*, 28–45).
95 For innumerable contemporary examples, see Elias, Garfield, and Gutschera, *Characteristics of Games*; Sicart, *Play Matters*; Galloway, *Gaming*.
96 On animal play, see Brown, *Play*, 15–45.
97 Kant, *CJ*, 5: 207, 229.
98 See Brown, *Play*, 15.
99 In his reading of the third *Critique*, Derrida multiplies and deconstructs Kant's distinctions, but he takes up Kant's distinction of work and play without noting the extent to which the concept of a game renders this distinction unstable. See Derrida, "Economimesis," 5, 17. The opposition of work and play is also apparent in de Man's reading of Kant (*Aesthetic Ideology*, 84).

100 For Turner, the distinction between play and work is a modern one (*From Ritual to Theater*, 32), and both Sicart (*Play Matters*, 19–34) and Brown (*Play*, 123–55) emphasize that it is a mistake to oppose play to work.

101 Loesberg's *Return to Aesthetics* makes the point more broadly that, despite all the poststructuralist critiques of Kant, important elements of post-structuralist thought are first worked out in Kant's third *Critique*.

102 See Brown, *Play*, 31–45.

103 In her essay "The Sublime and the Good," Murdoch worries about our allergy to judgment, and she is also concerned about Kant's determination of art as play (*Existentialists and Mystics*, 206, 211). However, she does not offer a sustained analysis linking the two. The link is somewhat clearer in "The Sublime and the Beautiful Revisited" (*Existentialists and Mystics*, 281).

104 Huizinga, *Homo Ludens*, 4.

105 Elias, Garfield, and Gutschera, *Characteristics of Games*, 6.

106 Huizinga, *Homo Ludens*, 17, see also 199; Turner, *From Ritual to Theater*, 39; Brown, *Play*, 15, 51, 55. Sicart also privileges play over games (*Play Matters*, 2, 5, 51, 73). Elias, Garfield, and Gutschera's *Characteristics of Games* is the exception to this tendency, since it is written from the perspective of players and designers of games rather than that of a hermeneutics of play.

107 Galloway makes a similar point about the tension between games and play in Huizinga (*Gaming*, 19–20), though he is more interested in the medium and formal structure of games than the phenomenology of judgment embodied in them (21). Huizinga also assimilates play to games in certain ways. For him, all play creates order and is structured by rules (*Homo Ludens*, 10–11), but this obscures the category of pure play. Caillois's continuum from *paidia* to *ludus*, from more spontaneous to more structured forms of play, captures something of the distinction between games and play (*Man, Play and Games*, 13, 27–8).

108 See Elias, Garfield, and Gutschera, *Characteristics of Games*, 29–36.

109 It is an essential, indeed defining, characteristic of judgment as I understand it that a judgment can be made otherwise. As scholars of games note, deterministic games quickly become uninteresting, and the uncertainty of outcome in games is crucial to keeping both players and spectators engaged. See Elias, Garfield, and Gutschera, *Characteristics of Games*, 34, 137; Caillois, *Man, Play and Games*, 7. But for me, it is not only the uncertainty of outcome that matters; for judgment to be at stake in a game, it must be possible to play the game *legitimately* (not just in terms

of the rules but in terms of strategies for winning) in more than one way. See Elias, Garfield, and Gutschera, *Characteristics of Games*, 139.

110 Clearly, my claims apply to games in which learned skills are a large component of the game. However, this does not mean that chance plays no roles in such games. Although it is commonplace to oppose games of chance and skill, Elias, Garfield, and Gutschera argue persuasively that these two characteristics of games are better understood as orthogonal than opposed (*Characteristics of Games*, 150–61).

111 See Elias, Garfield, and Gutschera, *Characteristics of Games*, 28.

112 See Soni, "Introduction," for some indications of how the logic of Kantian aesthetic judgments might shape certain aesthetic and political formations. But the case needs to be developed more fully.

BIBLIOGRAPHY

Addison, Joseph, and Richard Steele. *The Spectator*. Edited by Henry Morley. Vol. 2. London: George Routledge and Sons, 1891.

Arendt, Hannah. *Lectures on Kant's Political Philosophy*. Edited by Ronald Beiner. Chicago: University of Chicago Press, 1982.

– *On Revolution*. New York: Viking, 1965.

– "Thinking and Moral Considerations." In *Responsibility and Judgment*, edited by Jerome Kohn, 159–89. New York: Schocken, 2003.

Beiser, Frederick C. *Diotima's Children: German Aesthetic Rationalism from Leibniz to Lessing*. Oxford: Oxford University Press, 2009.

Berlin, Isaiah. "Historical Inevitability." In *Liberty*, edited by Henry Hardy, 94–165. Oxford: Oxford University Press, 2004.

Brown, Stuart, with Christopher Vaughan. *Play: How It Shapes the Brain, Opens the Imagination, and Invigorates the Soul*. New York: Penguin, 2009.

Burnham, Douglas. *Kant's Philosophies of Judgment*. Edinburgh: Edinburgh University Press, 2004.

Caillois, Roger. *Man, Play and Games*. Translated by Meyer Barash. Urbana: University of Illinois Press, 1961.

Carnes, Natalie. *Beauty: A Theological Engagement with Gregory of Nyssa*. Eugene, OR: Cascade, 2014.

De Man, Paul. *Aesthetic Ideology*. Edited by Andrzej Warminski. Minneapolis: University of Minnesota Press, 1996.

Derrida, Jacques. "Economimesis." *Diacritics* 11 (1981): 3–25.

Elias, George Skaff, Richard Garfield, and K. Robert Gutschera. *Characteristics of Games*. Cambridge: MIT Press, 2012.

Galloway, Alexander R. *Gaming: Essays on Algorithmic Culture*. Minneapolis: University of Minnesota Press, 2006.

Ginsborg, Hannah. "Aesthetic Judging and the Intentionality of Pleasure." *Inquiry* 46, no. 2 (2003): 164–81.

– "Reflective Judgment and Taste." *Nous* 24, no. 1 (1990): 63–78.

Henrich, Dieter. *Aesthetic Judgment and the Moral Image of the World: Studies in Kant*. Stanford: Stanford University Press, 1992.

Huizinga, J. *Homo Ludens: A Study of the Play-Element in Culture*. Boston: Beacon, 1950.

Hutcheson, Francis. *An Inquiry into the Original of Our Ideas of Beauty and Virtue in Two Treatises*. Edited by Wolfgang Leidhold. Indianapolis: Liberty Fund, 2004.

Kant, Immanuel. *Critique of the Power of Judgment*. Translated by Paul Guyer and Eric Matthews. In *The Cambridge Edition of the Works of Immanuel Kant*, edited by Paul Guyer and Allen W. Wood. Cambridge: Cambridge University Press, 2000.

– *Werke in zehn Bänden*. Edited by Wilhelm Weischedel. 10 vols. Darmstadt: Wissenschaftliche Buchgesellschaft, 1983.

Locke, John. *An Essay Concerning Human Understanding*. Edited by R.S. Woolhouse. London: Penguin, 1997.

Loesberg, Jonathan. *A Return to Aesthetics: Autonomy, Indifference, and Postmodernism*. Stanford: Stanford University Press, 2005.

Longuenesse, Béatrice. *Kant and the Capacity to Judge: Sensibility and Discursivity in the Transcendental Analytic of the "Critique of Pure Reason."* Princeton: Princeton University Press, 1998.

Makkreel, Rudolf A. *Imagination and Interpretation in Kant: The Hermeneutical Import of the "Critique of Judgment."* Chicago: University of Chicago Press, 1990.

Menke, Christoph. "Aesthetic Practice: Judgment That Hates Itself." Public lecture presented at Northwestern University, Evanston, Illinois, February 20, 2014.

Murdoch, Iris. "The Sublime and the Beautiful Revisited." In *Existentialists and Mystics: Writings on Philosophy and Literature*, edited by Peter Conradi, 261–86. New York: Penguin, 1997.

– "The Sublime and the Good." In *Existentialists and Mystics: Writings on Philosophy and Literature*, edited by Peter Conradi, 205–20. New York: Penguin, 1997.

Pfau, Thomas. *Minding the Modern: Human Agency, Intellectual Traditions, and Responsible Knowledge*. Notre Dame: University of Notre Dame Press, 2013.

– *Wordsworth's Profession: Form, Class, and the Logic of Early Romantic Cultural Production*. Stanford, CA: Stanford University Press, 1997.

Pocock, J.G.A. *The Machiavellian Moment: Florentine Political Thought and the Atlantic Republican Tradition*. Princeton: Princeton University Press, 1975.
Pippin, Robert B. "The Significance of Taste: Kant, Aesthetic and Reflective Judgment." *Journal of the History of Philosophy* 34, no. 4 (1996): 549–69.
Sandel, Michael. *What Money Can't Buy: The Moral Limits of Markets*. New York: Farrar, Straus and Giroux, 2012.
Schiller, Friedrich. *Letters on the Aesthetic Education of Man*. In *Essays*, edited by Walter Hinderer and Daniel O. Dahlstrom, 86–178. New York: Continuum, 1993.
Schmitt, Carl. *The Crisis of Parliamentary Democracy*. Translated by Ellen Kennedy. Cambridge, MA: MIT Press, 1985.
Shaftesbury, Third Earl of (Anthony Ashley Cooper). "*Sensus Communis*; an Essay on the Freedom of Wit and Humor." In *Characteristics of Men, Manners, Opinions, Times*, 37–93. Indianapolis: Liberty Fund, 2001.
Sicart, Miguel. *Play Matters*. Cambridge: MIT Press, 2014.
Soni, Vivasvan. "Can Aesthetics Overcome Instrumental Reason? The Need for Judgment in Mandeville's *Fable of the Bees*." In *Mind, Body, Motion, Matter: Eighteenth-Century British and French Literary Perspectives*, edited by Alison Conway and Mary Helen McMurran, 254–78. Toronto: University of Toronto Press, 2016.
– "Communal Narcosis and Sublime Withdrawal: The Problem of Community in Kant's *Critique of Judgment*." *Cultural Critique* 64 (Fall 2002): 1–39.
– "Introduction: The Crisis of Judgment." *Eighteenth Century* 51, no. 3 (2010): 261–88.
Starr, G. Gabrielle. *Feeling Beauty: The Neuroscience of Aesthetic Experience*. Cambridge, MA: MIT Press, 2013.
Strauss, Leo. *Natural Right and History*. Chicago: University of Chicago Press, 1953.
Turner, Victor. *From Ritual to Theater: The Human Seriousness of Play*. New York: PAJ Publications, 1982.
Zerilli, Linda M.G. "Toward a Democratic Theory of Judgment." In *Judgment and Action: Fragments toward a History*, edited by Thomas Pfau and Vivasvan Soni. Evanston: Northwestern University Press, forthcoming.
– "'We Feel Our Freedom': Imagination and Judgment in the Thought of Hannah Arendt." *Political Theory* 33, no. 2 (2005): 158–88.
Zuckert, Rachel. *Kant on Beauty and Biology: An Interpretation of the "Critique of Judgment."* Cambridge: Cambridge University Press, 2007.

6 In Frankenberg's Cafeteria: The Small Worlds of Highsmith's *The Price of Salt*

HEATHER LOVE

> The lunch hour in the coworkers' cafeteria at Frankenberg's had reached its peak.
>
> There was no room left at any of the long tables, and more and more people were arriving to wait back of the wooden barricades by the cash register. People who had already got their trays of food wandered about between the tables in search of a spot they could squeeze into, or a place that somebody was about to leave, but there was no place. The roar of dishes, chairs, voices, shuffling feet, and the *bra-a-ack* of the turnstiles in the bare-walled room was like the din of a single huge machine.[1]

Patricia Highsmith's 1952 novel *The Price of Salt* opens during the lunch hour in the staff cafeteria of Frankenberg's department store. The room is jammed with people, eating and looking for places to eat. Represented by the sound of their meaningless activity (chairs scraping, feet shuffling, turnstiles advancing), the people have no substance – they are just there to fill in the space by the cash register. Highsmith continues:

> Therese ate nervously, with the "Welcome to Frankenberg's" booklet propped up in front of her against a sugar container. She had read the thick booklet through last week, in the first day of training class, but she had nothing else with her to read, and in the coworkers' cafeteria, she felt it necessary to concentrate on something. So she read again about vacation benefits, the three weeks' vacation given to people who had worked fifteen years at Frankenberg's, and she ate the hot plate special of the day – a grayish slice of roast beef with a ball of mashed potatoes covered with brown gravy, a heap of peas, and a tiny paper cup of horseradish. She tried to imagine what it would be like to have worked fifteen years in Frankenberg's

> department store, and she found she was unable to. "Twenty-five Yearers" got four weeks' vacation, the booklet said. Frankenberg's also provided a camp for summer and winter vacationers. They should have a church, too, she thought, and a hospital for the birth of babies. The store was organized so much like a prison, it frightened her now and then to realize she was a part of it.
>
> She turned the pages quickly, and saw in big black script across two pages: "Are *You* Frankenberg Material?"[2]

The language of narration in the opening pages of *The Price of Salt* might have come out of the Frankenberg's employee handbook. The abstract quality of the people wandering the lunchroom is explained by the fact that they are more properly named as Fifteen Yearers and "Twenty-five Yearers," "summer and winter vacationers." Therese herself might be more accurately identified as coworker 645-A, the "name" with which she "signs" her fateful Christmas card to Carol, the woman she falls in love with after waiting on her at the doll counter.[3] The derealizing effect of the booklet's standardized language spreads throughout the passage, turning a slice of roast beef, gravy, peas, and horseradish into a "hot plate special." What we see is not a particular room but a "peak hour," a sample of "personal time." To be "Frankenberg Material" is, perhaps, not to be material at all.

I begin with this discussion of the opening of *The Price of Salt* in order to pose a question that is so simple as to perhaps seem disingenuous: What, if anything, is this passage a description of? One might answer that it is a description of Therese, of the people and events in a typical lunch hour at Frankenberg's, or more expansively, that it is a portrait of the prisonlike atmosphere of a great commercial institution. And yet, since we encounter Therese in a work of fiction, we must begin by acknowledging that there is no Therese, no lunchroom, and no Frankenberg's – however much these representations might suggest elements of real life (for instance, Highsmith's own experience working as a counter-girl at Bloomingdale's).[4] Even if we were to admit that this description is based on observations of a real place and time, the passage is in the first instance a textual object.

The most persuasive account of the passage, perhaps, is that it is a description of Therese's alienated experience of a fully administered world, what C. Wright Mills in 1951 called "the Great Salesroom."[5] The description begins in an apparently neutral register ("the lunch hour … had reached its peak"), but it is soon infused with Therese's irony and self-consciousness. However, while Therese's perspective adds a layer to the depiction of the scene – representing the affective experience of occupying this space – it also hides that scene from view: Therese can't stand to look. She uses the pamphlet to block out the lunchroom, and it is as if the pamphlet blocks the reader's view as well, its stereotyped and cliché-ridden language frustrating our ability to make sense of the space. If Therese finds it difficult to imagine what it would be like to work at Frankenberg's for years on end, we may find it difficult to picture with any specificity what it is like to work there for even one day. And the denuded, blank aspect of the description leaves open the question of Highsmith's attitude toward it. The ambiguity is inherent in accounts of realist form, as Fredric Jameson notes in *The Antinomies of Realism*: "It is never very clear whether [the realist novel] simply registers the advanced state of a given society or plays a part in society's awareness of that advanced state and its potentialities (political and otherwise)."[6]

The question remains, what is the opening description of *The Price of Salt* a description of? In light of the dubious ontology of the scene, it seems tendentious to identify this opening passage as an example of description at all. And yet, certain details – the precisely rendered sounds, the weight of the pamphlet against a sugar dispenser, the placement of a "tiny paper cup of horseradish" on the lunch-plate – suggest a desire to represent this world in its concrete specificity. In this moment, we might recall that Therese is not only an alienated and self-absorbed young woman but also an aspiring set designer, adept at the imagination and realization of interiors.

In recent reflections on what he calls the "Official World," Mark Seltzer considers the importance of description in Highsmith's work. Although he does not treat it directly, Frankenberg's lunchroom might be considered one of Highsmith's "microworlds": these small theatrical spaces offer, in Seltzer's view, both a "scale model" and a "working model" of the social world.[7] In this account, based on an engagement with the concept of reflexive or second modernity as articulated by Ulrich Beck and Anthony Giddens, the opening of *The Price of Salt* is not descriptive but self-descriptive. According to Seltzer, Highsmith's accounts of surveillance and detection take place in the "overlit public sphere [with] its media of observation and self-observation."[8] In this self-organizing world, every scene of observation is doubled, a commentary on its own protocols. "There is nothing deeper than the observation of how one observes and how he observes or fails to observe that," Seltzer writes, "but that is observed, too."[9] For Seltzer, the "minimalism" of Highsmith's descriptions suggests "what the face-to-face encounter between persons has come to look like in an unremittingly indoor, reflexive, and official world."[10]

In recent years, critics have attempted to formulate accounts of the world as something other than a textual phenomenon or a social construction. These approaches have been taken up in arenas that would appear least hospitable to them, including fields such as media studies, queer theory, feminism, science and technology studies, transgender studies, disability studies, critical race studies, and affect studies. These are fields where challenges to stabilizing regimes of truth have been crucial because of the long-standing links between epistemological realism and bodily and identity essentialism. Yet these fields have led the attempt to develop new forms of realism and alternatives to critique. With the waning of the linguistic turn, the political promise that critics once saw in performativity and the subversion of norms is now associated with concreteness, ontology, surface materialities, and the liveliness of things.[11]

We witness a striking turnabout in the case of Bruno Latour. One of the key figures in developing an account of the social construction of science, Latour has become an advocate for new empiricism and postcritical methods over the last decade. In his much-cited polemic against critique, "Why Has Critique Run Out of Steam? From Matters of Fact to Matters of Concern" (2004), Latour looks back on the reception of science and technology studies and suggests that this work was misinterpreted as scepticism about the material basis of reality and scientific facts. Given popular and official scepticism about science and expertise, Latour argues for the need for new, more robust descriptions in order to shore up facts (especially about climate change). Latour attributes the misunderstanding partly to his failure to emphasize the constructive (rather than deconstructive) aspects of his method. "The mistake we made, the mistake I made, was to believe that there was no efficient way to criticize matters of fact except by moving *away* from them and directing one's attention *toward* the conditions that made them possible."[12] As a countermeasure, Latour asks scholars to take a break from critique and to collectively cultivate a "*stubbornly realist attitude.*"[13]

The publication of the "Science Wars" issue of *Social Text* in 1996 is a significant event in the reevaluation of critique. In an essay reflecting on what was known as the Sokal affair, John Guillory offers an explanation for the misinterpretation that Latour bemoans in "Why Has Critique Run Out of Steam?" Guillory proposes that Left critics have responded to the decline of the humanities by battling with the social sciences over the territory of "the human world."[14] Since the 1970s, this battle over cultural authority has been waged on the ground of methodology: with the rise of poststructuralism, cultural studies scholars have asserted the superiority of interpretation over description and have conflated anti-realist epistemology with progressive politics. In a discussion of the "spontaneous philosophy" of the critics, Guillory argues that complex accounts of scientific practice such as Latour's 1979 book with Steven Woolgar, *Laboratory Life*, have been taken up in the context of the humanities as polemics about epistemology. Latour's empirical account of the making of scientific facts has become, in the context of the culture wars, a polemic against facts. Latour's increasingly polemical statements about the realism of his method – "from now on *everything is data*" provides a representative example[15] – might be seen as a way of guaranteeing that his work will not be misappropriated by anti-realist thinkers. Latour's reception in the humanities is now curiously divided: on the one hand, there are scholars who join him in polemics on behalf of new forms of realism (though without any more grounding in practice than the anti-realist humanists who previously championed his work); on the other hand, many scholars see in Latour's recent work evidence of his positivism.[16]

In his 2012 book *Fantasies of the New Class*, Stephen Schryer describes the divergence between US social sciences and literary studies in the period after World War II. The distinction between sociology and literature was less clear before the war, for instance in borrowings between Chicago School sociology and literary naturalism. Schryer describes increasing disciplinary specialization, evident in the rise of New Criticism (with its simultaneous critique and imitation of the sciences) and of structural functionalism. As a result of this disciplinary separation, literary critics became increasingly focused on the aesthetic realm and on questions of subjectivity, value, and interpersonal ethics. At the same time, fueled by a postwar surge of state funding, sociologists sought a path to professionalization through abstraction, generality, and systematicity. Schryer sees an exception to this split between literary studies and the social sciences in the work of postwar "maverick sociologists" such as C. Wright Mills and Paul Goodman, who attacked the increasingly technocratic and specialized role of sociology and attempted to imagine a public, humanist, and transformative role for the social sciences.[17]

In my current book project, *Practices of Description*, I complicate this narrative by attending to concrete practices of observation and description in the humanities, social sciences, and the arts after World War II. During this period, sometimes known as the "golden age of microsociology," humanists and social scientists engaged in extended, fine-grained practices of description that complicate the divide Schryer identifies. By focusing on practice – on acts of observing, describing, recording, and analysing the "human world" at the microscale – I find common ground among ethnomethodologists, linguists, novelists, ethnographers, animal ethologists, documentary filmmakers, and others. I consider these observational practices in the context of recent debates about interpretation, description, and critique in literary studies, arguing that we can see in extended acts of attention an example of social scientists engaged in reading – or close reading – the social world. This work has sometimes been seen as positivist, reductive, or objectifying. I argue instead that these researchers modelled self-reflexivity and patience; that they practised a form of observation attuned to complexity and ambiguity; and that their work was governed by values of fidelity and care. Attending to this history complicates the opposition between unremitting self-reflexivity and naïve realism: these scholars were attentive to the complexities of framing and perspective but also to the concrete details of environments, situations, behaviours, and interactions.[18] Attending to this history also promises to relax the dominance of interpretation in literary studies, opening a space for literary critics to grapple – once again – with the referential ambitions of the novel.

To suggest what I mean, I will return briefly to the opening of *The Price of Salt* and to its curiously vague account of Frankenberg's lunchroom. Through Therese's distracted, self-absorbed perspective, the lunchroom and the people in it seem remote and unlikely. But the scene does not end that way. Therese tries to distance herself from her surroundings by "think[ing] of something else"[19] – considering other job prospects, mulling over her unsatisfactory relationship with her boyfriend, Richard, remembering the gloves her teacher Sister Alicia gave her – but in the end her strategy fails: "Someone moved the sugar container, and the propped booklet fell flat."[20] In this world populated by coworkers, "someone" is still capable of making contact, of moving the furniture. Behind the pamphlet, a woman's hands: "plump, aging hands, stirring her coffee, breaking a roll now with a trembling eagerness"; "the hands were chapped, there was dirt in the parallel creases of the knuckles, but the right hand bore a conspicuous silver filigree ring set with a clear green stone, the left a gold wedding ring, and there were traces of red polish in the corners of the nails."[21] This pair of hands (soon revealed to belong to Therese's beaten-down coworker Mrs. Robichek) are, as so often in the novel, a spur to desire and interest; they also reground description. Language in this moment is not a screen blocking the world; instead, like dirt in the creases of knuckles or traces of polish lingering in the corners of nails, it limns the world, outlining and infusing it, bringing out its concrete particularity. The description at the beginning of *The Price of Salt* is a description of description; it is also, I want to argue, a description of the peak hour at Frankenberg's.

Highsmith has long posed a challenge for literary criticism because of her status as a writer of genre fiction, her distance from the category of woman (and lesbian), and her personal nastiness. In the last decade or so, however, her reputation has been solidified through a publication revival, the release of two biographies (including Joan Schenkar's critically acclaimed 2009 *The Talented Miss Highsmith*), and an outpouring of scholarly articles. Tom Perrin, the editor of a December 2012 special issue of the online journal *Post45*, justifies his choice of Highsmith as topic by asserting that she is "'hot' right now."[22] The *Post45* special issue is instructive, because it is in large part a renewed critical attention to the cultural and literary history of the Cold War that has spurred interest in Highsmith. In this recent scholarship, her work has been read in relation to key aspects of the period such as domesticity, commodification, mass culture, surveillance, the closet, violence, bureaucracy, McCarthyism, masculinity, and strategic containment. I have been particularly influenced by Seltzer's work on reflexive modernity and Highsmith's indoor worlds (which he links to the small worlds of microsociology); by David Alworth's related work on the postwar novel as a form of microsociology that produces knowledge about concrete social sites; and by Michael Trask's work on Highsmith in relation to dramaturgical accounts of the self.[23] In his book *Camp Sites*, Trask focuses on Highsmith's refusal of the "demand for motive," linking her permissive attitude toward the serial killer and forger Tom Ripley to the focus on social roles and the self's "social entailments"[24] in postwar sociology. By "prioritizing the self's instrumentality" rather than its "authenticity,"[25] Highsmith creates a zone of freedom, modelling a refusal of the imperative to self-revelation.

Recent work on Highsmith tends to focus on her "murder games and what might be called [her] cold war."[26] The Cold War Highsmith is anti-humanist, ironic, ruthless; she is the writer of suspense fiction, a dispassionate observer of human cruelty and self-delusion. With its sustained attention to the relation between Therese and Carol and the highly unlikely happy ending it imagines for them, *The Price of Salt* is hard to enlist in an argument about the gamelike and empty world of Highsmith's fiction. The novel concerns surveillance, but it contrasts Therese's obsessive attention to Carol with the cold view of the detective Carol's estranged husband hires to follow the two women. Highsmith represents the crushing normativity of marriage and family in a consumer society, but it also tells the story of two heroines who steal away. Victoria Hesford reads the novel in the context of Cold War domesticity, arguing that Highsmith exposes the violence and dehumanization at its heart. While that topos appears throughout Highsmith's novels, in *The Price of Salt* she gives her protagonists two other sites – the road and New York City – in which to explore the possibilities of eroticism and love. If homosexual love does not escape the law of the land – Hesford sees Therese and Carol at the end of the novel as "two of many 'like them' who must live with and against the claims of national heterosexuality"[27] – it does offer a loophole, a space that offers new "possibilities for social expansion and human interaction" – the "ability to love."[28]

Mary Esteve comments on the exceptional status of Highsmith's lesbian novel in her essay "Queer Consumerism, Straight Happiness: Highsmith's 'Right Economy,'" which was featured in the *Post45* cluster. Esteve begins her essay by citing Highsmith's comments in the afterword to the 1990 edition of the novel, in which she recalls the fan letters she received after its original publication. In response to outpourings of gratitude about the novel's nontragic representation of same-sex relations, Highsmith wrote back to some readers with advice about where to seek out others like them. Esteve comments, "There is agreeable irony in this image of Highsmith – whom biographers portray as orneriness incarnate, sexual predator, misanthrope, and habitual racist – embracing the novel's therapeutic and educative effects. Like any good liberal, she not only affirms the interpretation of the novel's happy ending but also accepts as legitimate the values this ending reflects."[29] Esteve obeys an unwritten law about the conservation of coldness in Highsmith's oeuvre: where irony is lacking, Esteve provides it. However, what sets Esteve's work apart from other readers of Highsmith is that she reads the happy ending of *The Price of Salt* as a reflection of its Cold War context rather than as an escape from it. Focusing on the question of consumer desire in the novel, Esteve reads Therese and Carol's relation as an early instantiation of queer liberalism, placing the novel's gesture toward their happiness in the context of the United Nations' 1948 Universal Declaration of Human Rights' commitment to "the full development of the human personality."[30] Esteve cites a scene – a "consumerist epiphany" – in which Therese looks at a shop window, "optically revel[ing] in all the precious and erotic uniqueness" of a tiny gold candlestick holder with "'a gold ring at the rim for the finger.'"[31] Esteve reads that ring as a nuptial band, linking Therese and Carol's precarious romance to the more established unions of contemporary gays and lesbians.

The significance of consumer desire in *The Price of Salt* is undeniable: as Esteve reminds us, Therese and Carol meet over the sales counter of a department store. But the fact of such a focus, and its link, in Esteve's reading, to an emergent homonormativity, tends to obscure the unsettled and unsettling erotic force of these moments. In a reading of Todd Haynes's 2015 film adaptation of the novel, *Carol*, Patricia White notes the pleasures of consumer goods in the film, focusing in particular on the proliferation of surfaces ("notably the soft leathers and furs of Carol's bourgeois accouterments: scarves and suitcases, purses and, especially, gloves").[32] Rather than seeing such images as consolidating an emergent lesbian and gay market, White reads them as signs of a fugitive eroticism embodied by Carol, who poses a danger to the social order by effortlessly passing and by combining "shopping with tricking."[33] The glimpses of happiness represented in *The Price of Salt* do not only index postwar human rights or presage gay marriage; the novel's range of perverse and ambient desires do not all fit into the category of consumer desire. In the scene Esteve reads, Highsmith describes the candlestick holder: "Most of its porcelain surface was painted with small bright lozenges of colored enamel, royal blue, and deep red and green, outlined with coin gold as shiny as silk embroidery, even under its film of dust. There was a gold ring at the rim for the finger."[34] This little object, with its enamel lozenges and silken coin gold, a film of dust quivering over its surface, "quench[es] some forgotten and nameless thirst inside [Therese]."[35] Therese thirsts for things, and her desire for Carol is mixed with and mediated by consumer desire. It's possible that this desire is also mixed with a desire for the security, recognition, and stability promised by marriage – though such a longing, barred by social impossibility, does not strike me as normative. But the desire for Carol is also a physical, erotic desire, focused through the hands, here evoked by association. Therese is window-shopping, and she comes back the next day to buy the candlestick as a gift for Carol, but the point is not so much to own it as to touch it, to put her fingers on it and in it.

By insisting on Therese's erotic desire, and arguing that by translating it into a consumerist desire we lose too much, I realize that I may also be losing some of my audience. Erotic longings – for objects and bodies – are by definition minor: corporeal, fleeting, situated within and between individuals, and inconsequential to those who are not experiencing them; they look small and insignificant, especially alongside larger issues of commodification, carceral domesticity, queer liberalism, and international human rights. It is this scaling down of critical claims that Seltzer worries over in his account of the "incrementalist turn": "With respect to the novel, there is a turn to the study of minor characters; with respect to affect, minor feelings; with respect to political forms, little resistances, infantile subjects, minute, therapeutic adjustments; with respect to perception, the decelerated gaze and a prolonged attentiveness; and so on."[36] Other critics have expressed similar concerns about the turn to postcritical methods in literary studies.[37] They argue that the reading practices developed by critics such as Stephen Best and Sharon Marcus ("surface reading") and Eve Kosofsky Sedgwick ("reparative reading") are too local and too invested in their objects to account for geopolitics, historical change, or ideology. What is the point of lingering on particular objects, particular bodies? What is the cost if attention to Therese's desire drops out on the way to make an argument about the growth of US liberalism and human rights?

Therese discovers the world through desire: the highly specific, even fetishistic nature of her desire for Carol constitutes not a narrowing of her world but an expansion of it. "It was a matter of that particular enchantment that came from Carol," Highsmith writes, "and seemed to work on all the world around them."[38] Therese's obsessive attention to Carol resembles surveillance, but it is also driven by fidelity and care. Attending to this way of looking can help to reframe observational practices in the postwar period. What Therese has in common with postwar social scientists is patience, attention to gesture and interaction at the microscale, and an attempt to describe the full range of human and social experience from the outside. Highsmith doubles Therese's extended practices of attention with her own observant gaze – this is narration by stakeout. Rather than simply collapse this observational realism into Cold War forms of surveillance, objectification, or commodification, I want to attend to the specificity of the desire that animates looking in the novel, and to suggest that it might rewrite taken-for-granted assumptions about the ethics of observation and description.

Observation is ethically ambiguous – at the very least – in *The Price of Salt*. Highsmith's key thematics of surveillance, paranoia, and detection make observation central and link the novel to naturalism and the late nineteenth-century detective novel. Highsmith comments on the value of observation in her 1983 book *Plotting and Writing Suspense Fiction*. She recommends "notebooks for writers,"[39] suggesting that the observation of real-world details as well as immersion in fictional worlds is necessary to flesh out setting and characters – who must "be seen as clearly as a photograph – with no foggy spots."[40] Realization depends on the use of the senses and the evocation of details in order to capture "how a house smells, the general color of a room – olive green, musty brown, or cheerful yellow. And sounds – that of a tin can being blown down a street, of an invalid coughing in another room."[41] It also depends on dwelling in worlds of one's own making long enough to lend them concreteness and believability: the author's "invented people must seem real,"[42] and the only way to achieve this end is by living with them.

Realization and verisimilitude also depend on sociological observation: Highsmith devotes a short section of the book to "other professions," discussing the difficulty (and necessity) of becoming intimately familiar with different fields, settings, and contexts. Highsmith points to her experience at Bloomingdale's: "I once took a job during Christmas rush at a department store in Manhattan. Here was a scene chaotic with detail, sounds, people, and a new tempo – pretty hectic – an unending stream of little dramas that one could observe in customers, fellow workers and the management, which was full of self-importance. I made good use of this new scene in my writing. A writer should seize upon every new scene that comes his way, take notes, and turn it to account."[43] By turning her attention to these "little dramas" and the welter of details, Highsmith suggests that one may build up a picture of the social world through minute attention to the small worlds that constitute it.

The figure most identified with observation in *The Price of Salt* is the detective hired by Carol's husband to trail the two women on their cross-country road trip. The detective is the villain of the novel; a hired hand, he is the one who does what Carol calls the "very dirty business"[44] of surveillance and who most directly blocks the happiness of the two women. Highsmith's representation of this figure suggests the close links between the private investigator and the social scientist conducting field research. The business of the detective is to observe the women, to inquire after their whereabouts, to take notes about their activities, including "times and places,"[45] and to record, with the aid of a Dictaphone, their conversations and activities, especially their sexual activities. His relation to the women is portrayed as being both predatory and parasitic; it also appears that the practice of surveillance has a deadening effect on his person. Highsmith notes several times the fact of his dead eyes – "like round gray dots"[46] – as if the activity of recording has assimilated his personality to the apparatus. When Carol confronts him by the side of the road, Highsmith writes, "The detective looked at her with a false and meaningless smile, not like a person at all, but like a machine wound up and set on a course."[47]

This meaningless, machinic existence sets the detective apart from the vibrant eroticism that flows between Carol and Therese. The detective is unshakeable, but his presence cannot interrupt the flow of attention and sensation between them. "The detective was still following them, half a mile behind them, back of the horse and farm wagon that had turned into the highway from a dirt road. Carol held Therese's hand and drove with her left hand. Therese looked down at the faintly freckled fingers that dug their strong cool tips into her palm."[48] A woman's hand rendered in fleshy particularity again acts as a conductor for live human presence in a dead world. Again and again in the novel, the reanimation of the world is enabled not just by the charge of eroticism but also by a shift to the microscale.

Despite the significance of this current between Carol and Therese, it must be said that the two women are more than followed by the detective – they are doubled by him. He is synched up with their activity, taking the same road trip and staying in the same tourist hotels they do. But the detective travels on the clock – in this he recalls Therese's stint at the doll counter at Frankenberg's (Highsmith describes his "dead little eyes … like a doll's blank and steady eyes"[49]). When Carol first confronts him, asking, "Do you like our company or what?" the detective responds, "I'm doing my job, Mrs. Aird,"[50] suggesting how Therese too in the midst of this love affair might just be doing her job, continuing to wait on Carol. An especially unsettling moment of doubling also suggests that possibility: when the women see him at dinner in the hotel restaurant in Salt Lake City, he is "reading a book that he had propped up on the metal napkin holder."[51]

Therese in the Frankenberg's lunchroom; the detective in the Salt Lake City restaurant: these are scenes of isolation and alienation, passivity and self-consciousness, that highlight the deadening effect of being an observer of the world rather an actor in it. That state is characteristic of being employed, of living on other people's time. But it is also linked to the experience of social and sexual marginality or deviance. Before they embark on the trip, Carol accuses Therese of "prefer[ring] things reflected in a glass" and of having only "secondhand" experiences; she wonders whether Therese will "really enjoy this trip," if she will "even like seeing real mountains and real people."[52] Therese is crushed by the comment, which she takes as an attack on her unsubstantial way of life: "Carol made her feel that she had done nothing, was nothing at all, like a wisp of smoke. Carol had lived like a human being, had married, and had a child."[53] Therese's withdrawal, her watchfulness, what Carol calls her "rather subjective"[54] approach to making set designs – Highsmith links these traits to Therese's social vulnerability, her dislocation, her half-orphan status, and her non-normative – excessive, fetishistic, and homoerotic – desires.

But if observation is linked to surveillance and to psychopathology in the novel, it is also linked to a capacity for attention and to a transformative cathexis of the world. Therese experiences her encounter with Carol as a pervasive enchantment and even as a justification for the existence of the world. In the hour in the hotel room before Therese sleeps with Carol for the first time, the world takes on a powerful charge:

> In the room, she lifted her suitcase from the floor to a chair, unlatched it and left it, and stood by the writing table, watching Carol. As if her emotions had been in abeyance all the past hours, or days, they flooded her now as she watched Carol opening her suitcase, taking out, as she always did first, the leather kit that contained her toilet articles, dropping it onto the bed. She looked at Carol's hands, at the lock of hair that fell over the scarf tied around her head, at the scratch she had gotten days ago across the toe of her moccasin.[55]

Carol kisses her a moment later and then goes out. "Therese waited by the table while Carol was gone, while time passed indefinitely or maybe not at all, until the door opened and Carol came in again. She set a paper bag on the table, and Therese knew she had only gone to get a container of milk, as Carol or she herself did very often at night."[56]

There is nothing special in these scenes; what distinguishes them is the pervasive sense that the world is perfect as it is. This sense characterizes all the time that Therese spends with Carol. What is deadening about the habitual and ordinary in Carol's absence is transfigured in her presence: taking a case out of her bag, buying a bottle of milk – no habit is too minor to be transfigured by Therese's attention. The novel traces the tidal shifts in the enchantment and de-enchantment of the world, correlated with Carol's presence and absence. After Therese and Carol have been exposed and Carol flies back east to fight the custody battle, Therese wanders around Sioux Falls remembering their time together. Highsmith writes, "In the middle of a block, she opened the door of a coffee shop, but they were playing one of the songs she had heard with Carol everywhere, and she let the door close and walked on. The music lived, but the world was dead. And the song would die one day, she thought, but how would the world come back to life? How would its salt come back?"[57] The passage points to the origin of the novel's title in "The Sermon on the Mount": "You are the salt of the earth. But if the salt loses its saltiness, how can it be made salty again? It is no longer good for anything, except to be thrown out and trampled underfoot. You are the light of the world. A town built on a hill cannot be hidden. Neither do people light a lamp and put it under a bowl. Instead they put it on its stand, and it gives light to everyone in the house."[58] If the associations of the "salt of the earth" – everyday people doing everyday things – tend to inspire revulsion in Therese, Carol has the power to illuminate that ordinariness with the light of her presence. When she is absent, the world loses its salt.

"How would its salt come back?" *The Price of Salt* offers a view of the world as disenchanted, a place where, in C. Wright Mills's words, "the salesman's world has ... become everybody's world, and, in some part, everybody has become a salesman."[59] But desire has the power to animate the world. Observing the world with desire enlivens it, gives it body and intensity, lighting up even its dead patches, its zones of habit and entropy. The power of the erotic is not merely in the way that it helps to form an attachment to the world but also in the way that it makes it real. In an early encounter with Carol,

> the dusky and faintly sweet smell of her perfume came to Therese again, a smell suggestive of dark green silk, that was hers alone, like the smell of a

> special flower. Therese leaned closer toward it, looking down at her glass. She wanted to thrust the table aside and spring into her arms, to bury her nose in the green and gold scarf that was tied close about her neck. Once the backs of their hands brushed on the table, and Therese's skin there felt separately alive now, and rather burning. Therese could not understand it, but it was so.[60]

Eroticism is the power of attraction, what brings Therese closer to Carol, but also closer to the world. And this close encounter seems to depend on a shift in scale, a zooming in that makes visible the concrete specificity of the world. Given Therese's blurred, subjective view of the world, her distance from things, the way that she is blocked from its light, her love for Carol can seem less like the culmination of her longing than an occasion for an encounter with the world, for an affirmation of it. *Therese could not understand it, but it was so.*

The methods that the microanalysts developed in the postwar period to capture social life and communication at its most ephemeral and complex offer a compelling model for a descriptive literary criticism. In pointing to such practices as forms of reading, or close reading, the social world, I hope to question taken-for-granted agreements about the value of empiricism, objectivity, observation, and social science methods more broadly. Attention to the practices of observation and description in the novels in this period might help us to account for the novel's ambition to describe the social world.

Erving Goffman sets a possible research agenda for this program in the introduction to his 1974 book *Frame Analysis: An Essay on the Organization of Experience*. Goffman describes all of reality – from chess games to track meets to surgical operations – as amenable to the procedure of frame analysis. This mode of analysis adds a potentially endless number of frames to an indelible "strip" of behaviour.[61] While those frames add complexity and complicate the ontological status and significance of the original event, they do not cancel it out. Goffman, in a move that we can trace to Gilbert Ryle and to his uptake by Clifford Geertz in his work on thick and thin description, imagined dizzying complexity – irony, fictionality, reflexivity and self-reflexivity – as integral to behaviour. He did not question the existence of behaviour as a ground for those reframings, however. By beginning with this concept of a strip of behaviour, Goffman set limits on self-reflexivity – acknowledging its importance without allowing it to take over. He writes: "Methodological self-consciousness that is full, immediate, and persistent sets aside all study and analysis except that of the reflexive problem itself, thereby displacing fields of inquiry instead of contributing to them."[62] For Goffman, frame analysis, in all its permutations, was still best understood as an attempt to answer the question, "What is it that's going on here?"

I do not anticipate that frame analysis will displace other methods of literary criticism. The question is whether we are willing to see Therese, sitting in the Frankenberg's lunchroom, reading an employee brochure propped up against a sugar dispenser, and stirred to life by a close encounter with a woman's hands, as a "strip" of behaviour – or as something else entirely. Treating these lines of text as not merely a description of description but also as a description of a world means suspending the other tools that we have for making sense of literature – interpretation, critique, formal analysis, and evaluation. But there is more to learn from fictional texts by asking the question, "What is it that's going on here?" (even if we shy away from the question of what is *really* going on here).[63] Highsmith took great pains to make these small worlds; I think one thing we might do when we read them is to look at them, to see how they work, to describe them, and to get closer to them.

NOTES

1 Highsmith, *Price of Salt*, 11.
2 Ibid., 11–12.
3 The card reads: "Special salutations from Frankenberg's." Highsmith, *Price of Salt*, 44.
4 For an account of Highsmith's encounter with Kathleen Senn (the model for Carol) in Bloomingdale's and its aftermath (including the writing of an early version of *The Price of Salt* [*The Bloomingdale Story*] and Senn's later suicide), see Schenkar, *Talented Miss Highsmith*, 267–71. For an account of working in Macy's that similarly adopts the language of retail to describe personal experience, see Jackson, "My Life with R. H. Macy."
5 See Mills, "Great Salesroom."
6 Jameson, *Antinomies of Realism*, 4.
7 Seltzer, "Daily Planet."
8 Seltzer, "Official World," 738.
9 Ibid., 745.
10 Ibid., 739. For Seltzer, there is no escape from this indoor world. To opt out of such overlit spaces of observation and self-observation is to light out for the "great outdoors." "Official World," 729.

11 The bibliography is extensive and various; many of these critics do not or would not see eye to eye. And yet across a range of fields, critics are interested in approaches that put pressure on critical hermeneutics and emphasize experience, affect, and thingliness. For some key examples, see Tobin Siebers's new realism of the body in *Disability Theory*; Anne Cheng in *Melancholy of Race* and *Second Skin*; Saidiya Hartman in *Scenes of Subjection* (and broader debates about Afro-pessimism that turn on the question of ontology); Susan Stryker, "My Words to Victor Frankenstein above the Village of Chamounix"; Rosi Braidotti's *The Posthuman*; Elizabeth Grosz's *Becoming Undone*; Mel Chen's *Animacies*.

12 Latour, "Why Has Critique Run Out of Steam?" 231 (italics in original).

13 Ibid. (italics in original).

14 Guillory, "Sokal Affair," 482.

15 Latour, *Reassembling the Social*, 133 (italics in original).

16 See, for instance, Hensley, "Curatorial Reading and Endless War." Hensley sees Latour's work as an example of the "so-called new materialism" and argues that "deferring uncritically to objects … ensures a reiterative, even positivistic relationship to the items under observation, since any merely descriptive method must perforce narrate in other terms what already is, however rich or variegated that extant reality might be" (62–3).

17 Schryer, *Fantasies of the New Class*, especially chapter 1 ("The Republic of Letters: The New Criticism, Harvard Sociology, and the Idea of the University"). British cultural studies, represented by the work of figures such as Richard Hoggart and Raymond Williams, is another site for the rise of a maverick sociology in the period.

18 For further reflections on the middle ground between self-reflexivity and empirical observation, see my essay "The Temptations: Donna Haraway, Feminist Objectivity, and the Problem of Critique."

19 Highsmith, *Price of Salt*, 12.

20 Ibid., 14.

21 Ibid.

22 Perrin, "On Patricia Highsmith." Perrin is citing an essay by Leonard Cassuto in *The Chronicle of Higher Education* ("Reality Catches Up to Highsmith's Hard-Boiled Fiction"). Victoria Hesford commented on the neglect of Highsmith in a review essay published the year before Cassuto's piece. See Hesford, "Highsmith: A Romance of the 1950's."

23 Like Seltzer and Trask, I pair Highsmith with Goffman. See Seltzer, "Daily Planet," "Official World," and "Parlor Games." See also Trask, "Highsmith's Method," and *Camp Sites*.

24 Trask, *Camp Sites*, 134.

25 Ibid., 146.
26 Seltzer, "Parlor Games," 121.
27 Hesford, "Patriotic Perversions," 230.
28 Ibid., 228. Castle arrives at a similar conclusion in "Pulp Valentine." Commenting on the links between *The Price of Salt*, *Strangers on a Train*, and the Ripley novels, Castle writes, "The same dark intelligence is at work in *The Price of Salt*, a novel in which pulp-fiction plotting, '50s paranoia, and heavy doses of authorial cynicism combined, somehow miraculously, to produce a louche and stunningly erotic McCarthy-era love story." Patricia White, reflecting on Todd Haynes's 2015 adaptation of the novel, *Carol*, also locates the difference in the film's representation of eroticism. She writes: "The poignance of Carol's desire resonates with Haynes's other films about women's thwarted lives, but her recognition and embrace of it goes further to figure a significant historical rupture. When she beholds Therese's body after undressing her for the first time, Carol gasps: 'I never looked like that,' remarking more than age difference, signaling the advent of something other, something new" ("Sketchy Lesbians," 16).
29 Esteve, "Queer Consumerism, Straight Happiness."
30 Quoted in Ibid.
31 Ibid.
32 White, "Sketchy Lesbians," 11.
33 Ibid., 15.
34 Highsmith, *Price of Salt*, 247.
35 Ibid.
36 Seltzer, "Official World," 727.
37 See, for example, Bartolovich, "Humanities of Scale."
38 Highsmith, *Price of Salt*, 201. My argument that it is by looking at and touching Carol that Therese grasps the world runs counter to Esteve's argument about the dangers of Therese's "idiosexual" or "Carol-specific" desire.
39 Highsmith, *Plotting and Writing Suspense Fiction*, 13.
40 Ibid., 37.
41 Ibid., 95.
42 Ibid., 137.
43 Ibid., 96.
44 Highsmith, *Price of Salt*, 206.
45 Ibid., 227.
46 Ibid., 223.
47 Ibid., 224.
48 Ibid., 225.

49 Ibid., 223.
50 Ibid., 223–24.
51 Ibid., 217.
52 Ibid., 177–78.
53 Ibid., 178.
54 Ibid., 163.
55 Ibid., 188.
56 Ibid., 189.
57 Ibid., 260.
58 Matt. 5:13–16.
59 Mills, "Great Salesroom," 161.
60 Highsmith, *Price of Salt*, 51.
61 Goffman, *Frame Analysis*, 10. Goffman writes: "The term 'strip' will be used to refer to any arbitrary slice or cut from the stream of ongoing activity, including here sequences of happenings, real or fictive, as seen from the perspective of those subjectively involved in sustaining an interest in them. A strip is not meant to reflect a natural division made by the subjects of inquiry or an analytical division made by students who inquire: it will be used only to refer to any raw batch of occurrences (of whatever status in reality) that one wants to draw attention to as a starting point for analysis."
62 Ibid., 12.
63 Thanks to Sharon Marcus for this formulation.

BIBLIOGRAPHY

Alworth, David J. *Site Reading: Fiction, Art, Social Form*. Princeton, NJ: Princeton University Press, 2016.

Bartolovich, Crystal. "Humanities of Scale: Marxism, Surface Reading – and Milton." *PMLA* 127, no. 1 (2012): 115–21.

Braidotti, Rosi. *The Posthuman*. Malden, MA: Polity Press, 2013.

Cassuto, Leonard. "Reality Catches Up to Highsmith's Hard-Boiled Fiction." *Chronicle of Higher Education*, February 20, 2004. http://chronicle.com/article/Reality-Catches-Up-to/8824.

Castle, Terry. "Pulp Valentine: Patricia Highsmith's Erotic Lesbian Thriller." *Slate*, May 23, 2006. http://www.slate.com/articles/news_and_politics/pulp_fiction/2006/05/pulp_valentine_4.html.

Chen, Mel. *Animacies: Biopolitics, Racial Mattering, and Queer Affect*. Durham, NC: Duke University Press, 2012.

Cheng, Anne Anlin. *The Melancholy of Race: Psychoanalysis, Assimilation, and Hidden Grief*. Oxford: Oxford University Press, 2001.

– *Second Skin: Josephine Baker & the Modern Surface*. Oxford: Oxford University Press, 2013.

Esteve, Mary. "Queer Consumerism, Straight Happiness: Highsmith's 'Right Economy.'" *Post45*, December 18, 2012. http://post45.research.yale.edu/2012/12/queer-consumerism-straight-happiness-highsmiths-right-economy/#identifier_39_2883.

Felski, Rita. *The Limits of Critique*. Chicago: University of Chicago Press, 2015.

Goffman, Erving. *Frame Analysis: An Essay on the Organization of Experience*. Hanover, NH: Northeastern University Press, 1974.

Grosz, Elizabeth. *Becoming Undone: Darwinian Reflections on Life, Politics, and Art*. Durham, NC: Duke University Press, 2011.

Guillory, John. "The Sokal Affair and the History of Criticism." *Critical Inquiry* 28, no. 2 (2002): 470–508.

Hartman, Saidiya. *Scenes of Subjection: Terror, Slavery, and Self-Making in Nineteenth-Century America*. Oxford: Oxford University Press, 1997.

Hensley, Nathan K. "Curatorial Reading and Endless War." *Victorian Studies* 56, no. 1 (2013): 59–83.

Hesford, Victoria. "Highsmith: A Romance of the 1950's, and: Beautiful Shadow: A Life of Patricia Highsmith (review)." *MLN* 118, no. 5 (Dec. 2003): 1311–17.

– "Patriotic Perversions: Patricia Highsmith's Queer Vision of Cold War America in *The Price of Salt*, *The Blunderer*, and *Deep Water*." *Women's Studies Quarterly* 33, no. 3/4 (2005): 215–33.

Highsmith, Patricia. *Plotting and Writing Suspense Fiction*. New York: St Martin's, 1981.

– *The Price of Salt*. 1952. New York: Norton, 2004.

Jackson, Shirley. "My Life with R. H. Macy." *New Republic*, December 22, 1941. http://www.newrepublic.com/article/books-and-arts/75022/my-life-r-h-macy.

Jameson, Fredric. *The Antinomies of Realism*. New York: Verso Books, 2013.

Latour, Bruno. *Reassembling the Social: An Introduction to Actor-Network-Theory*. Oxford: Oxford University Press, 2005.

– "Why Has Critique Run Out of Steam? From Matters of Fact to Matters of Concern." *Critical Inquiry* 30 (2004): 225–48.

Latour, Bruno, and Steven Woolgar. *Laboratory Life: The Construction of Scientific Facts*. Princeton: Princeton University Press, 1979.

Love, Heather. "The Temptations: Donna Haraway, Feminist Objectivity, and the Problem of Critique." In *Critique and Postcritique*, edited by Elizabeth Anker and Rita Felski, 50–72. Durham, NC: Duke University Press, 2017.

Mills, C. Wright. "The Great Salesroom." In *White Collar: The American Middle Classes*, 161–88. Oxford: Oxford University Press, 1951.

Perrin, Tom. "On Patricia Highsmith." *Post45*, December 18, 2012. http://post45.research.yale.edu/2012/12/cluster-introduction-patricia-highsmith/#identifier_0_2773.

Schenkar, Joan. *The Talented Miss Highsmith: The Secret Life and Serious Art of Patricia Highsmith*. New York: St Martin's, 2009.

Schryer, Stephen. *Fantasies of the New Class: Ideologies of Professionalism in Post-World War II American Fiction*. New York: Columbia University Press, 2011.

Seltzer, Mark. "The Daily Planet." *Post45*, December 18, 2012. http://post45.research.yale.edu/2012/12/the-daily-planet/.

– "The Official World." *Critical Inquiry* 37, no. 4 (2011): 724–53.

– "Parlor Games: The Apriorization of the Media." *Critical Inquiry* 36, no. 1 (2009): 100–33.

Siebers, Tobin. *Disability Theory*. Ann Arbor: University of Michigan Press, 2008.

Sokal, Alan. "Transgressing the Boundaries: Toward a Transformational Hermeneutics of Quantum Gravity." *Social Text* 46/47 (1996): 217–52.

Stryker, Susan. "My Words to Victor Frankenstein above the Village of Chamounix: Performing Transgender Rage." *GLQ: A Journal of Lesbian and Gay Studies* 1, no. 3 (1994): 237–54.

Trask, Michael. *Camp Sites: Sex, Politics, and Academic Style in Postwar America*. Stanford: Stanford University Press, 2013.

– "Highsmith's Method." *American Literary History* 22, no. 3 (2010): 584–614.

Warner, Michael. *The Trouble with Normal*. Cambridge, MA: Harvard University Press, 2000.

White, Patricia. "Sketchy Lesbians: Carol as History and Fantasy." *Film Quarterly* 69, no. 2 (Winter 2015): 8–18.

PART IV

Recounting: Literary Evidence and Liberal Narration

7 The Proletarian Thirties and Canadian Literary History

ANDREA HASENBANK

The On-to-Ottawa Trek had all the elements of a great Canadian story. In the spring and summer of 1935, a group of young unemployed men gathered together on the West Coast and set off to bring their plight to the nation's capital. This group, mixed in origin, ethnicity, and background, traversed the prairies along the CPR rail line, invoking the symbolism of the Last Spike and the railway's nation-building power. Along the way, communities turned out in full force to support "the boys," with food, money, and large celebrations. The group stopped in Regina, Saskatchewan, while a delegation of its leaders completed the trip to Ottawa and successfully met with Prime Minister R.B. Bennett. The delegation's return came on July 1, the national holiday then called Dominion Day.

In reality, the Trek played out in reverse of every national myth: the trekkers returned from the frontier crippled by poverty; their delegation was forcibly ejected by the prime minister; and Dominion Day in Regina erupted into violence as the RCMP turned horses and clubs against Canadian workers. This story, in many ways a stand-in for the period as a whole, is not one that fits easily into larger Canadian narratives, nor do its animating forces of class conflict, deprivation, racism, and state-sponsored violence find much representation in the country's histories. Like the Trek within political history, the proletarian texts[1] that address the tensions of the Depression era are regarded as aberrant within a literary tradition equally structured and policed by liberalism. However, during the 1930s in Canada, an emergent network of Left political groups, organizations, labour unions, cultural bodies, and publications (dominated by but not limited to the Communist Party) transmitted and amplified an increasingly politicized response to the precarious position of ordinary people. A handful of key events – the legal battle against the repressive Section 98 of the Criminal Code, the On-to-Ottawa Trek, and, in the latter half of the decade, the global fight against fascism – were tirelessly relayed and repeated in print campaigns designed to provoke working people into a state of resistance energized by anger. The language and speech of the pamphlets and manifestos produced by these groups infused the organizing power of their political and social movements with urgency, drawing variously on socialist and populist modes of address to project a proletarian public onto the Canadian populace. Equally, Canadian poets, novelists, journalists, and jurists grappled across genres with the economic and social conditions of strife lived out in the workplace, the relief office, the picket line, the courtroom, and the jail.

What might be described as "the proletarian thirties" captures the particular confluence of economic hardship, agitation among workers and the unemployed, strict laws surrounding immigration and political protest, and the rise of challengers to the Canadian political firmament on both the left and the right. The cultural impact of these phenomena was mediated through a discrete set of writers, publishers, artists, and critics – many of whom were actively involved with these protesting labour and political groups, or who had at least expressed sympathies with them. Individually and organizationally, they collaborated to share the resources that comprised public communication: workspace, performance space, publication space, shops and shelf space, presses, distributors, even readers, down to being reproduced side by side on the same pages. Together, their interactions and relationships formed a network that made class legible within the politics and the literature of the decade.

This ethos of collaboration and the shared labour of cultural production were certainly not unique to the Canadian scene.[2] However, the ways in which Canadian literary history has been made blind to this proletarian thread are very particular. Canadian culture remains uneasy with both its colonial/colonizing origins and its modern multicultural face. Canada's cultural production has been caught between the influences of Britain and the United States, superpowers alternately aligned in the Canadian national discourse with tradition and invention, inheritance and commercialism, effacement and corruption. In order to grapple with these conditions, the federal and provincial governments established a system of specifically Canadian institutions immediately following the Second World War, supported by a national communications network. The postwar period saw the dominance of a liberal political ideology that was able to be enacted, and reproduced, through these networks, while also being enforced through political institutions. This dominance was maintained culturally by tacit policing on three fronts: What is "Canadian"? What is "literature"? What supports the liberal project of Canada? These questions have contributed to the erasure of proletarian texts *as* literature from the narrative of Canadian literary history. To the extent that these texts have found an audience at all, they have been legible only as historical documents and not as part of an ongoing literary tradition.

A different methodological lens may help in making the proletarian readable within Canadian literary history. As I employ it, book history has allowed me to view the production, circulation, and reception of texts in social and material terms; and indeed, this disciplinary orientation shares some elements with labour history and histories of working-class culture. By taking the book as the material intersection of a set of social relationships, this approach has a sense of collectivity with the potential to reconfigure liberal assumptions about the circulation of ideas, the composition of the public sphere, and the operations of a given text. As a methodology, it draws first on the thick descriptive powers of bibliography, setting these into an understanding of "the book" (or any print object) as embedded in a fluid set of processes, themselves operating within a specific economic, political, legal, and social context.[3] Proletarian texts often exist outside of the book form: with their authors having limited resources to publish, and limited access to the cultural capital that deems some texts as worthy of attention and others not, my materials are more likely to be found in newspapers, handmade periodicals, or typewritten broadsides. Compounding the exclusion, these texts are less likely to be preserved in libraries and archives and more likely to be destroyed, lost, or illegal. The inclusion of non-book texts as objects of study is crucial to understanding proletarian literature as operating within the same conditions and conduits as mainstream Canadian literature but also to recognizing how different types of privilege have altered its trajectories. The very concept of "literary" history excludes the majority of proletarian writing while replicating problematic power relationships among writers, readers, critics, and legislators: the discipline itself is complicit in the exclusion of the proletarian. Critical book history has the necessary tools to address proletarian texts as they appear at the juncture of literature and documentary; in this view, I am interested in returning material questions to literary studies, while also emphasizing the formal, narrative, and figurative elements of proletarian writing that make these texts so appealing as historical accounts.

Ronald Liversedge's memoir, *Recollections of the On-to-Ottawa Trek,* is itself highly appealing, both as a narrative text and as a colourful adjunct to the documentation of a historical event. Furthermore, the publication history of the *Recollections,* first in its proletarian form as a local memoir produced by volunteer labour and shared among comrades and then in its documentary form as part of a paperback edition of historical evidence relating to the Trek and the Regina Riot, clearly reveals the multiple circuits through which proletarian texts are circulated – and diverted. My reading of Liversedge's text allows me to push on definitions of both "proletarian" and "literary" in ways that show these attributions to be a function of how the text is framed and read. The *Recollections* can be significantly dated to 1935 (the context of the memoir), 1963 (the first publication as a pamphlet/booklet), and 1973 (the release of the Carleton Library edition edited by Victor Hoar). Each of these dates marks the confluence of various cultural networks and institutions at different points in the development of Canadian literary history, and the situation of the *Recollections* at each juncture illustrates the ways in which proletarian texts can be "written out" of literary history while being "read into" political and social history. A fresh focus on proletarian texts stemming from the 1930s, such as Liversedge's *Recollections,* has the potential to destabilize liberal assumptions about what counts as Canadian literary history, as these texts allow critics to address issues of exclusion in the dominant narrative, including colonialism, classism, and elitism more broadly.

Liberal Interventions in Canadian Literary History

Beginning with the decisive 1935 election that saw William Lyon Mackenzie King defeat millionaire R.B. Bennett's Conservatives, Canada's politics were dominated by a liberal ethos, in both the small-l and capital-L varieties, through to the end of the century. Between 1935 and 2005, Parliament was led by the Liberal Party for a total of fifty-five years.[4] However, historians have traced the role of liberalism in shaping not just the political and economic concerns of Canada but also its social and cultural development over a much more expansive span of time. Ian McKay's reworking of Canadian history, first set out in "The Liberal Order Framework," has been transformative to conventional Canadian historians, and we are now beginning to feel its effects on the formulation of literary histories as well. McKay takes up the "liberal order" as the "project of liberal rule" deriving from the central concepts of liberty, equality, and property: that is, as an ideology manifested in institutions, practices, language, and social organization rather than one embodied strictly within those core concepts.[5] In this way, he configures Canada as a Gramscian political terrain, organized not in terms of a fixed top and bottom but as a centre and a periphery pressing ever against each other: rather than rulers and ruled, we have the insecure leadership of the liberal order and its resistors.[6] McKay's framework is intended as a method for reinvigorating the fractured writing and study of Canadian history, but it provides a necessary scaffold for Canada's literary history as well. Indeed, what McKay calls the "Canadian nationalist myth-symbol complex" is especially applicable to reworking received literary histories and the role of state institutions in shaping Canada's cultural production.[7] Reimagining Canada as a project perpetually on the make demands an awareness of *how* it is made, rather than acquiescing to false depictions of Canada as an essentialist nation or as an empty geographic space. A focus on making preserves the complex network of very human endeavours so needed to read Canada's proletarian current as one of many possible histories.

By invoking the term "liberal" to displace other ideological monoliths – capitalism, modernity, the bourgeoisie, the democratic system – historian Jeffrey McNairn claims McKay's "Liberal Order Framework" makes a shift to an intellectual framework for Canadian history rather than a political or economic one.[8] This framework emphasizes the imaginative work of structuring the nation, as well as the shared creativity of sustaining it. The received narrative of Canadian literary history as the necessary façade of national identity construction upheld by state-building projects such as transportation, communication, and industrial networks situates Canadian literature as one institution among many governed by state policies and regulated by gatekeeping functionaries. Canadian literature, in this telling, exists to shore up Canadianness, which is a civilized, contained, and above-all middlebrow enterprise. McNairn finds that McKay's focus on the entity called Canada, rather than North American or even transatlantic relationships, risks "re-privileging the nation-state" in a way that may not be productive for understanding the circulation of ideas and culture.[9] However, I would argue that the intense focus of the state on Canadian cultural institutions and industries in the postwar era, including the Royal

Commission on National Development in the Arts, Letters and Sciences (the Massey Commission), the Canadian Broadcasting Corporation, the National Film Board, the Canada Council and others, and the influence of those formations on Canada's literary history, renders the nation-state a necessary component of any historical analysis of Canadian literature. The study of national identity is certainly adjacent to the study of these institutions, but the position of such institutions as producers, distributors, responders, and preservers along the communications circuit makes them central to addressing textual questions.

The Massey Commission has been ascribed a gravitational pull for its reconfiguration of the mid-century Canadian cultural firmament.[10] Certainly, the commission's 1951 report is one of the key elements of the postwar liberal order, but its intervention into the cultural industry must be read within the political conjuncture of the same moment for a more complete view of the ways in which earlier proletarian texts were effaced by the construction of a particular kind of national identity. In this way, the Massey Report goes hand in hand with the 1947 Citizenship Act, sharing the work of shoring up the state by shaping ideas of the nation and the citizen as a unified body. The creation of the national narrative itself is the primary struggle of liberal Canadianness. Not only is class unavailable as a category of identity, but the elements that define proletarian literature – transience, instability, and radical politicization – actively threaten the national narrative. As such, proletarian texts, and the decade to which they are connected, became increasingly illegible within Canadian cultural history in the postwar period.

In an address marking the passing of the Citizenship Act, Justice A.M. Manson of the British Columbia Supreme Court posits citizenship as connoting "something more than mere nationality; it has to do rather with the individual's attitude and conduct ... One wonders how many of the twelve million odd people in Canada are real Canadian citizens and how many are merely inhabitants of our country."[11] Manson goes on to put the new legislation within a lineage of Roman, Anglo-Saxon, and then British ideas of the public and of justice. His version of history leaps over the suffering and exclusion of the Depression and the great changes to public life more generally in the interwar period. A contemporary pamphlet, "How to Become a Canadian Citizen," produced by the newly formed Canadian Citizenship Branch of the federal government, offers a similarly truncated narrative. The guide moves straight from the Treaty of Versailles to the Second World War, covering the 1930s with only a cursory mention of the Statute of

Westminster.[12] Caren Irr remarks that during this period, in between the Statute of Westminster and the Citizenship Act, Canada attained the status of a nation, but that nationhood was marked by a "confusion of practices."[13] This confusion was formally resolved for an emergent Canada in the figure of the citizen, distinct from both British subjects and immigrant masses. Paul Hjartarson has pointed to efforts by the state to "'Canadianize'" allophone cultures in between the First and Second World Wars through legal measures. Indeed, the Conservative government revised the Immigration Act and the Criminal Code in the 1920s and 1930s in order to continue policies enacted under the War Measures Act to restrict immigration and censor the importation, printing, publication, or circulation of any seditious materials, particularly those published in an "enemy language" or the equally suspicious Russian, Ukrainian, and Finnish – a project continued by the Liberals in the postwar era. These materials, and their assumed connection to politically radical groups of newcomers who entered the country following the Bolshevik Revolution, were notably targeted. To further uproot the influence of both publications and speakers who might be more concerned with participation in Canada's economic and political life than in upholding its self-told story, the state engaged in "assimilative work on the children of immigrants [through] compulsory schooling in English language and culture."[14] This suspicion of foreigners generally, and especially of their perceived connection to Communist radicalism, played a significant, though underexamined, role in the extinguishing of proletarian texts from this period. Reflecting on this fractured relationship among ethnicity, language, and class identity, Irr comments on the potential of the skills and social knowledges immigrants attained through activity within local formations to undo other collective identities: "Some argue that the assimilation tactics immigrants learned in left groups helped participants to move into the middle class, thus defusing the political potential of both ethnicity and class in Canada."[15] The loss of language continuity, as well as printing houses and readerships in these languages, severed a potential throughline of resistance for generations.

In both Manson's speech and in the citizenship pamphlet, as in Canadian law during the interwar period, non-Anglo immigrants are treated with wariness. Manson points to various nationalities of European origin and labels them "regrettable … cells of foreign born," capable of becoming "good Canadians if only we will take them in hand, and naturalize them culturally, politically, and spiritually."[16] The Citizenship

Branch pamphlet, presumably aimed at many of these same groups, refers only to "people, drawn from every racial group, [who] are welded into a mighty democratic force through their love of freedom, hatred of oppression, and the steadfast determination that the powers of government shall be exercised by and through the people for the common benefit of all."[17] Linguistic heterogeneity, and especially the possible taint of radical politics concealed within unfamiliar tongues, was a source of anxiety for Canadian officials; rhetorically, citizenship represented an erasure of difference, though it was the ideological work of the liberal order that produced these populations as potential sites of disruption.

As book history has oscillated between particular case studies and large-scale national projects, it has given attention to the role of printing and reading among the linguistic practices that support the nation-state. The *History of the Book in Canada* project, completed in 2007, shows the tension between the more totalizing narratives of state and nation and the more pluralistic accounts of the one-to-one relationships between readers and text objects that comprise the history of Canadian print. The third volume of the collection, which covers the period 1918–1980, examines modern print production and circulation, ranging beyond the book – in fact, editors Carole Gerson and Jacques Michon identify Canadian book publishing as a late development, growing out of earlier newspaper and periodical presses only in the second half of the twentieth century.[18] However, proletarian texts, particularly those dating to the 1930s, still remain underserved in this history. In relation to publishing, Gerson and Michon summarize the decade thus: "The Great Depression of the 1930s led to stagnation in publishing activity as some firms set up in the previous decade were forced to close. However, the decade also saw the development of new forms of solidarity as collective publications and small magazines brought together socially committed writers and artists, many of whom would become prominent during and after the Second World War."[19] The editors figure the postwar moment as the full maturation of modern Canadian print, particularly under the influence of the "decisive impact" of governmental inquiry and guidance.[20] Indeed, Canada as an object of reflection and study became possible only when demographic shifts and the corresponding boom in Canadian universities solidified Canadian literature as a field of study, supported by professor-writer-critics and a newly posited canon of texts.

The Canadian literary canon began to take shape in this moment, addressing itself to a homogenized version of the Canadian citizen defined against outsiders, both geographic and ideological, and connected to the nation through the new state media. Furthermore, postwar prosperity and population change saw greater investments in education, including universities, as part of this social project. It is this audience in particular that is marked out by this nationalist framing. Perhaps most durably, Northrop Frye has been linked with the erstwhile dominant narrative of Canadian literary history. Frye situates his narrative of literary history within a recognizably liberal historiography: "Like other kinds of history, it has its own themes of exploration, settlement, and development, but these themes relate to a social *imagination* that explores and settles and develops."[21] What this account of history lacks is an agent and a sense of the active social struggle that propels this development. Frye offers a cogent account of the interconnected institutions and formations that supported and governed Canadian literature at mid-century: "Scholarships, prizes, university posts, await the dedicated writer."[22] Frye's history follows Donald Creighton's Laurentian thesis, which locates the Saint Lawrence Seaway as the throughline of Canadian development, both geographically and economically.[23] Creighton's idea, a driving force in conventional Canadian history even up to the present moment, in turn draws on Harold Innis's staple theory, first synthesized in *The Bias of Communication*.[24] Both ascribe centrality to colonial relationships with Britain and France, extended into the twentieth century by trade with First Nations, resource extraction, and agriculture. From this historical narrative, dominated by geographical immensity and mediated by transplanted and isolated colonial subjects, Frye posits his own theory of Canadian literature as rooted in a "garrison mentality," to use his now infamous term.[25] For Frye, the garrison is an insular community, tightly bound by law and order (both political and moral), up against unknowable natural threats as well as the more human threat of outsiders. Sectarian fractures drive conflict inside the garrison, whereas class consciousness and action remain always on the outside. To Frye, the role of the "creative mind in society" – and by extension the role of the critic – is to help cohere a national identity[26] rather than to challenge the Canadian firmament.

Legible and Illegible

Locating ideologically charged texts within Canada's literary history is not just a problem of retrospection; marking and claiming proletarian writing posed a challenge to critics in that period as well. Ruth McKenzie's 1939 article in the *Dalhousie Review*, "Proletarian Literature in Canada," offers an inside view of the difficulties with identifying the "proletarian" in a Canadian context, particularly when critics are equally invested in identifying a distinctly national literature. McKenzie, asking whether such an object exists, defines proletarian literature as "literature which describes the life of the working class from a class-conscious and revolutionary point of view," in which "the worker is regarded as the victim of capitalistic exploitation; as the instrument of revolution by which a new social order will be ushered in. He, himself, is of more importance as a factor in society than as an individual."[27] Again, issues of authorship and authenticity are central to such evaluations. McKenzie pointedly states that proletarian writing is not limited to working-class authors – not with an eye to inclusiveness, but because "few members of the labouring classes are articulate in the literary sense."[28] This assessment is preoccupied with determining the characteristic marks of proletarian writing, mingling class identity with value judgments. McKenzie's definition of proletarian literature revolves around the portrayal of the worker as "the instrument of revolution" rather than an active voice circulating through the text.[29] Her survey takes in a range of forms, genres, and authors but concludes that although numerous Canadian writers show "proletarian interest," "very few of their works are truly proletarian according to our definition."[30] As well, she identifies two barriers to a large-scale movement toward proletarian fiction in Canada: a limited pool of writers who are both talented and concerned about the exploitation of workers (in McKenzie's estimation) and few outlets for publication.[31] Alternatively, those works showing the dynamic revolutionary force of the worker are "generally lacking in literary value."[32] McKenzie's consideration of proletarian writing is not open to unpolished or populist texts; her critique is invested in a schematic that privileges poetry over fiction while also claiming a typically "romantic tradition" for Canadian writing.[33]

The apparent gap between political commitment and literary prowess is also a point of contention for Earle Birney, whose writing as literary editor for the *Canadian Forum* takes a charged view of the ideological significance of proletarian fiction. Commenting on the *Forum*'s 1937 short story contest, Birney raises the issue of craft over content, stating that "to be a 'proletarian' artist it is not enough to voice the protests of workers; it is necessary also to be an artist, to shape material painstakingly into an illusion of life."[34] Writing style becomes a figure of class conflict, through which assumptions about education, intelligence, and intrinsic worth are played out. Birney takes the reverse position of McKenzie: rather than looking to the poor outputs of working-class writers, he decries the condescension of middle-class authors who "seem to think that the 'lower classes' should be written about only in words of not more than five letters ... with a careful absence of anything unusual in phrasing."[35] This serves only to propagate "ignorance about the complex realities of [a] working-class character," who is neither "simply, incoherent, passive" nor a "mechanized man."[36] The tendency to portray the working classes in stock types or to use revolutionaries for "atmosphere and fashionable value" is a way to signify proletarian sympathies,[37] as in McKenzie's discussion, while denying the agency and energy of actual proletarians.

Both Birney and McKenzie look to social revolution only in a future state, seeing "ripples of revolutionary thought," but no "vigorous current threatening to sweep the stream out of its placid course."[38] Writing pessimistically from the end of the 1930s, both critics concede that with prosperity seemingly just around the corner, Canadian writers are likely to return to traditional, romantic themes. Notably, as judge of the *Canadian Forum* fiction contest, Birney selected Luella Creighton's "The Cornfield," a naturalistic story of children on a Mennonite farm, rather than any of the more markedly proletarian submissions.[39] Indeed, Irr notes that few literary works were produced that met the criteria set forth by Birney and McKenzie or that met the criteria American proletarian writers were debating among themselves.[40] The task of contemporary critics is to follow this path even as it is trampled over by the histories of war and the welfare state. We must seek out obscured texts and work through the impact of the 1930s on Canadian cultural and public discourse afterward.

For literary history, the proletarian problem is doubled: in its own era, running alongside and occasionally intersecting with modernism, the proletarian was read as insufficiently sophisticated or self-conscious about its language. The elements of what make a text proletarian can often be used as criteria for excluding it from the literary realm: we see this tension in McKenzie and Birney's evaluations, and we see it in the work of the critics that followed in the postwar generation. However, in the period of canon formation, the proletarian was read as dangerous or challenging, and as such was something to be segregated. The liberal order has maintained a strong influence over Canadian literary historiography, particularly since the Second World War; however, it would be a mistake to read the liberal narrative as a totalizing one. As a contributor to the *1965 Literary History of Canada*, published just prior to the celebration of Canada's first centennial (the same volume containing Frye's influential essay), Frank Watt positions his history of protest literature against the "conservative act" of Confederation and the national narratives that followed. Instead, he traces a current of resistance that "was almost, but never entirely, stifled" by the practices of nation-building.[41] Indeed, taking a dialectical view, Watt claims that Canadian cultural maturity could be achieved only by the collision of that conservative ideal with a counternarrative of struggle.[42] Watt traces the early reception of Marx and the circulation more generally of socialist ideals among Canadian writers, finding revolutionary expression among a set of late-Victorian "poetasters" and journalists who linked creative power to a "proletarian aesthetic."[43] Despite the limited literary value of these works, Watt insists their "existence is worth recording because [they] remained alive to a range of ideals and social experiences largely ignored by the respectable Canadian tradition of the period."[44] This current continued to find channels among a growing working class in Canada's economic boom during the early twentieth century and grew more forceful through the period of post–World War I disillusion, flowing beneath modernist expressions of moral and intellectual critique. However, it is with the crisis of the Great Depression in the 1930s that Watt asserts that "what had been an insignificant proletarian minority swelled in numbers and power and became, for the first time, of major literary and cultural significance."[45] Watt primarily discusses little magazines and newspapers as the key outlets for proletarian writing – sources bound by periodicity and marked by an ephemerality that necessarily limits their long-term visibility. His history does not extend beyond the end of the 1930s: arguably, the dialectical collision he depicts between national ideal and protest generated a kind of cultural synthesis, which was neatly incorporated into postwar liberalism as the state came to manage key institutions for funding, producing, disseminating, and critiquing Canadian literature. Still, by repositioning the appearance of expressions of rebellion and radicalism past the early days of Confederation, Watt makes the case for a Canadian proletarianism coexisting with the birth of Canada itself.

Liversedge's *Recollections*

The history of Ronald Liversedge's Depression memoir, *Recollections of the On-to-Ottawa Trek*, animates these narratives of canonical formation and exclusion in illustrative ways. In its original edition, the *Recollections* is a clear example of a proletarian text: written by a non-professional, framed by the rhetoric of Communist Party activists and labour agitators, presenting a personal narrative shot through with a clear political didacticism, produced cheaply and poorly in small numbers, and forgotten to all but a few specialized collectors. However, Liversedge's text was taken up first by the academic realm and then by the apparatus of Canadian mass cultural institutions – both of which have effectively shaped liberal histories since the mid-twentieth century – and in the process it was reframed away from its proletarian origins.

Liversedge's *Recollections* narrates his experiences as a British immigrant turned itinerant labourer in Western Canada during the 1930s. The memoir is particularly focused around the 1935 relief camp strikes, beginning in Vancouver, which broke out into the On-to-Ottawa Trek of May and June 1935 and ended in violent clashes with the RCMP and local police on Dominion Day in what quickly became known as the Regina Riot. The text itself offers little biographical information about the author. Liversedge describes himself as a veteran of World War I and a trade unionist who emigrated from England in 1927, fleeing unemployment and widespread deprivation due to depressed conditions in the Lancashire cotton and Welsh mining industries, which gave rise to the UK's general strike of 1926.[46] Additional background material, particularly relating to Liversedge's work as a writer, is largely absent from this first edition and its later republication; for this, we must look to another scholarly recuperation. David Yorke's introduction to *Mac-Pap*, Liversedge's later memoir of the Spanish Civil War, fills in some of this authorial context. *Mac-Pap* traces a narrative common to two centuries of working-class autobiography: a labouring background, an early experience of war and conflict, self-education in the literary classics, and a socialist initiation. The biographical narrative continues as an emigrant's tale, taking Liversedge from England to Australia and back, and then to Canada following the 1926 general strike, as Liversedge himself relates in the *Recollections*; Yorke, however, provides a historian's detail and sourcing. From there, Liversedge's story merges into the collective narrative of jobless men moving west during the Great Depression. The text is tersely narrated, following a loose and episodic structure. Indeed, Liversedge takes on the role of a drifting anti-hero, consciously or not falling into a pattern that recurs in other modernist and masculinist Canadian novels of the same period (especially Douglas Durkin's *The Magpie* and Frederick Grove's *Settlers of the Marsh*), as well as later novels that draw on experiences of the

Depression (such as Hugh Garner's *Cabbagetown* and Dyson Carter's *Fatherless Sons*). His writing process, too, is rooted in the experience of this upheaval. Liversedge began writing in the late 1950s while in recovery from alcoholism, setting down lengthy, descriptive memoirs of the Trek and the Spanish Civil War almost entirely from memory.[47] It is not clear how much of the early *Recollections* went through editing, if it did at all; the Hoar edition appended a great deal of material to surround the memoir but did not alter the core narrative text.

The first publication of the *Recollections* is not entirely transparent in its presentation. The introduction to the memoir is written by Tom McEwen, who played a significant role in all of the key events concerning the Communist Left during the 1930s. McEwen was an organizer for the Communist Party across the Western provinces before becoming a founding member and general secretary for the party's "red union" arm, the Workers' Unity League. McEwen was among the eight Communist leaders arrested and tried under the Criminal Code's section 98 provisions against unlawful assembly, the issue that dominated proletarian protest through the first half of the decade. Following the release of the so-called "Kingston Eight," McEwen was instrumental in organizing a series of relief camp strikes on the West Coast and was one of the leaders of the On-to-Ottawa Trek. At the time of the *Recollections*' original publication, McEwen continued to be active as a Communist politician (later representing the renamed Labor-Progressive Party as well) and journalist in the Vancouver area.[48] Accordingly, his introduction to Liversedge's text carries a great deal of weight: it establishes the author's proletarian bona fides while also tying the *Recollections* to a particularly potent formation of West Coast radicalism, both at the time of the narrative's events and enduring into the moment of publication.

The publication and printing of the first edition of the *Recollections* offers a window into the often ad hoc methods of producing proletarian texts. It is a utilitarian piece of work.[49] The book is roughly octavo, measuring 5.5 inches by 8.5 inches, equivalent to letter-sized paper folded in half. It is 174 pages, staple-bound, and mimeographed. This edition is often referred to as "the yellow book" for its coated cardstock cover, which features a sketch of marchers in silhouette with the Parliament buildings in the background and a hand-lettered title in the foreground. Inside, several documents contemporary to the Trek are reproduced: two photos, showing May Day 1935 demonstrations in Stanley Park, Vancouver, and a line of marchers entering Calgary as part of the Trek,[50] and a handbill calling for an assembly of marchers at Gore Avenue,

Vancouver, June 3, 1935.[51] The only publication detail given is a note at the end of the introduction, indicating that "this Booklet [was] produced by Voluntary Labor."[52] There is no date, no named organization, and no indication of the size of the original print run. Yorke notes that Liversedge initially submitted his manuscript to Progress Books, then the publishing arm of the Communist Party of Canada;[53] however, the memoir was rejected, ultimately placing it at a greater remove from the "official" purview of the CPC than many other Canadian proletarian texts. Instead, the memoir was produced by friends and in a small edition of one thousand copies – entirely without Liversedge's knowledge.[54] The University of Alberta Library, which holds a copy in its Special Collections, gives the publication date as 1961, noting that the book was published by "a group of private citizens." Certainly, internal references to the experiences of boilermakers in Vancouver in 1960 indicate that it cannot have been published before this date.[55] Bibliographer Peter Weinrich gives a publication date of 1963, which corresponds to the date given in the Canadian National Catalogue (AMICUS).

With such limited publication information, it is difficult to trace either distribution or circulation. Catalogue searches show a few scattered copies, mostly held in special collections sections of university libraries across the country. An inscription in ink on the inside cover of my own copy, reading "D. Godfrey \ 4149 Sardis St \ Burnaby \ 161-6801," provides at least some evidence that the text did circulate in the Vancouver area before its re-publication. The readership and overall reception remain largely unknown, although Yorke claims that the memoir "was the first, and at the time the only full description of the Trek."[56] This first edition of the text came to greater prominence – and ultimately entered the circuits of the larger academy – when it reached the attention of Victor Hoar, professor of English at the University of Western Ontario. Hoar used Liversedge's later memoir of the Spanish Civil War (which was not itself published until Yorke's 2013 edition) as a source text for his research into the Mackenzie–Papineau Battalion, and through that text he came to the *Recollections*.

Hoar's editorial work in producing the *Recollections* for the Carleton Library Series in 1973 diverts the original cycle of the text into one dominated by academic institutions and oriented around formal, state-centric narratives of history. Despite Hoar's position as a literary scholar, his introduction to the Carleton edition offers very little in the way of narrative analysis or biography of its author. Instead, it sets out a historical background for the relief camps and the On-to-Ottawa Trek itself.

This version of the memoir was published with a number of other governmental records and documents relating to the Trek, the Regina Riot, and the political aftermath, as a sort of Depression case study. Here, the *Recollections* becomes only one document among many – a colourful "memory book,"[57] but not an authoritative stand-alone account. When they are recovered in this way, however infrequently, proletarian texts are severed from their networks of origin, and much of the context of circulation and readership is erased. Furthermore, the subsumption of the narrative elements of the text into a documentarian frame transforms a body of literature into the records of a social movement and of labour history. Without a doubt, publications in this form produce valuable and necessary scholarly work to which studies of working-class life and culture in a number of fields are heavily indebted; however, this disciplinary shift also renders many proletarian texts invisible to the lens of literary history.

To the extent that it is made reference to at all, Liversedge's *Recollections* appears in histories of radical politics and working-class movements rather than in appraisals of narrative forms. Indeed, the work of making proletarian literature legible within a general Canadian literary history has necessarily been engaged with a particular kind of historiography that has opened the way for cultural studies and textual objects like Liversedge's text. On one hand labour history in Canada, particularly since the 1970s, has responded to the work of E.P. Thompson and the questions of the Birmingham School, while on the other hand it has been built up and out from the practices of local history. Much of this work intersects with concurrent work in publishing and theatre, some at the local level and some reaching larger national audiences. For example, the leftist publisher New Hogtown Press, which sprang out of the student movement in Toronto during the 1960s, publishing radical pamphlets and later going on to re-publish collections of plays and short stories taken from the leftist periodicals of the 1930s,[58] was a significant resource through the 1970s for publishing the work of young Marxist historians (and former student radicals).[59] The products of this research – bibliographies, publication lists, connections among formations and groupings, oral histories, artefacts – are also foundational to reconstructing a more materially focused literary history.

In 1973, Russell Hann and collaborators Gregory Kealey, Linda Kealey, and Peter Warrian recorded a number of archival collections, newspapers, pamphlets, and government documents in their bibliography,

Primary Sources in Canadian Working-Class History 1860–1930. The compilers position themselves as working to fill in the "blindspots created by the Laurentian approach to Canadian social history,"[60] as well as the union-centric focus of much contemporary labour history. Hann et al. reconfigure the "virgin territory" of Canadian geography as the uncharted historiography of the Canadian working class,[61] disrupting the received narratives with their imagery. Following on this first attempt, Peter Weinrich's massive 1982 bibliography, *Social Protest from the Left in Canada, 1870–1970*, decisively pushes scholarly consideration of proletarian print beyond the book and the little magazine, taking account of the pamphlet and periodical press as well as government documents and manuscript/archival collections across Canada. Significantly, Weinrich extends the view of this body of material well beyond the 1930s, right up into the moment of labour history's emergence in the 1970s (a formation in which Hann and his collaborators were central participants). In his commentary, Weinrich reflects on the ways in which the limited survival of proletarian print, ephemeral and materially fragile, belies its actual prevalence; the "survival rate bears no relation whatsoever to its distribution and impact at the time of publication,"[62] the fact of which has led to an underestimation of the amount of material and hence to a critical underestimation of the role played by particular groups, organizations, and institutions in the political and cultural currents of the 1930s. Bibliographic projects such as these provide an essential resource for recomposing these narratives, tracking the primary sources and material details vital to labour historians and literary historians alike. In particular, by acting as a point of reference as well as an archival directory, the bibliographies of Weinrich and Hann et al. have enabled those scholars engaged in print history to make a particularly generative contribution to re-evaluating the proletarian moment in Canadian literary history.

The labour historians emerging out of this materialist turn have advanced new considerations of class and culture as relevant to history; unsurprisingly, these scholars have also looked to literature as a contributor to this historiography. Bryan Palmer points to Watt's work as a breakthrough for the study of Canadian literary radicalism side by side with that of working-class cultural formations.[63] With this new visibility for proletarianism in literature, Palmer identifies a valuable framework for working-class history, particularly for a moment of Canadian history previously dominated by much more conservative narratives that reproduce Innis's blind spot regarding the influence of labour. Conversely, with Marxist history gaining ground in the subsequent decades, Palmer sends a warning about the appearance of a more nationalistic literary criticism; this, he says, crowded out class-oriented readings just as they began to appear and obscured the "left underside of the Canadian literary legacy."[64] This critique extends to literary histories as well, if not to the body of texts that could conceivably be called a Canadian literature.

The liberal narrative of Canadian literary history has proved to be remarkably elastic, incorporating new forms of identity and hybridity with each successive decade. Liversedge's own memoir places the Trek within the recuperation of a liberal order rather than as the surge and failure of a radical populist challenge. In this telling, the fact that the Conservatives were "swept into oblivion"[65] in the next election is enough of a victory, particularly as questions of unemployment were swept away by the advent of world war and as the welfare state offered a safety net against the worst impacts of the Depression in the postwar era. Just as Canadian political history after 1935 has been able to subsume the Trek within a narrative of citizenship and state-centric social support, literary history has largely subsumed the proletarian era, reducing it to the stuttering of an immature Canadian cultural expression. In this, a subsumption rather than a dialectic, the liberal order and the proletarian challenge operate in entirely different modes. However, it would be a mistake to take subsumption as obliteration: within the liberal order, as McKay and Watt have outlined, a distinct organ of proletarian energy remains. It is my hope that by making the processes that have obscured it more transparent, it will thrive in the light.

NOTES

1 In her study of Depression-era US fiction, *Radical Representations*, Barbara Foley asserts that the question of class consciousness must be "central to both rhetoric and representation" (x) for a text to be called "proletarian," a general guideline that I will also maintain.

2 See Denning, *Cultural Front*; Wald, *Exiles from a Future Time*; and Foley, *Radical Representations* for in-depth considerations of American proletarian networks during the interwar period. For the UK context, Hillier's work on left-wing publishers is a recent addition to a long critical history on working-class writing.

3 See Darnton, "What Is the History of Books?" and Adams and Barker, "A New Model for the Study of the Book" for detailed theorizing of the communications circuit.
4 Significant interruptions to Liberal rule came under the Diefenbaker Conservatives (1957–1963) and the neoliberal resurgence of the Conservatives under Brian Mulroney (1984–1993).
5 McKay, "Liberal Order," 627.
6 Ibid., 638.
7 Ibid.
8 McNairn, "Hope and Fear," 65.
9 Ibid., 68.
10 The mandate of the commission, both forward- and backward-looking in scope, is as follows:

> That it is desirable that the Canadian people should know as much as possible about their country, its history and traditions; and about their national life and common achievements; that it is in the national interest to give encouragement to institutions which express national feeling, promote common understanding and add to the variety and richness of Canadian life, rural as well as urban.
>
> There have been in the past many attempts to appraise our physical resources. Our study, however, is concerned with human assets, with what might be called in a broad sense spiritual resources, which are less tangible but whose importance needs no emphasis. (Canada, *Royal Commission*, 4.)

11 Manson, "Canadian Citizenship," 4.
12 Canadian Citizenship Branch, "How to Become a Canadian Citizen," 37.
13 Irr, *Suburb of Dissent*, 68.
14 Hjartarson, "Government Policy," 25.
15 Irr, *Suburb of Dissent*, 147.
16 Manson, "Canadian Citizenship," 12.
17 Canadian Citizenship Branch, "How to Become a Canadian Citizen," 37.
18 Gerson and Michon, introduction to *History of the Book*, vol. 3, 3.
19 Ibid., 6.
20 Ibid., 3.
21 Frye, conclusion to *Literary History of Canada*, 822. Emphasis in original.
22 Ibid., 823.
23 See Creighton, *Commercial Empire of the St. Lawrence*.
24 See Innis, *Bias of Communication*.
25 Ibid., 830.

26 Ibid., 833.
27 McKenzie, "Proletarian Literature in Canada," 49.
28 Ibid.
29 Ibid.
30 Ibid., 63.
31 Ibid., 56.
32 Ibid., 63.
33 Ibid., 59.
34 Birney, "Short Story Contest," 96.
35 Ibid.
36 Birney, "Proletarian Literature," 58.
37 Ibid., 59.
38 McKenzie, "Proletarian Literature in Canada," 63–4.
39 Birney, "Short Story Contest," 97.
40 Irr, *Suburb of Dissent*, 145.
41 Watt, "Literature of Protest," 457.
42 Ibid., 473.
43 Ibid., 461.
44 Ibid., 465.
45 Ibid., 469.
46 Liversedge, *Recollections* (1963), 3–4.
47 Yorke, introduction to *Mac-Pap*, 21.
48 See McEwan's biography, *The Forge Glows Red*.
49 The bibliographic details that follow are based on my own copy of the 1963 *Recollections*, which I picked up for $50 at MacLeod's Books in Vancouver in October 2011.
50 Liversedge, *Recollections* (1963), i.
51 Ibid., ii.
52 Ibid., 4.
53 Yorke, introduction to *Mac-Pap*, 22.
54 Ibid.
55 Liversedge, *Recollections* (1963), 7.
56 Yorke, introduction to *Mac-Pap*, 22.
57 Hoar, introduction to *Recollections*, xi.
58 See, for example, Wright and Endres, *"Eight Men Speak"*; Phillips, *Voices of Discord*.
59 Diemer, "New Hogtown Press," n.p.
60 Hann et al., *Primary Sources*, 10.
61 Ibid., 13.
62 Weinrich, *Social Protest*, x.
63 Palmer, "Rhyming Reds and Fractious Fictions," 100.

64 Ibid., 104.
65 Liversedge, *Recollections* (1963), 174.

BIBLIOGRAPHY

Adams, Thomas R., and Nicolas Barker. "A New Model for the Study of the Book." In *A Potencie of Life: Books in Society*, edited by Nicolas Barker. London: British Library, 2001. 5–43.

Birney, Earle. "Proletarian Literature: Theory and Practice." *Canadian Forum* 17, no. 196 (1937): 58–60.

– "Short Story Contest – A Report." *Canadian Forum* 17, no. 197 (1937): 96–7.

Canada. *Royal Commission on National Development in the Arts, Letters, and Sciences 1949–1951*. Ottawa: King's Printer, 1951. Last modified 27 January 2000. https://www.collectionscanada.gc.ca/massey/h5-400-e.html.

Canadian Citizenship Branch. *How to Become a Canadian Citizen*. Ottawa: King's Printer, 1947.

Creighton, Donald. *The Commercial Empire of the St. Lawrence*. Toronto: Ryerson Press, 1937.

Darnton, Robert. "What Is the History of Books?" In *The Book History Reader*, edited by David Finkelstein and Alistair McCleery, 9–26. New York: Routledge, 2002.

Denning, Michael. *The Cultural Front: The Laboring of American Culture in the Twentieth Century*. New York: Verso, 2010.

Diemer, Ulli. "New Hogtown Press: After Retrenchment, A Few Steps Forward." *Radical Digressions* (blog). Last modified 2010. http://www.diemer.ca/Docs/Diemer-Hogtown.htm.

Foley, Barbara. *Radical Representations: Politics and Form in U.S. Proletarian Fiction, 1929–1941*. Durham, NC: Duke University Press, 1993.

Frye, Northrop. Conclusion to *Literary History of Canada: Canadian Literature in English*, edited by Carl F. Klinck, 821–49. Toronto: University of Toronto Press, 1965.

Gerson, Carole, and Jacques Michon. Introduction to *History of the Book in Canada*. Vol. 3, *1918–1980*, edited by Carole Gerson and Jacques Michon, 3–9. Toronto: University of Toronto Press, 2007.

Hann, Russell G., Kealey, Gregory S., Kealey, Linda, and Warrian, Peter. *Primary Sources in Canadian Working-Class History 1860–1930*. Kitchener, ON: Dumont Press, 1973.

Hillier, Christopher. "Producers by Hand and by Brain: Working-Class Writers and Left-Wing Publishers in 1930s Britain." *Journal of Modern History* 78, no. 1 (2006): 37–64.

Hoar, Victor. Introduction to *Recollections of the On to Ottawa Trek*, by Ronald Liversedge, vii–xv. Edited by Victor Hoar. Toronto: McClelland & Stewart, 1973.

Hjartarson, Paul. "Government Policy and Allophone Cultures." In *History of the Book in Canada*. Vol. 3, *1918–1980*, edited by Carole Gerson and Jacques Michon, 24–9. Toronto: University of Toronto Press, 2007.

Innis, Harold. *The Bias of Communication*. Toronto: University of Toronto Press, 1951.

Irr, Caren. *The Suburb of Dissent: Cultural Politics in Canada and the United States during the 1930s*. Durham, NC: Duke University Press, 1998.

King, Thomas. *The Inconvenient Indian: A Curious Account of Native People in North America*. Minneapolis: University of Minnesota Press, 2013.

Liversedge, Ronald. *Mac-Pap: Memoir of a Canadian in the Spanish Civil War*. Edited by David Yorke. Vancouver: New Star Books, 2013.

– *Recollections of the On-to-Ottawa Trek*. Lake Cowichan, BC, 1963.

– *Recollections of the On to Ottawa Trek*, edited by Victor Hoar. Toronto: McClelland & Stewart, 1973.

Manson, A.M. "Canadian Citizenship." Vancouver, BC: Kiwanis Club of Vancouver, 1946.

McEwen, Tom. *The Forge Glows Red*. Toronto: Progress Books, 1974.

McKay, Ian. "The Liberal Order Framework: A Prospectus for a Reconnaissance of Canadian History." *Canadian Historical Review* 81, no. 4 (2000): 617–45.

McKenzie, Ruth. "Proletarian Literature in Canada." *Dalhousie Review* 19 (1939): 49–64.

McNairn, Jeffrey L. "In Hope and Fear: Intellectual History, Liberalism, and the Liberal Order Framework." In *Liberalism and Hegemony: Debating the Canadian Liberal Revolution*, edited by Jean-Francois Constant and Michel Ducharme, 64–93. Toronto: University of Toronto Press, 2009.

Palmer, Bryan. "Rhyming Reds and Fractious Fictions: Canada's Heritage of Literary Radicalism." *American Review of Canadian Studies* 34, no. 1 (2004): 99–128.

Phillips, Donna, ed. *Voices of Discord: Canadian Short Stories from the 1930s*. Toronto: New Hogtown Press, 1979.

Smitka, Kristine. "Canadian Writers, McClelland & Stewart, and the Paperback Book: Remediation, Publishing, and Cultural Content." PhD diss., University of Alberta, 2014.

Wald, Alan M. *Exiles from a Future Time: The Forging of the Mid-Twentieth Century Literary Left*. Chapel Hill: University of North Carolina Press, 2002.

Watt, Frank W. "Literature of Protest." In *Literary History of Canada: Canadian Literature in English*, edited by Carl F. Klinck, 457–73. Toronto: University of Toronto Press, 1965.

Weinrich, Peter. *Social Protest from the Left in Canada 1870–1970: A Bibliography*. Toronto: University of Toronto Press, 1982.

Wright, Richard, and Robin Endres, eds. *"Eight Men Speak," and Other Plays from the Canadian Workers' Theatre*. Toronto: New Hogtown Press, 1976.

Yorke, David. "Introduction: Ron Liversedge and His Writing." In *Mac-Pap: Memoir of a Canadian in the Spanish Civil War*, by Ronald Liversedge, 9–25. Vancouver: New Star Books, 2013.

8 The Corporate Reconstruction of American Literary History

JASON POTTS

Perhaps no critic in recent memory has been more interested in the project of American literary history than Jonathan Arac. Over a series of essays, Arac has wondered aloud about everything from the relation between literary history and theory; to the place of literary history in a global age; to the connection between literary and cultural history and identity; to the historical situation of theories of the novel; to the canonization of works in literary history; and to the writing of national literary histories themselves. Taken as a set, these essays serve as a compendium to anyone interested in the problems that have vexed literary historians over the past twenty-five years. But it is Arac's 2008 essay, "What Good Can Literary History Do?," that I want to lean on here in order to think about how we might understand the importance of American literary histories written in the latter half of the nineteenth century.

In this essay, Arac lays out neatly the various different models of literary history (as narrative, as reference archive), their differing principles of organization (by the encyclopedic principle of alphabet, by chronology), and their ongoing negotiation between part and whole (in studies limited to a specific time; in works with an extended chronological range but focused in terms of theme; in those studies that try to relate national part to global whole). It is his discussion of the potential effects of the *Cambridge History of American Literature*, edited by Sacvan Bercovitch, however, on which I want to pause. After acknowledging that "it is too soon to say what difference in the long run the *Cambridge History* will make," Arac equivocates over its future effects. "We may hope to be good for those who live after us," he says encouragingly, but we can't know that we will be, insofar as "ambitious original composition" moves in Nietzchean "untimely" rhythms.[1] What we can believe, he argues, making reference to Lionel Trilling, is "that when politics is inescapable, the alternatives of imagination are necessary. In this area, too, literary history may do some slow good."[2]

Or bad. It is the "may" that matters. This paper originated from an interest in the motivations behind the writing of American literary histories.[3] But what became of particular interest to me was the way in which literary histories written in the latter part of the nineteenth century looked to mitigate any concern about conflict resulting from economic inequalities. This seemed to me a peculiarly underdeveloped discussion. What I am going to argue is that while the impact of literary histories is not the kind of thing one can measure exactly, these works clearly contributed to helping develop a form of cultural nationalism in which the issue of difference (and not economic inequality) was the primary concern. Far from treating existing economic inequalities as inconsistent with national ideals, the histories written in this period understand these kinds of inequalities as natural, inevitable, and consistent with the founding principles of the nation.

This narrative runs counter to standard accounts of American literary history that treat a commitment to a more comprehensive equality as a given. For example, in their introduction to the very recent *The American Novel to 1870*, Gerald Kennedy and Leland Person argue that "the novels ostensibly most 'American' in character manifest a patriotism quite at odds with uncritical nationalism – a candor that acknowledges distinct failures of the early nation while recalling its democratic promise." They claim that "the landmark narratives examined [by their contributors] variously expose the gap between US founding ideals and sociohistorical realities."[4] For Kennedy and Person, then, inequality is what falls off the national ideal of equality; "uncritical nationalism" is less American, not because it is inegalitarian but because it isn't committed to a strong enough form of egalitarianism. The idea that forms of inegalitarianism might be consistent with American ideals is simply ruled out.

Working in a slightly different mode, Kerry Larson (rightly) tries to reorient Americanist criticism away from its interests in studies "of race commended for [their] discussion of the topic but faulted for slighting gender," or "of gender praised for [their] insights but faulted for neglecting class," toward a criticism that treats equality, following Tocqueville, as a "social psychology that permeates the beliefs and desires of citizen and non-citizen alike." Attempting to reorient Americanist criticism away from "treating equality as a political or social good that may be won or lost" in order to think of "equality as a social norm whose presence was already well established and pervasive in the antebellum era,"[5] Larson creates much more complicated (and interesting) discussions about America's egalitarian commitments. But these discussions are made possible only by conserving the idea that at the heart of an American literature is a national egalitarian psychology. So while Larson acknowledges that constituencies in antebellum America were committed to inequality – he devotes an entire chapter to the efforts by Southerners to give inegalitarianism a theoretical grounding and draws a comparison between Tocqueville and Marx in his final chapter – his commitment to the Tocquevillian model of equality of condition occludes any in-depth discussion of economic inequality. As he notes, to follow Tocqueville means to follow an idea of equality that is "something less than the shared ownership of resources envisioned by socialism."[6]

What strikes me about accounts like these is that while they recognize inequality as a persistent feature of American nationalism, they wind up, in their emphasis on egalitarianism, covering over the inegalitarian aspects of American nationalism. The desire to present American literature and its literary history as committed to a comprehensive version of equality – at least in their "good" forms – shades over any real discussion of forms of inegalitarianism that might run alongside more egalitarian imaginings. In this regard, their desire to normalize equality as a value, albeit well intentioned, seems almost willful.

But perhaps putting things this way is a little too harsh. In one respect, these critics are simply making good on the claim of Rufus Griswold who, writing in 1847 in *Prose Writers of America*, prefigured Arac in pointing out that it is the shaping of national literary history that matters. In an assertion that seems more in line with twenty-first-century thinking about literary history than nineteenth, Griswold argues that

> there never was and never can be an exclusively national literature. All nations are indebted to each other and to preceding ages for the means of advancement; and our own, which from our various origin may be said to be at the confluence of the rivers of time which have swept through every country, can with less justice than any other be looked to for mere novelties in art and fancy. The question between us and other nations is not who shall most completely discard the Past, but who shall make best use of it.[7]

Standing opposed to those looking to fashion a uniquely American literature like Ellery Channing, Evert and George Duyckinck and, especially, William Gilmore Simms (who saw immigration as a threat to the creation of an American literature), Griswold saw that the value of an American literary history didn't lie in simply anthologizing works or in accurately describing the national character; it involved moulding the past into a narrative for future effects.

It is with Griswold's claim in mind that I want to turn back to the literary histories written near the end of the nineteenth century to examine how they contributed to fashioning the national egalitarian narrative. What strikes me about these works is that they were much more reluctant to suggest that equality really was a national ideal or a normative value than today's critics. In fact, they were more interested in making sure that an interest in economic equality *didn't* become a national value. From the perspective of these literary histories, any opposition like the one Kennedy and Person identify in an important strain of American literature isn't the consequence of a misfit between ideal and reality; it is simply the complaint made by those who either hold a different interpretation of the positions reflected in documents like the Declaration of Independence or those looking to substitute an alternate set of principles for those they dislike. These literary histories, in other words, developed out of a particular sense that the political equality and the individualism that made these sorts of complaints possible went hand in hand with a political culture that was relatively unconcerned with economic inequality. Larson may well be right to claim that egalitarian concerns had become commonplace in American culture, but it is equally important to see that this form of egalitarianism may not simply have envisioned "something less" than socialism; it may have actually discouraged more robust attempts to redistribute resources.

To see how these ideas play out, I want to begin not with the literary histories themselves but with a discussion of Horace Kallen's important 1915 essay, "Democracy versus the Melting-Pot." I begin here because that essay has – at least since Werner Sollers's contribution to *Reconstructing American Literary History* – been so central to twentieth-century American literary historiography. I want to show, moreover, that the tenets of the cultural nationalism Kallen espoused were already being worked out in the literary histories some twenty-five years before his essay. Kallen was, of course, not a literary historian; he was a philosopher. But insofar as he was exposed to the ideas underwriting the literary histories and their historians – Milton Konvitz goes so far as to say it was "under the influence" of the literary historian Barrett Wendell at Harvard that Kallen "turned to his Hebraic heritage"[8] – it is not far-fetched to see in Kallen's thinking ideas informed by these histories (a Nietzchean untimely rhythm, if you will), especially because he saw literature as the expression of a culture, not a class. I'm not interested, in other words, in trying to work out an even more nuanced reading of Kallen's conception of culture and its relation to ethnicity and race.[9] Nor am I arguing that the attention these issues have received is undeserved, uninteresting, or unimportant. Rather, I'm interested in how positions such as Kallen's – ones that set aside economic issues regarding birth, wealth, and merit in favour of a discussion of cultural egalitarianism – were made possible in part by there being an existing script to follow.

Kallen's work is an especially useful starting point for this discussion given that he was, on the one hand (at least in the earlier portion of his career), such a staunch defender of the idea that cultural difference needed to be protected and, on the other, as indifferent to economic inequality as the Anglo-Saxon majority he critiqued. Dismissing A.E. Ross's contention that immigrants posed a threat to "Americanism" near the conclusion of his essay, Kallen declares that Americanization was responsible for "liberati[ng] of nationality." "The institutions of the Republic," he writes, "have become the liberating cause and the background for the rise of the cultural consciousness and social autonomy" of immigrant ethnic groups. "What troubles Mr. Ross and so many other Anglo-Saxon Americans is not really inequality," Kallen famously asserts; "what troubles them is *difference*."[10]

Critics have understood this passage as an attempt to disarticulate "American" from "Anglo-Saxon" in order to make cultural difference a value in and of itself. And this makes sense because this interpretation is in keeping with Kallen's efforts to ensure that those whose first language wasn't English were treated equally. It lines up with his comparison of America with a symphony: "There is nothing so fixed and inevitable about its progressions as in music, so that within the limits set by nature they may vary at will, and the range and variety of the harmonies may become wider and richer and more beautiful." It also helps explain why he believed an inclusive "'American civilization' would bring about the perfection of ... 'European civilization.'"[11] Indeed, Kallen more or less asked for this interpretation by concluding the second part of his essay with the question: "Do the dominant classes in America want such a [pluralized] society?"[12]

But understanding Kallen's delineation of inequality and difference only within the context of cultural pluralism has the effect of blinkering us to the initial set of commitments on which his polemic develops. The question that concludes "Democracy versus the Melting-Pot," in other words, points forward toward multicultural futures unrealized but also back to the nation's origins. In this sense, it functions as a bookend to a set of overlooked premises outlined in the first part of his essay. These premises have less to do with America's cultural make-up and more to do with its founding economic principles, ones that Kallen clearly understood to be inegalitarian in nature.

In fact, the first pages of "Democracy versus the Melting-Pot" begin with a discussion of the Declaration not in terms of difference but in terms of inequality and not with a focus on culture or ethnicity *per se* but on political and economic inequality. Kallen emphasizes the fact that those who signed the Declaration were not egalitarians. They were, he points out, well aware of the fact that their cohort included those who owned slaves; many who were "eminent by birth"; "many by wealth"; and "only a few by merit." Despite the fact that their inequalities were largely unearned, the Declaration's signatories would "probably have fought their [the inequalities] abolition," Kallen argues, on the grounds that the inequalities that separated themselves from others were not incompatible with the Declaration's principles. The Declaration, according to Kallen, was not committed to "abstract principles" or even to "formal logic."[13] Rather, it was an "instrument in a political and economic conflict" meant to establish the colonists as political equals to their counterparts in England. And the colonists could claim that they were England's equals in 1776 because they "*were* actually, with respect to one another, rather free and rather equal" insofar as they were, despite "great differences in wealth," "*like-minded*." Because they "were possessed of ethnic and cultural unity" and were homogenous "with respect to ancestry and ideals," they shared, Kallen claims, a unified "self-consciousness."[14]

The emergence of this form of national self-consciousness not only left untouched the existing economic inequalities it acknowledged; it also conserved the individualism and liberty on which America was founded. A political egalitarianism based on cultural equality did not, in short, necessitate any redistribution of resources or restrictions on individuals. As such, it served as an established model for Kallen's version of cultural egalitarianism. Just as Anglo-Saxons had claimed like-mindedness as the grounds for their political equality, so too could the different ethnic groups populating America in increasing numbers. And they could do so while embracing the values of individualism and liberty that defined the nation.

The ethnic groups could use this model, that is, so long as the individuals constituting these groups understood themselves as like-minded. And here we might see how class identity looked like a threat to Kallen. If individuals began to see themselves in terms of their class rather than their culture, they might lose their sense of like-mindedness. So it comes as no surprise that Kallen rested his case on the belief that when individuals weighed the strength of convictions they held for the groups to which they could understand themselves belonging, they held a much stronger allegiance to their culture than they did their class: "The history of the 'International' in recent years ... indicat[es] how little 'class-consciousness' modifies national consciousness."[15] In contrast to class, ethnicity made a permanent imprint: "Because no individual is merely an individual," Kallen writes, "the political autonomy of the individual has meant and is beginning to realize in these United States the spiritual autonomy of his [ethnic] group."[16]

In pointing out that Kallen thought culture, and not class, was the primary modifier of national consciousness, I do not mean he was ignorant about the issue of economic inequality in America. He claimed that the history of post–Civil War America proved the astuteness of "Marx's generalizations concerning the tendencies of capital towards concentration of the few."[17] And he was careful to note the extensiveness of the problem of poverty in America, especially in immigrant communities. But I do mean to highlight the fact that he thought the lack of class consciousness in America counted as evidence that the material effects individuals felt as a consequence of their poverty did not amount to their experiencing themselves as a class or in identitarian terms. In contrast, the fact that immigrants tended to locate themselves in communities that were ethnically homogeneous (in "stripes," not "stipple[s]"[18]) was proof that people were hard-wired to their culture in ways that prominent proponents of the "melting pot" like Mary Antin and Jacob Riis hadn't understood. Indeed, he argued that efforts that were made toward creating a more equal distribution of wealth were in service not of preempting class strife but of preventing ethnic conflict. Progressive parties (led by wealthy Anglo-Saxons) might promise to limit the trusts, regulate industry, and establish minimum wages and safety conditions in order to alleviate economic inequalities and to create better working conditions, but this attention was "not socialist, of course."[19] Instead, these Anglo-Saxon elites were concerned with their culture being overrun by the Continental labour force needed to satisfy their "greed." The fact that elites were indifferent to the status of poor whites and the African American population was indication enough to him that the concern over immigration was "primarily ethnic and not economic."[20]

The reason for this divergence in feeling between Kallen and Antin and Riis was simple. Whereas ethnicity was intrinsic and thus permanent, the "economic individualism" and "pioneer virtues" associated with Americanism were environmental and external. Anglo-Saxons had simply benefited from arriving in America first. It was merely "primacy in time," Kallen argues, that gave "[Anglo-Saxons] primacy in status ... so that what we call the tradition and spirit of America is theirs."[21] For the very same reasons, the ascendency of the English language in America was not inevitable but the consequence of its having been made the language of the public school system and of the need for a lingua franca in a society that emphasized mobility. Eventually, these external factors would run their course and one could expect similar social and economic outcomes for immigrants (just not Anglo-Saxonization).[22] And once they did, immigrant communities would experience the same economic mobility that had prevented strong class identities from forming in America: "What poverty and unemployment exist among us," Kallen argued, "is the result of unskilled and wasteful social housekeeping, not of any actual natural barrenness."[23] Time would, in short, transform the immigrant population from "an occasion" into "a force."[24]

Kallen's emphasis on the importance of aggregates was symptomatic of the period's ongoing reorganization of the scale of the units of economic production away from individual producers and toward corporate entities. The Progressive period, Martin Sklar argues, was distinguished by its leaders' belief that "capitalism as an economic system, or as a mode of production, evolved according to indefeasible economic law, from small-scale competitive to large-scale corporate enterprise, and society in its sociopolitical, intellectual, and cultural dimensions must adjust to that evolution in an appropriate way or suffer retrogression."[25] The most obvious example of this involves the Supreme Court's legitimation of corporate personhood on the grounds that corporations were merely "associations of persons united for a special purpose"[26] and so were entitled to constitutional protections. But we can also detect a similar impulse in the renovation of political parties as "cross-class, cross-strata construction[s]."[27] "Rather than ... being permitted to divide along class lines, with all the apocalyptic implications," Progressive Era party politics were, Sklar argues, "sustained as a mode of inter-class alignment and cooperation." This alignment, he contends, not only disabled the emergence of a labour party; it also allowed "upper- and middle- class leadership [to] preside over progressive reform as the alternative to reform or revolution from below," thus ensuring that "state direction and state ownership" never became a threat.[28]

From this perspective, Kallen's claim that "no individual is merely an individual, the political autonomy of the individual has meant and is beginning to realize in these United States the spiritual autonomy of his group" captures an important feature of corporate personhood. For it both identifies the ways that cultural groups, like other corporate organizations, gain coherence through a common purpose and captures how cultures, like political parties, get their integrity in part by repudiating any identifications on class lines.[29]

Formulations like these help us understand why Griswold thought that the realization of an exclusively American literary history was an implausible dream: while individuals might have understood themselves as American, it seemed they were beholden to their individual cultures. But what Griswold hadn't considered was that American literature could be reconceptualized as a collection of culturally distinct literatures. Thought of in this way, American literature was actually advantaged. The "indebted[ness]" between nations that Griswold identified as responsible for literature's "advancement" would happen internally, within America itself.[30] The freedoms afforded by the American political system that underwrote its individualism would allow for the creation of new forms of art (while at the same time making economic inequality part of the American way of life). This is why "art, literature[,] culture" should also be understood as the expression of the group, as the product of a common cultural "like-mindedness and self-consciousness."[31]

The literary histories written in the latter half of the nineteenth century map this progression in thinking about America as a culturally diverse nation: from the implausibility of an American literature, to its possibility as an Anglo-Saxon literature, to its origins as a multicultural literature (albeit with a privileging of Anglo-Saxon literature). Especially notable here is Moses Coit Tyler's influential *History of American Literature* (1878), in which Tyler promised to chart the "unfolding of the American mind"[32] by taking "the scattered voices of the thirteen colonies" and shaping them into "an utterance … [of] a single nation only, with all its great hopes and great fears in common, with its ideas, its determinations, its literature, in common likewise."[33] Tyler's *History* is important for a number of reasons, not the least because where others had simply anthologized American works or provided bibliographies, Tyler reputedly read "every American writer of the colonial time, in his extant writings" in order to provide "our literary history only ... that is, the history of those writings, in the English language, produced by Americans, which have some noteworthy value as literature, and some real significance in the literary unfolding of the American mind."[34] Tyler's *History,* in other words, was really the first history of Anglo-Saxon American literature (and not only Northeast literature).

But what I want to draw attention to is the fact that the difference that mattered to Tyler had nothing to do with culture; it involved differentiating American from English literature. And what made American literature different, despite its also being written in English, was its authors having shared the experience of relocating to the United States. American literature therefore begins, for Tyler, when ships left harbors destined for the New World: "It is that year 1607, when Englishmen, by transplanting themselves to America, first began to be Americans."[35] But to put the point this way is to understate the force of Tyler's intentions, for emigrating to the New World did not just provide people with different experiences than they would have had if they remained in England; from Tyler's perspective, it made them a different people with their own culture.

Which is not to say that Tyler was interested in cultural difference; the only culture that matters in Tyler's *History* is Anglo-Saxon culture. Indians are, for example, for Tyler, merely "fierce dull biped[s] standing in our way."[36] That is one reason why it is remarkable that by the time Charles Richardson wrote his *American Literature* (1887), it was already necessary to provide an alternate accounting for the various groups in America. Richardson's history – which served as the model for subsequent literary histories – was committed, like Tyler's, to the idea of the melting pot. But where Tyler's conception of Americanness turns on the question of experience, Richardson's turns on inclusiveness: "In regard to the perspective of American literature," he writes, "it must never be forgotten that deck-hands, 'longshoremen, and stage-drivers, Californian miners, Chinese, highway robbers, buffaloes, and Indians are but a part of our civilization, and that literature *may* concern itself with such themes as God, duty, culture, and Eastern lakes or rivers, and still be distinctively American."[37] And so while today

Richardson is dismissed by scholars as an artefact of American literary studies' prepubescence – even his most ardent current appreciator calls the history an "inarticulate commentary on the literary text [that] represented the state of literary analysis and judgment in the American academy well into the 1940s"[38] – the history is still useful not so much for its judgments of authors and texts but for its indexing of a shift in thinking about the internal composition of American literature. When Richardson turns to talking about the "race-elements" in American literature, he treats "Mound-Builders, perhaps the ancestors of the North American Indians," as irrelevant not because they were not persons but because "they had no poet, and they died."[39] In contrast, "aboriginal American literature," though "scanty," "deserves mention" (albeit only as an "influence" on American progress). "Indian oratory," Richardson argues, "sometimes possesses force, or even sublimity" and "is not undeserving of study by the speakers of other languages," but the Indian race "has not been one which has created or preserved a literature, in any large sense."[40] "The materials of literature have been about the race," he claims, "in nature and life, but these materials have lacked the shaping force of an indigenous culture."[41]

In their survey of earlier literary histories, the editors of the important *Cambridge History of American Literature* (1917) argued that Richardson's history "protest[ed]" Tyler's work insofar as its intention was not "historical enquiry and elucidation but aesthetic judgment."[42] And this is certainly right insofar as Richardson thought that American literature had developed to the point that a less appreciatory, more canonizing history was needed. But to see Richardson as opposing Tyler misses how Richardson actually amplifies Tyler's Anglo-Saxonism. "Behind literature is race; behind race, climate and environment," Richardson makes clear on his first page.[43] Thus Howard Mumford Jones was right to say that Richardson's primary contribution is to what he called "the racial school"[44] of American literature insofar as Richardson demonstrates what Kermit Vanderbilt rightly describes as a "pervasive Anglo-Saxon bias."[45]

Noting that Richardson's work has served as the prototype for most subsequent literary histories, David Shumway argues that, for Richardson, the "relevant conditions" for creating distinctive national literatures "are mainly what we would call cultural."[46] Shumway's is a useful description not only because it captures how Richardson's discussion of different immigrant groups prefigures Kallen's some twenty-five years later but also because it clarifies Richardson's history's major innovation. While only Anglo-Saxons have culture in Tyler's history, Richardson acknowledges that all the different ethnicities that comprise America have cultures. Where Indians appear in Tyler's history only to vanish as part of the process of making immigrants into Americans, Richardson takes time to weigh their contributions. But where Kallen treats ethnicity as immutable, Richardson, as a proponent of the melting pot, insists that immigrants lose their ethnicity over a period of time. Thus "the American Irishman, or German, or Frenchman, notwithstanding his love for fatherland, soon loses somewhat of his former nature, under the potent influence of new conditions of the dominant Saxon temper." "Their past and future in America," Richardson claims, "belongs to the social historian, not to the literary recorder."[47] And while one might pause here to note that Richardson was, in one sense, right – no literature department teaches or hires in Irish American, German American, Italian American, or French American literature – he was right here not because these ethnicities disappeared but because ethnicity was racialized such that we now think of Irish, German, Italian, and French American literatures as literatures written by white people and Asian American, Latino American, and Native American literatures as written by people of colour.

What gets lost in this process of racialization, however, is the fact that the melting pot was not only a technology meant to transform people of all ethnicities into Anglo-Saxons; its operations were also meant to prevent Anglo-Saxons from becoming economically subservient. Richardson's goal of producing an "American thought more sound than the institutions and thought of people less favorably situated" was not simply an assertion of Anglo-Saxon superiority; it was also an effort to protect those threatened by "the growth of wealth." Here America benefited, Richardson argues, from the fact that "even the denizens of 'shanty-town' in New York City … [did] not want a communistic distribution of their goats and geese." Because they "own[ed] some property" and had gone through the "Americanizing process through which the immigrant soon passes," they were "peaceable." So long as immigrants were "tolerably well-educated" in the "principles of Anglo-Saxon ethics, developed by education," Richardson claims, American institutions would remain stable despite the fact that "America [would] have fewer leaders in the years to come; but … as many workers."[48] This would be true even though the nation was becoming increasingly culturally diverse. A "sound and general education," Richardson maintains, ameliorated both the "sharp distinctions of race and competence" in the

South and kept New York from becoming "the receptacle of the residuum of a part of a debased foreign society."[49] America, he claims, was "liberal and tolerant and [was] rapidly becoming more so."[50] So long as everyone received an education and so long as the nation remained committed to freedom of religion – such that individuals would not be "oppressed for conscience' sake" – there was reason to believe America was "in little danger of atheism, communism, or the 'Goddess of Reason.'"[51]

Richardson's position on education and class is often lost today, of course, because the class issue resolved itself in a way he never imagined possible. Whereas Richardson thought that giving the poor (regardless of their cultural heritage) a universalized Anglo-Saxon education would dampen any revolutionary spirit, the deemphasizing of class identifications (that Kallen documents) in favour of cultural identity made this concern unnecessary. In part because America became so focused on issues of cultural identity, discussions about culture and education have often been about ensuring the diversity of the social elite within educational institutions, not the elimination of that elite.[52]

This point notwithstanding, Richardson emphasized a universalized education not because he was a class warrior but because he was afraid of the possible consequences of not providing one. When Richardson looked south and saw millions of poor, uneducated African Americans, he did not see a people who might someday rise to fight a race war; he saw millions of poor people who might rise up and fight as a proletariat in a class war. Thus he argues that the South's illiteracy rates, not just amongst blacks but also whites must be addressed through a strong public school system in order to bring the South into the nation and to align them with "the national type." It was the South's economic structure in the first place, he claims, "the planter-life, the semi-baronial system, the sharp distinction of classes (even among the whites), the absence of large towns or centres of culture" that "tended to give the South a literature of its own."[53] And as the expression of a people, a revamped literary education was an essential part of this reeducation: "The Southern critic has made too much of the idea of State Pride," Richardson argues, "and has favored the sectional when he ought to have encouraged the universal."[54]

If conditions were created in which Southern writers could have an "increasing share in the making of American (not Southern) literature," Southern writers could, Richardson argues, "rest their claims for fame upon their works, rather than upon their place of birth or residence."[55]

And this shift would help bring about a social movement that would harmonize the South's economic system with the nation's: "With the removal of slavery and the development of education," he says, "inventive genius appears, factories and schools and libraries rise side by side, and literature begins to share in the strength once monopolized by law and politics."[56] For example, if such a program were followed, the Creole author of *The Grandissimes*, George Washington Cable, "the first Southern writer since the war, and the one whose books gain most from their source and scene, would be the last to claim any attention *because* he [was] a 'Southerner' or Louisianian."[57]

That Cable seemed to favour such an outcome for himself was proof, from Richardson's perspective, that such a transformation – from Southerner to American – was not only possible but also desirable. He therefore cites – in one of the very few footnotes to appear in *American Literature* – Cable's claim that

> Webster is ours as well as Clay; Everett and Sumner are ours as truly as Randolph and Calhoun. Is not Irving ours, and Prescott, and Halleck, no less than Poe? The honored Hawthorne is ours, Emerson is ours, Longfellow is ours.... The South should no longer dream of a separate literature. While treating home subjects, let it be done for the whole nation; and you shall put your own State, not the less, but the more, in your debt; earn a double portion of her gratitude and love; add to these the general thanks of a vast country; and give the sisterhood of States a new interest in that sister whom you delight to call your mother and who will be proud to call you her son.... We want to purge ourselves of provincialism and stop speaking of 'the new South'; – what we must have in view is the 'no South.'[58]

Only when literature "instantly [becomes] the property & voice of the nation,"[59] Cable claims, will a truly national literature be realized.

But the "new South" could be turned into the "no South," Cable argues, only when "South" "receded to its original meaning of mere direction and location."[60] And the South could be turned into a direction only when the South developed a middle class. It hadn't done so because slavery divided the people from themselves, creating differences not only between black and white and between North and South but also, in the South, between a "caste" and a "fixed peasantry." The South, he says, had only an aristocracy that had "no fear of falling" and a peasantry that had "no hope of rising"; it was, he complains, a "people without a middle class."[61]

At stake in the development of a middle class was the social and economic mobility – the lack of fixity – that Kallen would identify as an important and peculiarly American trait. Without mobility, Cable contends, a "man's status [becomes] fixed by his birth."[62] It was imperative, then, that the "stronger classes" not be allowed "to assume that the classes below should allow the stronger to think and act for them" lest America develop into a version of British society that featured a "supremacy of class over class."[63] And so Cable advocated for educational reform because it is education that provides man with a taste for things like literature that in the North and Canada "r[un] from [the] top of the social scale to the very bottom."[64] The shared cultural capital people develop from reading literature establishes "consanguinity"[65] between those otherwise divided by the illusion of race, the dissemination of literature bringing into relation those who "inhale it – who feed upon it."[66]

Cable's rhetorical puffery notwithstanding, his position isn't exceptional. William Dean Howells would echo the idea that equality is predicated on individuals from different classes socializing with each other in "Equality as the Basis for Good Society." Both men shared the idea that it was compartmentalization that put the country at risk. "That order of society is best, and that order of society only is American," Cable claims, "where the intelligent are so hemmed in with the unintelligent that they cannot afford to let them rest in their unintelligence."[67] "Not fit for self government?" Cable quotes approvingly an American writer as saying, "no people is fit for any other."[68] But this phrasing takes on special import when the idea of the nation becomes attached to the idea of everyone being middle class and when the middle class becomes identified with mobility rather than a class interest. In the middle-class nation, there isn't any class interest, because everyone is, potentially, in motion. Rising and falling takes place within the middle class, not between classes (a psychologized version of class that has little to do with economics, but one that maintains its power today).[69] This would be one reason, then, that despite an Anglo-Saxon education and despite persistent economic inequality, it has been easier in America for individuals from different classes to identify in cultural terms than it has been for individuals from the same class to identify in class terms.

Recently Gavin Jones has argued that there is "a substantive evasion of the socioeconomic" in American literary analysis.[70] Whereas "race and gender [are treated as] insurmountable absolutes," Jones claims, the idea that class operates with a "normalcy of mobility" sanctions critics to treat the lower class as though it has "an inherently negative value."[71] Larry Griffin and Maria Tempenis have demonstrated that "relatively little of [*American*] *Quarterly*'s pages have ever been used to explore social class (the most conservative estimate of this is very low indeed), and articles exploring one facet or another of gender and race, or framed by either or (increasingly) both, have, at least since the late 1960s, greatly outnumbered those overtly motivated by class."[72] And Brook Thomas has claimed that the failure of a class subject to emerge in American literature is tied to issues generic to the novel and its rise to prominence in the latter half of the nineteenth century. Thomas contends that it is difficult to "express the rising influence of all sorts of associations within American culture (including labor unions, ethnic groups, and professional organizations, as well as corporations) in a genre that demands individual characterization."[73] Yet the fact that plots are generated by individual characters has not stopped critics of other national literatures from identifying characters in novels as representatives of their classes. (Commentators have no trouble, for instance, identifying Eliot's and Dickens's characters as representing class positions.) And it also hasn't been a problem for racial and ethnic groups in America to identify literary characters as surrogates for their communities.[74]

As I've tried to show here, the problem isn't one of communities but rather one of the construction of forms of community. And while Larson is perfectly right to say that we should think about equality, in the nineteenth century, as a social norm whose presence was already felt in the antebellum period, it was a presence that emerged out of a complicated and imbricated dynamic, one that depended, as Kallen put it, on the idea that "the poor of two different peoples tend to be less like-minded than the poor and the rich of the same peoples."[75] My gambit here has been to say that American literary history – and in particular the literary histories on which American literary history has been built subsequently – has been, in the main, indifferent to the consequences of this formulation. In its efforts to frame American literature as egalitarian – first between America and England and second between the different ethnic cultures operating in America – it licensed a psychology of class that continues to play its way out. Surely, as Arac puts it, working within this framework of equality did some "good for those who [lived] after" the Progressive Era.[76] But it surely did some bad too.

NOTES

Research for this article was supported by a St Francis Xavier University University Council for Research grant.

1 Arac, "What Good Can Literary History Do?," 8.
2 Ibid., 10.
3 On the history of American literary histories, see Claudia Stokes's excellent *Writers in Retrospect*.
4 Kennedy and Pearson, introduction to *The American Novel to 1870*, 5.
5 Larson, *Imagining Equality*, 1.
6 Ibid., 2.
7 Griswold, *Prose Writers of America*, 50.
8 Konvitz, "Horace Meyer Kallen," 31.
9 For a summary of the different positions on Kallen's racism, see Tim Parrish's *Walking Blues*, particularly the chapter "What Difference Does the Difference Make?," 17–56.
10 Kallen, "Democracy: Part II," 219.
11 Ibid., 220.
12 Ibid.
13 Kallen, "Democracy: Part I," 190.
14 Ibid., 191.
15 Ibid., 194.
16 Kallen, "Democracy: Part II," 219.
17 Kallen, "Democracy: Part I," 193.
18 Ibid., 192.
19 Ibid., 193.
20 Ibid.
21 Ibid., 194.
22 Kallen gives two reasons why, within any ethnicity, those who are best off economically will help those – like new immigrants – who are worse off. First, Kallen believes that because culture trumps class, those on top will give a hand down to those who prove their merit. Second, because people of the same ethnicity tend to settle in the same area, they create their own demand for doctors and lawyers to serve their community. As a result, some people within the ethnicity will "naturally" rise to the top of the socioeconomic hierarchy within the ethnicity simply by meeting this demand.
23 Ibid., 192.
24 Ibid., 193.
25 Sklar, *Corporate Reconstruction*, 5–6.

26 *Pembina Consolidated Silver Mining Co. v. Pennsylvania*, 125 U.S. 394 (1886).
27 Ibid., 35.
28 Ibid., 39. For a brilliant accounting (to which I am indebted) of how aggregate personhood became a problem for the novel and for liberalism, see Daniel Stout's *Corporate Romanticism*.
29 On the many different compromises made within liberalism, see Edmund Fawcett's excellent *Liberalism*.
30 Griswold, *Prose Writers of America*, 50.
31 Kallen, "Democracy: Part I," 191.
32 Tyler, *History of American Literature*, vol. 1, vi.
33 Ibid., v–vi.
34 Ibid., vi–vii.
35 Ibid., 11.
36 Ibid., 10.
37 Richardson, *American Literature*, xv.
38 Vanderbilt, *American Literature and the Academy*, 122.
39 Richardson, *American Literature*, 1–2.
40 Ibid., 3.
41 Ibid. In *Writers in Retrospect*, Claudia Stokes argues that American literary histories are "conspicuously silent about Native peoples and their narrative traditions" (33). Stokes doesn't spend much time with Richardson, whose account, I think, complicates this position. While my position is in general agreement with Stokes, it is important to see the positioning of Native literatures as part of a larger movement within American literary history and corporate liberalism, one that would see the positioning of these literatures as consistent with the fate of others.
42 Trent et al., *Cambridge History*, viii.
43 Richardson, *American Literature*, 1. It is worth noting here that Richardson makes no strong distinction between racial, ethnic, and cultural identity.
44 Jones, *Theory of American Literature*, 101.
45 Vanderbilt, *American Literature and the Academy*, 114.
46 Shumway, *Creating American Civilization*, 70.
47 Richardson, *American Literature*, 22.
48 Ibid., 45–7.
49 Ibid., 46.
50 Ibid., 50.
51 Ibid., 48, 50.
52 For Barrett Wendell, the Harvard professor who trained Kallen and whose *American Literature* (1901) was far more racist than Richardson's history, what mattered was not that non-Anglo-Saxons were given

an education that would keep them out of the slums but that the "literary character of America" (525) be consistent with New England character. This commitment to an Anglo-Saxon literature was entirely consistent with his commitment to economic inequality. Where European democracy has, on Wendell's account, "been dominated by blind devotion to an enforced equality" (529), America has "kept faithful to the principle that, so far as public safety may permit, each of us has an inalienable right to strive for excellence" (530). For an excellent account of Wendell's history, see Stokes.

53 Richardson, *American Literature*, 58.

54 Ibid., 59.

55 Ibid.

56 Ibid.

57 Ibid.

58 Ibid., 59–60.

59 Cable, "Address to the University of Mississippi," 11.

60 Ibid., 12.

61 Ibid., 13.

62 Ibid., 14.

63 Ibid., 22–23.

64 Ibid., 14.

65 Ibid., 11.

66 Ibid., 11.

67 Ibid., 23.

68 Ibid., 23. Both quotations attributed by Cable to the American writer.

69 The legacy of this type of psychologizing of class has long been characteristic of American thinking and continues through today. A recent Pew Research Center survey showed that 90% of Americans still identify as middle class. As Richard Reeves of the Brookings Institute puts it, "there is a very big difference between the psychological self-definition of class and anything approaching a useful economic definition of class." Patricia Cohen, "Middle Class but Feeling Economically Insecure," 10 April 2015, accessed 25 April 2016, http://www.nytimes.com/2015/04/11/business/economy/middle-class-but-feeling-economically-insecure.html?login=email&smid=tw-nytimes.

70 Jones, "Poverty and the Limits of Criticism," 767.

71 Ibid.

72 Griffin and Tempenis, "Class, Multiculturalism," 90.

73 Thomas, *New Historicism*, 149.

74 One can see why, given this amalgamation of terms, race would become the term that would structure debates about inequality insofar as the law has discriminated against it.

75 Kallen, "Democracy: Part I," 194.

76 Arac, "What Good Can Literary History Do?," 8.

BIBLIOGRAPHY

Arac, Jonathan. "What Good Can Literary History Do?" *American Literary History* 20, no 1–2 (Spring/Summer 2008): 1–11.

Bourne, Randolphe. "Trans-National America." In *Critics of Culture*, edited by Alan Trachtenberg, 145–64. New York: John Wiley & Sons, 1976.

Cable, George Washington. "Address to the University of Mississippi." In "George W. Cable's Revolt against Literary Sectionalism," edited by Arlin Turner. *Tulane Studies in English* 5 (1955): 5–27.

Fawcett, Edmund. *Liberalism: The Life of an Idea*. Princeton: Princeton University Press, 2014.

Griffin, Larry J., and Maria Tempenis. "Class, Multiculturalism, and the *American Quarterly*." *American Quarterly* 54, no. 1 (March 2002): 67–99.

Griswold, Rufus W. *The Prose Writers of America: With a Survey of the History, Conditions and Prospects of American Literature*. Philadelphia: Carey and Hart, 1847.

Jones, Gavin Roger. "Poverty and the Limits of Literary Criticism." *American Literary History* 15, no. 4 (Winter 2003): 765–92.

Jones, Howard Mumford. *The Theory of American Literature*. Ithaca: Cornell University Press, 1948.

Kallen, Horace M. "Democracy versus the Melting-Pot: A Study of American Nationality, Part I." *Nation*, 18 February 1915.

– "Democracy versus the Melting-Pot: A Study of American Nationality, Part II." *Nation*, 25 February 1915.

Kennedy, J. Gerald, and Leland S. Person. Introduction to *The American Novel to 1870*. Oxford: Oxford University Press, 2014.

Konvitz, Milton R. "Horace Meyer Kallen (1882–1974): In Praise of Hyphenation and Orchestration." In *The Legacy of Horace M. Kallen*, edited by Milton R. Konvitz, 15–35. Madison: Fairleigh Dickinson University Press, 1987.

Larson, Kerry. *Imagining Equality in Nineteenth-Century American Literature*. Cambridge: Cambridge University Press, 2008.

Parrish, Tim. *Walking Blues: Making Americans from Emerson to Elvis*. Amherst: University of Massachusetts Press, 2001.

Richardson, Charles F. *American Literature 1607–1885*. New York: G.P. Putnam's Sons, 1887.

Shumway, David R. *Creating American Civilization: A Genealogy of American Literature as an Academic Discipline*. Minneapolis: University of Minnesota Press, 1994.

Sklar, Martin J. *The Corporate Reconstruction of American Capitalism, 1890–1916: The Market, the Law, and Politics*. Cambridge: Cambridge University Press, 1988.

Stokes, Claudia. *Writers in Retrospect: The Rise of American Literary History, 1875–1910*. Chapel Hill: University of North Carolina Press, 2006.

Stout, Daniel. *Corporate Romanticism: Liberalism, Justice, and the Novel*. New York: Fordham University Press, 2017.

Thomas, Brook. *The New Historicism: and Other Old-Fashioned Topics*. Princeton: Princeton University Press, 1991.

Trent, William Peterfield, John Erskine, Stuart P. Sherman, and Carl Van Doren, eds. *The Cambridge History of American Literature*. New York: G.P. Putnam's Sons, 1917.

Tyler, Moses Coit. *A History of American Literature*. 2 vols. New York: G.P. Putnam's Sons, 1878.

Vanderbilt, Kermit. *American Literature and the Academy: The Roots, Growth, and Maturity of a Profession*. Philadelphia: University of Pennsylvania Press, 1989.

Wendell, Barrett. *A Literary History of America*. New York: Scribner's, 1901.

PART V

Culturing: Economics, Institutions, and the Imagination

9 The Empire Digs Back: Kew Gardens, the Assistant for India, and the Problem of Knowledge Production after Empire

SINA RAHMANI

"Surrounded by the red roofs of Londoners' homes is Kew Gardens. It's a world garden, for in it grow flowers and shrubs and trees from every country in the world. It's also a playground where Londoners, seeking a moment of release from war and work, may rest while their children play." Thus opens *World Garden* (1942), a short educational film profiling the Royal Botanic Gardens, Kew. Part of a series of documentary shorts sponsored by the British Ministry of Information, the ten-minute-long film explores the two principal ways in which the institution sitting on a three-hundred-acre site on the western edge of the English capital lives up to the title "world garden." The first half surveys the global collection of plant life housed both literally and figuratively on the site. Outside in the various pavilions, visitors can enjoy "flowers from the topless Himalayas, the Rockies, the Andes, and the Alps," while "a gallery of nature's most exotic creations from tropic, swamp, and jungle" awaits them inside the myriad greenhouses.

The second half shines a spotlight on another, less visible kind of globality, for "while the people sit beneath the trees as the clouds drift by, the real work of Kew is going on behind the scenes." This "real work" refers to Kew's position in the botanical sciences as the "great centre for naming and classification of the world's plants." The camera ventures inside the nerve centre of the operation, the Herbarium, where "parcels of specimens arrive every week from scientific workers and collectors from all over the world. After sorting, they are passed to the mounting staff, who gum or stitch them to these stiff paper mounts. They are then ready to be examined, classified, and added to the collection. Now many of these specimens have been sent by botanists from other institutions abroad to have their names checked and confirmed by Kew's staff … When all [the various] features agree with those of an authentically named specimen and with descriptions in reference books, the identification is complete." With remarkable accuracy, the film captures the duality of Kew's worldliness: an institution at once local and global, a place of "play" for Londoners where they can enjoy "nature's most exotic creations" as well as the "great centre" for the "real work" of botanical classification and research.

While not intending to denigrate the film in any way, I would propose that *World Garden*, as a snapshot of the zenith of the plant sciences, is more interesting for what it omits about its subject. This chapter explores two specific elisions and the insights each offers into a topic that has received some scholarly attention in recent years, Kew's relationship to British imperialism. In the first half, I answer a question that the film itself poses but ultimately fails to address when the camera moves "behind the scenes." The Edenic serenity of the grounds is replaced by the image of a cupboard, which, as the narrator explains, once housed "the private flower collection of Sir William Hooker, who in 1841 was invited to organize Kew as a centre for the study of the world's botany." Situated against the triumphant declarations of the importance of Kew's "real work" that follow, this brief reference to the institution's origins begs an obvious question: how did Kew transform over the course of a century from "a centre" to "the great centre" of botanical research? Although this transformation has been addressed directly in accounts of the institution and some of the eminent figures connected to it, my answer frames the story of Kew's rise as a case study of what I will be calling the fiction of Victorian imperial sovereignty. The second half of the chapter zooms in on one of the many nameless, faceless employees labouring "behind the scenes" in the Herbarium at the time of the film's production. A founding father of modern Indian botany, Kailas Nath Kaul arrived at Kew in 1939 and spent several years as the "Botanist for India" before returning to his native country. Drawing on archival documents, I reconstruct the remarkable story of his tenure at Kew, more precisely the events that led to his hiring and the historic significance of the post he inaugurated. More than a watershed moment in the institution's history – he was the first Indian to be hired as the resident expert for the subcontinent, a role that had been hitherto occupied for nearly six decades exclusively by white men – Kaul's appointment provides a different kind of perspective on the vexed questions of postcolonial knowledge production that literary scholars have mapped for decades. Namely, what is to be done with the tools (languages, institutions, hermeneutics) left behind by the master after he has abandoned his colonial house, and what role do indigenous knowledge forms and practices play after independence? And while the study of plants certainly cannot (and should not) be subsumed *tout court* under the broad banner of literary history, the reclamation of this body of knowledge in South Asia, as I will show, confronted many of the same fundamental dilemmas that writers, novelists, and playwrights did in their struggle to culture their newly liberated nations.

Taken together, the two intertwined halves of this chapter test Richard Drayton's claim that "through the story of a garden we may explore the history of the world."[1] On the one hand, inscribed into the narrative of Kew's emergence as "the great centre" of botany is an example of nineteenth-century British thinking that imagined the country's colonial possessions as a single "world garden" that could be cultivated to serve the empire's needs. On the other hand, the decades-long exclusion of Indians from "the real work" taking place in London underscores how one of the most cherished liberal justifications of imperialism – the cultivation of colonial subjects through the free and global circulation of knowledge – conflicted with another, less noble aspect of the British liberal imagination: the inherent inferiority of the native. However, since this contradiction has become a locus of decades of thinking from across the disciplinary spectrum, I focus on another lesson offered by Kaul's stint at Kew. At the conclusion of the chapter, I refract this story through Frantz Fanon's landmark essay "On National Culture" in order to show how the distinction between the institutions of scientific research and those of artistic creation is not as stark as commonly presumed. In other words, I make a case for greater critical attendance to the broader semantic range of the word "culture" beyond the traditional boundaries of textual forms. Although the emergence of ecocriticism in the last two decades has brought renewed attention to the role of green lifeforms and ecosystems in literary history, few have considered professional botany's participation in culturing the nation. But in order to pursue this more global line of thinking, the particularities of Kew's transformation into an imperial institution in the early Victorian period need to be outlined.

The Queen's Two Gardens

Any attempt at answering the question of how the assemblage of brick buildings, glass greenhouses, and green fields on the outskirts of London emerged as the preeminent institution of the plant sciences must begin with a clarification. Kew was indeed "a centre" of botany long before Hooker's arrival. In fact, this "King's Garden" had flourished under the patronage of George III and the labours of the institution's two founding figures, William Aiton and Joseph Banks. By the 1780s, it had come to house the "*de facto* national collection" of plant life,[2] to and from which flowed seeds, bulbs, rhizomes, clippings, seedlings, and dried specimens harvested by a network of mostly amateur plant enthusiasts. Unfortunately, the deaths of Banks and the monarch in 1820 coupled with the fact that the latter's two subsequent successors did not share his enthusiasm for scientific research sent the institution into a tailspin. Two decades of mismanagement and neglect took their toll, and by 1840 it was, as Drayton puts it, "a slightly shabby park" sitting on a small parcel of land largely disconnected from London metropolitan life.[3] Other than its impressive collection of plants, "a great botanical exchange house for the empire," to use Banks's oft-cited phrase, could claim little more than "ten stoves and greenhouses in varying states of disrepair."[4]

And yet by the 1870s Kew was unrivalled as "the great centre of the world's botany," as the film puts it. No other plant institution could approach either the size or the globality of its collection – a crown it still sports today. William Thiselton-Dyer, who headed Kew during the last two decades of the nineteenth century, was not exaggerating when he described it as "a garden in which a vast assemblage of plants from every accessible part of the earth's surface is systematically cultivated – imitating as far as possible their various physical conditions of growth – for the purpose of showing visitors, within a compendious space, what the different types of vegetation are like which the surface of the earth affords."[5] Alongside this function as what Thiselton-Dyer calls "a living museum," by the turn of the twentieth century Kew held under its auspices a vast amount of the world's botanical knowledge.[6] Be it in its expansive library and archival holdings, in the periodicals, books, and pamphlets it published, or in the minds of its employees, Kew housed the largest and most advanced depository of information about plant life in history.

As miraculous as this phoenix-like transformation may seem, Kew's Victorian renaissance is neither difficult to explain nor historically unprecedented. As was the case for the British Museum and other similar Victorian projects that sought to collect, classify, and curate the world's infinite diversities, the key to Kew's ascension was the synergistic bond between colony and metropole.[7] It could never have achieved such great institutional heights without the staggering expansion of British imperial might during the second half of the nineteenth century. Botanists regularly tagged along as the Union Jack unfurled itself across large swathes of the world, conducting research and sending their findings and specimens back to Kew.[8] And thanks to improvements in oceanic transportation and the "Wardian case," a self-enclosed glass terrarium popularized by Nathaniel Bagshaw Ward in the 1830s, the number of samples that survived the perilous boat journey to London dramatically increased.[9] So even though Banks must be credited with pioneering the global network of collectors, it was only during the Victorian era that Kew could justifiably call itself a "world garden."[10]

The combination of this massive influx of plant life and Hooker's shrewd boosterism helped make Kew one of Victorian London's most popular attractions. In 1848, it drew more visitors than Windsor Castle and the Tower of London.[11] Thousands flocked to see the world's first indoor flowering of the titan arum in 1889, one of the most rare and impressive botanical spectacles. Nicknamed the "Corpse Flower" for the strong stench of rotting flesh it emits during its infrequent blooms, it had never even existed outside of its native Western Sumatra before Kew's staff managed to cultivate one. One contemporary account called it an "incredible spectacle which the wise and the learned have been coming from afar to see," and news of the flowering spread across the British Isles and beyond.[12] A French science journal published an illustrated account of this "very rare phenomenon" and described Kew's achievement as "unique in the annals of agriculture."[13]

All this excitement notwithstanding, the real action at Kew was taking place backstage. The global biodiversity streaming into the institution gave some of Britain's leading botanical minds an opportunity to study exotic species in the safe confines of London. And this was not simply a matter of knowledge for knowledge's sake. As a number of studies have pointed out, Kew played an instrumental role in the industrial development of rubber, quinine, and sisal[14] and contributed indirectly to countless other commercial crops like citrus, orchids, and tea.[15] The intense focus on commodity crops was certainly not unique to Kew; it was part of a global shift in the plant sciences beginning in the 1730s toward "economic" botany. Largely as a result of the influential writings of Carl Linnaeus, botany acquired during this time period two interrelated "economic responsibilities."[16] Botanists now found themselves tasked with discovering new exploitable resources

L'INFLORESCENCE DE L'« AMORPHOPHALLUS TITANUM ».

Figure 9.1. Artist's rendition of titan arum flowering, from *La Science Illustrée*. Courtesy of the Bibliothèque nationale de France.

and more productive methods of cultivating plants that would enrich the nation's financial and political power. Furthermore, since the ever-expanding population of the modern nation-state required a stable food supply, agriculture around this time became a top priority for governments across Western Europe.[17] Research into plants was not just supposed to make nations wealthier and more powerful; it came to assume a pivotal role in their very survival. The botanical garden could therefore no longer operate as it had done for centuries, as a private domain divided between the medical sciences and aristocrats yearning for a respite from the chaos of urban life. It was now a site of national importance.

The story of Kew's nationalization is noteworthy in two respects. First, it came about as a result of the budget crisis that Queen Victoria inherited from her profligate predecessors. Assigned to investigate the management of green spaces owned by the Crown, the Royal Gardens Committee sent the well-respected botanist John Lindley to survey Kew and provide some suggestions for its future.[18] The resulting report, to put it mildly, painted a bleak portrait of this once-hallowed ground. Notwithstanding the "many very fine specimens" they contained, the collections were "too much crowded," and "no systematical arrangement was observable."[19] Many of the plants were either poorly labelled or unnamed, and the stoves and greenhouses were built "in an irregular manner."[20] Ultimately, Lindley decried an institution that failed to provide the public with a site of "science and instruction," what he calls "the first features in a botanical garden."[21] Lindley put forward two options: either put an end to this "royal pleasure-ground" permanently and sell it off or convert it into what he calls a "National Botanical Garden," something "worthy of the country" that could offer "a powerful means of promoting national science."[22]

The other noteworthy aspect of Kew's transformation into a national entity was the international role Lindley's report envisioned for the garden. As the country's flagship botanical garden, Lindley explains, Kew "would be the centre around which all those minor establishments should be arranged; they should be all under the control of the chief of that garden, acting in concert with him, and through him with each other, reporting constantly their proceedings, explaining their wants, receiving their supplies, and aiding the mother country in everything that is useful in the vegetable kingdom. Medicine, commerce, agriculture, horticulture, and many valuable branches of manufacture, would derive considerable advantages from the establishment of such a system."[23] According to Lindley, Kew's future rested on its directly taking up the imperial sceptre of the British state, an inheritance that would distinguish the institution from its counterparts in Europe. While it is undeniable that the botanical sciences across the continent reaped countless benefits from imperialism, Kew was unique insofar as it crowned itself the reigning monarch over 115 gardens scattered across the empire – many of which were far older and larger (at least at the time of the report's publication) than the "mother" institution in London.[24]

Clearly the implications of Lindley's ideas extend far beyond the problems confronting a single plant institution. Indeed, this short, obscure bureaucratic text penetrates to one of the truly universal questions beguiling the study of nineteenth-century Britain. Namely, how did seemingly rational individuals, nursed on liberalism's fundamental belief in human rationality and free will, come to believe that they had not simply the duty but the very ability to rule over vast swathes of the world, oftentimes violently so, from a "silly little island of Europe"?[25] Read through this question, Lindley's report is a reminder that a prerequisite of any kind of imperial undertaking is a straightforward act of the imagination. Before the military expeditions and settlements, the ceremonial planting of flags and redrawing of maps, was the imaginative fabrication of "the centre." By declaring Kew the site "around which all those minor establishments should be arranged,"[26] Lindley effectively conscripted the botanical garden, something literally rooted in the local, into the global enterprise of Victorian imperial sovereignty. Therefore, in addition to the two bodies that had historically constituted her juridical authority as a monarch, Queen Victoria, insofar as she was the head (formal or otherwise) of a global empire, held in her possession two gardens. That is to say, Kew bloomed in the second half of the nineteenth century into a double entity: a physical institution consecrated as a "living museum" of the world's plant life and something more conceptual, the central node of a global network of British botanical gardens.

The monarchial vestiges underlying Kew's Victorian renaissance are evident in the institution's leadership during the period. Beginning with the aforementioned William Jackson Hooker in 1841, followed by his son Joseph Dalton Hooker, who was in turn succeeded by his son-in-law, William Turner Thiselton-Dyer, a single family reigned for nearly seven decades. Each member of the house of Hooker ranked among the most well-known men of science of his day, rubbing shoulders with the learned and the political elite. They travelled extensively and were feted by dignitaries and politicians wherever they went, receiving countless prestigious distinctions in the process. These men embodied an era in which the "science of plants found new allies in the age of the Pax Britannica, as it garlanded imperial power with a natural legitimacy."[27]

No discussion of Kew's relationship to Victorian imperialism is complete without a look at Thiselton-Dyer's essay cited earlier, not least because of its title ("The Botanical Enterprise of Empire") or the venue where it was first presented (the Colonial Institute). After a broad overview of early modern botanic gardens, Thiselton-Dyer states that he is less interested in providing an account of Kew's history than analysing "the position it occupies in an extensive system."[28] He quotes the same passage of the Lindley report reproduced above and outlines Kew's role as a central resource for colonial botanical gardens, describing his astonishment "at the readiness with which we are able to supply specimens of even the most unlikely plants."[29] Beyond its services as a "sort of botanical clearing-house or exchange for the Empire," Kew manages "larger operations ... undertaken in connexion with plants of special importance."[30] He then turns to Kew's botanical mapping in the colonies, proudly announcing how the "representation of the Indian flora now at Kew is more complete than anything which exists, even in India itself."[31] He closes out this section with a description of two different ways Kew connects the world to the ecosystems of Britain's colonial possessions. Through the Museum of Economic Botany and the dedication with which the institution's employees respond to the voluminous inquiries arriving by mail from across the country and the world, Kew offers the general public a "repertory of information of everything connected with plants."[32]

Both Thiselton-Dyer's essay and Lindley's report exemplify precisely the argument Thomas Richards makes in the first sentence of *The Imperial Archive: Knowledge and the Fantasy of Empire* (1993): "An empire is partly a fiction." The imagination of Kew as "the centre" of "an extensive system" of colonial botanic gardens articulates what Richards calls "the fictive thought of imperial control."[33] As he reminds us, an "empire is by definition a nation in overreach, one nation that has gone too far, a nation that has taken over too many countries too far away from home to control them effectively."[34] The British Empire was certainly no exception. Even during its heyday in the second half of the nineteenth century, it was "largely a sham," as John Darwin succinctly puts it.[35]

That the kind of totalizing global control dreamed up by Lindley's report was impossible has unfortunately been overlooked in some recent scholarly engagements with Kew's place in imperial history.[36] How could a botanic garden, literally a living space in need of daily maintenance and decision-making, be administered in any meaningful sense of the term by individuals living thousands of kilometres away who could communicate only by mail? The fictionality of Kew's self-fashioning as an imperial control centre full of levers and buttons is confirmed by Donal P. McCracken's *Gardens of Empire: Botanical Institutions of the Victorian British Empire* (1997), the only serious exploration of this "extensive system": "Kew had no satellite Botanic Gardens; colonial botanic gardens were never controlled from Kew. Kew's impact on the empire was based on the concept of mutual interest: Kew could advise, placate or persuade colonial curators; it could not dictate to them."[37] Indeed, Thiselton-Dyer himself admits that Lindley's "thorough-going scheme" required a "degree of administrative centralisation" that "was probably not very possible forty years ago, and is certainly far from being so now."[38]

But the sentence that directly follows this frank admission is even more illuminating. Although it was impossible for Kew to live up to the emperor's role it imagined for itself, Thiselton-Dyer tells his audience that "the principle needs greater enforcement than ever, and the importance of a larger degree of organised co-operation amongst the botanical institutions of the Empire is the chief point which I wish to impress on your attention in this paper."[39] The "chief point" of Thiselton-Dyer's essay, presented during the heady days of "the scramble for Africa," makes clear that the fiction of Victorian imperial sovereignty was openly acknowledged as such by members of the country's intellectual elite. At the same time, the heir apparent to one of the country's leading scientific institutions affirms the "principle" underlying this fiction – British political dominance – and applies it to the field of botany.

Taking this line of thinking further, Thiselton-Dyer's disclosure of the fictionality of the British imperial power prefigures the far more famous articulation of this "principle" in Joseph Conrad's *Heart of Darkness* (1900), specifically the moment when Marlow tells his audience that what redeems the ugly realities of "the conquest of the earth" is "an idea at the back of it; not a sentimental pretence but an idea; and an unselfish belief in the idea – something you can set up, and bow down before, and offer a sacrifice to."[40] Here Marlow is making a distinction between modern British imperialism with its "efficiency" and the brutishness of Roman "conquerors" who preceded it. As a recent reading of this passage argues, Conrad "implicitly shifts the emphasis of conquest from discreet acts by individual actors to the smooth functioning of a system. In so doing, he removes any fundamental distinction between the elements of that system – men and steamships, bullets and rivets, flags and lies. All are elements of the system that enables the corporate body to function as a single machine. And, like all systems, empire is ultimately and exclusively self-referential."[41] The connection between the "machine" or "system" of empire and the "enterprise" of Victorian botany comes into view here. But rather than a simple erasure by way of a "machine" of the actually existing individual components that results in a generalized "belief," the "exclusively self-referential" nature of imperial thinking relies more correctly upon the *compost* of all these parts into a single, fictional whole operating "at the back of it": sovereignty.

So even if the British Empire was in a very real sense a "sham," the cultivation of vast swathes of the globe (both in terms of terrain as well as people) under the imaginative auspices of the Union Jack certainly was not. Indeed, some of the matter (organic or otherwise) that this violent terraforming naturally produced over the course of centuries found its way into the living admixture shorthanded as "British." And as the next section of this chapter demonstrates, those engaged in the postcolonial reclamation of those terrains understood their own independence as an appropriation of not only the land but also the tools to cultivate it.

One aspect of Kew's performance as the ultimate authority over plant life was undoubtedly more convincing. As mentioned, Kew became under the Hookers the largest and most advanced library of botanical knowledge in the world, and a crucial feature of this was the vast archive of dried specimens collected from around the world. This drive to map the biodiversity of the globe manifested a larger historical shift that distinguished Victorian imperialism from its predecessors, both British and otherwise. Beginning in the 1860s with the rise of the new imperialism, there was a general recognition that the empire was "united not by force but by information."[42] In effect, the Victorians augmented the Romantic notion of comprehensive knowledge – the world could be known and accounted for universally and systematically – with a form of knowledge that Richards calls "positive," a belief that this global body of information "could be controlled and controlling."[43]

The merger of these two modes of understanding the world "made possible the fantasy of an imperial archive in which the control of Empire hinges on a British monopoly over knowledge."[44]

At Kew, this merger took shape in human form through a number of assistant positions responsible for one specific part of the world. Between the 1880s and 1940s, Kew employed assistants for India, Africa, South Africa, tropical Africa, and Western Australia. The men who held these positions consulted with the institution's gardeners, answered queries from commercial nurserymen and the general public, and dispatched samples to other parts of the British Isles and across the world. In a word, these assistants rooted the colony in the metropolis and vice versa and were living proof that British global rule was constituted in part as a collection of local expertise.

A closer look at the oldest of these specialist roles, the assistant for India, is worthwhile for the lessons it offers. For starters, its establishment in 1883 highlights the fact that despite all the claims to transhistoricality that seemingly underwrite them, imperial archives are very much products of the contemporary and therefore susceptible to the political and financial currents of their locality. The closure in 1880 of the now long-forgotten India Museum, a fixture of the London cultural scene since opening eight decades earlier, resulted in the dispersal of its collections to different museums around the city and beyond. Kew's Herbarium received its extensive botanical holdings and some financial support to hire a special curator to assist in their management.[45]

More interesting, however, is the position's undoing half a century later, not only because of the first man to hold the newly minted title of "Botanist for India" – eventually renamed the Indian botanical liaison officer – but also for the series of events that preceded his hiring. K.N. Kaul's tenure at the "great centre" represents one aspect of Kew's imperial history that has received no serious consideration, specifically how the institution responded to the empire's dismantling. This shift from assistants to liaison officers offers an illuminating case study of postcolonial knowledge production.

Cross-Pollinations: Knowledge Making after Empire

Tucked among announcements for a bibliography compiled by the American Dietetic Association, a Cambridge zoology professor's lecture on "animal locomotion," and the appointment of an emergency committee by the Eugenics Society, the paragraph-long notice titled

"Assistant for India at Kew" published in a November 1939 issue of the journal *Nature* does not appear all that extraordinary. Reading like a typical retirement announcement, it summarizes the distinguished career of one C.E.C. Fischer, a Bombay-born Anglo-Indian botanist who, following a long and distinguished career with the Indian forestry service, spent fifteen years as Kew's resident expert for the subcontinent, "responsible for the identification of material from all parts of the Indian Empire."[46]

Most of the men who had preceded Fischer in the position had also spent years in the British colonial service, and those who had not resembled their peers in another important way: they were white. This information underlines the importance of the two closing sentences of the notice in *Nature*: "On Mr. Fischer's retirement in December, he will be succeeded by Mr. K. N. Kaul, who has already spent nearly six months at Kew. Mr. Kaul is a graduate of the University of Lucknow, where he has worked under Prof. B. Sahni." The plain, bureaucratic tone belies the historic significance of Kaul's appointment, for it marked the end of the assistant for India and the beginning of a new era at Kew in which Indians were hired as the experts responsible for the subcontinent.

Also missing from the article is the fact that Kaul's arrival in London was the final link in a chain of events that stretched back four years to the Third Imperial Botanical Conference, the final such gathering of plant scientists representing nations connected to the empire. During the conference, one of the two Indians in attendance, Shankar P. Agharkar, put forward a daring suggestion to Arthur W. Hill, Kew's all-powerful director. Agharkar was irked by Hill's announcement that the Australian government had agreed to fund a "liaison officer" at Kew. Despite its name, the new position was essentially identical to the assistant for South Africa established in 1918. In contradistinction to its older Indian counterpart, as Hill would later write in *Nature*, the position of assistant for South Africa was occupied by "a botanist on the staff of the Union Government" who had been "sent to work at Kew on the historical South African collections."[47] The most important difference was that this South African botanist would eventually "return[] to his duties" after "two or three years."[48] The temporary posting at Kew – which Hill not immodestly names as "the Mecca" and "headquarters of botanical work for the Empire" – granted young "Empire botanists" invaluable experience that would help them improve the botanical institutions in their home country.[49]

No stranger to the politics of race,[50] Agharkar challenged Hill on the obvious double standard. Flanked by his colleague Bilal Sahni, he pointed out to Hill and the other delegates that although funding for the assistant for India had been drawn from Indian coffers since its 1883 inception, no Indians had been consulted on the matter, let alone offered the job. It was time, Agharkar announced, for the end of the assistant for India and for the creation in its stead of a liaison officer position, one to be occupied by an Indian chosen by his peers. As so often is the case when powerful men are confronted by less powerful ones, Hill suppressed the motion from any official discussion. Agharkar and Sahni, however, refused to let the issue be buried and coauthored a polite yet terse letter to the editor in response to Hill's article in *Nature* about the new initiative. The two men did not mince words: "It was pointed out" at the 1935 Imperial Botanical Conference,

> and we do so here again, that the Assistant for India at Kew has always been a retired official, who has never served in India after his period of appointment at Kew. *The knowledge and experience that he gained at Kew has thus not been directly available to India.* The result has been that we have not so far been able to train a single Indian Botanist in return for the money spent from Indian revenues during the fifty-four years that the post … has been in existence.
>
> We are of the opinion that the time has arrived for the abolition of the post of the Assistant for India and Kew and its replacement by Liaison Officers of the type recommended for the Dominions of South Africa, Australia, Canada, and New Zealand. These officers should be comparatively young men who should return to India after their experience abroad.[51]

Unfortunately for the two dissenting "Empire botanists," the editor of *Nature*, Sir Richard Gregory, was a personal friend of Hill and refused to publish what he saw as an "undesirable" letter.[52] Instead, he forwarded it to Kew's director, who took it upon himself to write the men privately. Hill explained that although he was "fully in sympathy with [Agharkar's] proposal" at the conference, he could not publicly support the abolition of the position.[53] For Hill, the problem was less political than personal, since "it would not have been fair on [Fischer] to suggest his being replaced before his time of service [was] completed."[54]

As it turns out, though, Hill informed the men that horizon was not too far off, for Fischer was just two years from mandatory retirement. So,

> if India should wish to follow the procedure adopted by the Government of the Union of South Africa, it would be very much to the advantage both of India and Kew. I should be very pleased to have one of the young Indian systematic botanists working in our Herbarium for two or three years, who would then return enriched, I hope, by all he had learnt here, to be replaced by another for a like term of service as a Liaison Officer for India, and I hope arrangements may be made by your Government to this end.[55]

Thus came about the hiring of the first "Botanist for India" four years after Agharkar first broached the topic at the conference. Sahni put forward the name of his "best student," K.N. Kaul, a thirty-three-year-old "Kashmiri Brahman of a respectable family with a robust physical constitution."[56]

A glance through Kaul's personnel files makes it abundantly clear that the posting at Kew was no walk in the park. His inexperience with systematic botany forced his predecessor to stay on an extra year, double what had been planned. The strains caused by his meagre salary were compounded by the difficulties he faced with landlords reluctant to rent to an Indian. Hill, who initially expressed doubts about the possibility of finding a capable Indian for the position only to end up becoming Kaul's vocal advocate in London, died in a riding accident in November 1941. England's declaration of war on Germany barely two months after Kaul's arrival only complicated matters further. As bombing raids became an all too familiar reality for Londoners, Kew sent staff members and parts of its collections to safer corners of the country. Kaul's wife and child were forced to flee the city as well after the family's Brentford flat was hit by a bomb. And since the war made any return journey to India an extremely dangerous venture, his stay in London ended up running five years long, more than double the length originally planned.[57]

Viewed at a distance, this overlooked fragment of Kew's history is proof that in addition to the foundational role botany played in British colonial policy, the science was also conscripted into the nationalist agitation against empire. Kaul was intimately connected to the struggle for Indian independence; his brother-in-law was none other than Jawaharlal Nehru, and his widow, Sheila Kaul, was one of the oldest living figures connected to the Indian National Congress until her death in 2015. Kaul had direct experiences of the lengths to which colonial administrators would go to stifle it. In 1933, he was arrested and jailed for six months for raising an Indian flag, and during his time in jail he set up a school for his fellow prisoners.[58]

Beyond the individuals involved in its demise, the assistant for India position penetrates to one of British liberalism's most cherished justifications for the empire: the global, unencumbered circulation of knowledge as a catalyst for civilizational progress. As Uday Singh Mehta argues, the "tutorial and pedagogic obsession of the empire and especially of liberal imperialists [was] all part of the effort to move societies along the ascending gradient of historical progress."[59] Although the humanistic aspects of this project have been well documented – most famously by Gauri Viswanathan's *The Masks of Conquest* (1989) – little has been said about how the plant sciences figured into the rhetoric of cultivating colonized natives into civilized subjects. One example is offered in a text cited in Viswanathan's study, a report filed by the president of the Board of Education at Bombay in April 1853: "We will expand your intellectual powers to distinguish truth from falsehood by the aid of Logic and Mathematics; and we will, in the sciences of Astronomy, Geology, Chemistry and Botany, lay open to you all we know of the firmament above, of the nature of the earth on which we live, and the organization of the flowers which enamel its surface; and with your perceptions of the power and wisdom of your God and ours, thus cleared and enlarged, we may safely leave you to distinguish truth for yourselves."[60] By highlighting the fact that the "knowledge and experience" that the assistant for India gained at Kew had "not been directly available to India," Sahni and Agharkar were effectively calling the institution to task for breaking this promise to teach Indians about "the organization of the flowers." Along the same lines, the decades-long exclusion of Indians from the post confirms Richards's claim that the feverish Victorian push to archive the globe hinged not simply on the accrual of the maximum amount of knowledge but also on the monopolistic control of that information. The short note composed by Kaul's predecessor – titled "Note on Messrs. Agharkar and Sahni's Diatribe" and clearly intended only for Hill – confirms this, for in it Fischer confesses that the "desirability of the [Assistant] for India serving *in* India after appointment escapes me; surely it is only desirable *before* appointment."[61]

Fischer's utter bafflement here exemplifies how the liberal rhetoric of educating the colonized can be understood as an important subplot running through the fictitious narrative of Victorian imperial sovereignty. (Fiction, I should add, throughout this chapter does not necessarily signify that which is not reality, but rather a product of an imaginative act.) Obviously, this is not to deny the existence of the sprawling apparatus of training and education erected in India and other parts of the British Empire. Nor is the absence of Indians from one particular career path symptomatic of a transhistorical fact of British imperial rule. Rather, the inability to hire Indians at Kew is clear evidence that the pledge to cultivate colonials was compromised when it involved granting them access to the central corridors of knowledge.

Another obstacle that impeded the realization of this promise was a different fiction woven into the fabric of nineteenth-century British liberal thought: the inherent superiority (racial, intellectual, and political) of the colonizer over the colonized. Botany was certainly not immune to this belief, as evidenced by "The Sudanese Gardener, His Characteristics, Customs and Tools," an article in a 1932 issue of the *Journal of the Kew Guild*. It opens with a casual remark about the infectious laziness of the setting: "This is a country for doing things 'Bookra,' which means to-morrow, and the native is not always the only one affected by the creed."[62] The prototypical national gardener makes his backwardness obvious when he chooses to work: "The Sudanese gardener is not a man who requires many tools in a garden."[63] And the few tools he has in his repertoire are not used properly, as "hoeing is a job which is not fully understood by the Sudanese gardener, and it is very seldom carried out in a proper manner or at the right time."[64] It would be unfair to extract generalizations about either Kew or the British botanical establishment from a single text. Nevertheless, this "profile" of native gardening practices in one part of the empire is a reminder of a somewhat obvious fact: modern botany, like all the other ostensibly "scientific" fields of inquiry forged on the anvil of liberalism's quest for truth through the rational study of actually existing reality, was susceptible to the reigning fairy tales of racial superiority.

Conversely, the article also underlines the symbolic importance of Kaul's hiring as one very literal example of Indian self-determination. It was a significant victory for the Indian botanical community to have one of its own stationed at the most prestigious institution of the field.

This much is articulated by a pair of articles published before and after Kaul's arrival in the country's leading interdisciplinary science journal, *Current Science*. Around the same time that Sahni and Agharkar fired their salvo at Hill's article in *Nature*, the head of Calcutta's Royal Botanic Garden, Kalipada Biswas, published a glowing profile of Kew. He describes the Herbarium as a "sanctuary of Systematic Botany," where "specialists from all over the world" travel in order to "solve their doubts."[65] However, the victory of Kaul's hiring lay just as much in the David and Goliath drama that preceded it, a battle over the racist presumption that Indian botanists were inherently incapable of understanding and managing plants that originated from their backyard, as it did in the fact that an Indian had infiltrated the *sanctum sanctorum* of professional botany. *Current Science*'s account of Kaul's appointment also points out another "glaring anomaly" about the absence of Indians from the position, namely the fact that "the post has been maintained from Indian revenues."[66]

Interestingly enough, *Current Science*'s announcement of Kaul's posting in London is guilty of its own glaring inaccuracy in the article's title, "Liaison-Officer for India on the Staff of Royal Botanic Gardens, Kew." According to the staff list published annually in the *Journal of the Kew Guild*, both Kaul and his direct successor were officially known as the "Botanist for India." Inexplicably, only later did the institution rename the position as the Indian botanical liaison officer. To confuse things even further, Hill and others at Kew refer to Kaul's position as "the Assistant for India" in a number of different correspondences. Nevertheless, the article's closing sentence makes clear that more important than its title was the purpose of Kaul's assignment: "We hope that Dr. Kaul will fully utilise the opportunities offered to him during the next 2½ years so as to enable him to understand a part of the work of identification of Indian plants in India itself."[67] To put it another way, Kaul's tenure at Kew was a definitive sign that Indian intellectuals were no longer going to assist the British Empire. "This appointment," the piece declares in the first paragraph, "marks a new departure in filling this post, which is likely to promote very greatly the study of systematic botany in India, and enable India, in course of time, to have a number of systematic botanists trained at Kew and having first-hand knowledge of the Collections of Indian type material available at Kew and other European herbaria."[68] Irrespective of the official status bestowed upon them, Kaul and those who followed him in the following decades were all "botanists for India."

In *Western Science in Modern India: Metropolitan Methods, Colonial Practices* (2004), Pratik Chakrabarti argues that despite their myriad differences, the many scientists and academics who became active in the nationalist fight shared a "dual commitment – towards science and towards the nation."[69] According to Chakrabarti, "one of the main issues of this nationalist scientific endeavor was the need to locate European science within its own cultural context."[70] But when understood in the strictest sense of the phrase, the location of European sciences in the Indian context is an idea that long predates the rise of the nationalist movement. In fact, it can be found in one of the paradigmatic statements of British colonial education policy, Thomas Babington Macaulay's 1835 "Minute on Indian Education": "We must at present do our best to form a class who may be interpreters between us and the millions whom we govern; a class of persons, Indian in blood and colour, but English in taste, in opinions, in morals, and in intellect. *To that class we may leave it to refine the vernacular dialects of the country, to enrich those dialects with terms of science borrowed from the Western nomenclature,* and to render them by degrees fit vehicles for conveying knowledge to the great mass of the population."[71] A post at Kew reserved specifically for Indian botanists seems to have acceded directly to this call to "enrich" Indian botany "with terms of science borrowed from the Western nomenclature." This is true in the literal sense insofar as the new position would "promote very greatly the study of systematic botany in India." There was also an abstract form of enrichment insofar as the exposure to the inner workings of Kew would undoubtedly help in the construction of national botanical institutions in the subcontinent. After his return to India, Kaul helped found the National Botanic Gardens of India in Lucknow, known today as the National Botanical Research Institute.

Putting aside the racialized dimensions of this issue, the underlying goal of knowledge production fundamentally distinguishes Macaulay's army of "interpreters" from the nationalist intellectuals of the twentieth century, something that also separates all the assistants for India from Kaul and those who followed him. While the former are clearly linked to a more global history of empires seeking out native participation in colonial governance, the latter imagined their work as part of a larger effort "for India." Before considering the precise contours and implications of the Indian nationalist reclamation of botany, a brief discussion of an example of science clearly *not* for India is useful. Moreover, the complicated and tragic history of what is now known as the Acharya

Jagadish Chandra Bose Indian Botanic Garden is directly connected to this chapter. Not only was the institution headed at one point by the subsequent botanist for India at Kew, Debabrata Chatterjee; its history also illustrates why gaining access to the Herbarium in London was so important to Indian botanists.

First proposed by Colonel Robert Kyd in 1786, the establishment of a botanic garden in Calcutta, one of the strategic hubs of the East India Company, received the enthusiastic backing of Joseph Banks. However, it very quickly became clear that Banks would not be able to exert control over the project in the way he liked. In the ensuing decades, the garden was largely left to the devices of the military personnel and colonial agents who ran it. Because the East India Company in the early decades of the nineteenth century was "a greater patron of the sciences than the government (or indeed any other body) in the mother country," the Calcutta garden eventually became one of the largest and most advanced in the empire.[72] But everything changed overnight when in 1828 the head of the gardens, Nathaniel Wallich, and an assistant boarded a boat to London, taking with them more than eight thousand samples held in the institution's museum. Wallich told his superiors that a sabbatical in London was necessary for his health and would afford him an opportunity to publish his long-delayed survey of rare Indian plants. He lived up to this promise, and the resulting text would establish him as one of the eminent botanists of his generation. Unfortunately, the pilfering devastated the Calcutta garden's museum, which over the course of five decades had amassed one of the largest plant archives ever assembled in Indian history, and it never returned to its former glory.[73]

Read against this historical backdrop, Kaul's time at Kew epitomized a nationalist drive to ensure that such blatant examples of colonial expropriation were never repeated. More than that, he was taking part in something that would play an important role in the Indian state created after empire – something in which his brother-in-law had a direct hand. While Kaul was mastering one particular set of "Western nomenclature" in London, Nehru was sitting in a prison cell in Ahmednagar authoring *The Discovery of India* (1946), a text that touches upon the issue of Indians acquiring foreign knowledge. Nehru, a proponent of modern secular education, makes a case for the importance of the "scientific temper" to the country's postcolonial future. Despite his "partiality for the literary aspects of education," Nehru argues that "some elementary scientific training in physics and chemistry, and especially biology, as also in the application of science, is essential for all boys and girls. Only thus can they understand and fit into the modern world and develop, to some extent at least, the scientific temper."[74] Not surprisingly, the book has come under attack in recent decades by a variety of readers who have justly questioned much of its rhetorical and argumentative logic, including the vague and muddled explanations of what precisely "scientific temper" signifies.[75] But when refracted through the lens of Frantz Fanon's "On National Culture," the landmark exploration of how formerly colonized societies forge their own spheres of artistic creation, the work of Kaul and those who followed him suggests that the boundary Nehru draws between "the literary aspects of education" and the "scientific temper" is much more porous than one might presume.

Fanon himself explicitly states that the construction of new imaginative terrains for postcolonial nations is a task applicable to all fields of intellectual inquiry: "A national culture is not a folklore, nor an abstract populism that believes it can discover the people's true nature. It is not made up of the inert dregs of gratuitous actions, that is to say actions which are less and less attached to the ever-present reality of the people. A national culture is *the whole body of efforts made by a people in the sphere of thought* to describe, justify and praise the action through which that people has created itself and keeps itself in existence."[76] Earlier in the essay, Fanon outlines a three-part schema for the development of a native intellectual, a process that helps foster what he calls "the national consciousness."[77] During the third phase, the native intellectual confronts a terrifying spectre: "At the very moment when the native intellectual is anxiously trying to create a cultural work he fails to realize that he is utilising techniques and language which are borrowed from the stranger in his country. He contents himself with stamping these instruments with a hall-mark which he wishes to be national, but which is strangely reminiscent of exoticism."[78]

Fanon's point raises questions about the men who took part in this botany "for India." What is to be done with the "techniques and language … borrowed from the stranger in his country"? Why did they choose to follow their colonial masters and join the ranks of systematic botany and Linnaean nomenclature? Could they have minted an entirely indigenous vernacular for "the organization of the flowers"? Alternatively, as Orientalist William Jones had done,[79] why didn't these Indian botanists fashion something that combined the hegemonic Linnaean system with names derived from Sanskrit or Persian? Fanon supplies one answer to these questions when he argues that the "responsibility of the native man of culture is not a responsibility *vis-à-vis* his national culture, but a global responsibility with regard to the totality of the nation, whose culture merely, after all, represents one aspect of that nation."[80] Kaul and his generation of thinkers and scientists sought to claim a seat for India in the global enterprise of research. In doing so, they proved that liberalism's cherished belief in the worldwide circulation of knowledge could be deployed in the fight against imperialism, a kind of reclamation of the means of intellectual production.

The sentence preceding Fanon's description about what is and is not a national culture cited earlier is particularly germane: "We must work and fight with the same rhythm as the people to construct the future and to prepare the ground where vigorous shoots [*pousses*, sprouts] are already springing up."[81] The botanical metaphor Fanon utilizes in his description of the "work and fight" of fostering a national culture after imperialism furnishes the key to deciphering the significance of the end of the assistant for India, for it underscores the necessity of a broader view of culture that transcends the limit placed on it by the suggestion that it represents "one aspect" of the nation. To reiterate, this story cannot be simplistically reduced to an exemplar of representatives of the marginalized gaining access to "the great centre." The Indian botanists who helped author it were preparing the ground for the botanical enterprise for India, one facet of a larger venture to culture the postcolonial Indian. And while the cultivation of any national culture is a far dirtier kind of work than Fanon's image of a mass of bodies digging in unison suggests, the essay nevertheless models the definitive boundary between the colonial and postcolonial as the difference between the fiction of imperial sovereignty and that of an imagined Indian community.

NOTES

This essay was written with the support of the Social Sciences and Humanities Research Council of Canada. I would like to thank Lorna Cahill and the entire staff of the archives of the Royal Botanical Gardens, Kew, for their invaluable assistance and knowledge. Mark Simpson and Corrinne Harol patiently read through multiple drafts of this essay and provided critical feedback along the way.

1 Drayton, *Nature's Government*, xii.
2 Ibid., 108.
3 Ibid., 173.
4 Ibid.

5 Thiselton-Dyer, *Botanical Enterprise*, 1–2.
6 Ibid., 2.
7 For more on the British Museum's debt to the empire, see Richards, *The Imperial Archive*.
8 The opening sentences of an 1880 report on Afghanistan's Kuram Valley provide a telling illustration: "In the winter of 1878 I accompanied the troops under General (now Sir Frederick) Roberts's command during the advance of the Kuram Field Force into the Kuram Valley, at the taking of the Péwárkotal, and during its further advance to near the Shutar-Gardan [*sic*]. From what I then saw of the country it appeared to me to be an interesting one in a botanical point of view." Aitchison, "On the Flora of the Kuram Valley," 1.
9 Brockway, *Science and Colonial Expansion*, 86.
10 For more on Banks and his global supply chain, see Miller, "Joseph Banks."
11 King, *Bloom*, 238–9.
12 For a contemporary newspaper account, see Anonymous, "A Fairy Flower."
13 "L'Amorphophallus Titanum," 280.
14 Philip, *Civilizing Natures*, 171–95; Brockway, *Science and Colonial Expansion*, 103–82.
15 Tasker, "The Role of the Living Orchid Collection"; Drayton, *Nature's Government*, 246–50.
16 Drayton, *Nature's Government*, 28, 72. For a contemporary account of the importance of economic botany to the Victorians, see Ellis, *Fifty Years of Economic Botany*.
17 Drayton, 69. The rise of economic botany was part of a more global development across all fields of scientific inquiry. As Londa Schiebinger puts it, "across Europe eighteenth-century political economists ... taught that the exact knowledge of nature was key to amassing national wealth, and hence power." *Plants and Empire*, 5.
18 For more on the work of the committee, see Meynell, "Kew and the Royal Gardens Committee of 1838."
19 Lindley, "Report," 1.
20 Ibid.
21 Ibid., 2.
22 Ibid., 5.
23 Ibid.
24 McCracken, *Gardens of Empire*, 19.
25 *My Beautiful Laundrette*, directed by Stephen Frears.
26 Lindley, "Report," 5.
27 Drayton, *Nature's Government*, 172.
28 Thiselton-Dyer, *Botanical Enterprise*, 7.

29 Ibid., 6.
30 Ibid., 6–7.
31 Ibid., 11.
32 Ibid., 13.
33 Richards, *Imperial Archive*, 1–2.
34 Ibid., 1.
35 Darwin, *Empire Project*, xi.
36 See, for example, Eugenia Herbert's *Flora's Empire* (2011) and Peder Anker's *Imperial Ecology* (2001).
37 McCracken, *Gardens of Empire*, 78.
38 Thiselton-Dyer, *Botanical Enterprise*, 5.
39 Ibid.
40 Conrad, *Heart of Darkness*, 107.
41 Oak Taylor, "Joseph Conrad and the Face(s) of Imperial Manhood," 197.
42 Richards, *Imperial Archive*, 1.
43 Ibid., 7.
44 Ibid., 7.
45 Desmond, *India Museum*, 180–9.
46 Anonymous, "Assistant for India at Kew."
47 Hill, "Royal Botanical Gardens," 422.
48 Ibid.
49 Ibid.
50 While studying at the University of Berlin, Agharkar was part of a group of Indian students interned after the outbreak of World War I. Only in late 1917 was he given permission to leave the camp and allowed to complete his degree, albeit under police supervision. Kundu, "Professor Shankar Purusottam Agharkar," 209.
51 Agharkar and Sahni, letter to the editor (emphasis added). All the documents related to Kaul's tenure can be found at the Kew Archives under the heading "Assistant for India."
52 Gregory, letter to Sir Arthur Hill.
53 Hill, letter to Professor Bilal Sahni.
54 Hill, letter to Professor S.P. Agharkar.
55 Hill, letter to Professor Bilal Sahni.
56 Sahni, letter to secretary of Inter University Board.
57 These details about Kaul's time in London have been culled from two separate documents: Hill, letter to W.D. Croft, and Cotton, "Report on Mr. Kaul's Work 1943 and 1944."
58 Bhushan, ed., "K.N. Kaul."
59 Mehta, *Liberalism and Empire*, 81–2.
60 Quoted in Viswanathan, *Masks of the Conquests*, 107.

61 Fischer, "Note on Messrs. Agharkar and Sahni's Diatribe" (emphasis in original).
62 Robbie, "The Sudanese Gardener," 148.
63 Ibid., 149.
64 Ibid., 150. Another example is furnished by a letter to the editor of the *Indian Gardener*, a short-lived horticultural magazine published in Calcutta during the 1880s: "In Beluchistan, where I am at present stationed, I find [a number of] fruit [trees] are grown by the natives ... But, with the exception of a few Syads [*sic*] near Quetta, who keep their science to themselves, the people are supremely ignorant of all gardening operations. Grafting, pruning, insect-killing, are unknown amongst them; and provided they can secure a large quantity of fruit, they seem utterly indifferent as to its quality." Anonymous, "Fruit Culture," 315.
65 Biswas, "Impressions," 139.
66 "Liaison-Officer for India," 355.
67 Ibid.
68 Ibid., 354.
69 Chakrabarti, *Western Science in Modern India*, 180.
70 Ibid., 122.
71 Macaulay, "Minute on Indian Education (1835)," 237 (emphasis added).
72 Sharma, "British Science, Chinese Skill and Assam Tea," 431. See also Harrison, "The Calcutta Botanic Garden"; Axelby, "Calcutta Botanic Garden"; McCracken, *Gardens of Empire*, passim.
73 This example neatly illustrates Eddy Kent's argument about the "corporate character" of British imperialism in India in *Corporate Character*.
74 Nehru, *Discovery of India*, 409, 512. The statesman's insistence on the national importance of scientific education has enjoyed a long afterlife in India. In 1958, both Houses of Parliament adopted the Scientific Policy Resolution, which extols the singular importance of nurturing advanced research. This was followed two decades later by an amendment to the constitution enshrining the coinage of "scientific temper" into the juridical heart of the Indian state. Among an array of "fundamental duties" now ascribed to citizens is the development of "the scientific temper, humanism and the spirit of inquiry and reform."
75 Nehru's prose soars, but the precise meaning of the term and its translation into everyday life remain elusive:

> It is the scientific approach, the adventurous and yet critical temper of science, the search for truth and new knowledge, the refusal to accept anything without testing and trial, the capacity to change previous conclusions in the face of new evidence, the reliance on observed fact and not on pre-conceived theory, the hard discipline of the mind – all this

> is necessary, not merely for the application of science but for life itself and the solution of its many problems … The scientific approach and temper are, or should be, a way of life, a process of thinking, a method of acting and associating with our fellowmen. That is a large order and undoubtedly very few of us, if any at all, can function in this way with even partial success. But this criticism applies in equal or even greater measure to all the injunctions which philosophy and religion have laid upon us. The scientific temper points out the way along which man should travel. It is the temper of a free man. We live in a scientific age, so we are told, but there is little evidence of this temper in the people anywhere or even in their leaders. (Nehru, *Discovery of India*, 512.)

For a more positive discussion of the term, see Mahanti, "A Perspective on Scientific Temper in India." A more hostile engagement with Nehru's views is offered by Nandy, "Science as a Reason of State."

76 Fanon, "On National Culture," 188 (emphasis added).

77 Ibid., 178–9.

78 Ibid., 180.

79 Styles, "Sir William Jones' Names of Indian Plants."

80 Fanon, "On National Culture," 187.

81 Ibid., 188.

BIBLIOGRAPHY

Agharkar, Shankar Purusottam, and Bilal Sahni. Untitled letter to the editor. 10 May 1937. 1/STAFF/74, Assistant for India 1883–1942, Kew Archives, Royal Botanical Garden.

Aitchison, James E.T. "On the Flora of the Kuram Valley &c., Afghanistan." *Journal of the Linnean Society* 18, no. 106–7 (1881): 1–113.

Anker, Peder. *Imperial Ecology: Environmental Order in the British Empire, 1895–1945.* Cambridge, MA: Harvard University Press, 2001.

Anonymous. "A Fairy Flower." *Star (Guernsey)*, July 1889, 4.

– "Fruit Culture." *Indian Gardener* 1, no. 26 (August 1885): 315–16.

– "Assistant for India at Kew." *Nature* 144 (November 1939): 829.

Axelby, Richard. "Calcutta Botanic Garden and the Colonial Re-ordering of the Indian Environment." *Archives of Natural History* 35, no. 1 (2008): 150–63.

Bhushan, Ravi, ed. "K.N. Kaul." In *Famous India: Nation's Who's Who*, 133. Delhi: Famous India Publications, 1975.

Biswas, Kalipada. "Impressions of the Royal Botanic Garden, Kew, London." *Current Science* 6, no. 3 (September 1937): 135–9.

Brockway, Lucile H. *Science and Colonial Expansion: The Role of the British Royal Botanic Gardens.* New York: Academic Press, 1979.

Chakrabarti, Pratik. *Western Science in Modern India: Metropolitan Methods, Colonial Practices.* Delhi: Permanent Black, 2004.

Conrad, Joseph. *Heart of Darkness.* In *Heart of Darkness and Other Tales*, edited by Cedric Watts, 101–87. Oxford's World's Classics. Oxford: Oxford University Press, 2008.

Cotton, Arthur Disbrowe. "Report on Mr. Kaul's Work 1943 and 1944." 12 May 1944. 1/STAFF/74, Assistant for India 1883–1942, Kew Archives, Royal Botanical Garden.

Darwin, John. *The Empire Project: The Rise and Fall of the British World-System, 1830–1970.* Cambridge: Cambridge University Press, 2011.

Desmond, Ray. *The India Museum, 1801–1879.* London: Her Majesty's Stationery Office, 1982.

Drayton, Richard. *Nature's Government: Science, Imperial Britain, and the "Improvement" of the World.* New Haven: Yale University Press, 2000.

Ellis, John W. *Fifty Years of Economic Botany: The Vegetable Substances Introduced into Britain for Use in the Arts and Manufactures, and as Food, during the Reign of Queen Victoria.* London: Royal Botanic Society of London, 1888.

Fanon, Frantz. "On National Culture." In *The Wretched of the Earth*, translated by Constance Farrington, 206–48. New York: Grove Press, 1963.

Fischer, C.E.C. "Note on Messrs. Agharkar and Sahni's Diatribe." 3 June 1937. 1/STAFF/74, Assistant for India 1883–1942, Kew Archives, Royal Botanical Garden.

Gregory, Richard. Letter to Sir Arthur W. Hill. 9 June 1937. 1/STAFF/74, Assistant for India 1883–1942, Kew Archives, Royal Botanical Garden.

Harrison, Mark. "The Calcutta Botanic Garden in the Era of Nathaniel Wallich." In *Science and Modern India: An Institutional History, c. 1784–1947*, edited by Uma Dasgupta, 235–54. New Delhi: Centre for Studies in Civilizations, 2010.

Herbert, Eugenia. *Flora's Empire: British Gardens in India.* Philadelphia: University of Pennsylvania Press, 2011.

Hill, Arthur W. "Royal Botanical Gardens and Empire Botanists." *Nature* 139 (March 1937): 422–3.

– Letter to Professor B. Sahni. 14 June 1937. 1/STAFF/74, Assistant for India 1883–1942, Kew Archives, Royal Botanical Garden.

– Letter to Professor S.P. Agharkar. 15 June 1937. 1/STAFF/74, Assistant for India 1883–1942, Kew Archives, Royal Botanical Garden.

– Letter to W.D. Croft. 7 November 1939. 1/STAFF/74, Assistant for India 1883–1942, Kew Archives, Royal Botanical Garden.

Kent, Eddy. *Corporate Character: Representing Imperial Power in British India, 1786–1901*. Toronto: University of Toronto Press, 2014.

King, Amy M. *Bloom: The Botanical Vernacular in the English Novel*. New York: Oxford University Press, 2003.

Kundu, B.C. "Professor Shankar Purusottam Agharkar, 1884–1960." *Taxon* 11, no. 7 (1962): 209–11.

"L'Amorphophallus Titanum." *La Science Illustrée* 96 (September 1889): 280.

"Liaison-Officer for India on the Staff of Royal Botanic Gardens, Kew." *Current Science* 8, no. 8 (August 1939): 354–5.

Lindley, John. "Copy of the Report Made to the Committee Appointed by the Lords of the Treasury in January 1838 to Inquire into the Management Etc. of the Royal Gardens at Kew." 1840 (292) XXIX.259.

Macaulay, Thomas. "Minute on Indian Education (1835)." In *Archives of Empire*. Vol. 1, *From the East India Company to the Suez Canal*, edited by Barbara Harlow and Mia Carter, 227–38. Durham: Duke University Press, 2003.

Mahanti, Subodh. "A Perspective on Scientific Temper in India." *Journal of Scientific Temper* 1, no. 1 (January 2013): 46–62.

McCracken, Donal P. *Gardens of Empire: Botanical Institutions of the Victorian British Empire*. London: Leicester University Press, 1997.

Mehta, Uday Singh. *Liberalism and Empire: A Study in Nineteenth-Century British Liberal Thought*. Chicago: University of Chicago Press, 1999.

Meynell, Guy. "Kew and the Royal Gardens Committee of 1838." *Archives of Natural History* 10, no. 3 (1982): 469–77.

Miller, David Phillip. "Joseph Banks, Empire, and 'Centres of Calculation' in Late Hanoverian London." In *Visions of Empire: Voyages, Botany, and the Representations of Nature*, edited by David Phillip Miller and Peter H. Reill, 21–37. Cambridge: Cambridge University Press, 1996.

My Beautiful Laundrette. Directed by Stephen Frears. UK: Working Title Films, 1985. DVD.

Nandy, Ashis. "Introduction: Science as a Reason of State." In *Science, Hegemony and Violence: A Requiem for Modernity*, edited by Ashis Nandy, 1–23. Delhi: Oxford University Press, 1988.

Nehru, Jawaharlal. *The Discovery of India*. 1946. Reprint, Delhi: Oxford University Press, 1989.

Oak Taylor, Jesse. "White Skin, White Masks: Joseph Conrad and the Face(s) of Imperial Manhood." *Conradiana* 44, no. 2–3 (2012): 191–210.

Philip, Kavita. *Civilizing Natures: Race, Resources, and Modernity in Colonial South India*. New Brunswick, NJ: Rutgers University Press, 2004.

Richards, Thomas. *The Imperial Archive: Knowledge and the Fantasy of Empire*. London: Verso, 1993.

Robbie, J. "The Sudanese Gardener, His Characteristics, Customs and Tools." *Journal of the Kew Guild* 5, no. 39 (1932): 148–51.

Sahni, Bilal. Letter to secretary of Inter University Board, Lucknow, India. January 2, 1939. 1/STAFF/74, Assistant for India 1883–1942, Kew Archives, Royal Botanical Garden.

Schiebinger, Londa. *Plants and Empire: Colonial Bioprospecting in the Atlantic World*. Cambridge, MA: Harvard University Press, 2004.

Sharma, Jayeeta. "British Science, Chinese Skill and Assam Tea: Making Empire's Garden." *Indian Economic Social History Review* 43, no. 4 (2006): 429–55.

Styles, B.T. "Sir William Jones' Names of Indian Plants." *Taxon* 25, no. 5/6 (November 1976): 671–4.

Tasker, Soo. "The Role of the Living Orchid Collection at Kew in Conservation." In *Modern Methods in Orchid Conservation: The Role of Physiology, Ecology and Management*, edited by Howard Pritchard, 159–62. Cambridge: Cambridge University Press, 1989.

Thiselton-Dyer, William. *The Botanical Enterprise of Empire*. London: Eyre and Spottiswoode, 1880.

Viswanathan, Gauri. *The Masks of the Conquests: Literary Study and British Rule in India*. New York: Columbia University Press, 1989.

World Garden. Directed by Robin Carruthers. Spectator Films, 1942. DVD.

10 "They Make Their Own Tragedies Too": Harvey Swados and Postwar Liberalism's Discourse of Dependency

SEAN MCCANN

Like most of the New York literary intelligentsia of his day, Harvey Swados fell hard for the work of the young Philip Roth. Writing of *Goodbye, Columbus* in an omnibus review in 1959, Swados remarked that Roth had "succeeded brilliantly" in making Newark, New Jersey, a subject of literary art. So faithfully did Roth render that world that his stories could "send the shivers down your spine." He would "soon become," Swados predicted, "one of our most important writers."[1]

Of course, that was not an unusual prediction in an American literary quarterly of the late 1950s and early 1960s. What makes Swados's enthusiasm notable is simply the source. For at the time, Swados seemed to many of his contemporaries a writer and intellectual somewhat out of step with his peers. By his own description, he remained a socialist radical in a land of craven liberals and a realist novelist in an era when artists and critics were embracing formal exuberance and psychological introspection.[2] Each of these stances seemed, at first glance, to put him at odds with a generation of aspiring writers who were marking their ambition by throwing off, in various ways, the trappings of conventional narrative form. Those slightly younger writers were forging, as Swados himself remarked of Roth, "a cranky prose-poetry" – "a nervous muscular [style] perfectly suited to the exigencies of an age … at once appalling and ridiculous."[3]

In the view of the era's dominant critics and artists, moreover, such efforts seemed to mark both a generational and an ideological shift that Swados himself appeared reluctant to embrace. In the eyes of the most prominent literary intellectuals of the 1950s and early sixties, as Thomas Schaub has most trenchantly explained, the postwar United States seemed a thoroughly new society – one that had left behind the political struggles of the wartime and prewar years and that was now shaped above all by the rampant growth of mass media, mass consumption, and mass bureaucratic institutions. Such a world called out, the era's leading artists and critics asserted, for new literary styles whose novelty could register the obsolescence of traditional social concerns and outworn political ideologies. For many among the most prominent writers of the 1950s (Baldwin, Bellow, McCarthy, Salinger, Updike), that had often meant a preoccupation with the intricacies of psychological history. Toward the end of the decade, as the Eisenhower era declined, a slight shift in emphasis led a cohort of bold younger writers (Barth, Ginsberg, Heller, Kerouac, Pynchon) to place increasing emphasis on the artist's struggle to grasp a manufactured reality and to negotiate the absurdities and the spiritual emptiness of a bureaucratic world.[4] In either of these often overlapping modes, however, the leading fiction writers of the postwar decades distinguished their work from the limits they perceived in conventionally realist or political fiction.

Amid these trends, Swados looked, at first glance, recalcitrantly out of step. He was, as Irving Howe remarked, "an unfashionable novelist" who remained stubbornly "committed to the tradition of realism."[5] Swados himself appeared to say as much. He dismissed the "liberal mush" that dominated mid-century intellectual life and invoked against it the demands of "programmatic realism."[6] Looking at "the kind of idiosyncratic novels" his slightly younger contemporaries were writing, Swados regretted their abandonment of the "large themes" of realist fiction, which he feared had been surrendered to "hack writers" like Herman Wouk. In his own work – especially in his most renowned book, the cycle of stories about auto plant workers titled *On the Line* (1957) – Swados claimed to be aiming at "something ... no one else was trying to do."[7] This writing focused not on the psychological torments and cultural anxieties of the young artist but on the gruelling and demeaning experience of blue-collar labour – the "hatred, shame, and resignation," as Swados put it in his renowned essay "The Myth of the Happy Worker" (1957), of "factory servitude."[8] While his contemporaries had become distracted by the rhetoric of "liberal self-congratulation," Swados suggested, his writing would speak more generally of "the human degradation attendant upon capitalism."[9]

And yet, as his enthusiastic response to Roth made clear, Swados nevertheless shared some fundamental premises with his most influential contemporaries. What informed readers should take from Roth's innovations in narrative form and voice, Swados remarked, was "gratitude and delight at the inexhaustible wealth available in the constant rebirth of this ancient art form for those of us who hunger for news of the human personality."[10] And the very terms in which Swados framed this appreciation make the terms he shared with Roth apparent. For the achievement of a human personality and the alliance of personality with the enduring wealth of art were primary concerns of *Goodbye, Columbus*, as they were more generally of the postwar decade's liberal intellectuals. ("Of course, the mystery of personality may be nothing less than a writer's ultimate concern," Roth wrote in his landmark essay "Writing American Fiction.")[11] And these were in fact precisely the terms dramatized by Roth's rueful coming-of-age narrative, which hinges almost explicitly on a contrast between the *exhaustible* wealth of America's consumer riches and the inexhaustible treasure of hard-won wisdom – between the shallow personal beauty exemplified by Brenda Patimkin's nose job and the deeper human personality revealed by Neil Klugman in the novel's closing scene.

In that moment, as Roth's protagonist examines his reflection in the window of Harvard's Lamont Library and sees beyond his figure to the library's shelved books and the heritage of learning and discipline they symbolize, Roth stages a particularly eloquent version of a scene repeated frequently in American literary fiction of the postwar decades – where a character's careful consideration of his self-image reflects the larger challenge to forge an authentic personal identity amid the shallow temptations of mass society.[12] Despite their other differences, Swados's enthusiastic response to *Goodbye, Columbus* suggests that he shared Roth's preoccupation with this concern. Indeed, as we'll go on to see, in *On the Line* and in his critical writings, Swados presented less an alternative to the ideological consensus of postwar liberalism than an unresolved struggle with its most influential convictions.

In this respect, he resembled a number of the era's dissenting voices – those of his friends C. Wright Mills and Irving Howe and his sometime sparring partner Norman Mailer and those of others among the avowedly anti-Stalinist radicals of mid-century New York, such as Michael Harrington, Dwight Macdonald, and Mary McCarthy.[13] Like those thinkers, Swados found himself in the 1950s and early sixties stranded between the old and new Lefts and perched uncomfortably on the margins of the liberal consensus. If he took pride in his unwillingness to bow to the hegemony of Cold War anti-communism and to the complacent defence of democratic pluralism that Mills denounced as "The American Celebration," he also shared some of his liberal contemporaries' most basic ways of understanding the world.[14] Indeed, his incomplete struggle to bend their shared premises to a vision of independent radicalism may reveal more effectively than many other examples the most salient characteristics of postwar liberal ideology and its profound influence over both public policy and cultural expression in the mid-century United States.

Harvey Swados's most celebrated work, *On the Line*, is a collection of eight linked short stories depicting the lives of nine men, from various backgrounds, who work in the finishing room of a vast automobile manufacturing plant in the suburbs of New York. Those workers include LeRoy, a young African American man from an aspiring middle-class family in Virginia who has come to New York to pursue his dream of singing opera; Kevin, an immigrant from rural Ireland who first falls in, and then out of, love with the cars he helps manufacture; Walter, the child of a downwardly mobile salesman who yearns for a college education and the chance to become an engineer; Buster, a long-time line-worker who has risen to the frustrating position of shop foreman; Harold, a one-time commercial artist whose life has been damaged by alcoholism; and Frank, a middle-aged failed entrepreneur who returns to factory labour to salvage his family's finances. Together these varied figures illuminate the range of lives that cross, without quite meeting, in the overwhelming environment of the assembly plant. Despite their differences, all of these men are alike in finding their work gruelling, tedious, and degrading, and all exemplify the sentiment that comes to Harold as an epiphany. Briefly viewing the factory from a distance, he realizes that it resembles "nothing so much as a splendid, progressive new prison, conceived and executed by an architect who knew how to use glass and aluminum to conceal concrete pillboxes and whirling searchlights."[15] Harold and his fellow workers, Swados suggests, are captives of a totalitarian factory system and of the delusional promises of American consumerism that justify and conceal the factory's brutal operation.

In this respect, Swados's collection of stories takes up the theme expressed more programmatically in his essay "The Myth of the Happy Worker" (1957). There, Swados challenged the widespread assumption that the successes of organized labour and the abundance of the postwar consumer economy had overcome the legacy of class hierarchy and made the United States a fluid and egalitarian mass society. As Swados summarized it, this common view held that "the worker's rise in real income … plus the diffusion of middle-class tastes and values … has made it increasingly difficult to tell blue-collar from white-collar worker." Drawing on his own experiences of factory labour – most recently at the vast new Ford plant in Mahwah, New Jersey – Swados dispatched this mistaken perception. Manual labourers in the 1950s, Swados acknowledged, might appear to "earn[] like the middle-class, vote[] like the middle-class, dress[] like the middle-class, [and] dream[] like the middle-class." But, Swados pointed out, there was nevertheless "one thing that the worker doesn't do like the middle-class: he works like a worker."[16]

On the Line makes the strongest possible case for the significance of this distinction by showing us that its characters are among the most fortunate of the US blue-collar workers at a historical moment when the American industrial workforce appeared to be thriving. As employees in the auto plant's finishing room, Swados's characters perform, for the most part, skilled labour in a full-employment economy. Their abilities are in demand, and high turnover and a booming economy help keep wages and overtime pay high. They are, moreover, unionized workers in a closed shop and enjoy not only the fruit of collective bargaining over wages but also job security and work rules that limit their vulnerability to abuse. Unlike an earlier generation of autoworkers, as Swados himself emphasizes, the characters of *On the Line* have little reason to fear arbitrary firing, threats, intimidation, or violence from company goons. They earn incomes that allow them, depending on their aspirations, to buy homes and cars and to save for the future. Nevertheless, in each story, Swados shows these rewards to be insubstantial, manual labour to be grinding, and the workers' experience of status to be humiliating. As one particularly astute character notes, "life in the factory seem[s] to be deliberately designed to lower your own self-esteem."[17]

But what precisely are the causes of this injury? Swados sometimes makes it seem that the answer to this question is a simple one. "The plain truth is that factory work is degrading."[18] But in fact *On the Line* shows its characters to be angered by a range of diverse, overlapping frustrations. In some places, Swados suggests that the assembly line by its nature robs labourers of control over their work and makes them vulnerable to their employers' arbitrary demands for improvements in productivity. Thus, for example, one character – Orrin – who takes unusual pride in his dedication to his work, feels emasculated when he comes to the realization that he is easily replaced, and another – the foreman Buster – is humiliated by the demands of engineers who impose misguided efficiency schemes. In other places, Swados goes beyond this complaint and implies that factory work is degrading not merely because it robs workers of control over their labour but because it limits their capacity to develop the full range of their abilities. Thus, the collection opens with the story of LeRoy, whose dreams of a musical career are cruelly ended when his throat is injured on the job; and LeRoy's story is later complemented by the tale of Harold, whose vulnerability to drink leads him to trade his unsuccessful career as an artist for the comfortingly lifeless routine of factory work. *On the Line* further implies that factory labour isolates and alienates its workers and robs them of any sense of mutuality. (The theme is emphasized not least in the very form of the book's eight separate stories, which plumb the personal histories of men who, although they work side by side, are nearly strangers to each other.) But to this complaint it adds the suggestion that manual labourers are damaged by the hidden injuries of status – that they feel inevitably shamed by what Swados elsewhere called "the chasm that separates those who *think* from those who *do*."[19]

Perhaps most insistently, Swados suggests that his characters endure all these related injuries only because they have unwittingly chained themselves to the delusions of the consumer economy. The implication is conveyed most melodramatically in "A Present for the Boy" – the story of the elderly immigrant worker Pops who labours and saves to buy a roadster for his teenage son, in which the boy soon crashes and dies. But it runs powerfully through each of the book's eight stories. The mysterious anarchist whose name gives the title to "Joe, the Vanishing American," and who serves as Swados's voice of wisdom, makes the point explicit when he explains to the naive Walter that factory labour is degrading because "people are serving production." The blue-collar worker, Joe explains, "gets suckered into believing that there's anything real behind the billboards[,] … so that he commits himself to … selling his life on the installment plan."[20] Joe's words echo Swados's contention in "The Myth of the Happy Worker" that life for the industrial labourer was different, and in some ways better, amid the brutal conditions of the earlier twentieth century. Before World War II, American industrial workers could view their grinding labour as contributing to a greater purpose, Swados claimed. They strove to escape poverty and political oppression in their homelands, or they struggled for the cause of organized labour or toward a socialist future. The worker's "long hours were going to buy him freedom." Now, in the postwar world,

Swados lamented, industrial workers had gained unanticipated wealth and security, but at the cost of significance. "For the factory worker of the Fifties," Swados complained, "his long hours are going to buy him commodities."[21]

How should we understand this complaint? For some of Swados's most attentive critics, *On the Line* resembles, in its depiction of the varied forms of the worker's alienation, the writings of the young Marx.[22] But we can grasp the logic underlying Swados's book equally well, and perhaps more appropriately, by noting that the vision of work running through his stories is also fully consistent with the most influential, liberal accounts of the American political economy in the mid-twentieth century. Those versions of liberal theory sometimes resembled the young Marx's emphasis on alienation. (After all, no word may have been more prominent in postwar intellectual discourse.) But, more importantly for our purposes, they shared a set of premises about the nature of economic and political life in the postwar United States that is consistent with all of Swados's main implications.

A revealing account of those premises can be found in the scholarship of Howard Brick, who argues that mid-century liberal thinkers converged on a "postcapitalist" vision of American society. As Brick explains, the era's liberal thinkers tended to assume that the extraordinary growth of the postwar economy, and the institutional and political arrangements that sustained it, had all but resolved the historical problems of economic scarcity, inequality, and class conflict. Rejecting what they viewed as outmoded theories that emphasized the power of social hierarchy, mid-century liberal thinkers assumed instead that, at its best, the United States was a "pluralist" society of jockeying institutions and interest groups. By the same token, they frequently suggested that the American public's new wealth had revealed the spiritual and psychological costs of abundance and the need for cultural and political transformations that could translate economic productivity into more widely shared happiness or a greater public good. These challenges, the era's leading liberal thinkers often contended, were especially evident in the numbing dissatisfactions of routinized work and in the shallow and manufactured gratifications of mass culture.[23] In short, what Swados saw in the lives of his factory workers was arguably a variation on problems that liberal thinkers in the 1950s and early 1960s saw everywhere.

As Brick makes clear, such premises informed a wide range of mid-century American social and political thought. But their single most influential expression probably came in John Kenneth Galbraith's vastly influential bestseller *The Affluent Society* (1958). In his earlier work *American Capitalism* (1952), Galbraith had fashioned a powerful, pluralist view of the American economic order, casting the postwar political economy as a continual negotiation among the "countervailing powers" of business, labour, and government. Now, Galbraith followed up with a social diagnosis of the effects of America's pluralist economy and the wealth that it had generated. In Galbraith's view, the economic boom of the postwar years indicated that the United States had entered a new stage of capitalism – one whose great productive capacities created a world of abundance and obviated the classical economic focus on scarcity. Amid postwar affluence, Americans no longer needed to be concerned with "the preoccupations of a poverty-ridden world."[24] Instead, a new set of problems confronted them. Inspired by a need for constant growth in productivity and no longer urged on by want, business interests responded by inventing new consumer desires, which were "synthesized, elaborated, and nurtured by advertising and salesmanship."[25] Beholden, meanwhile, to a lingering attachment to private property, Americans allowed their new consumer wealth to be diverted into a bounty of unnecessary and ugly consumer products, even as the "public goods" of education, health, and common safety were allowed to degrade. The contemporary United States, Galbraith famously declared, had become a land of "private opulence and public squalor."[26]

In response, Galbraith called for a return to "social balance," laying out a policy agenda that would eventually lead to the major domestic initiatives of, first, the Kennedy administration's New Frontier and then, more substantially, of Lyndon Johnson's Great Society. The goal of this agenda was, in effect, to enable Americans to overcome their submission to the manufactured and shallow gratifications of consumer culture. Rather than seeking out ever more tawdry private satisfactions, Galbraith contended, Americans should invest in education, health, public safety, public leisure, and public support for the arts. (Galbraith's friend Arthur Schlesinger Jr identified this program as "qualitative liberalism" to distinguish it from the "quantitative liberalism" that he believed had characterized the political priorities of the New Deal.)[27] On Galbraith's account, this was more than an appropriate policy agenda for a newly wealthy society; it also reflected a distinctive historical and political vision. For he assumed that a movement to restore social balance would be led by the rising cohort of white-collar workers that he labelled the "New Class."[28] In Galbraith's view, the rise of this new class foretold a profound change in economic life and political ideology. Professional and managerial workers earned their most important skills through formal education, Galbraith pointed out, so they understood that "investment in human as distinct from material capital" should be rewarded.[29] They laboured, he further believed, not primarily for mere pecuniary rewards but for "the respect, regard, and esteem of others."[30] Perhaps most importantly, Galbraith argued that white-collar workers possessed a distinctive attitude to their work, which presented a fundamental challenge to the time-honoured assumption that labour must involve "pain, fatigue, or other mental or physical discomfort."[31] Members of the new class took it "for granted," Galbraith claimed, that work would "be enjoyable. If it [was] not, this [was] a source of deep dissatisfaction or frustration."[32]

For all these reasons, Galbraith expected that an expanding population of white-collar workers would become the vanguard of a new society. They all but directly displaced from this role the industrial workers and organized labour that had once been seen as the core constituency of social democratic politics. On Galbraith's account, as in the view of his most influential contemporaries, organized labour had won all the victories it could meaningfully anticipate.[33] The workers' movement was no longer an insurgent force to transform the social order; it had become the institutionalized guardian of narrow self-interest that Daniel Bell jokingly identified as "the capitalism of the proletariat."[34] By virtue of its very accomplishments, organized labour had metamorphosed into a recognized partner in the postwar détente among big business, big government, and big labour. Its role now was merely to protect the interests of industrial labourers and to provide them opportunities for political voice and civic engagement. (Interestingly, Galbraith cited Swados's *On the Line* in support of this view.)[35] Liberal intellectuals and policymakers should thus no longer be primarily concerned with the economic questions that had been paramount during the New Deal era. Instead, they should invest their hopes in the new class and in the provision of public goods, which Galbraith believed this class especially valued. Indeed, he suggested, the "rapid expansion of this class" – and the concomitant minimization of the population required to do "routine and repetitive manual labor" – should be "*the* major social goal of the society."[36]

The visions of a new qualitative liberalism of which Galbraith and Schlesinger spoke were crucial to the postwar literary renaissance that

Harvey Swados plausibly saw exemplified by the work and the career of Philip Roth. This was so not merely in the sense that Roth's fiction, like that of most of his contemporaries, was preoccupied with the experiences and concerns of the professional class. (*Goodbye, Columbus* is nearly allegorical in this respect. For it shows Neil Klugman literally moving, by dint of his intelligence and sensitivity, beyond his working-class roots in the industrial city and being ultimately compelled to choose between a future of suburban wealth or a life of professional dedication and public service.) More fundamentally still, qualitative liberalism made literature and art seem crucial indexes of the achievement of the "social balance" necessary to a pluralist society. "As the problems of our affluent society become more qualitative and less quantitative," Schlesinger wrote, "we must expect culture to emerge as a matter of national concern."[37] Seen in this framework, literature and the arts more generally became examples of the kind of public goods that the new class was presumed to value and that public policy (indirectly, through federal support for the growth of higher education, and later directly, through the creation of the National Endowment for the Humanities and the National Endowment for the Arts (NEA)) could underwrite.

Such federal funding played a crucial role in the postwar literary renaissance that Harvey Swados witnessed. It was crucial, for example, to the rapid expansion of university training in creative writing that has led Mark McGurl to identify the postwar decades as "the Program Era." Perhaps not surprisingly, then, the concerns of qualitative liberalism are evident throughout the central aesthetic and ethical dramas of postwar American literature. As McGurl has compellingly shown, the MFA program's rapprochement of modernist aesthetics and mass higher education led to a regime of aesthetic education that stressed literature's complementary role to the bureaucratic institutions that sustained this education. In the tacit ideology of the program era, the aspiring writer must struggle to negotiate the demands of personal experience and professional training, bringing these two contrary forces together in the quest to fashion fully realized works that might take their place in a larger literary community. This was a form of training that, as McGurl shows, made the creation of literature and the realization of autonomous personhood seem like inseparable goals. In both its mode of education and in the artistic problems it foregrounded, the literature of the program era modelled the way "the collective life we live through institutions" could be complemented by the realization of "expressive selfhood."[38]

In short, program aesthetics as McGurl describes them appear as nearly an allegory of the pluralist "social balance" that qualitative liberals like Galbraith and Schlesinger thought should be the primary concern of mid-century political life. They made literature seem a model of the way that aspiring members of the new class could resist shallow gratification and bureaucratic regimentation and thus lead a rewarding and admirable life. To put the point differently, creative writing in the program era became what McGurl calls "a therapeutic educational enterprise."[39] It acknowledged the central concern that ran through postwar liberal thought – that, now that the liberal state had ostensibly conquered the problems of class and economic insecurity, its vast bureaucratic institutions would submerge the vital, pluralist dimensions of American life and produce a homogenous mass society. (Swados's friend and pupil, Dan Wakefield, recalling the anxieties he shared with Columbia University classmates, remembered this as a "typical fifties fear ... that we'd lockstep into some automated, sterile future.")[40] But it countered that fear with the reassurance that a dedication to craft – and thereby to education as trained self-realization rather than as indoctrination or routinization – could reinforce rather than submerge one's own distinctive gifts and thus contribute to the realization of "a diverse aesthetic democracy."[41] To quote Swados on Roth, the tacit ideology of the program era suggested that, by providing a counterweight to the consumer market and bureaucratic institutions, literature could allow one to fashion a "human personality."[42]

But such ways of thinking were far from limited to creative writing programs. As Stephen Schryer has shown, the New York Intellectuals and New Critics made much the same vision – in which art and literature were at once complements and antidotes to the bureaucratic routinization of mass society – staples of postwar cultural discourse and core elements of liberal education.[43] And liberal intellectuals and policymakers spoke of themselves in quite similar ways. Thus, Galbraith, for example, distinguished his work from the narrow technocratic specialization he feared the postwar university was eliciting in academic economics by defining himself as, above all, a public intellectual and a wordsmith. "Nominally I have been a teacher," Galbraith recalled of his professional career. "In practice I have been a writer."[44] Richard Goodwin, Galbraith's colleague in the Kennedy administration, likewise described himself, despite his long professional career in politics, as first and foremost "a writer." Sounding not unlike a New Critic, Goodwin declared that it was "a lifelong love affair with language, its content, and the rhythmically cadenced interior sounds of words themselves" that had preserved him from the "institutionalized mediocrity" and "coercive force" of the bureaucracies that he believed dominated American political life.[45]

Even intellectuals who sought to distance themselves from the midcentury liberal consensus often spoke in similar terms. Thus, Swados's friend C. Wright Mills, who shared the pluralists' concerns about the dangers of bureaucracy and of mass society, resembled Galbraith and Goodwin in tracing his own immunity to bureaucratic regimentation to his attention to literary style. In *The Sociological Imagination* (which he dedicated to Swados and Swados's wife, Bette), Mills emphasized the way his literary "craftsmanship" made his own work a near cousin to that of "the creative writer." Like his contemporaries, moreover, Mills indicated that his dedication to literary skill enabled him to achieve a rare variety of intellectual autonomy. "The intellectual workman forms his own self as he works toward the perfection of his craft."[46] He was still more direct in explaining to Dan Wakefield, the mutual friend he shared with Swados, how he had escaped becoming a prisoner of the massive state university where he had begun his academic career: "I wrote my way out of there!"[47] Like a wide range of liberal intellectuals and artists, Mills implied that the creative writer's quest for professional autonomy placed him in constant battle with the bureaucratic mass society that housed him and threatened to swallow him whole.

For a time, Harvey Swados skirted the institutions that liberal intellectuals believed had transformed postwar American society. During the same years that Mills was defining himself at Columbia and that the literary critics and writers were finding homes in the growing university system, Swados at first appeared to chart an unusual direction, quitting his job at a Manhattan public relations firm and supporting himself and his family working as a metal finisher at the Ford plant in Mahwah. But that alternative direction lasted only a short time. By the end of the fifties, Swados had found brief employment at the Iowa Writers' Workshop – where Roth, who had begun the stories in *Goodbye, Columbus* while studying at the University of Chicago, would also soon join the faculty. He went on to become a visiting professor at Sarah Lawrence College and later at San Francisco State University. He would serve off and on as a teacher of creative writing throughout the sixties, while also working as a journalist and lecturer and patching together a living from prominent fellowships and grants (among others, a Guggenheim fellowship, an American Academy of Arts and Letters award, and an NEA grant) before ultimately becoming a full-time faculty member at the University of Massachusetts Amherst in 1970.

Perhaps it is not surprising, then, that although he thought of himself as writing a different kind of fiction and having a different politics from most of his contemporaries, Swados shared some basic aesthetic premises with exemplary program era writers such as Roth. Like those writers, Swados cast the demands of art as an alternative to the regimentation, artificiality, and homogeneity he perceived in mass society – or, as he revealingly described it, the "cultural assembly line."[48] Indeed, echoing the mid-century liberal intelligentsia's preoccupation with the evils of mass culture, Swados claimed that postwar society had merged "the chains of cultural subordination with those of economic subordination" to enslave the working man. Consumer marketing, Swados warned, "expoit[ed] him culturally as ruthlessly as he was exploited economically a generation ago."[49] As he suggested in his remarks on Roth, moreover, Swados shared his friend Mills's view that literary skill could provide the means to a kind of professional autonomy and personal self-realization otherwise endangered by mass society. The artists he admired, Swados explained, were "writers whose primary devotion was not to their class or their credo but to their craft."[50] "That's the basis of the best art," the anarchist Joe adds in *On the Line*, "the fact that you recognize yourself in it."[51]

Those professional values are important to the stories told in *On the Line*. But equally importantly, they are closely linked in Swados's story cycle – as they are in program era literature more generally – to the pluralist vision of political economy made prominent by postwar liberal intellectuals. The image of organized labour that runs all through Swados's work, for example, is nearly indistinguishable from that proposed by Galbraith, Bell, and other mid-century intellectuals. In *On the Line*, the union offers workers a form of institutionalized protection that, although valuable in itself, is disappointingly unlinked to any higher purpose. In fact, in one of the book's implicit narrative arcs, *On the Line* suggests that such limited rewards are the best that industrial labourers can now hope for. In the collection's final story, "Back in the Saddle Again," the failed entrepreneur Frank learns to appreciate what the union can offer him. A middle-aged worker who returns to factory labour after a failed career as a merchant, Frank must put aside the sensitivity about class that makes him view manual work as a humiliating decline in status. He must likewise learn to forget his memories of the bullying he encountered from coworkers decades earlier, when the union he distrusted was fighting for recognition. In the story's climactic final scenes, Frank comes to realize the value of organized labour when he finds himself protected from layoff by Lou, a former antagonist and fellow labourer who has risen in the union to become a committeeman. When Frank then reluctantly accepts Lou's invitation to a union picnic, he is further surprised to find himself enjoying a sense of happiness and camaraderie among his coworkers. In the book's final lines, Frank and his wife stroll "leisurely through the friendly throng toward the last little victory of the waning afternoon."[52]

Such small victories, Swados implies, are not the stirring visions of collective power that the workers' movement once cultivated. Notably, Frank's sense of happiness comes to him not in the workplace or on the picket line or joined in solidarity with other labourers but at leisure and surrounded by his wife and grandchildren. The goals of organized labour now, Swados implies, are not to transform society but to provide industrial workers with the security and income that will allow them to enjoy the pleasures of a happy domestic life. Frank's hard-earned sense of belonging and relief make clear that such rewards are far from negligible, and his role as the last of Swados's main characters suggests that his minor victory is a meaningful conclusion to the book's larger narrative design.

Nevertheless, the implications of Frank's story are countered by the more forceful implications that run through every other tale in *On the Line*. All of Swados's critics agree, for example, that the mysterious anarchist who appears in "Joe, the Vanishing American" serves as Swados's ideological mouthpiece in the collection, and the message Joe communicates is directly at odds with that implicit in "Back in the Saddle Again." For Joe tells his listeners that the assembly line workers are not beneficiaries of wealth and security; they are "trapped" in the plant by their rewards and obligations.[53] "I'm a little freer" than those ordinary labourers, Joe asserts. "I just read a little more and ponder a little more than the average fellow ... I've had to make sacrifices for it – no dependents, no ties." "I feel sorry for them," he adds.[54]

Joe's words cast a kind of anticipatory doubt on Frank's sense of minor victory. They are consistent, moreover, with the implications of every other story in Swados's collection, and they chime in particular with Harold's sudden realization that, seen from the outside, the assembly plant resembles "a progressive new prison." As Harold implicitly does, Joe understands the factory less as a workplace, where labourers are subject to exploitation or where workers and managers might struggle for control, than as a totalitarian prison camp whose inmates have effectively accepted their own subordination. "The men make the machines," Joe informs the aspiring engineer Walter, "and they make their own tragedies too."[55] With the exception of "Back in the Saddle Again," every story in *On the Line* bears out this stern remark. All of Swados's characters, except Frank, are working at the assembly plant because they seek middle-class comforts or domestic satisfactions that keep them effectively imprisoned by their jobs. They have chosen their subordination.

Swados himself casts this view as an aspect of the radical commitment that he, unlike his peers and contemporaries among liberals and former leftists, maintained to the struggle for a socialist future. "What is needed," he asserted, "is a social order in which, most important of all, the masses of man will be protected against the swelling flood of 'entertainment' opiates in order that they may be energized to search freely for new patterns of spontaneous living."[56] But, in truth, his complaints against the seductions of a banal mass culture were not greatly different from those of other postwar intellectuals. His stories and his critical writing suggest that Swados, like the era's pluralist liberals, assumed that the United States had seen the rise of a mass society that had supplanted older questions of economic justice with newer problems of meaning and value – that had made "economic exploitation" ultimately less significant than "cultural subordination."

Among Swados's contemporaries the political consequences of that perception may have been most evident in the conceptual framework they employed to understand the newly conceived problem of poverty. For the era's pluralist liberals, poverty came to seem less an issue of the distribution of wealth than a problem of cultural deprivation. According to Galbraith, for example, the poor were stranded on an "'island' of poverty" amid a sea of affluence.[57] They had been marooned, he explained, less by systemic injustice than by the misfortune of being unprepared for the opportunities made available by an affluent society. They either suffered from an "inability to adapt to the discipline of modern economic life,"[58] or they were captive to a culturally impoverished "environment."[59] Michael Harrington made this point still more concrete – drawing both from Galbraith and from Oscar Lewis's recent account of the "culture of poverty." As Harrington explained in his seminal work *The Other America*, the poor had been mis-served less by the structures of American capitalism than by their own backgrounds and educations. "Their entire environment, their life, their values, do not prepare them to take advantage" of the opportunities of an affluent economy, Harrington wrote. They've "proved immune to progress."[60]

Implicit in this view was the assumption that the problems of poverty were, as Galbraith put it, problems of "human investment."[61] They could be best addressed not by efforts to increase the wealth and income of the poor but by attempts to repair their cultural deprivation. The poor called out, Galbraith and other postwar liberals thus claimed, for the very public goods – more schools, more hospitals and doctors, better parks and roads, more widely available arts and leisure – that Galbraith believed the new class most valued. By the same token, as Robin Marie Averbeck points out, mid-century liberal intellectuals viewed poverty in a manner deeply informed by their concerns about the dangers they believed beset the middle class. In effect, as Harrington's language makes particularly clear, in postwar liberalism's discourse of poverty, the poor became a mirror to the middle-class intellectual. The poor, that is, provided an image of the way that one might fail to achieve meaningful autonomy amid the opportunities and enticements presented by an affluent society. They thus became in the eyes of mid-century liberals, Averbeck demonstrates, less examples of the problems of inequity than of the dangers of "psychological dependency."[62]

Unlike his liberal contemporaries, Harvey Swados did not write much about the poor. In *On the Line* and in much of his journalism, he focuses rather on unionized industrial workers – people his contemporaries believed had already joined the American middle class. Nevertheless, in disagreeing with that assessment, Swados, like his character Joe, comes to view his coworkers much as his liberal contemporaries viewed the impoverished. They appear victims less of economic exploitation than of cultural deprivation, and they thus exemplify a crippling dependency that their apparent economic wealth conceals. As the anarchist Joe suggests, they have read a little less and pondered a little less than he has, and they seem to him therefore pitiably a little less free. In this respect, industrial workers play for Swados something very near to the ideological role that the poor came to serve for mid-century liberals. They are foils whose lives reveal by contrast the values of cultural autonomy that middle-class intellectuals are presumed to cherish. Indeed, in his critical writing, Swados makes this point all but explicit. What he sees in the industrial working-class, he writes, is "proof not of the disappearance of the working class but of the proletarianization of the middle class ... The white-collar man is entering (though his arms may be loaded with commodities) the gray world of the working man."[63]

In sentiments like these, Swados appears to effectively invert the perspective of Galbraith and other mid-century liberals. It is not the case, he suggests, that growing consumer wealth is bringing almost everyone into the middle class. Rather the delusions of consumer luxury conceal the fact that mass society is making even the middle-class professionals who once enjoyed control of their labour power members of a growing proletariat. Yet, as is often the case with such inversions, Swados's seeming reversal of the world view of mid-century liberalism manages to preserve its underlying premises intact. For, just as Galbraith did, Swados presumes that American society possesses the resources to free every person from demeaning, routinized labour. Therefore, the fact that so many people remain in its grasp becomes evidence of our ideological dependence on attitudes we need not retain but whose grip on us remains mysteriously powerful. As Joe, the Vanishing American implies, particularly when he one day just walks off the job, the lives of the working class show that we are all chained to the cultural assembly line, but for the same reason, they suggest that we could all free ourselves, if only we possessed Joe's critical intelligence and independent will.

In short, the more closely one looks at *On the Line*, the more it appears that Swados is less concerned with the lives and desires of the industrial working class than he is deeply anxious about the peril of the middle class's cultural proletarianization.[64] And, indeed, seen from this perspective, the stories in *On the Line* reveal a preoccupation with the danger of downward mobility amid the illusion of rising living standards. The collection opens, for example, with the story of LeRoy, whose aspiring parents managed to send him for two years to Hampton Institute, where, discovered by a visiting music professor, LeRoy "found himself."[65] But LeRoy's talent for operatic music is sacrificed to his need to make a living to support himself and his pregnant wife. He falls prey, that is, not just to the material but to the "cultural assembly line." The cycle continues with Kevin, an Irish immigrant who had worked as a schoolteacher in the old country before briefly – and, as he comes to believe, mistakenly – falling in love with the promises of American wealth. As the series continues, we go on to meet Walter, whose father is a former sales manager "come down in the world" and who is "desperately anxious to go away to college" to restore the family's class position. And Walter's story is followed by that of Orrin, who becomes an industrial labourer after a new highway project causes his filling station business to fail; that of Harold, whose alcoholism dooms his career as a commercial artist; and that of Frank, whose dreams of entrepreneurial success have been dashed by misfortune and bad decisions.[66]

Nearly all of Swados's characters, in sum, turn out to be victims of downward status mobility and have lost careers as professionals or independent merchants. As LeRoy's story in particular makes clear, they are most importantly victims of what Swados called "cultural subordination." With the loss of LeRoy's voice also departs the characteristics with which Swados invests him: difference, beauty, a love of art – all qualities implicitly sacrificed to the banal promise of domestic satisfaction. Indeed, the accident that ends LeRoy's career and kills his spirit happens immediately after LeRoy announces his wife's pregnancy and indicates that he will now "be growing into a responsible family man."[67] As Joe might point out, the implication is clear. LeRoy has chosen a life of middle-class domesticity – of "dependents" and "ties" – at the cost of his artistic talent. His arms loaded with commodities but his voice silent, he will become a permanent member of the grey world of the workingman.

In such moments, Swados has little to say about the small victories of organized labour. His narrator does not observe, for example, that it is because of the past victories and the ideology of organized labour that the assembly plant is an integrated worksite or that, despite a terrible industrial accident, LeRoy can rely on some health care and job security. Indeed, despite his avowals, it is hard in the light of stories like LeRoy's to see a profound difference between Swados and his liberal contemporaries. Like them, he appears at his most earnest to be concerned that American mass society creates a kind of cultural bondage that prevents the realization of professional autonomy – of what, praising Roth, Swados had invoked as "human personality." And like them, he ends up implying that unionized workers, like the non-unionized poor, are therefore victims – not of an inequitable distribution of wealth or power or opportunity, but of their own psychological dependency. "They make their own tragedies."

This perception is put most allegorically in "One for the Road," the story of Harold, the former commercial artist. Harold, we learn, was reared by his single father, an alcoholic business executive who, despite his negligent care of his child, leaves Harold a trust that permits him to attend college. But, as Harold muses over his past, he comes to the realization that he "muffed" his "great opportunity."[68] Shy and lonely at school, Harold had become convinced that "he was headed noplace in the fine-arts world," and he chose a life as a commercial artist in the advertising and comic book industries in response and became a self-destructive alcoholic.[69] During his solitary drinking sprees in the Village, Harold falls in love with Marie, whom he eventually marries, an aspiring sculptor who assumes a nurturing role toward him and eventually takes up work as a public school teacher "when it be[comes] clear that her sculpture [will] not go."[70]

But Marie's nurturing attitude does little to restrain Harold's drinking and, in fact, seems only to intensify it. Eventually, he destroys his career and marriage and in desperation flees his familiar haunts in the city to take a job on the assembly line. There he discovers that the very wearying routine of factory labour, along with the growing pile of money he is saving, allows him to bring his alcoholism under control. As the story develops toward its conclusion, Harold writes to Marie about his reformed state, and she encourages him to return to the city and to begin a new career in the growing television industry. He exults that "she wanted him to be a free and independent man at last, with his own identity" – a man who would live by "his poor wits" rather than "by his brawn."[71] As a token of her belief in his prospects, Marie mails Harold a leather wallet she has made in the hobby work that is the remnant of her failed artistic career. In the climactic passage, however, all goes tragically wrong when Harold opens this wallet and discovers that Marie has included a card indicating, "*In Case of Accident Please Notify* ..."[72] Harold returns to drinking on the spot and, we discover in later stories, to life back on the line.

A reader unaware of the preoccupation with cultural subordination that Swados shared with his liberal contemporaries might find it difficult at first glance to grasp what he is getting at in this strange denouement. But seen in light of the liberal intellectuals' preoccupation with the rewards and dangers of mass culture, the story's implications become clear. Harold is a weak man whose upbringing and personal characteristics do not prepare him to contend with the enticements and anxieties of mass society. In fact, his work on the assembly line, and his weary enjoyment of movies and TV after his long days of work, serve merely as displacements of the slavish self-obliteration he had pursued earlier through alcohol. Harold endures on the line, Swados tells us, only by "accepting the unreality of the present and forging ... a chain of the most delectable daydreams," which he anticipates on the way to work "just as he used to wait impatiently for the liquor store to open."[73] His lack of autonomous character, meanwhile, is only underscored by his wife's maternal attitude toward him, as it is by the value she places on the material rewards of his work – a value symbolized by the wallet she sends him, which is itself tellingly an emblem of Marie's loss of a career as a professional artist and of her acceptance of the implicitly shallow rewards of job security and a leisure-time hobby. Harold, in other words, implicitly suffers a more dramatic version of the humiliating confinement by middle-class domesticity hinted at in LeRoy's tale. That Marie includes an identification card in the wallet only reinforces this implication. For it implicitly signals to Harold that, however much she appears to encourage him, she also expects him to begin drinking again – an expectation he thus promptly confirms. In nearly every way possible, Harold's story is an allegory of the failed artist who becomes a prisoner of mass society because of his crippling psychological dependency.

Did Swados mean for us to recognize how similar his own first name was to that of his character? It's impossible to say, but certainly, Harold represents the inversion of everything that Swados valued most in his own literary career, and by the same token, Harold's career conceivably represents everything Swados might have feared for himself.

For the same reasons, Harold can be viewed as a virtual inverse of the "human personality" that Swados saw in Roth's work and that Roth suggested was exemplified by Neil Klugman.[74] Harold ends his story staring at the symbols – the prison-like factory, the wallet – that confirm his confinement. Neil Klugman ends his story looking at his reflection, and in doing so, asserting his claim to mould and possess his self. The contrast suggests that Swados may have done less to escape the postwar liberal ideology he frequently denounced than he did to demonstrate how dramatically it had reshaped the ways in which even avowedly left thinkers would conceive the issues of work, class, and status in the postwar United States.

The most striking feature of his writing, in retrospect, may thus turn out to be how little faith Swados, like his liberal contemporaries, placed in the power of organized labour or in its capacity to defend the values of social democracy. For, now that the role of unions in American economic and political life has so precipitously declined, the victories of organized labour and of postwar liberalism no longer seem so small. The concerns that Swados shared with his contemporaries among liberal intellectuals about the dangers of mass society and the psychological dependency it allegedly fostered appear, by contrast, ever less significant.

NOTES

1 Swados, "Good and Short," 458–9.
2 See Swados, *Radical's America*, ix–xvii and *passim*.
3 Swados, "Good and Short," 458.
4 This preoccupation is put nowhere more directly than in Roth's celebrated essay, "Writing American Fiction" (1961). There Roth approvingly quotes Benjamin DeMott's assertion that the "deeply lodged suspicion of the times [is] … that events and individuals are unreal, and that power to alter the course of the age, of my life and your life, is actually vested nowhere" and uses it as a way of framing the cultural alienation and stylistic brio Roth observes in contemporary fiction. Roth, *Reading Myself and Others*, 121. For the larger critical consensus Roth's comments reflect, see Schaub, *American Fiction in the Cold War*, 25–89. See also Belletto, *No Accident, Comrade*; Dickstein, *Gates of Eden*, 93–129; Trask, *Camp Sites*, 51–84 and *passim*.
5 Howe, "On Harvey Swados," 637; Howe is quoting here remarks he first published in the early 1960s. For a scholarly view of Swados's place among the New York Intellectuals – and the most astute critical commentary on Swados's major work, *On the Line* – see Wald, *New York Intellectuals*, 334–43.
6 Swados, *Radical's America*, 275, 273.
7 Feinstein, "Contemporary American Fiction," 87, 84, 86.
8 Swados, *Radical's America*, 112, 113.
9 Ibid., 223, 65.
10 Swados, "Good and Short," 459.
11 Roth, *Reading Myself and Others*, 130–1.
12 Roth, *Goodbye, Columbus*, 136.
13 See, for example, Stanley Aronowitz: "[C. Wright] Mills, … Swados, and Mailer were among a relatively small minority who stayed … outside the consensus" of anti-Communist liberalism in the 1950s and early 1960s. Aronowitz, "Considerations on the Origins of Neoconservatism," 64.
14 Mills, "Decline of the Left," 215.
15 Swados, *On the Line*, 163.
16 Swados, *Radical's America*, 112.
17 Swados, *On the Line*, 66.
18 Swados, *Radical's America*, 117.
19 Ibid., 127.
20 Swados, *On the Line*, 66.
21 Swados, *Radical's America*, 117.

22 Wald makes this case in *The New York Intellectuals*, 334–43, noting also the way that Swados anticipates some of the attention to the features of industrial labour and class that would appear in, for example, Braverman, *Labor and Monopoly Capital* (1974) and Sennett and Cobb, *The Hidden Injuries of Class* (1972); Wald's point about Swados's resemblance to the young Marx is extended by Robert Niemi in "'Dirty Industrial Dawn.'"
23 Brick, *Transcending Capitalism*, 152–218 and *passim*. On the crucial role that opposition to mass culture played in the self-definition of Cold War liberals, see also, among others, Pells, *The Liberal Mind in a Conservative Age*; Ross, *No Respect*, 1–64 and *passim*; Schaub, *American Fiction in the Cold War*, 3–24; Trask, *Camp Sites*.
24 Galbraith, *Affluent Society*, 14.
25 Ibid.
26 Ibid., 203.
27 Schlesinger, "Future of Liberalism," 9.
28 Galbraith, *Affluent Society*, 259.
29 Ibid., 268.
30 Ibid., 265.
31 Ibid., 263.
32 Ibid., 264.
33 See Lichtenstein, "Pluralism," 83–114.
34 Bell, "Capitalism of the Proletariat," 211–26; Bell's title quotes George Bernard Shaw in a phrase that Bell begins by calling a "half-truth" (211). The remainder of his essay, however, does little to qualify this statement.
35 Galbraith, *Affluent Society*, 266.
36 Ibid., 267, emphasis in original.
37 Schlesinger, "Notes on a National Cultural Policy," 320.
38 McGurl, *Program Era*, 71, 21, 19.
39 Ibid., 16.
40 Wakefield, *New York in the Fifties*, 33.
41 McGurl, *Program Era*, 74; for further discussion of the way in which McGurl's discerning account of program era aesthetics reveals their affinity with the pluralist liberalism that dominated the postwar university, see McCann, "'My Ghost Life.'"
42 Swados, "Good and Short," 459.
43 Schryer, *Fantasies of the New Class*, 1–28 and *passim*. Schryer's account stresses the reliance of postwar literary intellectuals on assumptions about the new class that mirrored those of Galbraith.
44 Galbraith, *Annals of an Abiding Liberal*, 286.

45 Goodwin, *Remembering America*, 418, 14, 22. Goodwin's self-conception mirrored the way liberal intellectuals in the fifties and early sixties conceived of their relationship to mass society, which, as Christopher Lasch notes, they demonstrated most directly in the aristocratic "style" they admired in JFK. Lasch, *New Radicalism in America*, 286–348.

46 Mills, *Sociological Imagination*, 196.

47 Wakefield, *New York in the Fifties*, 35. Mills also bragged to Swados that he possessed the "sensibilities of the novelist," and Swados offered a similar appraisal, praising Mills's *White Collar* as "poetry" (Gillam, "*White Collar* from Start to Finish," 7, 18). Gillam suggests that Mills's attitude was influenced by his concern about the judgment of critics and intellectuals like Lionel Trilling. Mills read Trilling and the other New York Intellectuals in the little magazines, such as *Partisan Review*, where the ideas discussed by Schryer were disseminated and where Philip Roth's early reputation was forged ("*White Collar* from Start to Finish," 7).

48 Feinstein, "Contemporary American Fiction," 86.

49 Swados, *Radical's America*, 69.

50 Ibid., 7.

51 Swados, *On the Line*, 67.

52 Ibid., 233.

53 Ibid., 62.

54 Ibid., 60.

55 Ibid., 62.

56 Swados, *Radical's America*, 110.

57 Galbraith, *Affluent Society*, 253.

58 Ibid., 252.

59 Ibid., 250.

60 Harrington, *Other America*, 9.

61 Galbraith, *Affluent Society*, 257.

62 Averbeck, "Greed of the Poor."

63 Swados, *Radical's America*, 118. Andrew Hoberek, in *The Twilight of the Middle Class*, discusses the significance of this concern to C. Wright Mills and, arguing that it was a reasonable perception of postwar economic life, contends that it was implicitly addressed in the major fiction of the fifties.

64 Swados personally had good reason to be concerned about the experience of downward mobility. He was raised as the child of a doctor and painter in Buffalo and attended the University of Michigan during the late thirties, before taking employment as a riveter in aircraft plants and then, during the war, joining the Merchant Marine. After World War II,

he worked in public relations and spent time living in a villa in the South of France, working on his writing, before he returned briefly to industrial employment in the mid-fifties.

65 Swados, *On the Line*, 3.

66 Ibid., 43.

67 Ibid., 17.

68 Ibid., 147.

69 Ibid.

70 Ibid., 148.

71 Ibid., 164.

72 Ibid., 165.

73 Ibid., 156.

74 It may be worth recalling here that, in the story's crisis, Neil demonstrates that autonomy by staking out a lonely independence from the tacit conspiracy against birth control that he perceives Brenda to have entered with her mother. That is, he defines himself against the domesticity by which LeRoy, Harold, and Swados's other characters are confined.

BIBLIOGRAPHY

Aronowitz, Stanley. "Considerations on the Origins of Neoconservatism." In *Confronting the New Conservatism: The Rise of the Right in America*, edited by Michael Thompson, 56–70. New York: New York University Press, 2007.

Averbeck, Robin Marie. "The Greed of the Poor: Dependency and the Post-War Political Imagination." Paper delivered at the Society for U.S. Intellectual History, 2014. *U.S. Intellectual History Blog*. 16 October 2014. http://s-usih.org/2014/10/the-greed-of-the-poor-dependency-and-the-post-war-political-imagination.html#more-8839.

Bell, Daniel. "The Capitalism of the Proletariat: A Theory of American Trade-Unionism." In *The End of Ideology: On the Exhaustion of Political Ideas in the Fifties*, 211–26. Cambridge, MA: Harvard University Press, 1960.

Belletto, Steven. *No Accident, Comrade: Chance and Design in Cold War American Narratives*. New York: Oxford University Press, 2012.

Braverman, Harry. *Labor and Monopoly Capital: The Degradation of Work in the Twentieth Century*. New York: Monthly Review Press, 1974.

Brick, Howard. *Transcending Capitalism: Visions of a New Society in Modern American Thought*. Ithaca, NY: Cornell University Press, 2006.

Dickstein, Morris. *Gates of Eden: American Culture in the Sixties*. 1977. New York: Norton, 2015.

Feinstein, Herbert. "Contemporary American Fiction: Harvey Swados and Leslie Fiedler." *Wisconsin Studies in Contemporary Literature* 2, no. 1 (1961): 79–98.
Galbraith, John Kenneth. *American Capitalism: The Concept of Countervailing Power*. 1952. New Brunswick, NJ: Transaction Publishers, 1993.
– *Annals of an Abiding Liberal*. Boston: Houghton Mifflin, 1979.
– *The Affluent Society*. 1958. Toronto: New American Library of Canada, 1963.
Gillam, Richard. "*White Collar* from Start to Finish: C. Wright Mills in Transition." *Theory and Society* 10, no. 1 (1981): 1–30.
Goodwin, Richard N. *Remembering America: A Voice from the Sixties*. New York: Harper & Row, 1988.
Harrington, Michael. *The Other America*. 1962. New York: Simon & Schuster, 1993.
Hoberek, Andrew. *The Twilight of the Middle Class: Post-World War II American Fiction and White-Collar Work*. Princeton, NJ: Princeton University Press, 2005.
Howe, Irving. "On Harvey Swados." *Massachusetts Review* 24, no. 3 (1983): 637–45.
Lasch, Christopher. *The New Radicalism in America: The Intellectual as Social Type, 1889–1963*. 1965. New York: Norton, 1986.
Lichtenstein, Nelson. "Pluralism, Postwar Intellectuals, and the Demise of the Union Idea." In *The Great Society and the High Tide of Liberalism*, edited by Sidney M. Milkis and Jerome M. Mileur, 83–114. Amherst: University of Massachusetts Press, 2005.
McCann, Sean. "'My Ghost Life': Russell Banks and the Limits of Aesthetic Democracy." In *After the Program Era: The Past, Present, and Future of Creative Writing in the University*, edited by Loren Glass, 195–218. Iowa: University of Iowa Press, 2016,
McGurl, Mark. *The Program Era: Postwar Fiction and the Rise of Creative Writing*. Cambridge, MA: Harvard University Press, 2009.
Mills, C. Wright. "The Decline of the Left." In *The Politics of Truth: Selected Writings of C. Wright Mills*, edited by John H. Summers, 213–22. New York: Oxford University Press, 2008.
– *The Sociological Imagination*. New York: Oxford University Press, 1959.
Niemi, Robert. "'Dirty Industrial Dawn': Alienation and Its Discontents in Harvey Swados's *On the Line*." *Reconstruction* 8, no. 1 (2008): 14 paragraphs.
Pells, Richard H. *The Liberal Mind in a Conservative Age: American Intellectuals in the 1940s and 1950s*. 2nd ed. Hanover, NH: Wesleyan University Press, 1989.
Ross, Andrew. *No Respect: Intellectuals and Popular Culture*. New York: Routledge, 1989.

Roth, Philip. *Goodbye, Columbus*. 1959. New York: Vintage, 1993.
– *Reading Myself and Others*. New York: Farrar, Straus and Giroux, 1975.
Schaub, Thomas Hill. *American Fiction in the Cold War*. Madison: University of Wisconsin Press, 1991.
Schlesinger, Arthur M., Jr. "Notes on a National Cultural Policy (1960)." In *The Politics of Hope and the Bitter Heritage*, 312–20. Princeton, NJ: Princeton University Press, 2008.
– "The Future of Liberalism." *Reporter*, 3 May 1956, 8–11.
Schryer, Stephen. *Fantasies of the New Class: Ideologies of Professionalism in Post-World War II American Fiction*. New York: Columbia University Press, 2011.
Sennett, Richard, and Jonathan Cobb. *The Hidden Injuries of Class*. Cambridge, MA: Cambridge University Press, 1972.
Swados, Harvey. "Good and Short." *Hudson Review* 12, no. 3 (Autumn 1959): 454–9.
– *On the Line*. 1957. Urbana: University of Illinois Press, 1990.
– *A Radical's America*. Boston: Little, Brown, 1962.
Trask, Michael. *Camp Sites: Sex, Politics, and Academic Style in Postwar America*. Stanford, CA: Stanford University Press, 2013.
Wakefield, Dan. *New York in the Fifties*. Boston: Houghton Mifflin, 1992.
Wald, Alan M. *The New York Intellectuals: The Rise and Decline of the Anti-Stalinist Left from the 1930s to the 1980s*. Chapel Hill: University of North Carolina Press, 1987.

Contributors

Jennifer Ashton is associate professor of English at the University of Illinois at Chicago. She is the author of *From Modernism to Postmodernism: American Poetry in the Twentieth Century* and the editor of *The Cambridge Companion to American Poetry since 1945*. Her articles on modern and contemporary poetry and theory have appeared in *ELH, ALH, Modernism/Modernity, Western Humanities Review, Chicago Review,* and *Interval(le)s*, among others. She is a founding board member of the online arts and political journal *nonsite.org* and a founding organizer, former chief steward, and proud member of UIC United Faculty (IFT-AFT-AAUP-AFL-CIO Local 6456).

Jonathan Flatley is professor of English at Wayne State University, where he was the editor of *Criticism: A Quarterly for Literature and the Arts* from 2007 to 2012. He is the author of *Affective Mapping: Melancholia and the Politics of Modernism* (Harvard University Press, 2008) and *Like Andy Warhol* (University of Chicago Press, forthcoming). He is currently working on a book called *Black Leninism: How Revolutionary Counter-Moods Are Made.*

Corrinne Harol is associate professor of English and Film Studies and literary director of the Orlando Project at the University of Alberta, where she teaches Restoration and eighteenth-century literature. She is the author of *Enlightened Virginity in Eighteenth-Century Literature* and has been working on the relations between literature and politics in 1688.

Andrea Hasenbank is a PhD candidate at the University of Alberta, where she is a Killam Memorial Scholar and a past doctoral fellow of Editing Modernism in Canada, as well as project coordinator for the

Proletarian Literature & Arts project. Her research is grounded in the area of print history with a focus on the intersections between print, politics, and propaganda. Her forthcoming dissertation, *Proletarian Publics: Leftist and Labour Print in Canada, 1930–1939*, examines radical pamphlets circulating in Western Canada during the Depression years.

Aaron Kunin is associate professor of English at Pomona College. He studies the English Renaissance and is writing a book about the old meaning of character. His books of poetry are published by Fence Books; the most recent is *Cold Genius* (2014).

Heather Love teaches English and Gender Studies at the University of Pennsylvania. She is the author of *Feeling Backward: Loss and the Politics of Queer History* (Harvard University Press), the editor of a special issue of *GLQ* on Gayle Rubin ("Rethinking Sex"), and the coeditor of a special issue of *Representations* ("Description across Disciplines"). She is currently completing a book project on practices of description in the humanities and social sciences.

Sean McCann is professor of English at Wesleyan University. He is the author of *Gumshoe America: Hard-Boiled Crime Fiction and the Rise and Fall of New Deal Liberalism* (2000) and *A Pinnacle of Feeling: American Literature and Presidential Government* (2008).

Michael Meeuwis is assistant professor at the University of Warwick. His research addresses English literature, political theory, and theories of performance. He is currently in the very late stages a manuscript project, *Everyone's Theatre: Literature and Daily Life in England, 1860–1914*, which considers the ubiquity of theatre and its effect on literature and daily life in England and its colonies in the years between 1860 and 1914. A new project, *Performing Novels*, reconsiders the Rise of the Novel tradition in light of the eighteenth- and nineteenth-century phenomenon of novels read out loud.

Jason Potts is associate professor of English at St Francis Xavier University, where he teaches American literature and cultural theory. He is the coeditor (with Dan Stout) of *Theory Aside* (Duke University Press, 2014). He is currently writing a book about happiness and the twenty-first-century American novel.

Sina Rahmani completed his PhD in the Department of Comparative Literature at UCLA. He was also a SSHRC postdoctoral fellow in the Department of English and Film Studies at the University of Alberta. His work has been published or forthcoming in *Iranian Studies, PMLA, boundary 2*, and the *Radical History Review.*

Mark Simpson is associate professor in English and Film Studies at the University of Alberta. His work takes up mobility's modern regimes. The author of *Trafficking Subjects: The Politics of Mobility in Nineteenth-Century America* (Minnesota University Press, 2004), he is coeditor of *English Studies in Canada* and a founding collaborator in the multidisciplinary research partnership After Oil.

Vivasvan Soni is associate professor of English at Northwestern University. His book, *Mourning Happiness: Narrative and the Politics of Modernity* (Cornell University Press, 2010), was the recipient of the Modern Language Association's eighteenth annual Prize for a First Book. He is working on a project that probes the long history of our discomfort with judgment, tracing its genesis in eighteenth-century discourses of empiricism and aesthetics.

Index

www.ingramcontent.com/pod-product-compliance
Lightning Source LLC
LaVergne TN
LVHW090150080826
844660LV00013B/740/J

* 9 7 8 1 4 4 2 6 3 0 9 0 1 *